D1447696

PRIVATE PROPERTY, GOVERNMENT REQUISITION AND THE CONSTITUTION, 1914 – 1927

PRIVATE PROPERTY, GOVERNMENT REQUISITION AND THE CONSTITUTION, 1914 – 1927

G.R. RUBIN

THE HAMBLEDON PRESS

LONDON AND RIO GRANDE

Published by The Hambledon Press 1994
102 Gloucester Avenue, London NW1 8HX (U.K.)

P.O. Box 162, Rio Grande, Ohio 45674 (U.S.A.)

ISBN 1 85285 098 1

© Gerry R. Rubin 1994

A description of this book is available from the British Library and from the Library of Congress

Typeset by The Midlands Book Typesetting Company, Loughborough

Printed on acid-free paper and bound in Great Britain
by Cambridge University Press

Contents

To Brenda
and Susanna Ruth

Introduction

The origins of this book can be traced back to a study which I published in 1987 and which examined government controls on labour during the First World War. It struck me then that a blueprint for legal controls, in the form of statutory provisions, offered no clear indication of how such controls might work out in practice. I decided to explore that theme further but, in respect to the present work, to focus not on wartime controls over labour but on controls over property. This study therefore investigates how the state sought to enrol land, buildings and other forms of property (though not capital in the narrow sense) into the gigantic war effort waged from 1914. It concerns itself with the conflicting claims of state and society to the application of private property for public purposes during wartime and to the question of compensation for private property owners whose properties had been requisitioned by the state for war purposes.

The structure of the book is to present in the early chapters an overview of the legal framework governing the requisitioning of private property in emergencies and of compensation issues arising therefrom. It also addresses, albeit briefly, the conceptual and philosophical issues raised in preparing for and enacting a code of regulations authorising state take-overs of private property. The book then proceeds by analysing individual case studies which constituted legal watersheds during the war years. Of these separate episodes, a number subsequently became legal *causes célèbres* and occupied lofty places in the pantheon of what lawyers like to call leading cases. The final chapters employ a more thematic approach, addressing how government departments sought to resolve more universal administrative problems; in particular, what general principles of compensation should apply in respect to property requisitioned for governmental purposes during the war.

In more detail, Chapter One examines the alternative conceptual approaches to emergency wartime legislation which government departments considered in the years prior to the outbreak of the First World War, when the War Office, in particular, was concerned with contingency emergency planning. Chapter Two raises some philosophical questions pertaining to state requisition of private property and to claims of entitlement to compensation for such acquisitions. It also offers a brief historical overview of the general doctrines applying thereto. Chapter Three looks in some detail at wartime Defence of the Realm Regulations which were widely employed by government departments to assist the war effort; in particular, to facilitate munitions production and the provision of accommodation for multifarious war-related purposes. In this chapter, I will also explore one of the features of this study, the phenomenon of the lawless state, that is, the reliance by government departments on legal powers of doubtful validity and of the awareness by such departments of their vulnerability to legal challenge.

Chapter Four, the first case study examined, explores the legal and administrative history of the take-over of Shoreham Aerodrome in Sussex. Although the airfield was an insignificant base in military terms, the government's reliance on the royal prerogative power to justify its requisition stirred up a hornet's nest of legal dispute and intrigue forcing government departments, faced with the prospect of legal condemnation by the judges of the House of Lords, to rethink their requisitioning strategies. This aspect is analysed more fully in Chapter Five which explores the bluffs, threats and manipulations of the law to which government departments were obliged to resort in order to circumvent the legal obstacles now erected in the path of effortless requisitioning of private property for the war effort.

Chapter Six, the second case study, examines that jewel in the modern-day constitutional lawyer's crown, the requisitioning of De Keyser's Royal Hotel in London for use by the Royal Flying Corps. The importance of the case has been compared with the great constitutional struggles between the Crown and Parliament supported by the common lawyers in the seventeenth century. John Hampden's resistance to the imposition of Ship Money by Charles I is the parallel which some commentators during the war drew with the government's claim to requisition the hotel without a legal duty to pay full compensation. In Chapters Seven and Eight, two more *causes célèbres*, also familiar to modern students of constitutional law, represented further legal defeats for the government's strategy of relying on emergency legal powers in order to take over private property, respectively the Ordnance Arms in Woolwich, owned by the Cannon Brewery Co. Ltd and rum requisitioned for the Navy from the Newcastle Breweries Co. Ltd.

Chapter Nine examines how the government sought to overcome with rapidity one particular legal set-back in its control over the market in beans, peas and pulse, promoted as alternatives to wheat, then in short supply. A government order had been successfully challenged in the courts as interfering with the freedom of contract. As the government's dim view of this 'freedom' was a freedom to make speculative profits, an emergency bill was quickly drafted which, after some delay, passed onto the statute book the following year.

Chapter Ten considers some of the intricate legal difficulties, especially in respect to compensation, to which the requisitioning of ships during the war gave rise, prompting the drafting of remedial bills which did not in fact proceed, for a mixture of political and administrative reasons. Chapter Eleven, yet another one-property case study, looks at the public controversy surrounding government plans to sell off Turnhouse Aerodrome in Edinburgh after the war. The land upon which the aerodrome was built belonged to the former Prime Minister, Lord Rosebery. His understandable outrage at what he saw as his property being sold behind his back offered newspaper readers of the day a delicious controversy to savour.

Chapter Twelve examines the institutional machinery set up by the government in early 1915 to offer *ex gratia* compensation to those whose properties had been requisitioned for the defence of the realm. But in the wake of the Shoreham Aerodrome and *De Keyser* rulings that compensation levels should in law have regard to a more generous market value, the government was forced, after the war, to a device which at the same time both questioned and endorsed parliamentary democracy. As further explained in Chapter Thirteen, it presented to Parliament an Indemnity Bill to confirm the principle of compensation basically only for direct loss and not for market value loss, for which its institutional machinery, the non-statutory Royal Commission on the Defence of the Realm (Losses), had made provision. The Indemnity Act 1920 now endorsed that principle in law and established the War Compensation Court, a division of the High Court, to adjudicate upon disputed claims.

As with the constitutional debate surrounding the case of *De Keyser's Royal Hotel Ltd*, with its overtones of outdated royal prerogative claims challenging the rights and liberties of the subject, the controversy over the Indemnity Act was couched in similar terms of high political principle.

Chapter Fourteen explores the transition from war to peace from the standpoint of the emergency wartime regulations and seeks to identify the legal difficulties faced by the government in attempting to secure as smooth a transition as possible. Given the continuing usefulness of a number of wartime regulations during the early years of peace, when shortages of essential commodities were still rife, a policy of retention was favoured by the authorities but disliked by politicians, for whom a command economy had no further justification in peacetime. Again, questions of principle, which some commentators saw as the choice between despotism and democracy, loomed large in the debates and, indeed, informed constitutional discourse into the 1930s. The chapter also looks at the possible linkage between land requisition during the war and post-war policies of land acquisition and valuation in order to create a 'land fit for heroes.' The optimistic hopes were not, of course, fulfilled and the lessons of the war in this sphere were quickly forgotten.

In order to glimpse a long-term legacy of the war experience, one would require to examine the Second World War practice of property requisition and compensation provision, to which brief allusion is made in the final chapter. In that chapter, the conclusion is drawn that the First World War experience in this sphere conformed to the efforts made elsewhere in a domestic economy grappling with new and daunting challenges. Lacking relevant pre-war experience, the state lurched from one expedient to another. As one door was shut by the judiciary, so another was jammed open by administrative subterfuge, fudge and hedge, failing which a pliant Parliament bowed to the wishes of an executive pleading the national urgency of its case and justifying rapid legislation thereby.

For those readers anticipating an extended discussion of property rights theory or of the history of property law in the early twentieth century, there will be disappointment. This writer professes no expertise in those areas but prefers to conceive of this book as a modest contribution to the history of constitutional law in this century, to the history of compensation and to the history of government administration during the First World War. No broader claims are made on its behalf.

Parts of Chapter One have appeared in Richard Eales and David Sullivan (eds), *The Political Context of Law* (The Hambledon Press, London 1987), Chapter Eleven, and parts of Chapter Five have appeared (in Spanish) in Carlos Petit (ed.), *Derecho Privado y Revolucion Burguesa* (Marcial Pons, Ediciones Juridicas, S.A., Madrid 1990). To thank one's secretaries for having undertaken the typing of one's book might occasionally seem like a ritual expression of gratitude. My gratitude to Hilary Joce, Rebecca Edwards and Kate Campbell is, I hope, anything but a ritual pronouncement. I would also like to use this opportunity to thank Professors Peter Fitzpatrick and A.W.B. Simpson for providing, unconsciously no doubt, those vital sparks of inspiration and support.

Crown copyright material in the Public Record Office appears by permission of the Controller of H.M. Stationery Office. Material from the Steel-Maitland papers in the Scottish Record Office appears by permission of Mrs. R. M. Stafford, Sauchieburn Estates Office, Stirling. The financial assistance of the Wolfson Foundation and of the Leverhulme Trust in the preparation of this study is gratefully acknowledged.

Canterbury   G. R. Rubin
April 1992

Abbreviations

cif	cost, insurance, freight
DLB	Disposal and Liquidation Board
DORA	Defence of the Realm Acts
DRLC	Defence of the Realm Losses Commission
H.C.	House of Commons
HLRO	House of Lords Record Office
K.B.	King's Bench
LTCC	Defence of the Realm (Licensed Trade Claims) Commission
P.P.	Parliamentary Papers
PRO	Public Record Office
PRO, AIR	Public Record Office, Air Ministry
PRO, BT	Public Record Office, Board of Trade
PRO, CAB	Public Record Office, Cabinet
PRO, HO	Public Record Office, Home Office
PRO, LCO	Public Record Office, Lord Chancellor's Office
PRO, MAF	Public Record Office, Ministry of Food
PRO, MT	Public Record Office, Ministry of War Transport
PRO, T	Public Record Office, Treasury
PRO, TS	Public Record Office, Treasury Solicitor
PRO, WO	Public Record Office, War Office
RAF	Royal Air Force
RCC	Railway and Canal Commission
RFC	Royal Flying Corps
SRO	Scottish Record Office
SRO, AD	Scottish Record Office, Lord Advocate's Department
SRO, HH	Scottish Record Office, Scottish Home and Health Department
WCC	War Compensation Court

1

Too Important to Leave to the Generals?

On 30 June 1914, just one month before the outbreak of the First World War, a sub-committee of the Committee of Imperial Defence (CID), which was the Prime Minister's standing advisory committee on defence matters, met to discuss what emergency powers, if any, would require to be enacted in the event of war being declared.[1] The War Office representative at the meeting, Colonel G. M. W. MacDonogh,[2] produced a list of powers which the army believed should be made available to it by statute for implementation in wartime, or during the 'precautionary period' prior to the actual outbreak. This, suggested MacDonogh, might cover a period of 'imminent national danger or great emergency', the phrase used in the Reserve Forces Act 1882. Such emergency powers, which were to be exercised against or in relation to the civilian population, covered the provision of supplies to garrisons, arrest powers, the taking possession of property, transport and communications controls, censorship, controls over 'warlike stores' and many other categories. Finally, legislative powers were sought in order to 'take all measures necessary for the public safety'.

At this point in the committee's discussion, the Attorney-General, Sir John Simon, expressed the view that the last-named requirement:

> covered all those that had preceded it, and was itself covered by the common law; for it was the duty of the military authorities in time of war to take such measures as might be necessary for the safety of the State.

His pointed remarks drew no response, as the committee members continued to discuss which novel powers ought to be enacted. The Attorney-General again intervened and insisted that:

---

1. Public Record Office, London [PRO], CAB 16/31/EP1, 'Sub-Committee of the Committee of Imperial Defence. Emergency Powers in War. Minutes of the 1st Meeting held on 30 June 1914'. Until indicated otherwise, subsequent quotations in the text are from this source. See also D. French, *British Economic and Strategic Planning, 1905–1915* (London, 1982), pp. 74–76.

2. George Mark Watson MacDonogh (1865–1942). Joined army 1884; Colonel 1912; Lieutenant-General 1919; General Staff Officer 1912; Adjutant-General 1916–18; Director of Military Intelligence 1916–18. Barrister (Lincoln's Inn) 1897; Vice-President and Member Executive Council, International Law Association; President, Federation of British Industries 1933–34. Photograph in J. H. Morgan, *Assize of Arms* (London, 1945).

it was important to consider without prejudice the main question before the Committee. This was whether it was expedient to pass legislation of the nature proposed or to trust to an act of indemnity.

During the period from about 1885 to 1914, there existed conflicting legal viewpoints, on the part of senior military officers on the one hand and government legal advisers on the other, over the kind of law deemed appropriate for use in relation to the domestic civilian population in wartime. There were differing perspectives as to the appropriate conceptual structure of the legal proposals advanced to meet the contingencies of war, differences which could not simply be attributed to conflicts over interpretations of existing law. The approach of the military authorities was to some extent grounded (perhaps not surprisingly) in the military preoccupation with precise forward planning, so that the supposed certainty of statute law, rather than the somewhat open-ended flexibility of the common law, as preferred by the lawyers, appealed to military planners anticipating operational needs, both in wartime and when armed conflict appeared imminent. What is presented here is neither a history of the doctrinal development of the relevant law, such as the nineteenth-century Defence Acts, nor an exploration of the doctrinal accuracy of legal arguments advanced at the time, such as the proper scope of alleged prerogative powers to take over land or property in appropriate circumstances. My concern, rather, is with different perceptions of existing law, not with whether the ensuing military criticisms of the civilian lawyers were doctrinally sound in juridical terms.

A series of nineteenth-century statutes, known collectively as the Defence Acts 1842–73, made provision for the compulsory military take-over of land. Under section nine of the principal 1842 Act, power was granted to the Secretary of State for War to lease or purchase lands for buildings 'for the Ordnance or Barrack Services or the Defence of the Realm', while section 16 authorised the military to enter upon, survey or mark out lands 'for the service of the Ordnance Department or for the Defence of the Realm'. In such circumstances, they had power to treat and agree with the owners for the absolute purchase of the land or for the possession or use thereof during the exigencies of the public service. In default of agreement, section 19 provided that fourteen days after failure to treat, the Secretary of State could require two justices or three deputy lieutenants (one of whom had to be a magistrate) to put the Secretary of State or his nominee into immediate possession of the lands. Such compulsory powers were limited to acquisition for the Ordnance service or for the defence of the realm generally. Two warrants, one authorising the military authorities to take possession, the other requiring the sheriffs to summon a jury to assess compensation, were then to be issued by the justices.

Though exercised for the 'defence of the realm', such powers were assumed to be applicable in peacetime. This partly explains why military acquisition was hedged around with limited procedural safeguards for landowners. Yet such peacetime powers were nonetheless considered sufficiently drastic to justify the Treasury Solicitor's observation that, 'the owner has really no voice in the matter at all'.[3] Even more draconian were the provisions in section 23. This granted power to the lord lieutenant or to two deputies or to the governor of the county or to two of his deputies to certify the necessity or expediency of a military take-over of land or buildings. A Treasury warrant authorising the take-over was also required. This procedure presumably would only occur in cases of emergency. Finally, section 23, not unexpectedly, dispensed with the need for a possession order under section 19 or a certificate under section 23 where the 'Enemy shall have actually invaded the United Kingdom'. The only circumstances in which a military officer could take immediate possession of land on his own initiative appeared to be once the enemy had landed. Otherwise, bureaucratic procedures, perhaps not conducive to defence preparations, were to be followed. Under the Military Lands Act 1892: 'It frequently takes over a year from the time when it is decided to take the land before the Secretary of State for War is in a position to serve Notice to Treat.'[4]

Though the Defence Acts were not as dilatory, none of the statutory codes met all the contingency needs of the military authorities. For what was most desired was, first, the ability to offer an immediate and flexible response on the basis of their evaluation of the military situation, whether or not war had been officially declared or whether or not an invasion had commenced. Secondly, the military wanted clear, statutory authority for such an instantaneous response. The varying procedural restrictions of the Defence Acts (apart from invasion) were an impediment to speedy military reaction to enemy threats.[5]

In 1885, for example, the Inspector-General of Fortifications had drawn attention to the fact that in the event of imminent danger of invasion, it would become necessary for the military to take certain defensive measures involving interference with private property. They might have to enter on lands, erect works, construct roads or demolish buildings. Given that the existing law, by which he presumably meant the Defence Acts, prescribed so many complicated formalities and imposed so many restrictions, he feared that the military authorities would, at a time of imminent danger, be seriously hampered

3. PRO, TS 27/62, 'Note on the Compulsory Procedures for taking land possessed by the Secretary of State for War, dated 1902'.
4. Ibid.
5. There were also criticisms of the limited scope of the Defence Acts even in respect to peacetime usage. For example, the inability of the military authorities to divert carriage roads led to suggestions in 1889 to widen the military's peacetime powers. The Secretary of State for War at the time, Edward Stanhope, was decidedly unenthusiastic. 'I cannot imagine', he minuted, 'any proposal more likely to provoke considerable opposition than this and I am inclined on the whole to leave the matter alone for the present.' See PRO, WO 32/9269, 'As to the compulsory powers of the Secretary of State for War, for acquiring land etc', minute of Secretary of State, 5 December 1889.

in the performance of their obvious duties.[6] International incidents, which might have given rise to mobilisation, had drawn the attention of military commanders to what they believed were deficiencies in their legal powers to deploy as they considered appropriate. Following the Fashoda Incident, when Britain was on the verge of war with France in 1898, Lieutenant-General Sir Frederick Stopford minuted that the want of information as to what the military authorities might or might not lawfully do on mobilisation had caused serious inconvenience. In one case, the General Officer Commanding (GOC) Home District had to enquire whether he was authorised to arrange for the quartering of troops for whom no government quarters or camp equipment existed. As Stopford lamented, it was, 'very unsatisfactory in reply to all these questions to have to state that no definite instructions can be given them, but that the question is under consideration'.[7]

In effect, military commanders were simply told to rely on their own discretion as to whether they ought to infringe private property rights once a mobilisation had been ordered. In 1911 all GOC's Home Command had been instructed that in the event of mobilisation, they

> should take all such steps as you consider necessary to occupy, or make use of, such land as may be required for camping, training, artillery practice, or musketry of the troops under your Command by arrangement with the owners, or otherwise, in anticipation of subsequent indemnity, either by the existing Defence Acts, or by emergency legislation.[8]

Of course, military commanders might reasonably doubt whether the Defence Acts provided any indemnity for illegal acts. They might also have preferred to see emergency legislation on the statute book, rather than being held out to them as an uncertain inducement. Yet the position was bound to be more obscure when a 'precautionary period', short of actual mobilisation, was in existence. Major R. E. H. James told the CID sub-committee in June 1914 that a precautionary period would be initiated by means of a warning telegram from the War Office to GOCs, 'but there were no specific instructions as to how far the military authorities would be justified on receipt of it in disregarding private rights'.[9]

How might this state of uncertainty be resolved? The military authorities throughout the last two decades of the nineteenth century made various attempts to obtain a statute conferring on them extensive powers to take steps necessary for the defence and security of the realm, both in the critical period pending a major conflict and after the outbreak of war. Such a bill was drafted

6. PRO, CAB 16/31/EP2, 'Memorandum by the General Staff of the Need for an Emergency Powers Bill', 1 May 1914, para. 1.
7. Ibid., para. 14.
8. PRO, WO 32/7112, R. H. Brade to all GOCs in C at Home and GOC London District, 9 November 1911.
9. PRO, CAB 16/31/EP1, p. 2

in 1888 on the suggestion of Colonel (later Major-General Sir John) Ardagh.[10]
It included provisions for the immediate military take-over of land and roads.
The bill was put aside on the understanding that it could be brought forward
when the circumstances were ripe, the intention being that the bill would be
passed rapidly through Parliament when the emergency existed.[11] This did not
appear to satisfy the War Department. The War Office subsequently wrote to
the Treasury that Stanhope, the Secretary of State for War, had,

> had it impressed upon him by his military advisers that, for the safety of the
> country, it is essential that Her Majesty should possess in a time of great national
> emergency, powers over lands, property, and persons of Her subjects which are
> far in excess of those which the common law confers. At the same [time], it
> is necessary, both for securing prompt obedience to the mandates of military
> necessity and for assuring military commanders against actions for things illegal
> done in the execution of their duty, that these extraordinary powers at an
> extraordinary crisis should be sanctioned by the law.[12]

It was at this point that the War Office came up against a powerful legal
opponent in the shape of Mr (later Sir) Courteney Ilbert (1841–1924), the
parliamentary draftsman.[13] Ilbert, before whom the measure was laid in
1891, intimated that he did not consider the Bill was necessary. The War
Department remained undaunted, and despite the lack of support from
Sir Henry Campbell-Bannerman, Secretary of State for War in 1895, it tried
again. Ardagh redrafted his bill of 1888 and once more it went to Ilbert, again
to receive the thumbs down. On this occasion, Ilbert submitted a lengthy
memorandum on the subject, dated August 1896, the essence of which was
that the Crown already possessed, under common law, the necessary powers.
He pointed out that in the event of an invasion of the realm or an imminent
risk of invasion, it was the duty of the military authorities to take all steps
necessary, in their opinion, for the defence of the realm; and that it would be
the duty of the civil authorities and of every subject to aid and support the
military authorities, significantly adding that compensation would be payable
to those suffering loss in such circumstances. Not only was this duty grounded
in common law but

> any attempt to specify in detail and to express in statutory language the powers
> exerciseable by the civil and military authorities under such circumstances
> might throw doubt on the prerogative powers of the Crown, and would

10. PRO, CAB 16/31/EP2, para. 8.
11. PRO, WO 32/7112, 'Martial Law in the United Kingdom. Case for the Opinion of
the Law Officers of the Crown', *c.* April 1913.
12. PRO, CAB 16/31/EP2, para. 9.
13. For details of Ilbert's career, see entry by G. R. Rubin in A. W. B. Simpson (ed.),
A Biographical Dictionary of the Common Law (London, 1984), pp. 267–68. A photograph of
Ilbert appears therein.

probably involve the imposition of restrictions and limitations which would be inconvenient and misleading, and which in practice it would be necessary to disregard.[14]

Ilbert not only placed his faith on the generality of common law prerogative powers to act in cases of necessity. He also considered that a statute might be positively harmful if couched in specific terms, for it might then be construed as derogating from general powers under the 'ordinary' law, an unhelpful situation where 'difficulties arising in due course of war or of preparations for war cannot be foreseen'. He warned: 'In the event of invasion or of imminent risk of invasion, it might, and probably would, be necessary to take much stronger steps than would be authorised by the War Office draft.' No doubt, if the government insisted, he observed, a statute 'adequate to the necessities of the case' could be prepared within the hour and passed through Parliament in a single day. He dismissively concluded that 'the elaboration of a statutory "emergency code" would appear to be an academic exercise on which a government official would not be justified in spending his time unless he happened to be in the enjoyment of superabundant leisure'.

Military criticism of Ilbert's opinion seems to have been informed by two related factors. First, as Ilbert himself acknowledged, the exercise of general powers at the discretion of military officers was to run the risk of exposing the latter to a continual danger of legal proceedings, as the boundaries of lawful action might not be capable of delineation with pinpoint accuracy in the event of tumult or disorder or chaos. The fate of Pinney, the mayor of Bristol, tried for neglect of duty, and of Colonel Brereton who as commander of the troops during the Bristol Riots in 1831 was court-martialed; and the martial law controversy involving Governor Eyre's handling of the Jamaica rebellion in 1865, haunted the military authorities.[15] The CID sub-committee in 1914 were reminded of the remarks in 1887 of the Commander-in-Chief, Lord Wolseley.

> To rely on General Officers taking all the necessary responsibility in an emergency would be the height of madness. The manner in which Government treated Governor Eyre is too fresh in the memory of the Army to admit of any reliance being placed on officers to break the law in a dire emergency. Some, doubtless, would do so deliberately, preferring to be treated as Governor Eyre was, to exposing the country to risk; but many law-abiding gentlemen would

14.   PRO, WO 32/7112, 'Emergency Powers. Memorandum by C. P. Ilbert, 5 August 1896', para. 2. Subsequent quotations in the text, until otherwise indicated, are from paras. 12, 11, 27(5) and 28, respectively, of this memorandum. See also Charles Townshend, 'Military Force and Civil Authority in the United Kingdom, 1914–1921', *Journal of British Studies*, 28 (1989), at pp. 262–79.
15.   On these episodes, see Charles Townshend, 'Martial Law: Legal and Administrative Problems of Civil Emergency in Britain and the Empire, 1800–1940', *Historical Journal*, 25 (1982), pp. 167–95.

not have the moral courage to do so. It is not fair deliberately to place an officer in such a dilemma.[16]

As MacDonogh had pointed out to his superior, Sir Henry Wilson, in 1911, the common law, as described in the *Manual of Military Law*, permitted the taking of 'exceptional measures in time of invasion as may be necessary' for the restoration of order. Such measures were limited by 'immediate necessity'. Therefore, he added:

> It does not seem that anything beyond this is allowed, and in addition to the fact that, human nature being what it is, many officers and others will in time of emergency either do the wrong thing or fail to do the right one, there is the further difficulty of dealing with the Civil Power as represented by the Courts. In the absence of an Act of Parliament it is too much to expect that the Courts will not hamper the military powers.[17]

Fears of exposure to legal proceedings might cause military officers to act indecisively, the consequences might be military disaster. Second, Ilbert's general approach was dubbed by the War Office as a policy of *laissez-faire* which was in direct conflict with that being pursued by the CID itself, with its preoccupation with contingency wartime planning. Legal preparations were as necessary, in the view of the military, as those concerned more directly with the fighting and security aspects. Since the law provided the framework for the latter activities, the law had to be got 'right'.

The difficulty was to persuade its political masters that the War Office's complaint of inadequate legal powers was real and not imaginary. During the first few years of the twentieth century the matter appeared to have been put to one side, perhaps because of the more immediate need to absorb the recruitment lessons of the Boer War. In particular, the political uproar caused by the revelations of the Interdepartmental Committee on Physical Deterioration in 1904 preoccupied the minds of the military authorities at the time. In 1911, however, attempts were made to interest the then Secretary of State, Lord Haldane, in the proposals. To no avail, for Haldane, the future Lord Chancellor, was content to place reliance on the flexible qualities of the common law. His successor at the War Office, Colonel Seely, agreed to refer the question to the Law Officers in 1913. MacDonogh busied himself with drafting a memorandum to this purpose, calling attention to the fact that English law, unlike its counterparts abroad, knew no concept of *l'état de siège*. This was an interim situation between normality and emergency, during which time precautionary powers might be exercised before an immediate necessity had arisen. The common law appeared to make no provision for such contingency. He ended by pouring scorn on Ilbert's advocacy of the

16. PRO, CAB 16/31/EP2, para. 22,
17. PRO, WO 32/7112, MacDonogh to Wilson, *c.* 27 May 1911.

sufficiency of prerogative powers, concluding that, 'the exercise of martial law [here meaning non-statutory emergency powers] being justified solely by necessity, which may have to be proved, the prerogative power is too doubtful to be relied on for practical service . . .'[18]

Yet again, the lawyers appeared to close ranks against the military. Once more the legal advisers came down on the side of the status quo; on this occasion, Rufus Isaacs, the Attorney-General, and Sir John Simon, Solicitor-General, expressing their agreement with the thrust of the Ilbert memorandum drafted seventeen years previously. Their concise 169 word opinion merely reiterated the malleability of the common law and the danger of enacting an exhaustive list of required powers. 'The great merit of the Common Law', they wrote, 'is that it will justify even an unprecedented course of action if it is fairly covered by the maxim *salus respublicae suprema lex*.'[19] For good measure, they added, a Bill of Indemnity could, if necessary, be passed. The apparent contradiction appeared to cause the law officers no problems of self-doubt (in that a Bill of Indemnity would appear to assume the strong possibility of an unlawful exercise of power).

MacDonogh was nothing if not persistent. Following the rebuff in July 1913, he tried once more, with the support of Sir Henry Wilson and of Brigadier-General David Henderson, Director of Military Training, to bring about a fundamental change of thinking on the part of the government.[20] By November 1913 there was light at the end of the tunnel. The Prime Minister, Asquith, eventually agreed to refer the whole matter to the CID sub-committee whose deliberations provided the point of departure for this chapter. Though the sub-committee papers were prepared in March–April 1914, the actual meeting did not take place till 30 June. Two days earlier, the Archduke Franz Ferdinand had been assassinated, though the significance of this event had not yet been grasped. Perhaps this is one explanation why Sir John Simon, who was by now Attorney-General, continued to play a similar legal refrain before the sub-committee to that which had accompanied the previous enquiries into the nature and content of emergency powers. When the chairman of the sub-committee, the Home Secretary, Reginald McKenna, enquired whether in the event of a 'precautionary period' being declared, the common law would not protect officers entering private property for the erection of necessary defensive works, the Attorney-General answered in the affirmative.[21] Yet at least he now recognised a difficulty facing the military. He acknowledged that, 'what the War Office wanted was some way of convincing officers', that their actions would be lawful when war had not

18. Ibid., 'Martial Law . . .', c. April 1913, p. 5.
19. Ibid., 'Martial Law in the United Kingdom. Opinion of the Law Officers of the Crown', 17 July 1913. French, who cites the Opinion (which was reprinted in CAB 16/31/EP2, appendix 2 for the CID Sub-Committee), wrongly dates it to 1914. See French, *British Economic and Strategic Planning*, p. 83n.
20. Ibid., MacDonogh to Wilson, 13 November 1913.
21. PRO, CAB 16/31/EP1, pp. 3–4 for this and subsequent quotations.

yet broken out. A bill, he suggested, would merely discourage the executive from taking action while it was going through parliament. A proclamation, Simon considered, would be more suitable since it would merely embody the royal prerogative power to defend the realm. It would state that

> whereas certain conditions had arisen necessitating the adoption of precautionary measures for the defence of the country, the responsible authorities might be compelled to take certain steps which were justified by the common law ... An advantage of the Proclamation would be that it would enlighten the public on the powers which it was lawful to exercise in time of emergency.

Simon thus maintained his consistent line that the common law was adequate to meet the necessity of the case. Inasmuch as the object was to 'reassure a timid General Officer', the War Office representative at the meeting, Major James, declared himself satisfied.

International events moved rapidly thereafter, especially from 24 July when Austria's ultimatum to Serbia was endorsed by Germany. A few days later, the British home fleet's orders to disperse after exercises were countermanded by Churchill, the First Lord of the Admiralty. So was there a proclamation forthcoming, indicating the common law powers which it was lawful for the military authorities to exercise in an emergency prior to the actual declaration of war? Since a 'precautionary period' was instituted less than a month after the CID meeting, such a proclamation might have been expected. Instead, Maurice Hankey, the secretary of the CID, recalled that:

> During the next few days I was extremely busy putting the finishing touches on the War Book – printing off copies of some belated instructions still in proof, working with MacDonogh and Parliamentary Counsel on the Defence of the Realm Regulations, and so forth.[22]

Within the space of five weeks, there took place a rapid about-turn in policy on the kind of legal framework required in wartime. The sub-committee had indeed been charged with considering what emergency legislation 'if any' was necessary or desirable during the precautionary period and in war. Actual discussions were, in the event, confined to a consideration of the legal framework only for the precautionary period. It appears that the War Office's shopping list of emergency powers for use during wartime itself managed to slip through the committee undebated and without challenge. A proclamation was published in the *London Gazette* for 14 August 1914, but it merely incorporated the defence regulations of 12 August issued under the authority of the first Defence of the Realm Act of 8 August, the statutory embodiment of that shopping list of emergency powers.

---

22. Lord Hankey, *The Supreme Command, 1914–1918*, 1 (London, 1961), pp. 153–54. The War Book contained all approved defensive preparations of the state including necessary orders-in-council, regulations, telegrams and other communications. See ibid., ch. xii.

The Defence of the Realm Act itself, Sir John Simon noted in his auto-biography, had passed through all its stages in Parliament on the first day of the war, even before there was time to circulate it as a bill. Far from bemoaning the failure to resort to a proclamation outlining the military authorities' common law powers, as Simon had recommended a month previously, he now remarked that the statute 'and much else beside, had been carefully prepared beforehand'.[23] His own ambiguous role in respect of such a general purpose defence statute passed without comment.

23.   Viscount Simon, *Retrospect* (London, 1952), pp. 103–4.

2

No Expropriation without Compensation

As has been seen, legal powers of property requisition for military use and for the defence of the realm were contained in a series of nineteenth-century statutes, the Defence Acts 1842–73 and the Military Lands Act 1892. In addition, the royal prerogative appeared to confer power on the Crown to requisition property in an apprehended emergency, though it might be inferred that the doctrine of necessity suggested that the right was not a legal power unique to the Crown but a power shared by and available to all subjects to combat the emergency.

It may be enlightening to pose a number of basic philosophical questions. First, could property be rightfully taken from an owner at all? Secondly, did the state, in the absence of parliamentary authority, possess a right to requisition private property or did such a right exist, if at all, only in circumstances of dire emergency? If such a taking of land or buildings or goods or chattels did occur, did the owner possess a legal right to compensation deniable only on the authority of Parliament? Or could the state take without paying compensation where Parliament remained silent on the question?

As to the first question, F. A. Mann concludes:

> The answer is clear: all the available evidence goes to show that at all stages of history, the individual owner was liable to have his property taken from him. Never and nowhere was there any support for the proposition that that property could not in any circumstances be taken, that it was sacrosanct, inviolable. Nor is there any evidence that in reality this was ever doubted. On the contrary, the long struggle about the conditions of and the restrictions upon expropriation could not have occurred had the right of expropriation not been assumed and treated as superior to the right of property.[1]

Ownership, that is *dominium*, was not incompatible in other circumstances with expropriation and with loss of *dominium*. Property rights were always qualified, suggesting the immanence of a social theory of property even if ownership was the least qualified right of property identifiable in a legal

---

1. F. A. Mann, 'Outlines of a History of Expropriation', *Law Quarterly Review*, 75 (1959), pp. 188–219, at p. 189.

system. When the state expropriated property, it did so by virtue not of ownership, though this may have been the theoretical basis of expropriation by feudal lords, but of sovereignty. As Mann states:

> it cannot be, and for some centuries has not been, doubted that it is by virtue of its sovereignty, by public or constitutional law rather than by virtue of ownership that the supreme authority in the State has the power to take private property ... It thus appears that it is not the existence or the source, but the exercise of the State's right to take private property which poses the real problems of legal significance.[2]

The problems to be tackled were therefore those concerned with the limitations imposed upon the exercise of the state's power of expropriation. Derived from the writings of the Dutch jurist, Grotius (1583–1645), and from ideas of natural law, the doctrine informing this power is reflected in American terminology today as 'eminent domain', the right which inheres in the Federal government, even in the absence of explicit provision in the written constitution: 'The right is the offspring of political necessity and it is inseparable from sovereignty, unless denied to it by its fundamental law.'[3] Eminent domain is a distinct doctrine to which there is no exact counterpart in English common law, though the extravagantly worded claims as to the scope of prerogative powers might overlap with it. According to one view, English law took no note of eminent domain because 'the power is included ... in the absolutism of Parliament'.[4] Integral to the American doctrine was that there could be no expropriation without compensation. In its English statutory variant, land could not normally be acquired compulsorily by the state or for public utilities unless under the authority of a private Act of Parliament passed for that purpose. Private acts were passed to acquire land compulsorily for the construction of canals, ports, roads, for road-widening and for the railways in the nineteenth century, latterly incorporating the model provisions and compensation scheme set out in the Lands Clauses Consolidation Act 1845. It complemented the compulsory powers of the Defence Acts, with this difference: the Defence Acts were the only general public as distinct from special or private statutes which permitted the compulsory purchase of land for those purposes already noted – for ordnance or for training purposes or, more generally, for the defence of the realm.

That compensation for dispossessed landowners in the nineteenth century bordered on the lavish simply attested to the power and influence that the landed interest could still exert on contemporary parliaments, on the

---

2. Ibid., p. 192.
3. *Kohl* v. *United States* (1876) 91 U.S. 449, at p. 451, *per* Strong J., cited in ibid., p. 193.
4. Carman F. Randolph, 'The Eminent Domain', ibid., 3 (1887), pp. 314–25, at p. 323.

arbitrators or magistrates who fixed the amounts of compensation, even on the judiciary who tended to confirm liberal awards. These were based on notions of market value plus a *solatium* for the hurt feelings caused by compulsory divestment of one's property, an amount which was conventionally fixed as an additional 10 per cent.[5] Expropriation was, in this mould, not merely a 'legislative or administrative act but a compulsory contract'.[6]

If relevant English legislation was silent as to compensation, the right of the owner to obtain compensation could not be denied. This had been confirmed in numerous judicial dicta. For example, Lord Justice Bowen in *London & North-Western Railway Company* v. *Evans* declared that:

> The legislature cannot be fairly supposed to intend in the absence of clear words showing such intention, that one man's property shall be confiscated for the benefit of others, or of the public, without any compensation being provided for him in respect of what is taken compulsorily from him. Parliament in its omnipotence can, of course, override or disregard this ordinary principle as it can override the former, if it sees fit to do so, but it is not likely that it will be found disregarding it without plain expressions of such a purpose.[7]

As Mann points out, this might be seen as a 'paramount principle of construction, though in truth [it is] a rule of constitutional law'.[8] No instances could be cited of English statutes authorising requisition without compensation or indeed requisition for purposes other than public ones. An intensive historical search undertaken among the dusty records of the Public Record Office for the Court of Appeal and for the House of Lords in the post-war 'Case of Requisition', *Attorney-General* v *De Keyser's Royal Hotel Ltd*, did not assist.[9] It failed to uncover cases where property had been taken without payment of compensation by the state under statutory authority even for military powers in the midst of war, such as the Napoleonic wars.[10] That was not to say that Parliament could not legislate accordingly, or even make

---

5. Juries asked to settle compensation disputes between landowners and railway companies tended to favour the latter. In 1845 a House of Lords select committee advocated an addition for *solatium* of at least 50 per cent. On these points, see W. R. Cornish and G. de N. Clark, *Law and Society in England, 1750–1950* (London, 1989), p. 153.

6. Mann, 'Outlines of a History', p. 196.

7. *London & North-Western Railway Co.* v. *Evans* [1893] 1 Ch. 16, at 28, and see the cases cited in Mann, 'Outlines of a History', p. 199n.

8. Ibid., p. 199.

9. *Attorney-General* v. *De Keyser's Royal Hotel Ltd.* [1919] 2 Ch. 197 (C.A.); [1920] A.C.508 (H.L.). The case is discussed fully in chapter 6, below.

10. For plentiful examples of statutes, commissions, proceedings, memoranda, instructions, warrants, letters patent and War Office records going back to 1512, but from which no examples of requisitioning without payment of compensation by the state could be found, see Leslie Scott and Alfred Hildesley, *The Case of Requisition: De Keyser's Royal Hotel Limited v. The King* (Oxford, 1920), pp. 220–304. See below for further reference to Leslie Scott.

provision for confiscatory levels of compensation; only that in order to do so, the statutory wording would require to be unequivocally precise.[11]

What if Parliament had not legislated? In English law, the Crown claimed a power under the royal prerogative, that collection of residual powers recognised at common law as inhering in the King, and latterly in his ministers on his behalf (or as A. V. Dicey inaccurately though familiarly defined it, that discretionary or arbitrary authority which at any given time is legally left in the hands of the Crown),[12] to requisition property. Authority for this claim has always been shrouded in uncertainty, leaving aside the added difficulty that property itself is an imprecise concept. What was freely acknowledged within legal authority was the right of the state under the royal prerogative to take those steps deemed necessary for the defence of the realm. Even this proposition could convey a misleading impression on two counts. First, the taking of steps to defend the realm might be limited to matters concerning the deployment of the armed forces, so that the taking of property by the state for this purpose could be unlawful as not falling within the scope of the royal prerogative. Yet the state, early in the war, relied on prerogative powers for this purpose; and during the crucial years was successful in deflecting legal efforts to declare such a procedure unlawful. The courts never authoritatively declared the purported exercise of such powers unlawful when faced with a case in which there was an absence of circumstances pointing to an immediate emergency. On the other hand, the House of Lords did not feel compelled to give its stamp of approval to reliance on the prerogative for purposes short of immediate necessity for the defence of the realm.

If, for the sake of argument, there was no doubt as to the existence of a prerogative power to requisition all manner of property, the equally critical matter of whether compensation for such a requisition by the state was legally due to the owner needed next to be addressed. This question was an unavoidable adjunct to the administrative arrangements made by the state during the war in respect to the requisitioning of properties taken over for military purposes, whether the take-over was under prerogative power assumed to be lawful or under statutory authority which might be silent or parsimonious as to compensation entitlement. If compensation for a prerogative taking was due *ex*

11. Cf. the decision of the European Court of Human Rights on the claim of United Kingdom shipbuilding and dock companies that the nationalisation of their firms, and the low levels of compensation offered, were in breach of the principle of no expropriation without adequate compensation and of the fundamental right to property enshrined in the European Convention on Human Rights, Article One of the Protocol to the Convention. See *Lithgow et al.* v. *United Kingdom* (1986) 8 E.H.R.R. 329. For the epochal influence of that *annus mirabilis*, 1789, see Mann, 'Outlines of a History', pp. 207–8. For England, the Civil War and the bloodless Revolution of 1689 have assumed significance for the rights of private property, a significance perhaps bordering on the extravagant. As J. W. Gough observed, 'Englishmen did not need Locke to tell them that the chief reason why civil government was established was to protect property'. See J. W. Gough, *Fundamental Law in English Constitutional History* (Oxford, 1955), p. 54, cited in Mann, 'Outlines of a History', p. 197.

12. A. V. Dicey, *Law of the Constitution* (8th edn, London, 1915), p. 420.

lege, then the quantum to be paid was outside the influence of the government. If no obligation to pay existed in law and if any payments were *ex gratia*, the amount was wholly within the discretion of the government, which could result in considerable savings to the Exchequer. The House of Lords was not required to rule on an application for compensation where the exercise of prerogative powers had been allegedly undertaken. In the *De Keyser* case, the matter of compensation had been settled on statutory authority. Consequently, judicial remarks on compensation entitlements under the prerogative were invariably obiter. In the leading cases, some of them dating from the sixteenth century, which declared support for a prerogative right to take over land, a legal obligation on the part of the Crown to pay compensation was nowhere admitted.[13] In the midst of the war, Lord Parker of Waddington declared in a House of Lords decision: 'The municipal law of this country does not give compensation to a subject whose land or goods are requisitioned by the Crown.'[14] By 1920, in the *De Keyser* case, the House of Lords judges seemed to express conflicting observations. One of the judges, Lord Dunedin, stated that the historical evidence as to compensation payments for requisitioning under the prerogative was, in his view, consistent either with *ex lege* or *ex gratia* payments.[15] Lord Moulton declared:

> Nor have I any doubt that in those days the subjects who had suffered in this way in war would not have been held to have any claim against the Crown for compensation in respect of the damage they had there suffered. The limited and necessary interference with the property of the subjects, of which I have spoken, would have been looked upon as part of the damage done by the war which had fallen to their lot to bear, and there is no reason to think that anyone would have thought that he had a claim against the Crown in respect of it.[16]

This proposition seemed to doubt payment of compensation *ex lege*. By contrast, Lord Sumner said of the historical searches at the Public Record Office:

> Many documents are forthcoming which relate to the taking of land for such purposes by agreement and on payment of compensation. None can be found relating to taking land as of right without any compensation at all, even in time of war.[17]

---

13. That is, *R v. Hampden* (1637) 3 How. St. Tr. 825, at 1195 (the *Ship-Money* case); *The King's Prerogative in Saltpetre* (1606) 12 Co. Rep. 12; and *Hole v. Barlow* (1858) 4 C.B. (n.s.) 334, among others.

14. *The Zamora* [1916] 2 A.C. 77, at p. 100.

15. [1920] A.C. 508, at p. 525.

16. Ibid., p. 552. As well as being a judicial member of the House of Lords, Moulton was a Fellow of the Royal Society and Director-General of Explosives Supply at the Ministry of Munitions.

17. Ibid., p. 563.

Lord Parmoor quoting the Master of the Rolls, Lord Swinfen-Eady in the Court of Appeal, found that on the basis of the searches undertaken: 'it does not appear that the Crown has ever taken subjects' land for the defence of the country, without paying for it; and even in Stuart times, I cannot trace any claim by the Crown to such a prerogative.'[18]

The limitations of the searches were acknowledged. Lord Moulton observed that no trace of a compensation claim *ex lege* for a prerogative taking could be found.[19] Lord Summer noted:

> No petition of right is to be found on which a suppliant seeks to recover compensation, but whether this be, as the Crown suggests, because no subject ever had the temerity to put forward such a contention, or, as the respondents argue, because the Crown never gave him occasion to do so, is a matter which remains unknown. There appears to be no reported case which has decided that the subject is entitled to compensation for lands taken by the Crown, in purported exercise of the prerogative, but to this circumstance the same observation applies.[20]

Nothing authoritative was established on this question during the war.[21] What of the question of whether the take-over of De Keyser's Royal Hotel on London's Embankment in order to house the clerical staff of the Royal Flying Corps (RFC) fell within the scope of the prerogative power? Was the emergency so immediate as to justify the exercise of that legal power? More generally, was the proposition relating to invasion and to the enemy being at the gate, which informed the seventeenth-century authorities such as *The King's Prerogative in Saltpetre*,[22] applicable in the age of huge government bureaucracies organising for 'total war', of Zeppelin attacks, of the trenches of the Western Front or of the national projectile factories of the Ministry of Munitions? On the specific question concerning De Keyser's Royal Hotel, Lord Moulton strongly hinted at the answer:

> This litigation itself is enough to show how debatable a proposition it would have been if the claim had been made that the ancient Prerogative of the Crown covered the taking of a hotel for the more comfortable housing of a military staff and its clerks and typewriters.[23]

---

18. Ibid., p. 573.
19. Ibid., p. 552.
20. Ibid., p. 563. The petition of right procedure enabled 'suppliants' to sue the Crown for breach of contract.
21. In 1935 Lord Justice Roche pointed out that a passage in Clarendon's *History of the Rebellion in England*, Book II, written between 1646 and 1648, suggested there had never been a requisition by the state without payment of compensation and that none of those arguing the requisition cases during the Great War seemed to have been aware of this source. See *Consett Iron Co. Ltd* v. *Clavering Trustees* [1935] 2 K.B. 42, cited in (Anon.). 'Requisitions – Clarendon's Opinion – "Carefully to be Repaired by the Public Stock"'. *Law Times*, 180 (1935), pp. 35–36.
22. *The King's Prerogative in Saltpetre* (1606) 12 Co. Rep. 12.
23. *Attorney-General* v. *De Keyser's Royal Hotel Ltd.* [1920] A.C. 508, at p. 549.

On whether the prerogative power had authorised the previous military requisitioning of Shoreham Aerodrome, Lord Sumner was more equivocal:

> Rightly or wrongly, the facts of the *Shoreham case* were assumed to have been analogous to the case of raising bulwarks. No question arose of the taking of buildings for the mere use of administrative officials, although employed in one of the combatant branches of the administration.[24]

It was a carefully worded statement which nonetheless remained noncommittal.

This was also the approach of the law lords to the scope of the prerogative in general. 'I do not think that the precise extent of the Prerogative need now be dealt with', insisted Lord Sumner.[25] 'It is not necessary', stated Lord Parmoor,

> to inquire into how far in certain cases of necessity for public defence the Executive has power to act without statutory authority, but a generalization of this wide character requires careful analysis in its application to special conditions such as have arisen in the present appeal.[26]

The questions therefore did not require answers, for, as noted earlier, existing statutory authority for both a take-over of the property and for payment of compensation *ex lege* was discovered. As Lord Dunedin concluded on the basis of the historical evidence adduced before the court: 'There is a universal practice of paying resting on bargain before 1708 and on statutory power and provision after 1708.'[27]

But *absente* legislation or of contract or even of *vente forceé*, would the prerogative have been applicable here? In the Court of Appeal in *De Keyser*, a distinction was drawn between property taken for the defence of the realm *stricto sensu*, which would be a prerogative taking, and property taken to facilitate the defence of the realm, which was thought to fall outside the ambit of the prerogative. The latter would be exemplified by the installing of the RFC headquarters in De Keyser's Royal Hotel. The former, thought the Court of Appeal, was demonstrated by the take-over of Shoreham Aerodrome by the War Office in December 1914 as an advance defence and warning station against Zeppelin incursion.[28] But the approval by the Court of Appeal of reliance on prerogative powers to requisition the aerodrome attracted, in its turn, the condemnation of the distinguished legal commentator, Sir Frederick Pollock, editor of the *Law Quarterly Review*: 'The dicta about lawful entry on a man's land to make a bulwark for the defence of the realm', wrote Sir Frederick, 'seem to us not to contemplate general military

24. Ibid., p. 564.
25. Ibid., p. 561.
26. Ibid., p. 568.
27. Ibid., p. 525.
28. *In re a Petition of Right* [1915] 3 K.B. 649 (C.A.). The case is fully discussed in chapter 4, below.

requisition but the precise emergency of apprehended attack on the spot.'[29] It is clear that this expression of opinion challenged not only the court's upholding of the Crown's refusal to award the aerodrome owners compensation *ex lege*, but also the very applicability to the case of the prerogative itself. By July 1916, the Crown recognised that the Shoreham Aerodrome ruling in its favour was a mere temporary advantage obliging it to compromise financially with the owners out of court.[30]

The divergence of opinion on the applicability of the prerogative to the take-over of land was also highlighted in two contributions to the *Law Quarterly Review* in October 1916 and April 1918. In the earlier paper, by F. C. T. Tudsbery, a strong claim was made for an expansive interpretation of the prerogative powers of the Crown to defend the realm in time of war. Thus he argued that: 'any action which would in time of peace be illegal would be justified provided that it can be shown that such action was reasonably necessary for the purpose of maintaining order and for the defence of the realm'.[31] The vagueness of the last dozen or so words is noteworthy. It was for the Crown to determine the manner in which such prerogative power was to be exercised, or, as Lord Justice Warrington put it in the Shoreham Aerodrome case,

> The only condition which it would appear must be fulfilled is that the act in question, having regard to existing circumstances, must be necessary for the public safety and the defence of the realm, and on this matter the opinion of the competent military authorities, who alone have sufficient knowledge of the fact, provided they act reasonably and in good faith, should be accepted as conclusive.[32]

The qualification 'provided they act reasonably and in good faith' was probably more theoretical than actual. It would require a litigant to assert that the 'competent military authority' had taken leave of its senses and had taken action which amounted to the imposition of martial law: paradoxically, the denial of regular law which Colonel MacDonogh had recognised in his note to General Sir Henry Wilson in 1911. Tudsbery's view was delightfully simple:

> The maintenance of an army in time of war naturally connotes the requisitioning of goods, the occupation of private property, and the doing of all manner of things which would be illegal in time of peace, and were it not for the prerogative rights of the Crown would be equally illegal in time of war.[33]

29. Sir Frederick Pollock, editorial, *Law Quarterly Review*, 32 (1916), p. 339.
30. Chapter 5, below.
31. F. C. T. Tudsbery, 'Prerogative in Time of War', *Law Quarterly Review*, 32 (1916), pp. 384–91, at p. 385. Major Tudsbery O.B.E., LL.M. was a serving officer in the Army and became secretary of the Surplus Government Property Disposal Board, attached to the Ministry of Munitions after the war. See *Surplus*, no. 3, 1 July 1919. See also chapter 14, below.
32. *In re a Petition of Right* [1915] 3 K.B. 649 (C.A.), at p. 665.
33. Tudsbery, 'Prerogative', p. 389. See chapter 1, above.

One answer to this claim was to question the generality of the proposition. It was acknowledged that:

> All the developments of modern warfare have made an extension of the meaning of invasion imperative. That has been realized by the courts [in the Court of Appeal ruling in the Shoreham Aerodrome case], but there is still necessarily a great deal of ambiguity about the degree of imminent danger to the realm which would justify the dispossession of land.[34]

Given the new vulnerability of the country to aerial attack, the maintenance of a state of readiness could theoretically warrant a prerogative taking of all land. The author clearly considered this an improbable interpretation and quoted an earlier source who advised:

> Emergencies may arise where it is necessary, for the safety of the State to commit additional powers to the persons entrusted with its defence. But when such cases occur, we are to be guided by considerations of reason and expediency in the powers we confer and not by vain and empty theories of prerogatives which the very act we are called upon to perform proves to be futile and unfounded.[35]

By the adoption of this dictum, the prerogative would be shown to rest upon the 'will of the people', and its modernisation at the behest 'not of a monarch but of an enlightened and progressive community.'[36] The implication of these remarks was that the more 'extravagantly archaic' were the Crown's claims on behalf of the prerogative, the more they possessed a 'Prussian taint', the more the constitution was weakened. The extremely cautious conclusion drawn by the author from a review of the pre-Armistice cases was that, 'the whole question of the Prerogative is left in a nebulous state'. As to the democratic urge, the 'will of the people' was respected by securing statutory power, 'which pays homage by saving the dignity of Prerogative while distrusting its authority'.[37]

That statutory authority for the requisitioning in an emergency of land, buildings and certain goods was available before the war, or was very rapidly enacted in the Defence of the Realm legislation from August 1914 onwards, is a matter of record. For land, the nineteenth century Defence Acts and the Military Lands Act 1892 have already been noted. For billeting purposes, section 108A of the Army Act 1881 (as amended) was available. For the

---

34. V. St. Clair Mackenzie, 'The Royal Prerogative in War-Time', *Law Quarterly Review*, 34 (1918), pp. 152–59, at p. 155.

35. *Allen on the Royal Prerogative* (1849), cited ibid., pp. 156–57.

36. Ibid., p. 156.

37. Ibid., p. 159. Events in Burma during the Second World War prompted a subsequent authoritative ruling from the House of Lords that compensation was payable to owners as a matter of law when their property was requisitioned under the prerogative. See *Burmah Oil Co. Ltd. v. Lord Advocate* [1965] A.C.75. The following year, Parliament nullified the effect of the ruling by passing the War Damage Act 1965.

requisitioning of vehicles, including carriages, animals and barges, section 115 of the 1881 Act provided the necessary authority.[38] For the commandeering of aircraft, power was inserted in the Army (Annual) Act 1913 after the Committee of Imperial Defence enquired as to the Army's legal powers of impressment of airships and aeroplanes,[39] while the prerogative power to requisition British ships for the defence of the realm was not disputed by owners. On 7 August 1914 the Army's right to requisition chattels (moveable possessions) was granted by the Army (Supply of Food, Forage and Stores) Act 1914, which amended section 113(2) of the 1881 Act accordingly. In all the statutory cases, the obligation to pay compensation, usually on the basis of fair market value, was laid down. The copious defence regulations issued under the Defence of the Realm Acts (DORA) were, less assuredly and less legitimately, a written refutation of expropriation without parliamentary representation. Regulations 2, 2A, 2B and 7, among many others, authorised, or purported to authorise, the requisitioning of property, whether land, buildings or chattels; in the case of Reg. 2B, it came to grief on the rocks of the *ultra vires* doctrine in the *Newcastle Breweries* case in 1920 when its niggardly compensation provision was successfully challenged.[40]

Subsequent chapters will explore the interplay between regular statutes, wartime legislation and the royal prerogative, not specifically from the standpoint of the lawyer, but from the perspective of the government administrator. We will be exploring the background debates, arguments, claims and policies pursued by the protagonists: the individual property owners and the various government departments involved in the process of requisitioning private property. Though departmental officials were, at the outset of the war, confident that their legal arsenals were adequately stocked for the purpose at hand, that is, to take over land and buildings 'for the public safety and the defence of the realm,' in the words of DORA, their confidence was undermined by the forced compromise over Shoreham Aerodrome in July 1916. From that time on, government departments were obliged to resort to various ploys, subterfuges or mere bluff, or to contemplate law reform proposals (effectively delayed till after the war), in order to ensure that following military requisition of private property, the government's financial burden in providing compensation to owners was kept within those bounds considered reasonable by the executive.

In one respect civil servants involved in legal administration appear not to have been too unhappy at the uncertain legal position in respect both to the requisitioning of private property, and to the payment of compensation therefor. The common law prerogative power was in part mysterious, mystical, divine, imprecise in scope, of obscure origin, of uncertain longevity; a recipe for delay, procrastination, intimidation of property owners and an instrument

38. For forms of requisition under sections 108A and 115, see PRO, WO 32/7088.
39. PRO, TS 27/24, 'Impressment of Airships and Aeroplanes', January 1913.
40. *Newcastle Breweries Ltd.* v. *R.* [1920] 1 K.B. 854. See below, chapter 3.

of bluff. Perhaps that state of affairs was not intolerable, even if it lacked the precision of statutory authority. Legislative powers *could* limit the actions of officials, while favourable provisions might risk judicial emasculation or, in respect to some defence regulations, judicial condemnation. To insist that at least statutory powers would be clearer would be to miss the point. Clarity could denote the limitation of powers just as easily as the conferral of powers on the executive. In anticipation of the object of Lord Hewart's attack on the 'New Despotism' in the inter-war years, executive discretion was something to be cherished by government administrators, not something of which to be wary.[41] For a number of citizens and property owners, it looked like lawlessness.

41. See below, chapter 14.

3

DORA, the Lady of Doubtful Legality

It is unnecessary to analyse all those emergency regulations which regulated the use and deployment of property during the war given that the aim of this study is to explore how government departments faced up to the task of regulating the war economy, and how they sought to overcome or by-pass legal obstacles in this endeavour. Thus a doctrinal analysis of wartime cases on the legality of Defence Regulations is not strictly speaking necessary. Instead, emphasis will be placed on the approaches of government departments and of ministers to particular legal difficulties as they emerged from time to time. There will be no attempt, consequently, to offer a comprehensive survey of wartime administrative law.

The first Defence of the Realm Act, passed on 8 August 1914, declared that His Majesty in Council had power during the continuation of the war to issue regulations as to the powers and duties of those responsible for securing the public safety and the defence of the realm. This included the issuing of regulations aimed at preventing espionage and similar actions and at securing the safety of means of communication, railways, docks or harbours.

Three weeks later, the Defence of the Realm (No. 2) Act added to the above military aims and also enabled regulations to be issued to suspend any restrictions on the acquisition or user of land or on any other power under the Defence Acts 1842 to 1875 or the Military Lands Acts 1891 to 1903. These restrictions, as already noted, related to the elaborate and lengthy procedures to be followed before a military take-over of land could be effected. Their lifting was designed to ensure that no undue delay in occupying land for military purposes was experienced. The Crown was prepared to argue in litigation that the lifting of such restrictions also implied the removal of any legal claim to compensation by property owners whose property had been acquired, an argument eventually rejected by the courts in *De Keyser's Royal Hotel Ltd.*

In the first three months of the war, a consolidation measure, the Defence of the Realm (Consolidation) Act 1914, repeated the first two measures, inserting for the first time provisions pertaining to the economic conduct of the war. It provided in section 1:

(3) It shall be lawful for the Admiralty or Army Council

(a) to require that there shall be placed at their disposal the whole or

> any part of the output of any factory or workshop in which arms, ammunition, or warlike stores or equipment or any articles required for the production thereof, are manufactured;
>
> (b) to take possession of and use for the purpose of His Majesty's naval or military service any such factory or workshop or any plant thereof; and regulations under this Act may be made accordingly.

Regulations could also be issued under section 1(1)(e), 'to prevent ... the successful prosecution of the war being endangered', a provision capable of extremely broad interpretation, possibly covering not only matters such as sabotage but also manufacturers' refusal to cooperate in producing certain items or other owners refusing to yield up land, buildings or other property. Whether such an interpretation was possible would depend on whether it fell within the scope of the wording of the appropriate regulation. It also depended on whether the regulation itself could be upheld as *intra vires* the vague terminology of section 1(1)(e) and as being for the public safety and the defence of the realm.

It may be observed that section 1(3)(a), merely enabled the military authorities (later extended to other government departments, especially the Ministry of Munitions) to requisition the munitions-related output of a factory, not to dictate to the manufacturer what the latter was obliged to produce. In terms of directing the production of specific commodities, section 1(3)(b) seemed to envisage that the factory itself be requisitioned from the owner, who, it might be assumed, would depart from the scene. The military authorities, and not the owner, would by regulation 'use' the factory for the 'purpose' (whatever this might mean) of military service. The Home Secretary, Reginald McKenna, justified the insertion of these provisions as aimed at ensuring that the government could obtain 'the highest maximum possible output' from munitions factories, though he added: 'These powers may not have to be used.'[1] One querulous voice was heard to enquire:

> What guarantee have you that the Army and Navy will be reasonable in their requirements? We know by experience that when you allow military gentlemen to take control of everything they are most unreasonable. The requirements of the civil population are just as important to the Crown as any other section of the population [Hon. Members: 'No!'] and there really ought to be a guarantee that the Army and Navy will not be the sole masters, and that some balance will be struck in the interests of the civil population.[2]

To the question posed by Lord Robert Cecil as to whether any damage suffered would be compensated, McKenna responded sharply, 'Oh, yes!', but did not expand on this answer.

A further expansion of statutory powers occurred in the Defence of the

1. H.C. Deb., 5th series, 68, 25 November 1914, col. 1275.
2. Ibid. (Richard Holt).

Realm (Amendment) (No. 2) Act 1915, passed on 16 March 1915. First, by section 1(1), it applied section 1(3) of the Consolidation Act 1914 to 'any factory or workshop of whatever sort, or the plant thereof'. Secondly, it added to section 1(3) that it would be lawful for government departments:

(c) to require any work in any factory or workshop to be done in accordance with the directions of the [department] given with the object of making the factory or workshop, or the plant or labour therein, as useful as possible for the production of war material; and

(d) to regulate or restrict the carrying on of work in any factory or workshop, or remove the plant therefrom, with a view to increasing the production of war material in other factories or workshops.

'War material' included, under section 1(3) of the 1915 Act, arms, ammunition, warlike stores and equipment, 'and everything required for or in connection with the production thereof'.

It can be seen that the added section 1(3)(c) to the Consolidation Act 1914 rectified, in a sense, the deficiency of the original 1914 provision in that it would ensure the continued functioning of the owner as a manager in his own factory, simply in order to fulfil the directions of the department. The new paragraph (d) which was later repealed by the Munitions of War Act 1915 section 10, which substituted a new paragraph (d), added to the powers of the department to order *what* kind of work was to be done or not to be done; whereas paragraph (c) was concerned with *how* particular work was to be carried out.

It was confidently claimed by two legal writers that between the enactment of the first Defence of the Realm Act 1914 on 8 August 1914 and the enactment of the Consolidation Act on 27 November 1914, 'we have been living under decrees [Defence Regulations] of the military and naval authorities which were absolutely illegal'.[3] They argued, in respect to the two measures of August 1914:

3. T. Baty and J. H. Morgan, *War: Its Conduct and Legal Results* (London, 1915), p. 102. Thomas Baty (1869–1954), D.C.L., LL.D., Joint Honorary Secretary of the International Law Association; Fellow of University College, Oxford; author of *International Law* (1909); *Polarised Law* (1914); *Vicarious Liability* (1916), and *Canons of International Law* (1930). See also entry by Steve Uglow in Simpson (ed.), *Biographical Dictionary of the Common Law*, p. 37. John Hartmann Morgan (1876–1955), Q.C. 1926; Barrister; legal editor of *Encyclopaedia Britannica*; Emeritus Professor of Constitutional Law, University of London; member, Executive Council of International Law Association; Liberal candidate in both general elections of 1910; Assistant Advocate General, Military Section of Paris Peace Conference; Deputy Adjutant-General and GOC Effectives Sub-Committee on Inter-Allied Military Control Commission in Germany, 1919–23; Vice-Chairman, Government Committee of Enquiry into Breaches of Laws of War; Home Office Commissioner with British Expeditionary Force, 1914–15; Staff Captain on Adjutant-General's staff; Publications included *The House of Lords and the Constitution* (1910); *The German War Book* (1915); and *Assize of Arms* (1945). One of his more unusual appointments was as third defence counsel at the trial of Sir Roger Casement for treason in 1916. As only two counsel were permitted under the Treason Trials Act 1696, Lord Chief Justice Reading allowed him to appear as *amicus curiae*. See *Solicitors' Journal*, 60, 1 July 1916, p. 582.

The Act does not say 'it shall be lawful for His Majesty in Council', but 'His Majesty in Council *has power*' to issue regulations. And regulations for what purpose? The Act says 'regulations *as to the powers and duties of the Admiralty and Army Council* . . . and other persons acting in his behalf for securing the safety and the defence of the realm'. It would be legislation by innuendo, and a great perversion of the ordinary rules of interpretation, to assume that these words create new powers. Power to issue regulations as to the powers of a particular body – whether the Army Council or a tramway company – means, on the face of it, power to regulate existing powers, not to create new ones.[4]

As a result, the authors claimed, the only new powers conferred on government departments by Defence Regulations issued under the authority of the two statutes of August 1914 were those falling squarely within the specific wording of the sections of the two August measures. The sections, as briefly noted earlier, authorised the issue of regulations designed to prevent persons communicating with the enemy; to secure the safety of the armed forces, of means of communication, and of railways, ports and harbours; to prevent the spread of false rumours; to secure navigation according to Admiralty instructions; and otherwise to prevent assistance to the enemy or interference with the successful prosecution of the war. They also authorised the lifting of restrictions on the acquisition or user of land as already noted. Any regulations falling outside the scope of those sections would therefore be *ultra vires*. For example, the authors cited an article (which was in fact Reg. 51) which provided that any person authorised by the competent military authority (that is, by the executive) could enter, if need be by force, any private house, and search it if there were reason to suspect conduct prejudicial to the public safety. But the authors complained that no legal power to authorise officials to enter private property had been conferred on the executive by Parliament. In other words, the primary DORA statutes of August 1914 did not specify that regulations could be issued by a minister permitting forced entry by his officials to private property in certain circumstances. Nor, presumably, would the common law so permit.[5] Consequently, they reasoned, the regulation was *ultra vires* and was not saved by the provision in those Acts empowering the authorities to make general regulations for the defence of the realm, on the ground that the latter did not specify the consequences of a breach of any such regulation (apart from those authorised by section one of the first DORA 1914). They neither prescribed penalties nor authorised arrest without warrant, unlike other regulations such as Reg. 55 whose legality could be challenged for the reasons given previously.

In respect to the relation between defence regulations and private property rights, the authors referred to Reg. 2 which declared that 'it shall be lawful' for

4. Baty and Morgan, *War: Its Conduct and Legal Results*, p. 75.
5. *Entick* v. *Carrington* [1765] 19 St.Tr.1030 was authority for the proposition that the common law permitted forced entry on private property only to search for stolen goods.

the authorities to take possession of any land or buildings or other property, and even to cause any property to be destroyed or, '(f) to do any other act involving interference with private rights of property which is necessary . . .' for the purpose of securing the public safety and the defence of the realm. They observed, however, that, 'these Regulations, which purport to give what the statute does not give, the power to destroy private property, are in our opinion wholly unwarranted'. Nor were they saved, in the authors' view, by a reference to the use of such powers 'where necessary' for public safety. This could only apply where a situation of imminent danger arose, such as the actual presence of the enemy, and could not apply merely to precautionary steps. This reasoning paralleled the debate on the applicability of the royal prerogative to wartime situations, and the common denominator, as Baty and Morgan interpreted the wording of DORA, was that the law-making role of Parliament was by-passed both in respect to the exercise of the prerogative and in respect to the promulgation of those regulations for which primary statutory authority was wanting. The abrupt and brief Reg. 3., stating that, 'The competent . . . authority . . . shall have right of access to any land or buildings or other property whatsoever', appeared, according to Baty and Morgan, to invite the authority to commit a trespass. No such arbitrary power of access existed at common law. Nor was such power to be found in the August 1914 DORAs. The 'truth of the matter' was that the statutes were brief without being terse, while the regulations were voluble without being explicit; the authors had never seen comparable regulations, 'which appeared to outrun so breathlessly the statutory powers actually conferred'.[6] The 'Henry VIII Clauses' were the nearest parallel involving legislation by proclamation.[7] While one could argue that the gravity of the wartime situation might prompt a relaxation of established rules of construction, in respect to the relation between primary and secondary legislation, to do so, argued Baty and Morgan, would be to 'dispense with the Rule of Law altogether and entrust the Cabinet with autocracy'.[8]

The Consolidation Act of 27 November 1914 transposed part of the wording of section one of the August 1914 measures. The earlier provisions, as already noted, had declared that the Crown 'has power . . . to issue regulations as to the powers and duties' of the military authorities, 'for securing the safety and the defence of the realm'. This formulation Baty and Morgan condemned for its legal ineffectiveness. The November 1914 version now declared that the Crown 'has power . . . to issue regulations for securing the public safety and the defence of the realm, and as to the powers and duties for that purpose'

6. Baty and Morgan, *War: Its Conduct and Legal Results*, p. 80.
7. For a consideration of the original clauses, see the sources cited in P. R. Roberts, 'The "Henry VIII Clause": Delegated Legislation and the Tudor Principality of Wales', in Thomas G. Watkin (ed.), *Legal Record and Historical Reality* (London, 1989), ch. 3. For an analysis of more recent examples, see Carleton Kemp Allen, *Law and Orders* (London, 1947 edn), pp. 100–2.
8. Baty and Morgan, *War: Its Conduct and Legal Results*, p. 80.

of the military authorities. Whether this transposition rendered the defence regulations legally watertight was not, in their view, wholly free from doubt. It would have been preferable if the statute had declared that, 'It shall be lawful for His Majesty in Council to issue regulations for securing the public safety and the defence of the realm and as to the powers and duties for that purpose' of the military authorities. The revision, Baty and Morgan concluded:

> meets nearly the whole of our criticism . . . and it is a remarkable confession of the illegality of the Regulations of the last four months. It is extraordinary, however, that no-one so far as we know, has during those four months pointed out these illegalities.[9]

It is likely that this contemporary observation was factually correct. The early faith in business as usual, the belief that the war would be over by Christmas and, to some extent, the xenophobic approval of harsh measures against potential spies and saboteurs, perhaps dulled lawyers' critical faculties. As a reviewer of Baty and Morgan's volume wrote in March 1915:

> Perhaps [the authors'] surprise is more rhetorical than real. Everyone accepted the regulations as honestly intended to meet a great emergency, and it would have been an unwelcome and useless task to criticize them too closely.[10]

On the other hand, the fact that the order of the wording of the Consolidation Act disclosed differences from its predecessors might indicate that legal advisers within government service became aware of the defects in the earlier measures. There were many occasions when self-doubt crept into government departments as to the legality of the powers they were exercising or intending to exercise. For example, the arrangements originally made between the War Office and the manufacturers of sandbags made of jute were regulated by Reg. 7 issued in March 1915. That regulation provided that the Admiralty or Army Council or Ministry of Munitions could by order require a manufacturer to place the output of his factory at the disposal of the department and that payment would be, 'such price as, in default of agreement, may be decided to be reasonable having regard to the circumstances of the case by the arbitration of a judge'.

In thus specifying arbitration by a judge, Reg. 7 was unusual and was similar to the provision in section 115 of the Army Act 1881 prescribing payment for requisitioned goods on the basis of 'fair market value'. For some time, the jute manufacturers in Dundee accepted the War Office interpretation of

---

9.   Ibid., p. 104. If the regulations had in fact been *intra vires*, then DORA alone would have been sufficient legal authority for actions such as restrictions imposed on aliens and the requisitioning of food and forage by the Army. There would have been no necessity for the enactment of the Aliens' Restriction Act 1914 or the Army (Supply of Food, Forage and Stores) Act 1914.

10.   (Anon.), 'The Legal Effects of War', *Solicitors' Journal*, 59, 6 March 1915, p. 314.

'reasonable' in Reg. 7, and voluntarily agreed to supply goods at prices around 25 per cent below the open market price. Meanwhile, the price of jute cloth was rising substantially from 2¼d per yard at the beginning of December 1914 to 4d. by March 1915, with further rises over the next few months. One large firm now intimated that it might soon resort to arbitration, which would, of course, undermine the agreement among manufacturers to maintain a lid on prices. The War Office then sought to impose price controls by law rather than by agreement. As one insider within the department, E. M. H. Lloyd, later wrote:

> This proved a task of considerable difficulty and complexity. The legal advisers of the Department were of the opinion that since the Defence of the Realm Act contained no provisions as to prices any regulation which purported to fix prices or to determine the basis on which they should be fixed, might be construed as *ultra vires*.[11]

While the War Office therefore wished a fixed rate of compensation to be set down, and while the lawyers demurred, a compromise solution was reached. Judicial arbitration would still be retained, but the principles which the judge was to apply were spelled out in a revised Reg. 7 issued on 15 February 1916. While the market price could be ignored, the arbitrator had to consider the cost of production, the pre-war rate of profit, whether that rate was unreasonable or excessive, and 'any other circumstances of the case'. As Lloyd observed:

> Whether a judge of the High Court appointed by the Lord Chief Justice of England would have regarded himself as bound by this amendment of the Regulation, or would have dismissed it as *ultra vires* ... was [not] at any time of very great importance.[12]

No reference to arbitration under Reg. 7 was known by the author. The provision was simply available in future negotiations with manufacturers. Whether it contained a fatal legal flaw was never tested. Lloyd attributed this to the patriotism and sense of justice of the majority, and to the threat of enforcing it if necessary (with its potential defect well hidden) in the case of less cooperative manufacturers. Here was an example of the use of a legal device as part of a gigantic bluff.

11. E. M. H. Lloyd, *Experiments in State Control: At the War Office and the Ministry of Food* (Oxford, 1924), p. 58. Lloyd had been with the Raw Materials Section of the War Office, and was Assistant Secretary, Ministry of Food.

12. Ibid., pp. 58–59. After the Armistice, ministers still expressed concern at the doubtful legality of the compensation provisions in Reg. 7. See PRO, CAB 24/70, G.T.6347, 21 November 1918, memorandum by Lord Milner, Secretary of State for War; CAB 24/72, G.T.6502, 17 December 1918, memorandum by Lord Cave, Home Secretary. Corrective measures in a Bill to continue emergency legislation after the termination of the war were proposed. Reg. 2B also continued to cause concern as to its legality. See chapter 14, below.

The same might be said about the accompanying provision in Reg. 7 enabling the authorities to inspect firms' books to ascertain the costs of production. As Lloyd remarks:

> No explicit reference was made to the compulsory production of books or the right to send officials into a factory to inspect them. The power was conferred in an almost casual manner by the insertion of the few unemphatic words, 'and may require such particulars to be verified in such manner as they may direct'.

This surreptitious approach was prompted by the opinion at one point that the power to examine companies' books was *ultra vires* DORA, and that the War Office was unwilling to obtain the approval of Parliament for such a proposal, as it felt certain that such permission would be denied.[13] Here was another tactic employed by the executive to secure powers whose legal basis might be questionable, that is, employ obfuscatory terminology and to trust that the spirit of wartime cooperation would hold strong.

The most 'comprehensive and drastic' regulation (in Lloyd's words) designed to secure state control over production and prices was Reg. 2E introduced in 1916. It enabled the authorities,

> to regulate, restrict or prohibit the manufacture, use, purchase, sale, repair, delivery of or payment for, or any other dealing in any war material, food, forage, or stores of any description, or of any article required for or in connection with the production thereof.

It did not specifically mention the fixing of maximum prices, but that was one of the prime objects. According to Lloyd, 'legal opinion was satisfied that it might be so used',[14] presumably by regulating 'sale' and 'payment for' goods. Perhaps a nagging doubt resided in his final observation on Reg. 2E that, 'Provided the whole Regulation was not *ultra vires*, there was virtually no measure of State interference with private property and freedom of trade, which could not be legally justified under its provisions.'[15] The prematurely terminated proceedings in the House of Lords in the Shoreham Aerodrome hearing in July 1916 brought home to the government the vulnerable legal basis on which property requisition and the payment of merely *ex gratia* compensation to owners was proceeding.

While the reactions of different government officials to these developments will be considered in detail in chapter five, one particular concern of the Director of Army Contracts may be noted at this stage, simply as an illustration of the kinds of legal difficulties envisaged by the departments.

---

13. Lloyd, *Experiments in State Control*, p. 61.
14. Ibid., p. 63
15. Ibid., p. 64. See below, chapter 4.

One area of concern to which he drew attention was the issuing by the Army Council of licences to merchants or manufacturers to enable them to deal in commodities. Reg. 2B, for example, forbade dealings by forage merchants except under licence. Similarly, Reg. 30A authorised dealings in war materials, but only under licence and the War Office used Reg. 30A to prohibit dealings in Russian flax and English wool. The area of legal uncertainty was whether it was *intra vires* for the department to attach conditions to the grant of licences, an example of a condition being the observance of a scale of maximum prices for sale. The Director noted that, in respect to Reg. 2B, it was assumed that it was competent for the department to attach conditions. As doubts were later expressed as to the *vires* of attaching conditions, an amendment to the regulation was made two months later to settle the point. In respect to Reg. 30A, it was also assumed that permits, either general or special, could be issued and that the attachment of a condition to observe maximum prices was valid. In connection with the purchase of the wool clip in Ireland, a general permit to deal was issued, though the condition of a fixed schedule of prices was attached. The Law Officers later expressed doubt as to whether the issue of general permits subject to such a condition of fixed prices was competent under Reg. 30A, since they envisaged the object of the regulation as being to restrict dealings rather than to impose limits on prices.[16] The promulgation of Reg. 2E on 8 October 1916 was designed to deal with the legal doubt and, as noted, contained references to 'sale' and 'payment'. The question of its *vires* was never decisively settled.

On a later occasion, the Law Officers of the Crown expressed concern about the legality of the various food control regulations.[17] In a Cabinet memorandum of 17 October 1917, they observed that where the regulations (which included Regs. 2B, 2E, 2F, 2G and 2J) made provision for compensation for requisitioned stocks (not, of course, at the market price), then their validity could not be impugned where they were regarded as modifications of a prerogative right to take without compensation. If the true view were that the subject had a legal right to compensation on different principles to those specified in the regulations, the validity of the latter would be open to grave question. The Law Officers also noted that when the government had decided in 1915 to impose liquor control, a new Defence of the Realm Act was passed, the No. 3 Act 1915. This appeared to imply that there were finite limits to what the original consolidated DORA of 1914 could authorise government departments to control by regulation, though they conceded that the enactment of the No. 3 Act 1915 did not prove that the original act was not sufficiently wide.

16. PRO, LCO 2/367, 'Defence of the Realm (Compensation for Loss) Bill: Appendix to Note by Director of Army Contracts'. See also Lloyd, *Experiments in State Control*, pp. 62–63.
17. PRO, CAB 24/4, G.165, 'Legality of Certain Acts Done Under the Defence of the Realm Regulations. Opinion of Law Officers of the Crown', 17 October 1917, for this and subsequent examples.

They also observed that some regulations could only be justified by a series of deductions, for example, Reg.2S which shortened the period during which stray dogs could be kept. This might be justified for the public safety and the defence of the realm in that it was presumably intended to conserve the food supply. They also referred to a regulation of 29 September 1917, which altered primary legislation, the Increase of Rent and Mortgage Interest (War Restriction) Act 1915.[18] The regulation, Reg. 2A(2), provided that in a designated 'munitions area', a landlord might be criminally liable simply for bringing legal proceedings to enforce his statutory rights. Such a regulation, opined the Law Officers, might not be unlawful, but might well be resented by otherwise loyal and cooperative citizens. Indeed, Reg. 2A(2) was later declared invalid by Mr Justice Darling in the post-Armistice case of *Chester* v. *Bateson* [1920] 1 K.B. 829, a 'somewhat belated discovery by the Bench', complained the *Solicitors' Journal*, 'that there are limits to the powers which the Executive could assume' under DORA.[19]

Generally speaking, the fears of the Law Officers in respect to the food control regulations were not realised (though the quaintly named Peas, Beans and Pulses Order of 1917 was an important exception.) The few legal challenges which occurred tended to be directed towards interpreting the compensation provisions in such a way that an arbitrator could take account of the market value of food requisitioned. Such attempts ended in failure.[20] Alternatively, it was claimed that food manufacturers were entitled to arbitration, even where the ministry paid compensation at the maximum scheduled price. This claim was also rejected.[21] Other challenges unsuccessfully contested the right of the Food Controller to fix the maximum prices of whisky[22] and tea[23] and the right of the Army Council under Reg. 2B to requisition raspberries after they had been gathered.[24]

---

18.   For another example of a regulation issued by the Crown by order in council which it was alleged overrode a statutory provision, see Reg. 34B enabling the Ministry of Labour to impose arbitration to settle industrial disputes. This appeared to by-pass arrangements made in the Munitions of War Act 1915. For cynical legal commentary, see *Solicitors' Journal*, 62, 24 August 1918, p. 749.

19.   *Solicitors' Journal*, 64, 7 February 1920, p. 250. No radical publication, the legal profession's weekly newspaper added, 'we cannot help wondering if the same decision would have been given when the German submarine menace was at its worst; or is it that the rights of property weigh more with the Divisional Court than the right to liberty?' This was a clear reference to the executive detention case of *R* v. *Halliday, ex parte Zadig* [1917] A.C. 260 on the legality of Reg. 14B. authorising detention of British citizens with 'hostile associations', a term capable of imaginative expansion. See A. W. Brian Simpson, *In the Highest Degree Odious: Detention Without Trial in Wartime Britain* (Oxford, 1992), ch. 2.

20.   See, for example, *Danish Bacon Company Ltd.* v. *Ministry of Food* (1922) 38 T.L.R. 507 (C.A.); *Swift & Co.* v. *Board of Trade* [1925] A.C. 520 (H.L.); ibid., [1926] 2 K.B. 131 (C.A.). For the Peas, Beans and Pulses Order, see below, chapter 9.

21.   *John Robinson & Co. Ltd* v. *The King* (1920) 36 T.L.R. 773 (K.B.).

22.   *Fowle* v. *Monsell* (1920) 36 T.L.R. 863 (K.B.).

23.   *Sainsbury* v. *Saunders* (1918) 35 T.L.R. 140 (K.B.).

24.   *Lipton Ltd.* v. *Ford* [1917] 2 K.B. 647. For the post-war doubts as to the legality of the compensation provisions in Reg. 2B see chapter 14, below.

One further illustration concerns the prohibition or restriction of the importation of goods from abroad. A special department of the Board of Trade was established to administer the system of restriction decided upon by the government, and to issue import licences. The legal authority for this power was contained in a pre-war statute, the Customs (Consolidation) Act 1876, which provided that: 'the importation of arms, ammunition, gunpowder or any other goods may be prohibited by proclamation or Order in Council.' According to a memorandum prepared in anticipation of a post-war Indemnity Bill, doubts arose as to whether this 1876 measure provided a sufficiently strong legal basis for the actions taken in pursuance of the import restriction policy.[25] In particular, was the phrase 'any other goods' to be interpreted broadly or *eiusdem generis* with arms, ammunition and gunpowder? If the department possessed wide powers of import restriction, then that could contribute to the purpose of promoting domestic industry. The section was also employed to authorise discrimination in the issue of licences to import in favour of particular countries and particular merchants. These matters were put before the Law Officers who advised, first, that the expression 'any other goods' could be construed as applying without qualification or limitation to all goods of whatever character. They also advised that it was not open to the Crown to discriminate against imports from any particular country or particular persons either in the proclamation of prohibitions or in granting licences for importation. It is not clear when these doubts first arose, or when the Law Officers drafted their opinion, though it does seem likely that it was towards the end of the military conflict or even after the Armistice. Certainly an internal Board of Trade memorandum from the Solicitor's Department admitted in 1919 that during the war, both the Board of Trade and the Customs department had been acting illegally (in view of the Law Officers' opinion) in prohibiting the import of goods of a specified origin.[26] It is possible to infer either that none in the department were aware of the legal flaw, or else that a conscious decision was made to continue to prohibit all kinds of goods or to discriminate in respect to particular countries or merchants in spite of the defect. The editor of the *Economist* during the period 1907 to 1916, F. W. Hirst, claimed much later (in 1934) that the Board of Trade's 'intricate system' of embargoes and licences on imports was 'generally supposed [to be] authorised by DORA', and that it was only some time after the cessation of hostilities that the illegality of the methods employed was discovered.[27] Businessmen then organised themselves into an Anti-Embargo League and received subscriptions in order to mount a legal challenge. In July 1919 the

---

25. PRO, LCO 2/440, 'Interdepartmental Committee on Indemnity Bill and Statute of Limitations. Memorandum no. 26. Note on the Position of the Board of Trade with regard to restriction of Imports', n.d. See below, chapter 13.
26. PRO, BT 103/32, 'Memorandum *re* Indemnity Bill', 4 October 1919.
27. F. W. Hirst, *The Consequences of the War to Great Britain* (New York, 1968 edn), p. 116 (originally published in 1934).

former Home Secretary, Sir John Simon, addressed meetings in the City of London and in Manchester, challenging the legality of the import quotas and the discriminatory grant of import licences. Observing that the powers were exercised by non-emergency nineteenth-century legislation, he claimed that:

> if therefore what is now happening is lawful at all, it could be done without the consent of Parliament at any time, to any extent, and without regard as to whether conditions of trade had been interfered with by war or not. That is a proposition which would have greatly surprised any constitutional lawyer in the past and one which I find it difficult to believe any competent authority would seriously maintain.[28]

In other words, an 1876 measure, designed to prevent the unrestrained importation into the country of munitions of war, no doubt justified in public policy terms of ensuring that government had exclusive oversight of commodities dangerous to public security, was being extended willy-nilly in pursuit of peacetime economic nationalism. Powers were being seized by a government department by dint of distorting grotesquely the rationale of an old statute, then applying it to an entirely different purpose. Parliament was not being consulted and indeed was treated as if its legislative authority no longer existed. *This* is what Simon believed would be offensive to constitutional lawyers.

The Board of Trade published a lengthy 'Consolidated List of Import Restrictions' in July 1919, which covered hundreds of goods. They included food, clothing, raw materials, tools, machinery and finished items, together with instructions as to the scope for obtaining import licences. As examples, women's clothing could only be imported up to 25 per cent of the 1916 figure, furniture was 50 per cent of the 1916 import level, stationery and tools were one-third of that level. Various committees such as the Hosiery Needle Committee or a section of the Ministry of Food would fix quotas. The periodical, *Common Sense*, described the list as 'the worst new tariff that has been introduced into this country for a century',[29] while Hirst observed at the time:

> It is not only unlawful, but in every respect irregular. It is altered day by day and week by week to the advantage or disadvantage of somebody or everybody. It is a tariff, and yet not a tariff; for its produces no revenue to the State, though it fills the pockets and swells the profits of individuals at the expense of the whole community. You can hardly find a large shop which is not selling numbers of articles at a higher price than they will fetch but for these embargoes, restrictions and licences.[30]

28. Quoted ibid., p. 117.
29. Quoted ibid.
30. Ibid., p. 118.

Sir John Simon went so far as to call the government's bluff on the question of the legality of the embargoes. He observed that in the issue of 16 August 1919 of *Common Sense*, a correspondent, Sir Herbert Samuel Leon (1850–1926), a chairman of Buckinghamshire County Council finance committee, had enquired how the legal position could be clarified. Simon replied the following week by referring to a letter he had just sent to the Solicitor to the Board of Trade. In that letter, he had announced that he was about to return to the United Kingdom from Spain and was proposing to bring with him certain foreign items whose importation was purportedly prohibited by a proclamation under the 1876 Act. He was not proposing to apply for an import licence and intended to resell the goods. The ball was now in the government's court and its bluff was being called. Two days later, Lloyd George told Parliament that the licensing system would be abandoned with immediate effect. Internal enquiries within the Board of Trade seemed to show that no legal authority for the policy existed, and the courts of law might look askance at the exercise of discretionary powers by the executive to interfere with the free flow of commerce where parliamentary authority was, to say the least, ambiguous.

At the end of 1919, Mr Justice Sankey *did* rule in *Attorney-General* v. *Brown* [1920] 1 K.B. 773 that the proclamation system was unlawful. In that case, a firm of chemical manufacturers had imported to Manchester six casks of pyrogallic acid aboard the S.S. *Bovic* from New York. On 29 August 1919, the Customs and Excise seized the goods as forfeit on the ground that their importation was in breach of the Prohibition of Import (No. 32) Proclamation of 25 June 1919, the 'notorious Proclamation No. 32', according to the *Solicitors' Journal*,[31] which forbade the import of all chemicals unless licensed by the Board of Trade. The company, however, claimed that the acid had been ordered from a firm in Montreal on 17 June 1919, that is, before the proclamation, and in any case imports from the Dominions were permitted. In response, the Customs and Excise pointed out that the shipping documents indicated that the goods originated from the firm's New York address. The Attorney-General now sought the court's condemnation of the goods.

When the matter reached the court, the company advanced two arguments. The first was the *eiusdem generis* argument to the effect that the import of arms, ammunition or gunpowder and only substances similar to those could be prohibited by proclamation; pyrogallic acid, used in photographic processes, did not fall into that category. Secondly, it was claimed that the proclamation was bad because it purported to express a dispensing power on the part of the executive, and the government had no legal power to make exceptions.

Mr Justice Sankey saw the issue in historical terms. The prerogative power to regulate commerce was overtaken by statute. Arms and ammunition had always been treated exceptionally in legislation. Acts of 1825, 1833 and 1845

---

31. *Solicitors' Journal*, 64, 27 December 1919, p. 159.

had prohibited the import of munitions except by licence. The Customs Act of 1845 was in fact a watershed for free trade, loosening the restrictions on general commerce imposed under the Navigation Acts and other mercantilist legislation. For example, the Customs Act 1825 had imposed an absolute ban on the import of beef, lamb, mutton, pork, sheep and swine. This was all swept away by the Customs Act 1845 which the 1876 Act reenacted. The 1845 Act was, according to Sankey, the 'Magna Charta of Free Trade' and section 41 enacted that, 'it shall be lawful to import into the United Kingdom any goods which are not . . . prohibited to be . . . imported'; provision for the prohibition by proclamation of 'arms, ammunition, gunpowder or any other goods' was made in a subsequent section. As Mr Justice Sankey observed:

> It is contended by the Attorney-General that this gives a right to His Majesty by Proclamation or Order in Council to prohibit the importation of every conceivable sort of goods. Having regard to the history of the circumstances under which the Act was passed, it is very difficult to follow this line of reasoning. It would be strange indeed at a time when the King's prerogative had been so carefully restricted, at a time when the desire of the country and the purpose of Parliament were to introduce a system of free trade as distinguished from a system of restricted trade . . . that . . . by means of a few general words at the end of particular ones, they should hand over to the Executive the power to prohibit absolutely the importation of every sort of goods.[32]

If power to impose a total prohibition had been sought, why specify arms, ammunition and gunpowder? The government's arguments therefore received short shrift and the final nail in the coffin of its embargo policy was hammered in.

It just remained to ensure that the Board of Trade, the Customs and Excise and their officials were protected against the consequences of pursuing an illegal policy and that claims for loss would not be maintained against them in the courts. This was effected by section 4 of the Indemnity Act 1920 in respect to actions taken before the introduction of the Bill in Parliament, by which time of course the practice had been abandoned. Section 4 therefore declared:

> Any proclamation or Order in Council issued or purporting to be issued under section forty-three of the Customs Consolidation Act, 1876, during the war and before the fifteenth day of April, nineteen hundred and twenty, prohibiting or restricting the importation of any goods into the United Kingdom, and any licence granted in pursuance of any such proclamation or order shall be, and shall be deemed always to have been valid, but nothing in this section shall be

---

32. *Attorney-General v. Brown* [1920] 1 K.B. 773, at p. 795. The Crown sought to argue that the allegedly statutorily authorised proclamation was declaratory of a prerogative power to prohibit imports. However, the legislation up to and including the 1845 Act arguably limited the prerogative to 'utensils of war'.

construed as rendering valid the continuance in operation after the fifteenth day
of April, nineteen hundred and twenty of any such proclamation or Order in
Council.[33]

What we have examined so far in this chapter are the recurring concerns
within government departments as to the legality of actions taken by them
under defence regulations, which those departments themselves were responsible for issuing. The safety valve of parliamentary scrutiny was lacking. But
management of total war, it is easy to argue, cannot be left to the cut and
thrust of open, democratic parliamentary debate. That public set-piece may
have a role of affirming or reproving the whole project, as a political or
moral choice. Technocratic decisions can be claimed as the domain of the
expert professionals. This line of reasoning can of course induce conceit and
a blinkered vision. Constitutional principles can legitimately be bent during
wartime so as to preclude, for example, a general election on the expiry of
a five-year stint. How much bending of a constitutional principle as central
as the rule of law can be permitted? The courts did not close during the
war, though severe modifications of the substantive law were made, relieving
parties from the legal consequences of, for example, breach of contract. It is
with the outer limits of the rule of law in its formalistic sense of rule by
regular law and not by decree that the judges in the DORA cases wrestled
during the war. Recognition that desperate times required desperate measures
was openly admitted, but so long as judges *were* judges of the courts of
law, they could not throw overboard the very essence of their professional
being. In construing defence regulations against the generalised benchmarks
of the primary statutes, they were conscious of the strains imposed by war
exigencies on their professional integrity. They bowed to the authorities not
just where conventional legal reasoning pointed in that direction but where the
authorities' claims were plausible. Such matters are questions of degree, not of
kind, the dividing lines are exceedingly difficult to pinpoint. We can only hope
to glimpse these dilemmas in the following illustrations of legal challenges to
executive action taken in the name of DORA.

---

33. The President of the Board of Trade, Sir Robert Horne, enquired about the possibility
of an indemnity if the grant of *export* licences by the Privy Council in derogation of a general
prohibition on exports were to be impugned. Questions had been raised in Parliament about
the validity of such practices by the Privy Council, where no statutory authority existed. The
matter was referred to the Solicitor-General, who presumably advised that the practice was
lawful as no indemnity was inserted in the Indemnity Act. See PRO, CAB 24/101, C.P.978,
27 March 1920, 'Bill of Indemnity and Statute of Limitations. Memorandum by the President
of the Board of Trade'; PRO, CAB 26/2, H.A.C. 54(3), 14 April 1920. On the Indemnity Act
1920 more generally, see chapter 14, below.

4

Those Magnificent Men and Shoreham Aerodrome

'I want to take over the Shoreham Aerodrome at once for training purposes', the Assistant Director of Military Aeronautics at the War Office, Major (later General Sir) W. Sefton Brancker, anxiously minuted to the department's Lands Branch on 22 December 1914. 'Will you tell me the correct procedure?'[1] As we shall see shortly, the Royal Flying Corps (RFC) already enjoyed limited facilities at Shoreham Aerodrome as a result of a tenancy agreement entered into in 1913. Four months into the war, however, the intention was to requisition the airfield for the sole use of the RFC.

Shoreham Aerodrome was owned by The Brighton-Shoreham Aerodrome Ltd, whose chairman was George Arthur Wingfield, a partner in the company's London solicitors, Messrs Wingfield, Blew & Kenward. Originally incorporated in 1909 as Aviators' Finance Ltd and having changed its name in 1912[2], the company's principal object was the development of aviation in the United Kingdom, at a time when British interest in flying was more or less confined to the sporting and recreational spheres.[3] The company acquired various parcels of land amounting to about 200 acres, and identified a site, known as New Salts Farm, which was suitable for all kinds of aircraft including seaplanes. It lay close to the sea and on one side was bounded by the River Adur, a public navigable river, which afforded a wide expanse of calm water, to which rights of access were obtained.[4] Between 1909 and 1914 the company sought to expand the aerodrome by building hangars and a club house and by encouraging the Pashley brothers, who operated a flying school on the site, to establish the Sussex County Aero Club, whose president, Lord Curzon, became a member of Asquith's coalition government in May 1915 and whose committee included George Wingfield.

In 1912 it issued a business circular which proclaimed that it was the largest

---

1. PRO, AIR 2/7, 'Taking over of Shoreham Aerodrome', 28 January 1915.
2. For the incorporation details, see PRO, BT 31/18802/102500.
3. For a brief mention of pre-1914 aviation, see Peter Fearon, 'The Growth of Aviation in Britain', *Journal of Contemporary History*, 20 (1985), pp. 21–40.
4. For these and subsequent details, see House of Lords Record Office, London [HLRO], 'Brighton – Shoreham Aerodrome Ltd', Main Papers no. 14, 14 February 1916. Unless otherwise indicated, the sources used hereafter are this extensive documentation for the House of Lords judicial hearing in 1916 and PRO, AIR 2/7, above.

aerodrome in the country, possessing an absolutely level surface with not a single tree. As the *Westminster Gazette* described the site: 'The ground is excellent, both from the geographical and flying point of view, and as flat as a pancake; while the manoeuvring limits are more spacious than any of the Aerodromes I have yet come across in this country.'[5] The circular added that similar favourable remarks had appeared in all sections of the press and that numerous aviators, both English and foreign, had testified to the aerodrome's 'exceptional advantages'.

A list of further advantages was appended. It was the only aerodrome (with its own 'Hydro-Aeroplane Water') on the English coast that was not in an area 'prohibited' by the Aerial Navigation Acts 1911 and 1913.[6] In winter and summer the area was practically free from fog and enjoyed the maximum of sunshine. There was even a railway station on the property (it was on the main line from London to Portsmouth, via Brighton, on the London, Brighton & South Coast Railway Company). The aerodrome could be reached in a few minutes from Brighton, Hove or Worthing, and from London in an hour and a quarter. It adjoined Shoreham Harbour, so that aeroplanes and materials could be brought on the spot from all parts of the world. It was particularly advantageous for seaplanes, given its location. There was an Exchange Telegraph Company office on the ground for dissemination of news. Local labour, it was claimed, was cheap. Finally, the company owned large areas of ground outside and adjoining the aerodrome and railway station for the erection of factories and repair shops.

The renting of its fourteen hangars at two guineas or at two pounds ten shillings a week, depending on size, was integral to the company's operations and was the basis of the tenancy agreement with the War Office. Alternatively, tenants could lease sites at ground rent and could then erect their own buildings, with the right to sublet. The company even offered to lend two-thirds of the capital cost on mortgage at 5 per cent per annum, repayable by instalments. For 'tourists' using the airfield, hangars and the services of mechanics, a separate tariff was available.

In August 1914, an inventory of the company valued its erections and outlays at £11,750. These included hangars;[7] other buildings including offices, workshops, restaurant, and judges' box; drainage; fencing; legal expenses; maintenance; and advertising. Rental income for the hangars produced £946 per annum. In respect to one arrangement, a tenancy agreement of 3 January 1913 with the War Office allowed the RFC use of a hangar and landing

5. *Westminster Gazette*, 25 May 1911.

6. For the restrictions on flying imposed by these statutes, see H. D. Hazeltine, 'The Recent and Future Growth of Aerial Law', *Flight*, 14 March 1918, pp. 295–96. The author was at the time Reader in English Law at Cambridge. He became Downing Professor shortly thereafter.

7. For a wartime rating case, concerning whether the aerodrome's hangars could be classed as houses and thus subject to a reduced sea defences rates levy, see *B. Aerodrome Ltd* v. *Dell* [1917] 2 K.B.381. The Court of Appeal upheld the company's contention on the ground that 'houses' did not mean only dwelling houses. See also *Flight*, 24 May 1917, p. 520.

and take-off rights on a yearly basis, subject to termination on six months written notice. The minimum annual rental payable by the War Office was considerably less than the amount charged to private customers and had prompted the company secretary, W. C. Littlewood, to write to the War Office in May 1914 terminating the tenancy as from 3 January 1915. If, however, the War Office were prepared to rent out a hangar at £100 per annum, then the company would be happy to enter into a new agreement. The Comptroller of Lands at the War Office, Edward H. Coles, wrote back on 8 July 1914 declining the new terms offered.

With the declaration of war on 4 August, it was clear that from the military point of view, it would be foolish to relinquish an aerodrome while a defensive posture was being worked out. The company recognised the intention of the War Office to retain its foothold in Shoreham and informed the Lands Branch on 24 August that it would allow the government to take a long lease of the land and business if the company were adequately compensated: 'those who have risked their money and worked so long ought to have some return, but this is not to be allowed to stand in the way of the Government's requirements in the present national crisis'. With hindsight, we can, perhaps, detect not merely a concern for the security of shareholders' long-term investments but a genuine fear that debenture-holders, deprived of interest on their loans as a result of war conditions, might foreclose. George Wingfield was alive to such a prospect, having personally guaranteed loans to the company. With the advent of the war, the promotion of aviation as a sporting activity for the upper and professional classes was beginning to look less and less like a profitable business venture, even though investors had recognised at the outset that adequate returns would not materialise for some years. On the other hand, the company were now sitting on an asset desirable to the state for the duration and anticipated a favourable offer. But first, an assessment of the airfield's suitability for military use had to be made.

On 17 December an inspection was carried out by Captain P. B. Joubert de la Ferté, RFC (later Air Marshal Sir Philip Joubert), accompanied by Lieutenant Fletcher. While his report recommended the acquisition of the aerodrome, the glowing praises sung by the company's circular of 1912 were not endorsed. The officers reported that the ground surface was good but that the area was small and was liable to be waterlogged in winter. The sheds were of poor construction and, except for two hangars, had earth rather than concrete floors. The much-vaunted club house of the Sussex County Aero Club was merely a small two-roomed building which, for the purposes of the RFC, could be used as a reading room. Unless the sheds were adapted for accommodation purposes, the nearest accommodation was Bungalow Town. As for the railway station at the aerodrome, this was in fact Bungalow Town Halt, not a station, just a couple of platforms and a shed. In respect to the existing tenants, Messrs Cedric Lee informed the inspecting officers that they were undertaking work for the Admiralty, but Messrs Pashley 'seemed anxious to get rid of their sheds'. Nonetheless, in spite of its shortcomings, the aerodrome was requisitioned under Defence Regulation 2 of the Defence of the Realm (Consolidation) Act 1914 (DORA), leaving the question of compensation to be settled by negotiation.[8]

After the War Office representative, Shand, met the aerodrome's manager on 24 December to effect the requisitioning under Reg. 2, the company secretary, William Littlewood, wrote to the War Office on 28 December, raising the question of a sale of the freehold of the whole site, presumably a reflection of Littlewood's pessimistic outlook in respect to the financial prospects for the company's investors. While he assessed the value of the site at £26,500, the War Office could have the lot, lock, stock and barrel, for £25,000, even though the shareholders considered they were entitled to an additional sum as goodwill.

If, however, as the War Office representative indicated, the RFC were interested only in a tenancy, the main difficulty for the company with this option was the question of damage to its commercial goodwill. The aerodrome would lose its existing tenants and would be prevented from securing new tenants, 'who are daily applying for accommodation'. If the War Office took over the exclusive tenancy, the company, on the tenancy's expiry, would merely receive back an empty aerodrome. The company therefore sought a premium of £5,000 and rent of £2,000 per annum as a *quid pro quo*, subject also to the War Office paying all outgoings, maintaining the upkeep of the aerodrome; and indemnifying the company against all claims for compensation by the existing tenants, by the aerodrome manager, John Bellham, who was on a five-year service contract, and by the local farmer whose livestock enjoyed grazing rights.

The War Office countered with a proposal to pay a rental of £1,500 per annum, plus a further £1,500 for depreciation when the RFC vacated the aerodrome. A further site visit on 5 January 1915 by Major Townsend, RE and Captain Ross-Hume, RFC, who proposed a number of ground works, including draining and constructing a road and a bridge, perhaps encouraged the Lands Branch to bid down the rental. The company, bolstered by a shareholders' resolution passed on 12 January stuck out for the higher figure. Its basic complaint was that the War Office's terms failed to recognise the peculiar financial investment of the shareholders in a venture which would require some years' patient development, 'before the enterprise would be a paying proposition'. The government's offer would deny them 'not only . . . all reward for their enterprise, but . . . the money which they have spent'. Thus the shareholders:

> feel very strongly that they should not be expected to lose money over the equipment and establishment of an Aerodrome which now is evidently necessary to the nation's need, and they appeal with some confidence to the War Office authorities to give them fair and adequate treatment.

8. For a modern assessment of the aerodrome's features, see Chris Ashworth, *Action Stations, 9: Military Airfields of the Central South and South East* (Wellingborough, 1985), pp. 254–60.

The War Office was not impressed. Captain H. C. Cole of the Lands Branch (not to be confused with the Comptroller, Edward H. Coles) advised that, 'they should be left to make the next move', while the existing offer remained on the table. That offer, it should be emphasised, was made on the strict understanding that payment would be an act of grace by the Crown and not a legal obligation, a position to which the department clung throughout this saga and of which the company was apprised by 1 February 1915 at the latest. The latter was politely reminded of the impending establishment of the Defence of the Realm Losses Commission (DRLC) with its remit to offer *ex gratia* compensatory payments.

With deadlock reached over the question of compensation (the company did not intend to deny the War Office access to the aerodrome), the matter was referred to the courts. The mode of proceeding against the Crown was by way of petition of right, sent via the Home Office and Treasury Solicitor, whereby the monarch consented, on the basis of an arguable, as distinct from an wholly specious, case that the Crown should answer the claim. The suppliants drafted their petition outlining their claim to compensation as of right and it eventually reached the War Office on 23 March.[9] Shortly afterwards, George Wingfield saw A. H. Dennis, the Treasury Solicitor, and requested the War Office, without prejudice to any question, to pay over a sum on account, equal to one-fourth of the £1,500 rent offered by the department. One can guess that this was prompted by debenture-holders' demands for interest payments but a War Office decision appears to have been postponed. The Permanent Secretary of the War Office, Sir Reginald Brade, also raised the question of referring the issue to the DRLC with the petitioners' consent, an approach favoured by the secretary of the Army Council. This possibility was put to the company on 12 May and was fielded with great care in their reply on 20 May. No reference to a commission in order to ascertain an *ex gratia* settlement would be contemplated, they insisted. However, if an agreement with the government over the amount could be struck, the company would be quite willing to treat the consequent payment as *ex gratia* compensation 'because there would be no object in litigating the question of legal right if you are willing, *ex gratia*, to pay as compensation the same amount as our clients would be entitled to if they established that right'.

As hinted earlier, there was a financial time-bomb ticking away at the aerodrome, which directly involved George Wingfield. For in 1916 debentures, personally guaranteed by Wingfield, were due for redemption. But as the business was now in abeyance, the holders, who included Wingfield's own clients, could not be paid off. He could invoke the protection of the Courts (Emergency Powers) Act 1914, which relieved debtors from liability on contracts disrupted by the war, but that would scarcely enhance his reputation. As part of a financial package, therefore, he proposed that the government should take over the debentures, pay them off when due, deduct that amount

---

9. PRO, HO 45/10770/274803 for petition of right.

from the rent due to the company from the department, and finally surrender that proportion of the debentures to the company which would represent the latter's loss of business.

These proposals, needless to say, received a frosty response from the Treasury Solicitor, who described the suggestions as 'preposterous'. He also (probably correctly) questioned the independence of the debenture holders and doubted whether they would actually enforce their rights in default of payment. On 29 May Edward Coles confirmed to A. H. Dennis that it was to be either litigation or the DRLC, with no compromise other than the possibility of paying something on account to the company, were the litigation option to be chosen by the aerodrome company.

That path was chosen and, less than one month later, a hearing took place before Mr Justice Avory in the High Court. The company were represented by L. F. Scott, who, with A. Hildersley, another barrister, later published *The Case of Requisition*, the narrative of the *De Keyser's Royal Hotel* case in which he also appeared. Leslie Frederic Scott (1869–1950) was Conservative M.P. for Liverpool Exchange between 1910 and 1929 and became Solicitor-General in 1922. During the war, he chaired the Acquisition of Land Committee 1917–19 whose reports led to the Acquisition of Land (Compensation) Act 1919 and the new Law of Property Acts in the 1920s. His interest in land use continued through the Second World War, when he chaired a committee on Land Utilisation in Rural Areas, 1941–42. Whether it was his interest in property requisition which inspired his selection as counsel for the aerodrome or vice-versa is not clear. His early legal experience in Liverpool revolved around commercial and maritime cases (one of his pupils there was F. E. Smith, the future Lord Birkenhead). His entry in *Who's Who* for 1927 declared he was 'interested in all questions of social and industrial reform, particularly in connection with the development of agriculture and the improvement of the conditions of life affecting the rural population'. He was undoubtedly an appropriate choice to engage in legal arguments with his former pupil, Sir F. E. Smith, the Conservative Solicitor-General in the Asquith coalition.

The company's argument, to reiterate, was that the power conferred on the executive to requisition the aerodrome under Regulation 2 did not imply a power to withhold compensation as of right from the company. This was because none of the wording of the Defence of the Realm (Consolidation) Act 1914, nor of the regulation itself, could be construed as denying the right of property-owners to compensation when their properties were commandeered. It was, the company insisted, implicit in the wartime provisions that the right to compensation for loss of property taken over by the military, a right enshrined in the detailed provisions of the Defence Act 1842, as amended, and the Military Lands Act 1892, could only be removed by express statutory wording. No such wording was contained in the wartime provisions, save a measure which counsel insisted was intended only to short-circuit the procedural delays in fixing compensation and not to remove the right to compensation. The Crown, for its part, relied not only on the statutory powers of requisition in DORA and Reg. 2 but also on the royal prerogative to justify the take-over of the aerodrome.

Four basic controversies in the law were therefore identified. The first was whether the take-over was necessary for securing the public safety and the defence of the realm. The second was whether, under statute, compensation was payable as of right in the circumstances of the case. The third was whether the royal prerogative, as distinct from any statutory authority, could authorise this particular takeover. Fourth, if the prerogative were held applicable to the case, was the payment of compensation a legally mandated accompaniment?

As to the first issue, the judge accepted that as 'we live in days in which there are liabilitites to raids from Zeppelins and so on', in the words of the Solicitor-General, the occupation of the aerodrome was justified from the standpoint of the defence of the realm. That opinion had been preferred in evidence by Captain Clive Miller, formerly on the War Office General Staff and latterly undertaking regimental duties with the RFC. The judge declined to know whether any enemy aircraft or airships had in fact been sighted in the vicinity of the aerodrome. He merely took 'judicial notice' of the existence of Zeppelin raids, without seeking further proof about their regularity or intensity or location. If the court hearing had actually taken place in December 1914, at the precise time when the RFC was officially taking over Shoreham, the judge would have been hard put to take judicial notice of any Zeppelin raids on British soil. The first such raids, against Yarmouth and surrounding villages on the east coast, north of the Thames Estuary, took place on the night of 19–20 January 1915; for the next six months, up to the hearing on 25 June, there were just half-a-dozen small raids, causing little damage.[10] Only from mid August 1915 was London threatened by Zeppelin raids, three such attacks during that summer causing relatively extensive damage and inflicting considerable loss of life. In all those cases, the southernmost crossing-point on the English coast for those Zeppelins was Kent, with Essex being the most frequent point of entry. The Sussex coast, where Shoreham was located, remained unpenetrated. Leslie Scott chose not to challenge Captain Miller's evidence.

What he did challenge vigorously was the proposition that the prerogative was applicable to the take-over of the aerodrome:

> The prerogative of the King in time of war to which my friend [the Solicitor-General] referred is not a prerogative that arises upon such a necessity as that. The exigency which gives rise to the prerogative to take property is the presence then and there of an urgent military necessity of an executive kind to take immediate steps at that place.

On the footing that the enemy were not 'at the gate', to employ the analogy from the seventeenth-century case law, in particular, the *Magdalen College*

---

10. Arch Whitehouse, *The Zeppelin Fighters* (London, 1972), p. 67.

case (1615) 1 Roll. Rep. 151 and the *King's Prerogative in Saltpetre* (1606) 12 Co. Rep. 12, the prerogative to requisition private property was inapplicable and statutory powers, if any, would have to be invoked. The judge enquired, 'Do you mean that it is not within the prerogative to anticipate future events in time of war?' Scott's reply was suitably guarded: 'In this context within the limitations that [sic] we are discussing the prerogative here, I do.' It therefore seemed that, if the prerogative claim was to be advanced with confidence by the Crown, the factual justification would have to be forthcoming: 'I think you had better give this evidence, Mr Solicitor.'

Presumably for security reasons, that evidence was reproduced neither in the expurgated report of the hearing published in the official Law Reports, nor in the printed 'Main Papers' on the case which went before the House of Lords. Indeed the publication of reports of the hearing of the petition before Mr Justice Avory had originally been prohibited by him, though there was no objection to the publication of the decision at which he arrived.[11] As we have seen, the evidence pointing to 'raids from Zeppelins and so on' by the time of the hearing was scarcely impressive. The eventual finding by the judge that the take-over fell within the scope of the prerogative may have flown in the face of the evidence. The more persuasive explanation is that Mr Justice Avory interpreted the prerogative power sufficiently broadly to enable it to 'anticipate future events in time of war', a proposition endorsed by the Court of Appeal but one which drew condemnation from other quarters.

In the event, on 6 May 1915, the War Office issued instructions to all RFC stations prescribing the type of aircraft and armaments to be maintained in anticipation of Zeppelin attacks. Apart from Shoreham, RFC aerodromes were located at South Farnborough, Brooklands, Hounslow, Joyce Green and Dover (there were also Royal Naval Air Service stations at places such as Detling, Westgate and Manston, all in Kent). The instructions were that one aeroplane should be maintained on constant alert at all sites. At Shoreham, No. 3 Reserve Aeroplane Squadron (RAS) had formed by the time of the take-over at the end of 1914. Its task was the elementary training of pilots and ground crews. The instruction of May 1915 was specifically directed at the air defence of London, with the Martinsyde S1 Scout biplane selected for this task. There is disagreement among writers as to whether the Martinsyde, which carried incendiary bombs, was a successful machine. Whitehouse comments that it was 'an immediate success' until the German Albatros and Halberstadt scouts later proved faster. Cole and Cheesman, by contrast, claim that it failed to meet expectations.[12] Whatever the truth, Shoreham's role in the period of the war was distinctly limited.

11. *Solicitors' Journal*, 59, 10 July 1915, p. 618. See also note 13, below.
12. Whitehouse, *The Zeppelin Fighters*, p. 69; Christopher Cole and E. F. Cheesman, *The Air Defence of Britain, 1914–1918* (London, 1984), p. 35.

In his judgment of 7 July, Horace Avory held that the Defence Act 1842 and the Military Lands Act 1892 were only intended to operate in peacetime, with the exception of section 23 of the former statute. That provision, he ruled, overrode the act's requisitioning provisions and its elaborate price-fixing arrangements only if 'the enemy shall have actually invaded the United Kingdom at the time when such lands . . . shall be so taken'. That was, he argued, simply a saving provision for the royal prerogative in wartime.

'But if I am wrong in this view of the operation of the Acts of 1842 and 1892', he added, then DORA and Regulation 2 conferred 'an absolute and unconditional power' to take over the property during the continuation of the war. Reg. 2, he ruled, also implicitly repealed for the time being any right to compensation, if such a right actually existed in time of war under the earlier acts, a proposition which presumably he denied. Finally, he dismissed the need in Reg. 2 for a specific suspension of any 'restrictions on the acquisition or user of land', by which he meant compensation under the nineteenth-century acts, even though DORA empowered the making of regulations providing for such suspension. The absolute and unconditional power in Reg. 2 was sufficient to suspend all such restrictions.

Perhaps the most controversial part of his judgment concerned the operation of the royal prerogative. He referred to the seventeenth-century authorities, *R.* v. *Hampden* (1637) 3 Howell's St. Tr. 825 (the *Ship Money* case) and the *Saltpetre Case* as tending to suggest the prerogative to take over private property operated only in the event of actual invasion. As late as 1858, Willes J. had stated in *Hole* v. *Barlow* (1858) 4 C. B. (N. S.) 334, at p. 345:

> Every man has a right to the enjoyment of his land; but, in the event of a foreign invasion, the Queen may take the land for the purpose of setting up defences thereon for the general good of the nation. In these and such like cases, private convenience must yield to public necessity.

These pronouncements, nonetheless, would seem to limit the operation of the prerogative to the most dire cases of immediate danger 'in the event of a foreign invasion' and would therefore be a check on the executive. Mr Justice Avory had other ideas. Probably impressed by the evidence sworn by Captain Miller, he reasoned that:

> the changed conditions of modern warfare must be taken into account, and the realm now requires protection from enemy aircraft and the long-range guns of enemy ships as in the old days it required protection from the landing of enemy troops.

He therefore found the prerogative applicable in the given circumstances and, moreover, held that no compensation was due. If the former finding appears, in fact, to have been scarcely argued, the latter appears to have been tacked on, without any argument, as a mere afterthought. Perhaps this legal recognition of the arrival of the era of total war prompted too hasty, too panicky and too subservient a reevaluation of the prerogative principle and its application.[13]

A week later, the matter came before the judges of the Court of Appeal. On 14 and 15 July, Leslie Scott and his junior counsel, Frank Gover, rehearsed their arguments before the Master of the Rolls, Lord Cozens-Hardy, Lord Justice Pickford and Lord Justice Warrington.

The company's principal argument was that although a statutory right to take was admitted, Reg. 2 was silent on the matter of compensation: that did not imply that no compensation was due as of right. For there was a rule of statutory construction upheld by Lord Esher in *Attorney-General* v. *Horner* (1884) 14 Q.B.D. 245, 'not to construe an Act of Parliament as interfering with or injuring persons' rights without compensation unless one is obliged to so construe it'. Therefore, it was argued, only express words in DORA excluding the right to compensation would be effective, and no such words existed. Moreover, it was submitted, the provision in DORA which allowed the executive to make regulations for the suspension of those restrictions on the acquisition of land contained in the nineteenth-century acts referred only to restrictions in respect to delay or notice, not as to payment of compensation itself.

On the prerogative question, the company again reiterated that the Crown's right to enter upon land only applied in cases of 'urgent military necessity', the emphasis being placed on the immediacy of the threat. The point was underlined by the argument that, whereas the particular prerogative claimed could only be exercised in time of war, the current situation was not, for purposes of the exercise of the prerogative, a time of war. Citing *Coke upon Littleton* (1628), 'the courts of justice are open . . . and may by law protect men from violence and wrong' (though this proposition may have confused martial law with prerogative powers). Therefore, one prong of the attack on the use of the Crown's prerogative was that the circumstances did not warrant the exercise of such powers. If that argument by the company were to fail, the question of compensation under the prerogative (as distinct from compensation under statute, which had already been raised) would arise. To justify the payment of compensation for the exercise of prerogative powers, the company, citing Blackstone's *Commentaries* and other early authorities, argued that no prerogative rights could be claimed which were not defined by statute or by immemorial use; and there was no prerogative right to take away a subject's property without compensation which might be so recognised. If the Crown had always possessed a prerogative, as it was claiming, to take land without compensation in anticipation of invasion, why had Parliament passed legislation in 1803 and 1804 (since repealed) enabling the Crown not only to

---

13. The case is reported as *In the Matter of a Petition of Right* [1915] 3 K.B. 649 which printed a limited version of the judgments. The HLRO Main Papers indicate that the Solicitor-General had originally requested that the press should not report the case. Mr Justice Avory directed that the judgment itself could be reported as long as the suppliants were not identified.

take over lands on which to construct defences (presumably including Martello towers) in order to repel an invasion by Napoleon, but also requiring it to pay compensation?

If the Crown had possessed such common law powers, why did it require to go to Parliament seeking identical powers to take now hedged with restrictions as to compensation? All these arguments supported the company's claim that the nineteenth-century statutory provisions in respect to compensation had not been removed by DORA and by Reg. 2. Additionally, even if the prerogative were applicable to the present case (which was denied), compensation would still be payable as of right. It was no satisfactory answer for the company to be told to refer its claim to the whims and fancies of the DRLC.

The Crown's case on statutory construction with respect to compensation was the obverse of the company's. Where a public official, having statutory authority to act for the public good, damaged an individual's property in so acting, that individual had no right to compensation except that which was expressly given by the statute. On the prerogative question, the Crown emphasised its redefinition of invasion to include bombardment and aerial attack by the enemy, which had already occurred, though only to a limited extent at the time of the court hearings and in areas distant from Sussex. As the military had already determined that this was an emergency situation, it was not for the court (nor, indeed, for anyone else) to challenge this view. Moreover, there had never been any successful claim for compensation against the Crown in such a case.

The Crown also pointed to the express provision for compensation in Reg. 7, which gave power to requisition the output of factories manufacturing arms and ammunition. By contrast, it was argued, since Reg. 2 made no mention of compensation, the inference to be drawn was that none was due under that regulation as of right. Indeed, when pressed by Leslie Scott for the company, the Solicitor-General sought to draw a distinction between the output of a factory, for which compensation was payable, and the taking possession and use of a factory for which no statutory provision for compensation was expressly set out.

On all other points of issue, the Crown simply repeated the arguments which had proved successful before Mr Justice Avory; evidently to good effect, for a week later, on 23 July, all three judges dismissed the company's appeal, upheld the legality of the aerodrome's take-over and confirmed that no compensation was due to the company *ex lege*.

Both Lord Cozens-Hardy and Lord Justice Warrington upheld the applicability of the prerogative to the case, while denying that a duty to pay compensation fell upon the state. Lord Justice Pickford, on the other hand, contented himself with justifying the take-over and denial of compensation with reference to the statutory provisions.

The decision prompted a fierce editorial comment by Sir Frederick Pollock in the *Law Quarterly Review* shortly thereafter.[14] He reminded his readers

---

14. *Law Quarterly Review*, 32 (1916), pp. 6–7.

that he had called attention in a previous issue to the extraordinary legal powers of the Crown in wartime, apart from those powers contained in DORA and in its accompanying regulations. In the light of the decision in the Court of Appeal, he added, that warning proved to be 'not unpractical', even though reliance was also placed on statute. Nonetheless, 'We cannot think it plain – we do not say it is not maintainable – that occupying and using an aerodrome for the continuance of the war is analogous to making a bulwark for the defence of the kingdom; but the Court apparently did.' It remained unclear, thought Pollock, whether the court considered that the prerogative applied not only when there was an apprehension of attack, but also when a general state of war existed within the realm. He concluded sardonically that 'there seems to be room for further education in the House of Lords'. One civil servant, writing after the war, was in no doubt of the practical impact of the prerogative. He concluded:

> The Royal Prerogative thus came to play an essential part in the development of control. It was by virtue of the absolutist theory that the subject had no legal right to compensation against the Crown, that the tyranny of market prices was 'overthrown'.[15]

Not surprisingly, the aviation magazine, *Flight*, viewed the decision with disgust.

> To most people [the claim to compensation *ex lege*] would not appear to be an unreasonable proposition, as after all, however loyal to one's king and fellow citizens one may be, it is not an honour to rejoice over that you should personally be practically wiped out for the general good – nominally the Crown – without the general purse being liable to share the honours by paying for the privilege.[16]

The 'one-sided bargain' was scarcely set off by the anachronistic offer of grace and favour compensation. This appeared to be a return to the 'dark days of feudalism', and given that the war was a 'people's war', the nation had a duty to furnish (and therefore property owners had a right to receive) fair compensation. While the editorial line was predictable and while it disavowed drawing distinctions between aviation property and property in general, it remains evident that particular concern was directed at the threat to the viability of aviation enterprise hitherto functioning as a going concern.

What effect did the Court of Appeal ruling have on the negotiations over compensation? The company continued to press the War Office for sums on account and did, in fact, receive some payments, in view of its own commitment to make interest payments to its debenture holders. But the

15. E. M. H. Lloyd, *Experiments in State Control*, p. 52.
16. *Flight*, 23 July 1915, p. 526. See also ibid., p. 544; ibid., 30 July 1915, p. 566.

War Office refused to increase the amounts, as it considered that the case was probably destined for the DRLC.

Edward Coles, the Comptroller of Lands at the War Office, was indignant at the company's approaches:

> The Company asked *far* too much. We offered what we considered very fair terms. The Co. refused these and went to law to test our legal powers. They have lost their case, and now complain of the delay in compensating them! . . . It is rather too much to expect us to keep them going by liberal payments on account while they make up their minds whether they will take their case to the House of Lords.

The company did, indeed, take its case to the House of Lords, but that hearing took place more than a year later. In the intervening period, negotiations between the increasingly antagonistic company and the complacent officials of the War Office were dragged out. The department was seeking to drive the company to the DRLC and the latter was proving obstinate. The company, in turn, was complaining that the War Office, although paying £33 a month to the company, was pocketing the rents being paid by the remaining tenants at the aerodrome, Cedric Lee & Co.[17] The department's reply, that it was awaiting clarification of the proper legal relationship between the company, the War Office and Cedric Lee, stung George Wingfield into retorting: 'To speak mildly, it is the most scandalously disingenuous letter that we have ever seen from a Government Department. We feel it is done on purpose to make the correspondence lengthy in the hopes that nobody will have the patience to read it.'

The principal short-term objective of the company was to receive a substantial lump sum on account, failing which it would publicise its plight, thereby 'exposing our villainy', as Edward Coles at the Lands Branch sarcastically noted. A letter from the company secretary, William Littlewood, duly appeared in the *Morning Post* in February 1916.[18] The letter referred to a speech in the House of Commons the previous week by Arthur Balfour, the First Lord of the Admiralty, in which the minister had claimed that although the needs of the armed forces for aeroplanes were identified, nonetheless, 'we cannot get the things'. According to Littlewood, this was not surprising, given the manner in which the government had been treating those 'who, with more foresight, spent years of labour and thousands of pounds in capital in developing the industry prior to the war'. Littlewood then rehearsed in public the long protracted struggle between the War Office and those affected by the requisitioning of Shoreham Aerodrome, underlining his case with repeated

---

17. Cedric Lee & Co. had apparently been taken over by the South Coast Aircraft Works whose proprietor was Sir Archibald Sinclair (1890–1970), the twenty-six year-old 4th baronet. A Liberal, he became Secretary for Scotland in the National Government (1931–32) and Secretary of State for Air in the Coalition government (1940–45).

18. *Morning Post*, 23 February 1916.

references to the 'pioneers of the industry' who had invested for the future when the government itself was not only neglecting but discouraging aeroplane development. Now, when the nation's needs had shifted, such far-sighted pioneers were being treated shabbily. 'Mr Balfour and the country must expect to cry out that they cannot get machines if the Government behave like this.'

Although every M.P. was circulated about the company's grievances, the resolution of the matter was finally left in the hands of Lords Loreburn, Parker of Waddington and Sumner in the judicial House of Lords, which heard the company's appeal in July 1916. Remarkably, before the hearing was completed, the Crown consented to the appeal being withdrawn on terms which effectively vindicated the company's legal argument. What had happened behind the scenes in the House of Lords committee room where the appeal was being conducted remains obscure. It is clear that the case was settled in the company's favour 'on the strength of an intimation [by the judges] to the Law Officers that the decision would go against them'.[19] As the Lord Chancellor, Lord Buckmaster, who, as a member of the government, had not sat on the hearing, observed in a note to the Cabinet:

> It is quite certain that no one of the Lords of Appeal who sat in the House of Lords on the hearing of this case would have accepted the view of the Royal Prerogative put forward by the advisers of the Crown.

As to the powers of requisition under DORA, he added,

> Assuming that the Defence of the Realm Acts conferred power by regulation to abolish rights to compensation [which he actually denied], it is difficult to identify any regulation which does so in express terms.[20]

As reported in *The Times*,

> The Attorney-General [Sir F. E. Smith] said that he had had an opportunity of considering this case since the adjournment on Tuesday [July 25], and he had come to the conclusion that in the special circumstances the suppliants had some ground for supposing that the Crown had proceeded under the Defence Act, 1842, which provided for compensation . . . Subject to the approval of the House, he proposed that the appeal should be withdrawn by consent on terms agreed upon by the parties.[21]

---

19. PRO, LCO 2/367, memorandum by Douglas DuBois Davidson, secretary of the DRLC, 22 August 1916.
20. Copy in PRO, LCO 2/367.
21. *The Times*, 28 July 1916. See also [1916] W.N. 311; *Solicitors' Journal*, 60, 19 August 1916, p. 694, *sub nom. Re Petition of Right of X.* The company were represented in the House of Lords by Scott, Gover and P. O. Lawrence (later Lord Justice Lawrence from 1926 to 1934). The Crown were assisted by the constitutional lawyer, Professor A. V. Dicey, making his last appearance at the bar.

Sir Frederick Pollock, commenting on the outcome in the *Law Quarterly Review*, could scarcely disguise his jubilation.[22] He noted that, technically, the settlement was only with regard to that particular case:

> Thus the high prerogative claim to occupy without compensation was waived in fact without prejudice to the question of law in any future case, and the construction of the Defence of the Realm Acts and Regulations was equally left open.

That latter statutory power remained potent in circumstances which might appear, *prima facie*, remote from *direct* involvement in military activities. Pollock undoubtedly believed that the prerogative proposition of the Crown had been damaged, perhaps beyond recall. He invoked John Locke, *On Civil Government* (1690) in support of the 'general constitutional principle which allows property to be taken for public purposes only with just compensation'.

The outcome of the Shoreham Aerodrome case was a reaffirmation of the fundamental principle of the sanctity of rights of property in the face of executive power. The government would now have to seek actively another test case to reshape the prerogative to its desire. The wider financial implications for the Treasury would prompt some drastic rethinking about procuring new powers from Parliament. Meanwhile, the immediate consequences of the hearing for the negotiations between the War Office and the aerodrome company had to be faced.

The company, whose costs would be met by the Crown, were now in a position to invoke the favourable compensation machinery in the Defence Act 1842 which, in the last resort, permitted arbitration to resolve any deadlock over terms. Immediate agreement was reached to pay over £3,000 on account which would 'relieve the claimants from certain embarrassment which they are suffering at the hands of a debenture holder'.[23] That was presumably a reference to a separate Court of Appeal judgment of December 1915 for £3,731 in favour of Florence Blew against George Wingfield and William Blew, whose names appear to indicate, *prima facie*, an absence of independence among the debenture holders, as the War Office had earlier suspected. Another £2,000 followed shortly thereafter.

From that point, the two sides remained far apart. General Brancker, the Director of Air Organization, had approved of the proposal to buy the aerodrome outright from the company, rather than retain it merely for the duration of the war. The former would be the more economical alternative and post-war retention could be justified militarily. The department was willing to offer £30,000 while the company were initially seeking £50,000 (a figure subsequently adjusted considerably upward), close to the amount the department suspected an arbitrator would award.

---

22. *Law Quarterly Review*, 32, 1916, pp. 339–40.
23. PRO, AIR 2/7, A. H. Dennis to War Office Lands Branch, 28 July 1916.

By October 1916 the company was sufficiently irritated by the delay in reaching a settlement that it commenced the compulsory arbitration process in the Defence Act 1842. Disagreement over the choice of arbitrator was recorded. Therefore an umpire, Edwin Fox, was appointed to resolve any potential deadlock between each side's nominee as arbitrator.[24]

By the time of the arbitration hearing at the end of July 1917, the company's financial demands had soared. The £50,000 originally sought had now risen to £178,000 as it creatively calculated not merely actual loss but prospective loss of business. In addition, it sought rent of £8,000 covering the period 30 December 1914 to 2 November 1916. Third, it wanted £50,000 compensation if deprived of the right to fly over adjacent land south of the railway line (the War Office wishing only to purchase the land north of the railway line). If not so deprived, and if permitted to continue its aeronautical development, then a figure of £5,000 was sought as compensation for damage to that adjacent land (on which it also held a lease).

Given these more precise demands, the Director-General of Lands at the War Office, Sir Howard Frank, sought clearer instructions from General Brancker. Faced with the greatly inflated demands of the company in the event of a buy-out, the War Office wanted to offer to give back the aerodrome six months (later reduced to three) after peace was declared. By making such an offer, the department would make it difficult for the company to refuse, 'without entirely discrediting the evidence they have given, which is to the effect that the aerodrome could be made to produce a nett income of no less than £22,000 a year'. If the offer were refused, it was explained, the the arbitrator's award would be reduced very considerably; and given that the department were now faced with a bill of up to £178,000 to buy out the aerodrome, it was obviously sensible to argue in this way. If the offer was accepted, then it would only cost the department around £1,200 per annum for the period of occupation, while the cost of reproviding the aerodrome elsewhere, as General Brancker thought acceptable, would be about £30,000. The offer to return the aerodrome was essentially a bargaining ploy to reduce drastically the purchase price which the department would have to pay.

The tactic appeared to succeed. Sir Gordon Hewart, the Solicitor-General, put the offer to the company which the latter declined. The arbitration then proceeded and the following awards were made. For the rental period, £3,235 (as against the £8,000 sought); the purchase price £20,240 (as against £178,000); and compensation for damage to the adjoining land, £2,290 (as against £5,000). The company retained the right to fly over the southern area and received in total £25,765.[25]

---

24. For additional financial preparations by the War Office for arbitration, see PRO, AIR 2/7/EASTERN/1597.

25. In early November 1917, Colonel Campion MP raised the matter of compensation for the aerodrome in the House of Commons. The Under-Secretary of State for War, Ian Macpherson MP, confirmed the award of £25,765 as against a total claim for £191,000. See *Flight*, 15 November 1917, p. 1209.

As the proceedings were under the Defence Act and not subject to the DRLC, this figure ought to have reflected the market value of the property, either at the date of the notice to treat or of the arbitration award. In either case, it ought to have taken account of the prospective profits to be earned as a result of increased demand for scarce resources during wartime. It ought not to have reflected simply the financial loss to the company, that is, the restoration of the company to the financial position it would have been in, had not the aerodrome been taken over. That was the approach of the DRLC which we shall analyse in more detail in chapter twelve. On the crucial question whether the company received considerably more for its property than it would have done had the matter gone to the DRLC, the answer must remain in doubt. The company's determination to fight on in the courts and not to be fobbed off with a reference to the DRLC was perhaps mostly due to the actions of George Wingfield. As an enthusiast, investor, financial guarantor and solicitor, he was perhaps fired up by the personal crusade which came from his own financial stake in the venture.

What did the War Office get for its outlay? As has already been noted, Shoreham became the base for No. 3 RAS. According to Chris Ashworth, they were flying a motley collection of aircraft.[26] Personnel from that squadron formed No. 14 Squadron on 3 February 1915, a reorganisation which interrupted the training of new pilots. The requirement to maintain at least one aircraft in readiness against Zeppelin attacks also hampered the aerodrome's training function. RAS eventually became No. 3 TS (Training Squadron) on 31 May 1917, putting novice pilots through an intensive six-week course for beginners. The minimum period set, of three hours accompanied and three hours solo flying, was, according to Ashworth, a 'recipe for disaster'.

By the time of the absorption of the RFC into the Royal Air Force in April 1918, No. 3 TS was flying Avro 504s. It departed in July 1918 and its role was taken over by the South Eastern Area Flying Instructors School. After the Armistice, some flying still took place at Shoreham until the disbandment of the school in 1919. The aerodrome was then made available to the Canadian Air Force, whose No. 1 Wing, comprising No. 1 (Fighter) Squadron and No. 2 (Bomber) Squadron was located there. When Canadian government policy shifted away from maintaining a peacetime air force, the planes and equipment were dismantled and shipped to Canada. In December 1921, the aerodrome was closed and Mr Trott (and his successors) could graze his farm animals on the ground once more.[27]

26. Ashworth, *Action Stations*, pp. 254–56.
27. Ibid., p. 255. For the revival of the aerodrome in the 1930s and beyond, see ibid., pp. 256–60.

5

The Departments Bluffed with Confidence

'The breakdown of this case on the appeal of the Shoreham Aerodrome to the House of Lords', minuted W. A. Bland of the War Office Finance Department, 'cuts at the root of all our actions under the Defence of the Realm Act, but I understand that this very important general question is being taken up separately.'[1] The outcome did indeed have awkward consequences for a number of government departments, prompting a general reassessment of the Crown's legal position.

There were new practical problems which government departments, including the Army, were now encountering in pursuing their property requisitioning policies, all of which forced the government to look for solutions, including legislative ones, to meet its dilemma and its crisis of legitimacy. Addressing the legal position in which the government now found itself, the Lord Chancellor, Lord Buckmaster, warned that following the aerodrome outcome, the government:

> must be prepared to see every act of the Executive with regard to the appropriation of property, made the subject of challenge in the Law Courts. Their power to take and their liability to pay and the measure of payment will all be the subject of acute controversy.[2]

In similar vein, Sir Claud Schuster of the Lord Chancellor's Office wrote to Edward Coles at the War Office Lands Branch, adding that both the Central Control Board (Liquor Traffic), which was responsible for buying up public houses in munitions factory districts, and also the Admiralty which had been requisitioning merchant shipping, were 'likely to be attacked at any moment'.[3]

Buckmaster had drafted a memorandum for the Cabinet in August 1916 expressing grave doubts as to there being any legal basis for the action of

---

1. PRO, AIR 2/7, W. A. Bland to Assistant Financial Secretary, War Office, 1 September 1916.
2. PRO, LCO 2/367, memorandum by Lord Buckmaster, c. October 1916.
3. Ibid., Sir Claud Schuster to Coles, 21 December 1916.

the War Office in requisitioning Shoreham Aerodrome, either under the royal prerogative or even under Regulation 2:

> The position is a grave one [although] the matter may be regarded as reasonably safe for the moment, since no case could well come before the House of Lords under nine months or a year and the *Court of Appeal seems to have supported a sufficiently extended view of the Royal Prerogative to warrant what has been done.*[4]

His own doubts concerning the applicability of the prerogative derived mainly from the Law Lords' view in the Shoreham case as to the preeminence of the Defence Act 1842, prompting Sir Frederick Liddell, the Parliamentary Counsel, to advise Sir Claud Schuster on 30 November 1916, that it was essential, in any proposed legislation dealing with the difficulty, 'to declare that the prerogative powers may be exercised notwithstanding the existence of statutory powers covering the same ground'.[5] As to the view that not even DORA and Regulation 2 might have authorised the take-over of the aerodrome, had such a decision by the Law Lords been necessary, that opinion was based on the belief that the general words in the 1914 Act, from which the regulation was derived, were 'merely a statutory declaration of the prerogative, and confer no additional powers'.[6] If the scope of the prerogative was in doubt, that is, if it were doubted whether it could justify the take-over of the aerodrome in anticipation of and indeed following occasional Zeppelin raids, as distinct from when one discovered the 'enemy at the gate', so also was the scope of the regulation. This interpretation of DORA did not subsequently find favour with the House of Lords judges in *De Keyser's* case, where Lord Moulton insisted that:

> Even the most fervent believer in the scope of the Royal Prerogative must admit that the powers of the Crown were extended by the Defence of the Realm (Consolidation) Act and the regulations made thereunder.[7]

In another case heard on 23 June 1916, Mr Justice Avory held that the words contained in Reg. 2, permitting the authorities to take over land, buildings or other property or to interfere with private rights of property where necessary for the public safety and the defence of the realm, could not be limited to operations of a strictly military character (or indeed chronologically). When the Ministry of Munitions wished to take over the premises of the Sheffield Conservative and Unionist Club in order to house ministry inspectors and their clerical staffs, this objective fell within the scope of Reg. 2 so long as

---

4. Ibid., Cabinet memorandum by Lord Buckmaster, August 1916. Italics in original.
5. Ibid., Sir Frederick Liddell to Schuster, 30 November 1916.
6. Ibid., 'Defence of the Realm (Compensation for Loss) Bill', February 1917.
7. *Attorney-General* v. *De Keyser's Royal Hotel Ltd* [1920] A.C. 508, at p. 549.

the competent military authority acted in good faith.[8] In so deciding, the judge rejected the contention of Leslie Scott on behalf of the plaintiffs, who were alleging a trespass by the authorities, that Reg. 2 could not extend to works which were only indirectly necessary for the defence of the realm. Avory was not convinced that a line could be drawn in this manner. Even were one to be drawn, the clerical tasks connected with the manufacture of munitions, which it would be 'ludicrous' to deny were necessary to the defence of the realm, were themselves part of that enterprise. Even if there were other premises which might have been taken over, this did not imply that the military authorities had acted so unreasonably as to suggest bad faith. Citing his own opinion in the Shoreham Aerodrome case, to the effect that Reg. 2 conferred an 'absolute and unconditional' power to requisition land or buildings and to repeal any existing right to compensation, Avory dismissed the plaintiffs' action. While this interpretation went far beyond what the House of Lords in *De Keyser* would admit as to the scope of Reg. 2, the timing of the outcome of the compensation question in the Sheffield case was unfortunate for the owners, the decision arriving only three weeks before the out-of-court settlement of the House of Lords hearing in the Shoreham appeal.

As to the reaction of the authorities to the outcome of that latter hearing, Buckmaster's pessimistic interpretation is perhaps evidence of the state of legal disarray in which the government now found itself. He was concerned that the attitude of the House of Lords in the Shoreham case, which addressed itself not only to the prerogative but also to the wartime and peacetime statutory frameworks, was now known to the public and that claims for compensation *ex lege* would, if allowed, cost the Exchequer 'enormous sums'.

The following year, in October 1917, the Law Officers, Sir F. E. Smith and Sir Gordon Hewart, drafted an opinion on the issue for presentation to the War Cabinet. They pointed out that owing to the transformation in the circumstances of war since 'former days', there was room for differences of opinion both as to the circumstances in which the prerogative could be exercised, and also as to the effect of its exercise once such a situation had arisen. In favour of the government's position was the 'remarkable fact' that prior to the current war, no one whose land or other private property had been taken in time of war for use in the defence of the realm had taken proceedings against the Crown, either for compensation or for a declaration that the taking was illegal. The difficulties should not be underestimated, they implied:

No one doubts that if a hostile force were actually marching across England, the Prerogative would enable the armed forces of the Crown to march across the lands of private owners in order to attack the enemy, to construct defensive works of all kinds, and to destroy buildings and other property on such land

8. *Sheffield Conservative and Unionist Club Ltd* v. *Brighton* (1916) 32 T.L.R. 598. See also *Solicitors' Journal*, 60, 1 July 1916, pp. 582–83.

which might be of use to the enemy or a hindrance to our forces. But from such a state of facts to such a case as the requisitioning of a set of offices for the more convenient or efficient housing of clerks in a Government Department, more or less directly connected with some matter of administration connected with the war, the urgency of the necessity for the acquisition of the particular property in question alters, in an ever-diminishing degree, until at last the taking of property, under the exercise of Prerogative power, appears to be a very harsh proceeding.[9]

They observed that the arguments against the validity of the exercise of the prerogative in the current war were that no urgent necessity for taking land had yet arisen and that the Defence Act had replaced the prerogative. Such arguments had been overruled by the lower courts, 'but they undoubtedly impressed the three Law Lords' in the Shoreham case. While reliance on the defence regulations had also been upheld in the alternative, these provisions, in the opinion of the Law Officers, did not 'carry the powers of the Crown any further than the Prerogative'. Nonetheless, they were adamant that if the prerogative enabled land to be 'acquired' (a term which they did not appear to distinguish from 'taken', though arguably there was a significant difference), 'no compensation is by law payable in respect of its use. The same result should logically follow from an acquisition under the Defence of the Realm Regulations'. Yet, despite the Shoreham ruling in the Court of Appeal, there were 'formidable arguments' for a contrary view.

Such was the none-too-optimistic view of the new legal position of the government. How did it affect individual departments? The Army Contracts Branch pointed out that the doubts following the Shoreham case, together with doubts expressed in Parliament by Arthur J. Sherwell on 15 February 1917 over the legality of the requisition of the wool clip,[10] meant that the legality of the defence regulations which the Army invoked to requisition commodities or to regulate their price could not be assured. It commented that:

> it will hardly venture to prosecute for offences against the existing orders for fear of the *vires* of the whole system of regulation being questioned in any proceedings. It must be remembered that an unsuccessful prosecution would not only render it impossible to maintain the present policy, but would also disclose the fact that the Department's past action had been illegal with the result that we should have to face an agitation which it would be very difficult to resist, for the reopening of thousands of past transactions which have only been acquiesced in because they were thought to be based on legal authority.[11]

9. PRO, CAB 24/4, G.165, F. E. Smith and Gordon Hewart, 'Legality of Certain Acts Done Under the Defence of the Realm Regulations, 17 October 1917'.
10. H. C. Deb., 5th series, 90, col. 831, 15 February 1917.
11. PRO, LCO 2/367, 'Defence of the Realm (Compensation for Loss) Bill. Note by the Director of Army Contracts', para. 5, February 1917.

In a revealing comment, Sir Claud Schuster wrote to his Treasury colleague, G. L. Barstow, in February 1917:

> You must remember that a good deal of the actions taken by the various Departments has succeeded because those who suffered were patriotic and still more because the departments concerned bluffed with confidence.[12]

The new difficulty was that the public were now becoming aware of the legal weakness of the government's position, and were also becoming less tolerant of the restraints imposed upon them.

The warning of the Army Contracts Branch pointed to the practical difficulties which government departments were now facing every time they eyed a particular property for occupation. In the case of negotiations between the government's Office of Works (the intermediary for the Army Lands Branch) and the owners of another hotel, the Metropole in Scotland, there was a financial gap of £13,625 between what the government was willing to offer by way of compensation on a voluntary basis and the amount demanded by the owners. Though the Office of Works had managed to bring down the Metropole's original claim from £120,000 to £47,625, negotiations became deadlocked thereafter. As a government official commented:

> The business has hung fire so long that it must, I think, be brought to a settlement one way or another. It would seem that we must either (1) break off the negotiations and leave them to such actions as they may be advised to take; or (2) in fact if not in name, regard the case as simply one in which we must drive the hardest bargain we can, endeavouring to safeguard the legal position generally, by getting the result of that bargain ratified as it stands by the Defence of the Realm Losses Commission.[13]

As to the first option, the writer acknowledged that, in the absence of further legislation, the government's legal position was 'dangerously weak'. Therefore, the second option had to be followed, even though, as Sir Lionel Earle, the Permanent Secretary to the Office of Works, observed, 'if our legal position is weak, we have little chance of getting anywhere down to bed rock terms'.[14]

The suggestion in the Metropole Hotel case, albeit discarded, of putting the onus on the claimants to institute proceedings and of letting *them* run the risks involved in taking on the government in the courts, was mirrored in negotiating the *Cannon Brewery* case,[15] where a government body, the Central Control Board (Liquor Traffic), had 'acquired' (rather than simply

---

12. Ibid., Schuster to G. L. Barstow, 26 February 1917.
13. Ibid., Memorandum by W. A. Robinson, Office of Works, 20 November 1916.
14. Ibid., Sir Lionel Earle to Sir Alfred Mond, First Commissioner, Office of Works, 20 November 1916.
15. *Central Control Board (Liquor Traffic)* v. *Cannon Brewery Co. Ltd* [1919] A.C. 744 (H.L.).

'taken possession of', as in the Shoreham case) a brewery at Enfield Lock, near Woolwich Arsenal. The government's Law Officers, conscious of the validity of the brewery's claim to compensation, as we shall see when we analyse the episode in detail in chapter seven, advised that the board:

> should endeavour (without waiving any rights) to agree the compensation or get it referred to some tribunal acceptable to both sides. If the Cannon Brewery Company are wholly unreasonable and will not listen to any fair settlement, the best course would be perhaps to let them develop their claim and realise the considerable difficulties which they too will have to face. It will be two years before the matter would reach the House of Lords.[16]

The Law Officers, Sir Frederick Smith and Sir George Cave (from December 1916, Viscount Cave and Home Secretary), emphasised the 'obvious inexpediency during the war of dislocating the whole work of the Royal Commission and the possibility of reopening cases supposed to be settled'. They concluded that the 'public interest evidently demands that the decision of the Court of Appeal in the Shoreham Aerodrome case should not be disturbed during the war'.

The reference to the work of the Royal Commission, the DRLC, is a reminder of the financial issues which existed below the surface of the high politics of property rights and the British constitution. The secretary of the DRLC, Douglas DuBois Davidson, drafted a lengthy departmental memorandum on the financial consequences of the Shoreham outcome.[17] He pointed out that the outcome of the case in the House of Lords had encouraged other owners of requisitioned properties not to accept the level of compensation offered to them by the DRLC on the *ex gratia* basis, a level calculated on the loss actually suffered by the owners. Instead, they were now holding out for compensation calculated on the more favourable market-rate basis, which could include loss of potential profits, somewhat inflated in the prevailing economic climate. For example, while the practice of the DRLC had been to refuse compensation to a landowner whose spare field at the time of requisition had not been rented out to a third party,[18] the significance of the Shoreham outcome was that the landowner would now be entitled to compensation at a market-rental rate. Those who were digging in their heels by refusing to refer their claims to the DRLC included the owners of the Metropole Hotel, De Keyser's Hotel and the National Club (probably a Protestant club of that name, with 600 members, which had premises at Queen Anne's Gate).

Davidson pointed out that in the approximately one thousand cases heard to date by the DRLC, the commission had awarded lump sum payments of

---

16.   PRO, TS 27/46, 'Law Officers' Opinion, 3 August 1916'.
17.   PRO, LCO 2/367, 'Defence of the Realm Losses Commission', 22 August 1916.
18.   See also the post-war parliamentary debate on the Indemnity Act 1920 in chapter 13, below.

£262,803 as against claims for approximately £561,405; and annual payments of £163,583 per year as against claims for £295,127 per year: 'The whole of this difference may be regarded as a net saving, for the claims can as a whole be said to have been fairly stated from the point of view of a commercial compensation.' He also noted that in many cases, especially the later agricultural cases, the claims were submitted on the 'loss' basis for sums some way below those which could be justified commercially. Where 'agreed' cases were concerned, the sums had usually been considerably reduced by the application of the 'loss' basis before they reached the DRLC.

There was a further factor. Knowledge of the loss basis had been widely disseminated, so that the War Office had been able to reach agreements on quartering troops at a saving of some millions of pounds over the previous winter. Those economies could not have been achieved under the 'original and wasteful' system of billeting or under hiring agreements on a commercial basis. Agreements entered into by the War Office ostensibly under the loss basis had even been modified by the commission, producing further savings to the Exchequer. The Shoreham Aerodrome settlement was now threatening to undermine this arrangement and would also make it 'increasingly difficult and invidious' to apply DORA powers, 'when their exercise is the exception rather than the rule'; while there would be 'not unjustifiable bitterness' among those who had settled for less prior to the Shoreham outcome.

Davidson drew attention to the unfortunate development now taking place whereby legal advice was being given by the Treasury Solicitor to various government departments to exercise only sparingly the defence of the realm legal powers, no doubt to minimise the risk of legal challenge. This course was being advocated in respect to the requisitioning of further accommodation for the *Commission Internationale de Ravitaillement*. The savings to the Treasury, running into hundreds of thousands of pounds, a result of the deliberately restrictive terms for compensation awardable by the DRLC, were now liable to be lost. The Army Lands Branch, for example, was having to revert to the extravagant system of renting from landowners accommodation for billeting at a commercial basis, instead of requisitioning under Regulation 2 and forcing the owners to apply to the DRLC for loss-based compensation.[19]

To these problems there were two broad solutions canvassed. One was advocated by Sir Claud Schuster who, in minuting on the Metropole Hotel matter, stated that his department's intention now was that a good case should be chosen and fought through the courts to confirm the Court of Appeal ruling in the Shoreham case. The proceedings should be expedited by every possible means to the House of Lords and should there be 'dealt with by a strong Court'.[20] It was an unwarrantably optimistic piece of advice given the acknowledgement of the soundness of the contrary indications by the House of Lords judges in that case. The only comfort to the government, when the

19. PRO, LCO 2/367, Edward Coles to Schuster, 20 December 1916.
20. Ibid., Schuster to A. McFadyean, Treasury, 27 November 1916.

'good case' of *De Keyser* was finally settled by the House of Lords in favour of the owners, was that it was decided long after the Armistice had been signed, when the distinctive pressures of wartime had vanished.

The other proposal was to enact new legislation which would have two main objectives. The first would be to remove any residual doubt as to the legal powers of the executive to take possession of land and buildings which they believed were required for the 'public safety and the defence of the realm'. The aim would be to buttress the prerogative power of the Crown and to move beyond the general words of DORA. Since that measure, on the basis of one not unreasonable interpretation, was merely declaratory of the existence of assumed powers, it would be advisable to enact a statute, and not just issue departmental regulations, which would expressly confer power on the executive to requisition property. The actual requisitioning powers, apart from those in the 1842 Act which guaranteed generous compensation *ex lege*, were themselves only contained in subordinate legislation, that is, in Regulation 2, while the DORA Consolidation Act of November 1914 did not in express terms confer any power to take over property. It merely stated, 'His Majesty has power . . . to issue regulations for securing the public safety etc . . .'[21] Inasmuch as Reg. 2 expressly conferred a power of take-over, it might be held *ultra vires* by the higher courts (no reference to the *Sheffield Conservative Club* case was made).

The second aim of the legislation would be to put the DRLC on a statutory basis and also to confirm the direct loss basis for assessing compensation. This would leave no choice to the dispossessed property owner whose claim would be confined to restoration in the same financial position as if his property had not been requisitioned. As Lord Buckmaster argued:

> It would, I think, be little short of a scandal if owners of real estate were able to insist on the extravagant terms provided by the Lands Clauses Act as a compensation for property which was wanted in times of national danger.[22]

A modest little bill would relieve the Treasury of the possible risk of having to pay compensation to property owners for rent foregone on the basis of notional inflated profits which market demand had stimulated. Buckmaster was convinced that Parliament would approve such a measure but, a year later, an alternative view was heard from a different source. The Secretary of State for War, Lord Derby, pointed out in a Cabinet memorandum in September 1917,[23] that if the courts were to uphold a claim for compensation on the nineteenth-century Defence Act basis (which applied the guidelines of the Lands Clauses Act), as this approach incorporated an element for loss of profit, a bill providing merely for direct loss compensation would be

21. Chapter 3, above.
22. PRO, LCO 2/367, Cabinet memorandum by Lord Buckmaster, August 1916.
23. PRO, CAB 24/27, G.T. 2153, 27 September 1917.

difficult to obtain from Parliament. The lack of any legal right to compensation announced by the Court of Appeal in the Shoreham case, was, he believed, 'felt to be a great grievance'. Despite some attempts, no legislation to underpin the loss basis of compensation favouring the government was enacted during the years of armed conflict. On the other hand, as the timetable of the *De Keyser* litigation reveals, the government managed to survive the remainder of the war without suffering a formal legal defeat in the House of Lords on the central issue, despite dreading such a reversal since the Shoreham *dénouement* in the House of Lords in July 1916. It appears that the Army Lands Branch and the Office of Works temporised in classic civil service style by producing a command performance of masterly inactivity in dragging out financial negotiations with those few property owners who had refused to apply to the DRLC.

It was perhaps as well that they were able to do so because the drafting of suitable legislative measures presented insuperable problems. A Defence of the Realm (Compensation for Loss) Bill was touted round government departments in 1916. This was replaced by a less ambitious Defence of the Realm (Acquisition of Land) Bill which did the rounds of the ministries in 1917, and which contained amendments to an unrelated 1916 Act of the same name. Though I shall look in more detail at their provisions shortly, it is worth observing at this point that, on both occasions, the government departments concerned thought better of displaying what their critics might have condemned as grasping acquisitiveness, by forcing property owners to settle for less than market value compensation.

There is no doubt that, during the war, the competing claims of high principle, between the rights of property and the rights of the state, also embraced the low principle of pounds, shillings and pence. As Sir Claud Schuster wrote to his Treasury colleague, R. S. Meiklejohn, in November 1917, 'The subject [the Defence of the Realm (Acquisition of Land) Act] is a dreary one, but I write this private note so as to bring to your attention the fact that there is a great deal of money in it.'[24] That observation was highly pertinent to the Defence of the Realm (Compensation for Loss) Bill. As Schuster explained to another Treasury official, G. L. Barstow, some months earlier,[25] the bill was necessary to deflect any legal challenges to the government's requisitioning programme. Some challenges were bound to succeed 'if the attack is pressed home'. With others, the government's chances were 'very doubtful', while in respect to a third category of claims, there was a 'fair fighting chance if the Court is favourably constituted and favourably disposed'. Perhaps that was an indication that certain judges might be relied upon to reach their decision first and find a justifying reason afterwards. Schuster made it clear that:

> The real question now at issue ... is not a legal one but one involving financial, administrative, and political questions. The question which we must

24. PRO, LCO 2/367, Schuster to R. S. Meiklejohn, 28 November 1917.
25. Ibid., Schuster to Barlow, 26 February 1917.

ask ourselves, but of course cannot answer, is roughly this: Is the amount of money which is at risk so large as to counter balance the political difficulties in carrying the Bill?

The options were, first, to do nothing; second, to legislate in order to make 'the past secure' and to establish a statutory compensation tribunal; or third, to legislate as above, and to indemnify the departments in the event of any future trespasses. Schuster, himself, was not confident that the courts would continue to find in favour of the government while the war continued. Even if the House of Lords delivered an adverse decision 'just when peace broke out', the compensation payable, already running into millions of pounds, 'might be multiplied indefinitely'.

The legislation proposed by Lord Buckmaster was presented by his successor as Lord Chancellor, Lord Finlay, in February 1917 to the Defence of the Realm Regulations Committee, a committee under the chairmanship of the War Office.[26] The previous month, the War Office had submitted a memorandum to the War Cabinet listing the points which the department wished to be included in the Bill.[27] It desired the bill to validate all that had been done under the authority of DORA, and to indemnify the Crown and its servants against all claims in respect of such transactions. It should give the force of law to all the regulations hitherto made under DORA and to all orders issued under the regulations. It wanted a broad definition of 'public safety and defence of the realm', as used in DORA, which should be expressly stated to cover the general regulation of trade, manufacture and all commercial operations, with a view to securing the best and most economical utilisation of the nation's resources. It should put the DRLC on a statutory footing and validate and render final all its adjudications. For the future, the bill should lay down compensation rules in respect to land and accommodation; agricultural or mineral produce requisitioned from the manufacturer; and goods requisitioned from persons other than the producer or manufacturer. In respect to land and accommodation, the basis of compensation was recommended to be the loss suffered by the owner (the bases for the other categories of property need not concern us at this stage).

Amplification of the War Office's position was provided in its observations on the Compensation for Loss Bill, which the Defence of the Realm Regulations Committee considered in late February 1917.[28] Given the doubts expressed about the legality of the department's action, not only in requisitioning the wool clip, as already mentioned, but also in controlling the prices of British and Colonial wool, Russian flax, hay, straw and some classes of

26. Ibid., 'Defence of the Realm (Compensation for Loss) Bill, Observations by the various Departments', 21 February 1917.
27. Copy in ibid., 'Requisition of Land and Commodities. Memorandum by the War Office, January 1917'.
28. Ibid., 'Defence of the Realm (Compensation for Loss) Bill, Observations by the various Departments', 21 February 1917.

hides, the Director of Army Contracts wanted it put beyond doubt that the Contracts Department's economic controls fell squarely within the scope of actions necessary for the public safety and the defence of the realm.[29]

He added that as public opinion was now acutely aware of the seriousness of the crisis in respect to essential supplies, including food, and as the public definitely supported 'calls for executive action in the direction of economic control', the time was ripe for corrective legislation. If the necessary measures were postponed till after the war, by which time the need and the crisis would have passed, 'a very different state of public opinion might have to be encountered, and there would be far more likelihood of effective criticism and opposition'.

Edward Coles of the Lands Branch acknowledged the extreme difficulty of framing and passing a bill, 'which will expressly legalise all we have done, or may want to do',[30] that is, to confer beyond doubt a power on the executive to take any property it desired. He expressed some doubts concerning the phrasing of crucial provisions, though advised accepting its general form.

These concerns were more clearly expressed in the Lord Advocate's submission to the committee.[31] Clause one, he noted, approved not merely the exercise of royal prerogative powers in acquiring property, but also the purported exercise of such powers, that is, action which professed to derive from such powers, but where the prerogative might not support such action. He could not recall a previous statute in which 'purported' had been employed, and considered it even more dangerous a word in statute than 'intended': 'But all such words are calculated to give trouble, for they let in, by a side wind, possibilities of abuse of power.' To obviate that danger, as he saw it, the Bill's scope should be extended (including changing its title) to provide that the powers of the prerogative should, during the war, that is, both retrospectively and prospectively, be held to include the taking possession and acquisition of any land, ship or other property, and interference with any business, for any purpose connected with the securing of the public safety and the defence of the realm.

Given the financial difficulties which were at the root of the legal conflicts faced by the War Office, both in the Shoreham and in the *De Keyser* case, it is scarcely surprising that the department examined the Bill's proposals on compensation with some care. It noted that the Bill stated that the DRLC, once put on a statutory basis, would act in accordance with the principles previously adopted. Those principles, listed in the First Report of the Commission, had confined compensation to the 'direct and substantial loss in arrears and damage sustained'. The proposed statutory commission, however, would consider the claims of 'any person whose property or business has been, or may be, affected by the action taken'. The War Office wanted clear authority that the two main

29. Ibid., p. 6.
30. Ibid., p. 11.
31. Ibid., p. 4.

principles of the Duke Commission, no compensation for indirect loss or for loss arising out of the enforcement of any order or regulation of general application, would continue to apply.[32]

Perhaps it had been put on its guard by Buckmaster's memorandum of August 1916 which had already suggested that 'all future compensations should be determined upon the basis of a fair value'. The phrase was unfortunate, given its imprecision as to the criteria to be adopted. It prompted A. J. Balfour, First Lord of the Admiralty, whose department's requisitioning activities were not dissimilar to those of the War Office, to write to Buckmaster. Balfour stated that he was unable to understand the meaning of the phrase 'fair value', to which Buckmaster replied that it was intended to be elastic, though the intention was to ensure that compensation was to be for 'actual loss', as at the date of requisition.[33]

Balfour's point and Buckmaster's reply only served to emphasise the ambiguity of the project. On the one hand, the aim was to facilitate the conduct of the war by enabling a trouble-free take-over of private property where the public interest so decreed. But that public interest was itself defined by an executive which invoked the support of public opinion for drastic measures. On the other hand, the denial of a right to compensation except on a loss basis would provoke the hostility of public opinion as expressed through opposition in Parliament to the proposal. While public opinion might support the principle of a government right to requisition under prerogative or DORA powers, the departments consulted were concerned that the public might not like the small print.

On 23 March 1917 an interdepartmental meeting held in the Lord Chancellor's room in the House of Lords concluded that there was an incompatibility between the increasing demands of government departments and the suspicions of Parliament. The Bill would have to be dropped for the moment.[34] If, as a result, any department found itself in difficulty over legal challenges, an *ad hoc* bill might be prepared and consideration given to its introduction. At the conclusion of the war an Indemnity Bill would be prepared, making provision for 'fair compensation'. Though this was stated as recognising that the 'individual loss was sustained for the protection of the whole community', its precise significance was not elaborated upon at that point.

Legislative proposals were put on one side for only six months. In September 1917 a more restricted measure was put forward for consideration as the Defence of the Realm (Acquisition of Land) Bill (not to be confused with the 1916 Act of the same name, which was concerned with the permanent acquisition of property by the government after the war). Lord Derby, the

32. For details of the approach of the DRLC, see chapter 12, below.
33. For this exchange of views, see PRO, LCO 2/367, memorandum by Lord Buckmaster, c. October 1916.
34. Ibid., 'Defence of the Realm (Compensation for Loss) Bill. Meeting of 23 March 1917'.

Secretary of State for War, urged its necessity, since, following the House of Lords hearing in the Shoreham Aerodrome case, there were now at least two petitions of right pending in which compensation was being claimed under the nineteenth-century provisions.[35] We may be sure that the *De Keyser* case was one of those two.[36] Derby commented that if the courts were to uphold compensation on that market value basis, it would be more difficult to persuade Parliament to pass legislation in favour of the loss basis, while an anticipated Private Member's Bill in support of Lands Clauses-level compensation should be forestalled in order to preempt the opening up of the approximately 50,000 awards and agreements reached so far.

The Law Officers, Sir Frederick Smith and Sir Gordon Hewart, felt that, as drafted, the legal right to compensation in the Bill might be construed by the courts in a wide sense, not confined to the loss basis.[37] Nor was there any time limit within which claims could be made. They concluded that Buckmaster's Bill, presented by Lord Finlay, his successor as Lord Chancellor, was preferable. The War Cabinet at its meeting on November 28 nonetheless approved the principle of Lord Derby's Bill, instructing the Law Officers, in consultation with the Lord Chancellor, to consider the necessary amendments.[38] Whether their discussions revealed further obstacles to wartime legislation is unclear, but no legislation was forthcoming prior to the Armistice.[39] Instead, all eyes concerned with the property acquisition question focused on the *De Keyser* case, while the final acts in the war on the Western Front were being played out.

35.   PRO, CAB 24/27, G.T.2153, 27 September 1917.

36.   By the time of the House of Lords ruling in *De Keyser*, twenty-three petitions of right were awaiting the outcome of that case. See list in PRO, HO 45/10952/330662.

37.   PRO, CAB 24/4, G.165, F. E. Smith and Gordon Hewart, 'Legality of Certain Acts Done Under the Defence of the Realm Regulations, 17 October 1917'.

38.   PRO, CAB 23/4, W.C.285 (14), 28 November 1917.

39.   In the draft bill, a tangential matter concerned the enhancement of land values brought about by government building in the neighbourhood, for example, for munitions factories. This was considered by the War Cabinet in January 1918. See PRO, CAB 23/5, W.C.318 (14), 8 January 1918.

6

At De Keyser's Hotel

There is no student of constitutional law who does not know of the case of *Attorney-General* v. *De Keyser's Royal Hotel Ltd.* [1920] A.C.508. A large number of those students will also know that the case concerned the military requisition of the hotel in order to house the headquarters of the Royal Flying Corps (RFC). Few or none of those students will have heard of Sir Polydore De Keyser, Mayor of the City of London (1887–88), who lent his name to the hotel, nor that the RFC headquarters in question was that of the Directorate of Military Aeronautics at the War Office.

Sir Polydore De Keyser was born on 13 December 1832 at Termonde (Dendermonde in Flemish), near Antwerp in Belgium.[1] He was the son of Joost Constant Fidel Keyser and of Catharina Rosalie Troch, the daughter of a respected surgeon of Termonde. Polydore came to England some time before 1849. He became a naturalised British subject on 17 December 1853. In 1862 he married Louise, eldest daughter of the late M.J. Pieron. She died of cancer in 1895 and was buried in the family vault at Nunhead Cemetery, London, one of the capital's most beautiful Victorian final resting places.[2] Sir Polydore himself died of the same illness, on 14 January 1898, and was buried beside his wife. They had no children of their own but Sir Polydore adopted his nephew, Mr Polydore Weichand De Keyser, as his son. It was Weichand who, until 1909, was chairman and managing director of De Keyser's Royal Hotel Ltd on the Victoria Embankment at New Bridge Street near Blackfriars Bridge.

The contemporary view when Sir Polydore became Lord Mayor was that the Royal Hotel had belonged to his father, but that at a relatively early age Polydore had taken over the management, and on his father's death, became sole owner. The evidence given before Mr Justice Peterson in the Chancery Division in March 1918, however, was that Sir Polydore had founded the

---

1. For this and the following information about Sir Polydore De Keyser, see *Pictorial News*, 8 October 1887; *City Press*, 29 August 1888. A 'Spy' cartoon is in *Vanity Fair*, 26 November 1887. For obituaries, see *City Press*, 19 January 1898; *The Times*, 17 January 1898. An account of his funeral is in the *Citizen*, 22 January 1898. For a recent biographical study (in Flemish), see M. Van Wesemael, 'Sir Polydoor De Keyser: Lord Mayor van Londen', *Ghendtsche Tydinghen*, 15 January 1981, pp. 28–43.
2. For a recent description of the cemetery, see the *Independent*, 27 July 1990.

hotel. Irrespective of this point, he personally ran the hotel from 1856 to 1887, during which time the mere 'Royal Hotel' became *De Keyser's* Royal Hotel.

Polydore had been active in local London politics and society. He was Sheriff of London and Middlesex (1882–83), and was elected an alderman to represent Farringdon Without on the Court of Common Council. He belonged to half-a-dozen City companies: the Spectacle Makers, Farriers, Butchers, Innholders, Poulterers and Gold and Silver Wire Drawers. He was also a governor of Bridewell, Bethlem and St Bartholomew's Hospitals. In October 1887 he was elected Lord Mayor of London, the first Roman Catholic since the Reformation to hold that office. Unusually for a Catholic, he was also a freemason. Prior to his election, local newspaper comment had questioned the appropriateness of someone of his faith holding such office. His reply was that in his official capacity he recognized but one religion, the Established Church; apart from that, his religion was his own property.

On a stately visit in August 1888 to his home town in Belgium, the Burgomaster of Termonde recounted some of De Keyser's achievements as Lord Mayor. For example, he proclaimed that, as a result of De Keyser's inspiring leadership, the City of London had remained calm in the midst of popular agitation, a reference to the unemployment disturbances of November 1887, which included the Trafalgar Square riot, for which the Labour and radical leaders, John Burns and R.B. Cunninghame Grahame, stood trial.[3] The Lord Mayor had received cordial support in his encouragement of the Paris Exhibition, while major charitable work was started at the Mansion House in support of the victims of London floods. He was knighted on 4 December 1888.

De Keyser's Royal Hotel had approximately 300 bedrooms and was well furnished.[4] It was largely used by foreigners visiting London, including Americans, Dutch, French and Belgians (perhaps appropriately, Sir Polydore could speak six languages). Its success apparently depended almost entirely on such clientele, but it was used also very largely for banquets among City companies, where no doubt Sir Polydore's membership of those companies listed previously produced added rewards.

The hotel property was leasehold, held under six leases, four from the Bridewell Hospital (of which, as previously noted, Sir Polydore was a governor), one from the City of London and the last from Spicer Bros Ltd, paper-makers, one of whom, Sir Evan Spicer (1849–1937), was an original member of the London County Council and chairman (1906–7), and another, Sir Albert Spicer (1847–1934), was a Privy Councillor and

---

3. G. D. H. Cole and Raymond Postgate, *The Common People, 1746–1946* (London, 1966), p. 422.

4. Unless otherwise indicated, the source cited is the Main Papers collection relating to *Attorney-General* v. *De Keyser's Royal Hotel Ltd* in the House of Lords Record Office (HLRO). The bulk of that material is not reproduced in the published law reports of the case. On the specific description of the hotel itself, see the testimony of Arthur F. Whinney, receiver to the company, presented at the High Court hearing on 21 March 1918.

Liberal M.P. (1892–1900 and 1906–18). The Bridewell leases were dated between 1874 and 1880, all running for 90 years. In chronological terms, the rents were for £1,450, £50, £350 and £750 respectively. The City of London lease, dated 27 April 1897, ran for seventy-eight years and nine months from 25 March 1883 at a rental of £127 8s. 7d., while the remaining lease, dated December 1906, was at a rent of £30. All the leases were due to expire at the same time, on 25 December 1961, and all except the last one were made with Sir Polydore himself. The annual rent was £2,757 8s 7d.

In January 1897, a year before his death, the business was incorporated and Sir Polydore sold the hotel to the new company. The directors were Sir Polydore, Weichand (who became managing director at £500 per annum on a five-year service contract), Ronald Herbert Savory, a stockbroker, Augustus Stenger, a 'gentleman', and Joseph Barker, a hotel manager. The share structure on incorporation comprised 12,000 preference shares of £10 each and 10,000 ordinary shares of £10 each, while 4 per cent debenture stock amounting to £150,000 was also issued. The price paid for the hotel was £367,500. This was paid, as to £52,500, by the issue to Sir Polydore of £50,000 of debenture stock at £105 for each £100 stock; as to £40,000, by the issue of 4,000 fully paid preference shares; as to £33,000, by the issue of 3,300 fully paid ordinary shares; and £242,000 paid in cash.[5] Sir Polydore appears to have exhausted much of this cash in his final year, as he left personalty of £137,353 18s 9d. on his death.[6] By June 1915, the share structure of the company was £145,000 worth of one pound preference shares, £100,000 of ordinary one pound shares and the debentures listed above. Shares to the value of £113,000 remained unredeemed after a further capital issue of £25,000 in 1900.

On the outbreak of the war the business fortunes of the company plummeted. The foreign clientele were no longer coming and, as a result, the receipts from the hotel were no longer sufficient to pay its rent, rates, taxes and expenses. On 25 June 1915, Arthur (later Sir Arthur) Whinney was appointed by the court as receiver and manager on behalf of the debenture holders. Whinney (1865–1927) was senior partner in Whinney, Smith & Whinney, a firm of chartered accountants which later became one of the largest firms in the country, Ernst & Whinney. He held appointments at various times as Adviser on Costs to the Admiralty, Assistant Accountant-General to the Navy, Adviser and Consultant to the Admiralty in Accountancy, president of the Institute of Chartered Accountants and chairman of Board of Trade committees into the safeguarding of industry.[7] He found that De Keyser's Hotel was incurring a loss of between £1,200 and £1,500 a month and quickly

5. For the sale price of the hotel, for certain incorporation details and for lists of shareholders, see PRO, BT 31/15719/50854. For the share structure on incorporation, see the winding-up papers in PRO, J 13/8453.
6. For this latter sum, see the *Citizen*, 19 February 1898.
7. See Edgar Jones, *Accountancy and the British Economy, 1840–1980: The Evolution of Ernst & Whinney* (London, 1980).

borrowed £5,000 from the bank on the security of the whole undertaking, to enable him to carry on the business. He borrowed a further £5,000 on 7 February 1916 to clear expenses to 25 February 1916. After a meeting with the debenture holders on February 16, he was given permission to carry on the hotel. He borrowed another £3,000 in May.

Meanwhile, he had also made application to the London County quarter sessions for a revised assessment of rates and local taxes, given the straitened circumstances of the company. The situation, it was argued before that court, was likely to persist during the continuance of the war and for some time thereafter. He nonetheless made other changes designed to eliminate a 'good deal of the extravagance which had been going on'. By altering the plans under which rooms were let, he managed to reduce the losses from around £1,200–£1,500 per month to about £350 a month. He calculated that the hotel was, as a result, losing only £4,000–£5,000 per annum, 'with a prospect that I should probably have been able to turn the corner altogether'.

Whether or not every cloud has a silver lining, the diminution of hotel custom coincided with an expansion of the general staffs of the armed forces, of the creation of new ministries and of the expansion of existing ones. Given the physical limits of existing government accommodation, new premises were required. What could be more appropriate than that government departments should turn their attention to underused hotel accommodation which might prove suitable to the administrative needs of such departments?

In the case of the War Office, it had become apparent by early 1915 that all departments, by virtue of their growth, were crowding out the available premises.[8] Instead of 1,500 personnel working at the War Office, there were by then 15,000. Further accommodation therefore had to be sought, a responsibility of the Office of Works in conjunction with the client government ministry. Temporary buildings provided one expedient. War Office departments were therefore housed in St James' Park and in the Embankment Annexe where Sir Guy Granet's staff, responsible for railway administration, were located.[9] In addition, the Admiralty and Ministries of Shipping and Munitions resorted to temporary accommodation. A 'loft' extension on the top of the War Office building was also built and given the homely name of Zeppelin Terrace.[10]

According to Major-General Sir Charles Heath, Deputy Quarter-Master-General and Director of Forces in April 1916 when the hotel was formally requisitioned, the overcrowding had begun to ease from around October 1915, as more departments of the War Office were located elsewhere. In the case of the RFC, the Director-General of Military Aeronautics, Brigadier-General

8. See the testimony of B. B. Cubitt, Assistant Secretary to the Army Council, presented at the High Court hearing in May 1918, in HLRO Main Papers.
9. Granet was also general manager of the Midland Railway, retiring from that post in December 1918. See *Daily Mail Year Book 1920*, p. 184.
10. For this name, see Maurice Baring, *Flying Corps Headquarters, 1914–1918* (London, 1930), p. 124.

David Henderson and his staff (which included Major Brancker) had occupied seven or eight rooms of the War Office at the outbreak of the war. Soon part of the department, which in effect was the organisational framework of RFC HQ, was relocated elsewhere. 'We had some in odd places', said Heath. 'There were a few of them at the Hotel Cecil at one time, and a few in other buildings.' Towards the end of 1915 the search commenced for a larger building to house the whole of the aircraft staff. The Inns of Court Hotel was inspected but found unsuitable. Then more staff were appointed in February 1916. Henderson and Brancker were planning for the expansion of the flying service to over 30,000 officers and 300,000 men.[11] To meet that further need, according to General Heath, possession was taken of a hotel and two other premises at 13, 14 and 15 Albemarle Street. But, as he added, 'the aircraft staff outgrew that almost immediately'. In the autumn of 1915, the Aeronautical Inspection Department at Farnborough was moved to London, accommodation being provided in Carter's Hotel.

By April 1916 the Army Council had come to the conclusion, according to Bertram Cubitt, the Assistant Secretary to the War Office, that it was now essential to the efficiency of the air service, indeed 'for the defence of the realm and public safety it was urgent', that the whole of the Military Aeronautics Directorate should be housed in one location. Cubitt therefore wrote to the Office of Works on 12 April indicating the accommodation required. It would have to contain a large number of small rooms (large rooms with partitions would be unacceptable), the rooms should be bright and well-lit, and the accommodation should be in a convenient location, which in effect meant reasonably near a main railway station.

The Military Aeronautics Directorate was subdivided into further departments. These were the Directorate of Air Organisation, Directorate of Aircraft Equipment and the Aeronautical Inspection Department. In addition, the HQ of the 6th (Home Defence) Brigade, RFC was to be located in the same premises. It was technically a training brigade and was, as Cole and Cheesman point out, 'under the direct operational control of the War Office'.[12]

The accommodation required was twenty-two rooms for Air Organisation, seventy-nine for Aircraft Equipment, fifty for Aeronautical Inspection and twelve for the 6th Brigade. Of those latter twelve rooms, four were allocated to the 18th Wing and two to the 39th Squadron, both of which were attached to the 6th Brigade. No. 18 Wing had been formed on 25 March 1916 at Albemarle Street and was commanded by Lt-Col. Fenton Vesey Holt, a thirty-year-old Old Etonian. On 15 April No. 19 Reserve Aeroplane Squadron (RAS) became No. 39 (Home Defence) Squadron, under the command of Major T.C.R. Higgins, flying many different types of machines. Aircraft of the

11. Sir Philip Joubert de la Ferté, *The Third Service: The Story Behind the Royal Air Force* (London, 1955), p. 36.

12. For this last point, see Cole and Cheesman, *The Air Defence of Britain, 1914–1918*, p. 95.

squadron were based mainly at Sutton's Farm and Hainault Farm, while the HQ flight was kept at Hounslow.[13]

How did it come about that De Keyser's Royal Hotel was selected as the HQ, and what was the dispute which gave rise to what is arguably the most celebrated case in constitutional law since the 'general warrants' controversy of *Entick* v. *Carrington* [1765] 19 St. Tr. 1030 in the eighteenth century?[14]

We noted earlier that the outbreak of the war had brought about a disastrous reduction in the number of customers using the hotel. This had prompted the directors of the company to resolve, on 29 April 1915, to contact the 'War Office Authorities' about a possible temporary occupation.[15] In consequence, the company secretary, Stephen Fabes, wrote to the Office of Works the following day, offering the hotel as government accommodation.

Some time after, a War Office official inspected part of the hotel and asked Fabes upon what terms the directors would be prepared to make it available to the department. There was later some dispute as to whether a particular amount was quoted, but at a subsequent board meeting on May 6, the directors resolved that a rental of £2,500 a month should be asked for the whole premises, and an appointment was made for the chairman, Sir Joseph Savory, to meet Colonel Peterkin, Deputy Director of Military Supplies. That meeting took place at the Horse Guards later the same day when Fabes, Savory and another director, Thomas Phelps, met Col. Peterkin and another officer. They put to the officers the offer of the whole building at £30,000 per annum, but two days later, the War Office wrote declining the offer.

On 19 May another director of the company, G.M. (later Sir George) Chamberlin (1846–1928), who was Lord Mayor of Norwich in 1916 and 1918, wrote from the Carlton Club to Bertram Cubitt at the War Office, apparently without the knowledge of Fabes. Chamberlin explained to Cubitt that he was on 'very intimate terms of friendship with your father', who, it was claimed by Chamberlin, was also interested in the matter. Chamberlin explained that a War Office representative (presumably Peterkin) had been approached concerning the possible letting of the hotel to the government for the recuperation of hundreds of wounded soldiers. He admitted that the war had hit the hotel's business badly, but suggested that the hotel's original terms were 'probably too onerous'. A few days later, General Heath replied, repeating that the rental of £30,000 per annum had been 'altogether prohibitive' and that it was not proposed to take the hotel as a military hospital. Undaunted, Chamberlin wrote back on May 27, assuring Heath that, 'if our hotel will be one of service to the nation at the present juncture, the rent *shall not* be "prohibitive"'. For the moment, the War Office was not interested.

---

13. Ibid., pp. 94, 464.

14. One contemporary view was that, 'The case has been compared in importance and scope to the great Ship Money case, by which JOHN HAMPDEN gained renown'. *Solicitors' Journal*, 63, 12 April 1919, p. 424.

15. For this and subsequent information, unless otherwise noted, see HLRO Main Papers.

That essentially remained the position until April 1916. Meanwhile, the hotel's financial crisis had caused the debenture holders to act, and Arthur Whinney had been appointed receiver and manager by the court in June 1915. For its part, the crisis of accommodation for the War Office was causing it to explore the market for further office space. In November 1915 Whinney wrote to Samuel Fane, a member of the staff of Sir Arthur Durrant, the Controller of Supplies at the Office of Works. Whinney had understood that Fane had called upon Stephen Fabes, the company secretary, a short time previously, enquiring about the availability of the hotel. At the court hearing in 1918, Fane referred to some pencilled notes he had made, which suggested that the rental proposal was now £10,000 a year. Again, nothing was done immediately to follow up the matter.

It was not, in fact, until April 1916 that the War Office finally decided the time had arrived when all the headquarters staff of the RFC should be brought together in one building in London. In consequence, Cubitt wrote to the Office of Works on April 12, giving the detailed breakdowns, already referred to, of the accommodation required to house the Military Aeronautics Directorate. This also included the whole of the Designs section already transferred *en bloc* from Farnborough. The accommodation at Albemarle Street, it was pointed out, had already proved inadequate. It was not feasible to expand within the proximity of Albemarle Street by, for example, taking over the Grosvenor Club. Nor would Imperial House, Kingsway, prove suitable, as it did not contain a sufficient number of small rooms.

Over the next few days, a number of premises were inspected by, among other government officials, Fane and War Office representatives. According to Fane's recollection, one of the first hotels examined was the Hotel Victoria. Another may have been the Grand Hotel, though probably not the Hotel Cecil (to which, ironically, the RFC HQ later transferred after staying eighteen months at De Keyser's). There were, thought Fane, probably no more than six suitable premises examined. When Bertram Cubitt was cross-examined by Paul Lawrence KC for the company, the latter enquired whether, apart from the physical situation of the building, the War Office had considered the position of the owners of the businesses that were being carried on. 'If possible', was the reply, and the case of the National Liberal Club was cited as an example, presumably implying that non-commercial premises, if suitably furnished, would be requisitioned first (the Grosvenor Club, for example, was rejected because it was too small). Lawrence persisted. Why had none of the other 'modern' hotels in London been taken? The Waldorf, for example, was mentioned by counsel, but according to Cubitt, it was too far away from a railway station, in contrast to De Keyser's (or Adastral House as it had been renamed for the duration).[16] The Holborn Viaduct Hotel was another venue mentioned by Lawrence. Did it not offer approximately the

16. The current Adastral House, housing Royal Air Force staff, is in Theobalds Road, London.

same accommodation as De Keyser's, he asked? Again, Cubitt fielded the question: 'I should not think it was as well lit'. But as he also conceded, a number of premises which, in comparison with De Keyser's, were not suitable at the time were later acquired for the public service, including the Metropole Hotel (acquired by the Ministry of Munitions), Imperial House, Westminster (for the War Office Contracts Department), Kingsway House and Alexandra House, both in Aldwych, and the new W.H. Smith building, beside the law courts.

The purpose of Lawrence's line of questioning is not immediately obvious. Perhaps it was to demonstrate that the War Office 'picked on' De Keyser's because it was thought to be financially vulnerable and therefore likely to be grateful to submit a claim for *ex gratia* compensation to the Defence of the Realm Losses Commission (DRLC). General Heath, in his evidence to the court hearing, certainly indicated that, 'to do things as economically as possible', he tended not to requisition the most flourishing hotels. In the case of De Keyser's, he had not in fact been aware of its financial situation at the time. The Office of Works may well have been better informed, as a result of which Heath, the competent military authority, was simply left with the requisition order to approve. If this was the motive of the department officials, they misunderstood the responsibility of those acting on behalf of company shareholders, whose duty was to secure the best return compatible with prudent business judgments. Perhaps the hotel was selected in the light of its association with foreign clientele, in part by a wartime feeling of hostility to foreigners. Perhaps the Waldorf was sacrosanct, viewed with deference and respect. These are, of course, speculations. So far as the Military Aeronautics Directorate were concerned, their new home was firmly fixed as De Keyser's Royal Hotel. Samuel Fane now entered into detailed discussions with Arthur Whinney in mid April 1916 to try to reach an agreed arrangement for vacant possession. This was to cover the rent, exclusive of rates and taxes, for the whole of the hotel, excluding the shops attached, to cover the period of the war, 'and, not improbably, say, for a maximum period of three months after the conclusion of peace'.

Whinney replied the next day, 19 April. He quoted a figure of £19,000 per annum for rent with a minimum one year rent. He later explained to the court that he had arrived at that figure by taking the capital value of the hotel as it had stood in the books and deducting the capital value of the shops which were not to be taken over. He then capitalised the value on a 5½ per cent basis. Conditions were, however, attached to this offer. These were that the cost of dismantling and reinstating the hotel was to be borne by the government; that the hotel's furniture and effects were to be removed and stored at the government's expense and redelivered by the government at the end of the tenancy; that the government insure the furniture and effects against fire and war risks; that the wines remain in the cellar at the government's risk, with reasonable access or right of removal given to Whinney; that the licence be preserved and kept alive at the government's expense; that the government return the hotel at the end of the tenancy in the same state as when originally handed over; and that it pay an agreed sum for loss of goodwill and to cover fair wear and tear. Approximately half of this was to be paid at the start of the tenancy and the rest at its termination. If the premises were destroyed or damaged in any way, reinstatement was to be at government expense, the rent to continue to be paid.

An alternative proposal put forward by Whinney was for the War Office to take over a part only of the hotel, that is, the north wing and a part of the east section of the hotel. They could be kept entirely separate from the remainder, with a separate entrance staircase, a lift to all floors, and 110 rooms including five measuring twenty three feet by fourteen feet. No goodwill payment would be sought, as Whinney would be able to carry on the hotel business, and the rent would be £7,500 per annum, plus a sum to be agreed for dilapidations and renovations, estimated at a further £2,500.

Whinney concluded his written offer by requesting Fane to keep the negotiations as secret as possible, 'as any reference to the matter may damage the goodwill and disturb the staff if it once gets about that the hotel may be closed'. He was especially concerned about this since the hotel's business had improved considerably and future prospects of more business were favourable.

Whinney actually visited Fane on April 28 at the Office of Works and later told the court that Fane had asked, 'Cannot you make it £17,500?' Whinney continued: 'We then beat about the bush a bit more, and I think he said he would have to go in and see his Board in the next room.' Whinney presumably appreciated that protracted discussions within the department would be necessary and told Fane to get in touch with him if an agreement was possible. In the event, the department resorted to emergency powers.

Just over a week later, Sir Arthur Durrant of the Office of Works wrote back to say that it would be to the advantage of all concerned if the financial matters were put before the DRLC. This was a prelude to the requisitioning order under Defence Regulation 2, which was duly communicated on 1 May 1916, with entry one week later ('In order to inconvenience you and your guests as little as possible . . .') As Samuel Fane claimed he had told Whinney, the requisitioning had been ordered, 'on account of the vital urgency of getting the premises with the least possible delay'.

Whinney in his reply to Durrant predictably failed to see a reference to the DRLC as being mutually advantageous, though for the moment, and subject to the consent of the Court of Chancery (from whom he received his appointment), he would facilitate the hand over of the hotel. He would arrange for his own representatives to attend while an inventory of the property was taken at the time of the take-over and requested to be allowed to stay on in the secretary's office for a short period to enable the book-keeping to be completed. He also mentioned to Durrant the position of the hotel's manager, Stephen Fabes, who, together with his wife and family, had occupied rooms in the hotel and would now have to vacate them on the loss of his employment.

Finally, he pointed out that there was an engineering staff of eight, responsible for heating and lighting the hotel by means of its own power units. The water supply, also, was drawn from the hotel's own well.

This communication of 1 May, as we saw, merely questioned the advantage to the hotel which would accrue from a reference of its claim to the DRLC, as distinct from reaching an agreement with the War Office on 'fair and reasonable terms'. On 3 May Whinney reminded Durrant that the steps he was taking to facilitate the take-over were 'without prejudice to the question as to whether the Army Council are within their rights in requiring possession' of the hotel under the requisition notice. On 5 May he amplified his position slightly. He questioned whether the acquisition of the hotel for office space was necessary 'for the purpose of securing the public safety or the Defence of the Realm', or that the acquisition was within the powers conferred under DORA. Nonetheless, he had no intention of hindering the military authorities, and had already given notice to all the hotel's guests in anticipation of the hand over.

Given that the hotel had an obligation to pay ground rent, he suggested that they negotiate over a fair rent for which reference should be made to arbitration. The question of compensation might also be left to some other tribunal. At the hand-over on 8 May Whinney made no secret of his anger at the turn of events.

> I protested very violently against the proceedings, because I was in this position – to a certain point they had been conducting negotiations to rent the place, and then suddenly they broke off and served me with this notice and I naturally protested against it.

As he explained on cross-examination by the Attorney-General, he had had some experience of the DRLC and of its guiding principles and believed that, as a result, he was going to receive nothing for the property. This belief was based on the understanding that the DRLC awarded no compensation where businesses, at take-over, were being run at a loss (though Whinney's belief may have been too dismissive of the DRLC's approach).

Nonetheless, it was agreed with Samuel Fane from the Office of Works that pass keys would be issued to Whinney and to a small number of his staff while the book-keeping duties were being completed, that Mr Fabes could remain on the premises for the present and that days should be fixed for the removal of the wines from the cellar after they had been put up for sale.

By 6 June Whinney had vacated most of the hotel, leaving behind 300 empty rooms, a lease with forty-five years left to run at a ground rent of £2,727 7s 6d. per annum, plus debenture interest payments of £5,640 (later corrected to £6,000) per annum. In the company's balance sheet, the hotel stood at £397,994 3s. 6d. What remained open to the public, was the restaurant whose changing fortunes, as we shall see, encouraged the company to pursue its legal claim.

It was the ground rent obligation which proved burdensome to a company with no substantial visible income. A bank loan upon the security of a first charge on the property was necessary, but agreement on a sum representing the War Office's occupation rent would considerably ease the difficulty, Whinney wrote to Durrant in early July. A figure of £17,500 had been quoted by the department in previous discussions and Whinney would find that acceptable. But he was addressing a brick wall, as Durrant merely directed him to the DRLC for compensation *ex gratia* for the direct loss suffered by the hotel.

By the middle of August, with no sign of the department shifting from its position, the directors and debenture holders themselves decided to become involved. They wrote to Sir Reginald Brade, the secretary of the Army Council, reminding him (as if the military authorities were unaware) that the army's action was denying them the 'ultimate benefit' which would derive from carrying on the business as a going concern, even at a temporary loss. While they were happy to acquiesce in the military take-over, 'it is both unfair and unreasonable that the burden of such action, which is for the benefit of the State as a whole, should have to be borne by the debenture and shareholders of the company'. Appeals to fairness, equitable treatment and just recognition of their claim marked their direct approach to the War Office, rather than an outright repudiation of the government's legal authority to requisition (the latter legal challenge had already been raised in Whinney's correspondence). On 20 September 1916, a meeting of shareholders and debenture holders, fully reported in *The Times*, took place at which it was resolved to 'approve of proceedings by Petition of Right being commenced, and, if necessary, prosecuted to the House of Lords . . .' However, such steps would not be taken if the 'Office of Works desire to make any communication which will be likely to meet the views expressed at such meeting, and thus relieve a position which in the interests of everybody will be far better avoided'.[17] This only drew from Durrant the information that if the department's accountants were to go over the company's books, the department would be in a position to formulate its position to the DRLC, which, he understood, would be able to consider and reply to any queries which the company might put to them. In Whinney's view, however, the government at this time, perhaps in contradiction to the Office of Works, 'were very desirous of not fighting this case out if it could be avoided'. While the department had refused to countenance any payments formally designated as 'occupation rent', Whinney conceived of the government's approach through the company's books as a means whereby he might obtain 'my £17,000 per year', no matter how it might be described.

Over the next couple of months (October-November 1916) a government accountant perused the books of the hotel. Hints to the War Office of improvements in the prospects of the hotel (which had by then been in the

---

17. *The Times*, 21 September 1916. See also the letter complaining of the injustice and tyranny meted out to householders denied compensation for requisitioned properties, in ibid., 29 September 1916.

hands of the government for six months) were dropped. Whinney was reluctant at this stage to put forward in writing evidence to this effect, which concerned improvements in the restaurant's business. As he intimated to Durrant in mid November, the company was contemplating legal proceedings in the absence of an 'adequate' offer. No doubt the implications of the outcome of the Shoreham Aerodrome case had been well digested by the company by that date.

Whinney put to Durrant further facts in mid December which he believed would enable the department to recommend to the DRLC the payment of an annual sum over and above the £3,200 which had apparently been agreed by the Office of Works as reasonable compensation for the hotel. These additional factors concerned a scheme for improving the fortunes of the hotel which had been hatched the previous April and announced in *The Times* on 27 April 1916. The plan was to transform the hotel into a residential one at inclusive terms of 3 guineas a week. This was thought by the company to be attractive to those who, 'by reason of war conditions and servant difficulties have had to give up housekeeping'. The company envisaged an increasing take-up as the scheme became more widely known, while the charges also would be increased over time. The scheme for this 'Home Hotel', as it was to become known, was welcomed by *The Times* but the advertisement had to be withdrawn almost immediately in view of the requisitioning of the premises a few days later. Whinney was of the opinion that the Office of Works, in calculating the compensation it would be prepared to offer, had ignored the financial potential of this scheme, consequently undercalculating the compensation payable.

Whinney also gave more details concerning the improved revenues from the kitchens. Luncheon and dinner bookings for May and June 1916 were good, and in the case of some of the clientele for which the hotel catered, such as functions of the Chartered Insurance Institute and of the London Savings Bank and the Wesleyan Methodist conference, a large number of hotel visitors would ordinarily have been expected.

Apart from the loss of anticipated profits from the conference trade, from the Home Hotel scheme and from improvements in the restaurant business, Whinney reminded the department of the extensive borrowings he had made in order to reduce significantly the company's losses. Due to the action of the government, 'a round sum of approximately £10,500 has therefore been uselessly squandered, leaving a heavy burden by way of interest, all of which comes out of the Debenture Holders' security'. Given that the annual interest on the debentures was £5,640, and given the position of the company generally, Whinney feared that he might 'have to take steps which will embarrass your Department at a time of national emergency', unless adequate compensation were forthcoming.

His appeal to high principle soon reached the new Prime Minister, Lloyd George, to whom he wrote on December 21. Since compensation according to the Army Council, he pointed out, was only payable *ex gratia* on the advice of the DRLC, and was strictly limited to the amount of loss incurred:

the property owner is placed in the position of having his property forcibly taken from him for the use of the State, while the State accepts no liability to pay either compensation for user and occupation rent. In this way, a burden is cast upon individuals, which ought in fairness to be borne by the State.

He added that as receiver appointed by the court, he was now involved in three 'large and important' cases, while other property owners had communicated with him with a view to litigating, 'to recover what we believe to be our rights'.

While the matter is addressed in the Lloyd George papers, the Prime Minister did not personally intervene in the dispute, and passed on the letter to the War Office. Cubitt formally replied on 26 January 1917, disputing the unfairness of compensating on a loss basis: 'On the contrary, that principle appears to [the Army Council] to be the one which most fairly preserves the balance between public and private interests.' As long as compensation on such basis was paid, he added, it did not seem very material that it was paid *ex gratia*.

What troubled Whinney in his reply of 6 February was not, perhaps, the fact that payment of compensation was an act of grace and not a legal entitlement, but the belief that the remit of the DRLC precluded the hotel, in view of its circumstances, from receiving any compensation at all. His reading of the *First Report* of the DRLC was that no payment would be made where premises had been occupied, with the result of suspending a business which had been carried on at a loss, or was capable only of being carried on at a loss. He effectively found himself in an impossible position. The Army Council would not consider any payment for occupation rent on the ground that the DRLC was responsible for all compensation matters. On the other hand, the hotel, which had been making annual profits of upward of £17,000 per annum prior to the war, was being run at a loss at the time of the take-over. Therefore, reasoned Whinney, the DRLC would be unable to make an award. It therefore followed, he concluded, that the government were getting the use of the hotel 'for nothing', hardly a fair balance between the public and the private interest.

He also found the position inconsistent with the treatment of shipowners and holders of securities: 'If the government takes ships, they pay hire; if they call for securities, they not only permit the owner to receive the interest, but supplement it by an additional payment.' As rent was 'only another name for interest on capital invested in land and buildings', he questioned why the hotel owners should be deprived of their interest while shipowners and security-holders were not. An answer was given on 28 February when Cubitt suggested that ships and securities were producing, or were capable of producing, revenue under war conditions. By contrast, he argued, the hotel was not; that is, the distinction was not between one form of capital and another, but between interest-generating and non-interest-generating capital. The hotel owners could hardly be deprived of non-existent interest on their capital.

But Cubitt did offer some comfort by suggesting (though he could not speak on their behalf) that the DRLC could award compensation for loss either of a temporary nature, for example, loss of mortgage or debenture interest, or of a permanent nature, such as damage to the premises or loss of goodwill, if these were a direct result of military occupation.

Whinney's response was to argue that the government's position made no allowance, in formulating its principle, for possible changes to be made in the capital asset, in order to render it interest-generating. It was manifest that the hotel, now let as offices, was capable of producing revenue (which would obviously shift it into the black either immediately or in the fullness of time). The Office of Works, after all, had commenced negotiations with the hotel to rent the premises, so compensation by way of an annual rent would seem in order even though Whinney took the view that the DRLC could not contemplate the payment of an occupation rent.

While this correspondence was all very interesting in exploring the nature of capital assets and their relationship to interest, the two sides were nowhere nearer agreement. In effect, the War Office had proved so intransigent that Whinney had little option but to go to law if his objective were to obtain a rental which reflected the market for office space or even for an hotel whose fortunes were beginning to change for the better at the moment of military requisition. There must also have been two other factors in the mind of Arthur Whinney. First, it is highly likely that he was aware of the promising outcome of the Shoreham Aerodrome case. Even the brief report in *The Times* in July 1916 would have prompted the intelligent to read between the lines of an out-of-court settlement. Secondly, he was unlikely to have innocently distorted the approach of the DRLC when he suggested that, as the hotel had been operating at a loss at the point of requisition, no compensation would be payable. He was probably disingenuous in so arguing. But, if so, why? Perhaps it was to shame the authorities into offering a reasonable settlement on which both sides could agree. Perhaps it was to justify publicly going to law, on the argument that there was no alternative, an argument which it is difficult to believe he himself endorsed, despite the points made to Cubitt at the War Office. Whatever the reasoning, the hotel now beat a path to the law courts and to immortality in the annals of constitutional law.

On 17 February 1917, the company presented its petition of right.[18] This rehearsed in brief the foregoing proceedings and correspondence, claiming, in particular, that the government's representative, on or about 28 April 1916, had made an offer to Whinney of £17,500 annual rent for the premises, and that Whinney would recommend this subject to the Court of Chancery's approval; that the following day, the government wrote back that the question of the amount should be for the DRLC, and that, while disputing the right of the government to requisition under DORA, Whinney voluntarily delivered up the property while reserving the company's rights in respect to compensation

18.   PRO, HO 45/10952/330662.

and rent. Thus the suppliants claimed (1) payment of an annual rent while the government continued in use and occupation of the hotel; (2) the sum of £13,520 11s. 1d. for use and occupation from 8 May 1916 to 14 February 1917; (3) in the alternative, an enquiry as to what was a fair rent of the premises, and payment of the sum so found; (4) a declaration that the suppliants were entitled to a fair rent for use and occupation by way of compensation under the Defence Act 1842; (5) compensation under the 1842 Act for such other losses and injurious consequences as aforesaid; and (6) such other declaration as to the suppliants' rights in the premises as the court might deem right and proper. The petition was signed by Leslie Scott and William Copping, the hotel's counsel.

The Attorney-General's answer and plea to the suppliants' petition raised the following claims. First, that in consequence of the state of war, it became necessary for the purpose of securing the public safety and the defence of the realm that the suppliants' land and premises be taken by the competent military authority. Second, that by virtue of that necessity, the property was thus taken, the legal authority being both the royal prerogative and the powers conferred by DORA. Third, the taking was only for the duration of the war and did not imply any claimed right or interest by the government in the property. Fourth, and perhaps most crucial, no rent or compensation was by law payable to the suppliants either under the Defence Act 1842, or at all, though application to the DRLC could be made if the suppliants wished to avail themselves of the opportunity. In effect, the government were seeking to argue anew the case which failed to impress the House of Lords in the Shoreham Aerodrome hearing.

At the factual level, they denied that an offer to rent the property at £17,500 per annum had been made. As Sir Lionel Earle, the Permanent Secretary at the Office of Works, pointed out on 24 March to the Under-Secretary of State at the Home Office, to whom the petition was first transmitted before going to the Attorney-General for his *fiat*, the discussions preliminary to the commandeering of the hotel were merely to ascertain the lowest terms on which the company's receiver would be prepared to let the premises. The ascertainment of this information would in turn be a preliminary to considering the advisability of requisitioning. Compensation, insisted the government, was for the DRLC but the government were willing to recommend to the DRLC compensation calculated on the basis of direct loss, making full allowance for possible loss of goodwill and possible loss of profits, given the later improvement in the hotel's business. Compensation on the basis of rent calculated on the value of the property was, however, resisted by the department. Earle added that the hotel company were the only parties with whom the Office of Works had dealt on the matter of requisitioning to have refused to refer their claim to the DRLC and to have challenged the legal basis of the requisitioning procedure (Shoreham Aerodrome was acquired by the War Office without the involvement of the Office of Works). Earle concluded by observing that the hotel's petition was couched in 'ambitious lines' as it interpreted the 1842 Act so as to entitle the company to compensation not only in the form of rent but also in the form of payments to cover the loss of goodwill.

Given the outcome of the Shoreham hearing in the House of Lords in July 1916, the greatest mystery is why the government contested the hotel's case at all. A convincing answer frankly eludes us, but it is instructive to note that it was long after the Armistice that the House of Lords conclusively ruled in *De Keyser* against the government on the matter of compensation, holding that it was due as of right and not merely on an *ex gratia* basis through the instrumentality of the DRLC. By that stage, the government had already made considerable progress in bringing forth an Indemnity Bill which would enshrine in law the obligation of property-owners to seek compensation before the DRLC (or, to be more exact, before its successor), but only on a direct loss basis. Essentially, the government got through the war years relying on the DRLC to deal with compensation claims. The more onerous financial burdens on the government, which the Shoreham Aerodrome outcome pointed to, did not materialise during the war itself. The timing may, indeed, have been crucial. For even though the Shoreham outcome did not augur well for the government in respect to the eventual conclusion to the *De Keyser* case, the government at least had a Court of Appeal judgment in the aerodrome case in its favour, and criticism of that judgment was merely *obiter* until it was authoritatively overruled. Thus if the hotel company were to go to law, the strong probability would be that the High Court would be bound by the superior authority of the Court of Appeal in the Shoreham case, on the footing that Reg. 2 of DORA and its significance for the compensation controversy governed both cases. This was so, even if it could be argued that the royal prerogative was inapplicable to the acquisition of administrative offices, as distinct from a coastal aerodrome.

A year after the petition of right was submitted, the petition was heard by Mr Justice Peterson in the Chancery Court on 20–22 March 1918.[19] He confined himself to judging the facts of the case, considering himself bound, as did counsel, by the interpretation of the law propounded by the Court of Appeal in the Shoreham case. He found that there had been no agreement between the parties as to the renting of the premises, whether for £175,000 or otherwise. The hotel had therefore been taken compulsorily. He also concluded that the occupation was indeed necessary for securing the public safety and the defence of the realm, thereby accepting the testimony of Bertram Cubitt and General Heath.

The date of the hearing was a considerable time after the lodging of the petition; no doubt the delay was welcome by the government. The judge's ruling was also received with satisfaction by the government, perhaps with more relief than previously envisaged. For the hearing coincided with the start of the German Spring Offensive on 21 March 1918, which threatened

---

19. *De Keyser's Royal Hotel Ltd* v. *The King* (1918) 34 T.L.R. 392.

to roll back the allied forces catastrophically. At the very least, the successful end of the war for Britain was not in sight and the necessity for continued occupation of private premises would not diminish in the short term. The prolongation of the legal proceedings was therefore not unwelcome to the government. In the event, the outcome of the hotel's appeal to the Court of Appeal was delayed because the petitioners themselves had instituted a search in the Public Record Office for evidence of the practices in respect to compensation which had prevailed in previous wars, the findings of which we examined in chapter two.

The Court of Appeal considered the suppliants' evidence on 20 July 1918, which suggested that no instance had been found in which the Crown had claimed, as a matter of right, to take and occupy the land of the subject, free from an obligation to make compensation. The Master of the Rolls, Sir Charles Swinfen-Eady, was intrigued by this evidence and promptly asked for more. On 22 October 1918 the Attorney-General, Sir Frederick Smith, sought a further adjournment on account of the complexity and number of the documents requiring examination. Six weeks later, junior Crown counsel, J. Austen-Cartmell, informed the court that while the search might proceed indefinitely, the time had come to call a halt as it was reasonable to conclude that further research would not produce different results. He did not add that, as the Armistice had been signed three weeks earlier, on 11 November 1918, the intense pressure on the government was now lifted; properties would no longer need to be requisitioned with the same urgency, if at all, and the upward climb of rents to grossly inflated levels, due to the wartime demands for suitable properties, could now be halted. The hearing then proceeded at a leisurely pace, though no longer deliberately prolonged by the government or by the judges. The Court of Appeal resumed its hearing on 21 January 1919, and delivered a majority judgment on 9 April 1919, in favour of the suppliants.[20] Such a decision a year earlier would indeed have put the cat among the pigeons so far as the government were concerned. The delayed legal process had been a god-send in avoiding this calamity. The following year, in March 1920, the House of Lords heard the Crown's appeal and, after ten weeks of deliberation, unanimously dismissed it.[21]

Given the focus of this book on government administration of, and responses to the exercise of, wartime emergency powers, a close analysis of the Court of Appeal and House of Lords judgments in *De Keyser's Royal Hotel* is unnecessary. Some brief points may, however, be highlighted. First, as the Shoreham Aerodrome ruling had been delivered before the researches in the Public Record Office were conducted, it was possible for the House of Lords simply to conclude that that decision had been erroneous for want of complete legal analysis. For the Court of Appeal in *De Keyser's*, however, it was sufficient for the majority to distinguish the facts of the Shoreham

20. (1919) 2 Ch. 197.
21. *Attorney-General* v. *De Keyser's Royal Hotel Ltd* [1920] A.C. 508.

case from those in the hotel case. The aerodrome case was considered to be analogous to the *King's Prerogative in Saltpetre* scenario, of entering upon private land to construct bulwarks to repel invaders. This parallel, reasoned the Court of Appeal judges in *De Keyser's*, could not be extended to the take-over of a building for accommodation for War Office clerks. Thus, whereas the House of Lords in *De Keyser's* concluded that the Shoreham Aerodrome decision of the Court of Appeal was wrong, the majority in the Court of Appeal in *De Keyser's* argued that it was not relevant.[22] Interestingly, the dissenting judge in the Court of Appeal, who upheld the government's claim to requisition without paying compensation as of right, was Lord Justice Duke, who had been the first chairman of the DRLC. At least one can say that his judgment was consistent with the administrative task he had previously been performing, though whether that explains his dissenting judgment is impossible to establish.

Secondly, an oddity worth observing is that it was admitted by both sides without argument that the act of taking the property by the Crown was lawful. The latter's claim was, of course, grounded both in DORA and under the prerogative. But why should the hotel company admit any such thing? Were they not claiming at various intervals that the government's actions were predatory and were denying Englishmen their property rights? There are two answers to this. First, the company were not objecting to the take-over of the hotel itself. Indeed, as business was not booming (though there had been some recent improvement in trade and in the hotel's prospects), the company may have welcomed the War Office's interest. Their objection was to being short-changed in respect of its occupation by the department. The second point is more technical but can be stated briefly in the words of Lord Dunedin. A lawful requisitioning

> must necessarily be admitted by the respondents [i.e. De Keyser's], for if taking in itself was purely illegal, then it would be a tort not committed by the Crown, who cannot commit a tort, but by the officers of the Crown, and the petition of right would not lie.[23]

Naturally, the amount of compensation sought was likely to be beyond the pockets of most civil servants or even of some ministers of the Crown. To obtain a remedy against the Crown, which possessed the greater financial resources, the hotel had to admit the taking was lawful, then raise the question of compensation by means of the petition of right.

Third, by the time of the Court of Appeal hearing, the Crown had narrowed the basis of its argument, by justifying the take-over by the power of the

22. For comments about the differing modes of reasoning of the Court of Appeal and the House of Lords, but which led to the same result, see Sir John Simon, 'Introduction', in Scott and Hildesley, *The Case of Requisition*, p. xxi.

23. [1920] A.C. 508, at p. 523. Not until the Crown Proceedings Act 1947 could the Crown, as distinct from ministers individually, be sued for tort.

prerogative alone. The reason for this seems to have been because the Crown now accepted (without admitting it) that the compensation rights enshrined in the Defence Act 1842 had not been removed by DORA and its accompanying Reg. 2. The war legislation had not explicitly removed such a right, a point which seemed to have impressed the House of Lords in the Shoreham hearings. Consequently, the Crown now focused solely on the prerogative in order to argue two points. The first was that the prerogative remained applicable until expressly removed by Act of Parliament (which had not occurred). Second, it did not expressly import a right to compensation. Therefore, none was due to the suppliants *ex lege*. On both points, their Lordships ruled otherwise. Lord Dunedin observed that the Defence Act 1842 covered both the permanent and temporary taking of property and offered compensation therefor:

> Inasmuch as the Crown is a party to every Act of Parliament, it is logical enough to consider that when the Act deals with something which before the Act could be effected by the prerogative and specially empowers the Crown to do the same thing, but subject to conditions, the Crown assents to it, and, by that Act, to the prerogative being curtailed ... It is therefore impossible, in my opinion, to say that the whole field of the prerogative in the matter of the acquisition of land or rights therein was not covered by the Act of 1842. It follows from what I have said above that there is no room for asserting an unrestricted prerogative right as existing alongside with the statutory powers authorizing the Crown to acquire on certain terms. The conclusion is that the Crown could not take the petitioners' property by the powers of the prerogative alone.[24]

Three final points may be noted. First, even where the taking over was authorised by Reg. 2 of DORA, there was, according to Lord Dunedin, 'no necessity for the public safety or the defence of the realm that payment should not be made'. Indeed, he ventured, suppose the regulation authorising the taking over of land had had the additional provision, 'without making any payment therefor'. The scope of the regulation would certainly have been clearer from the standpoint of interpretation, but a deeper question would have been posed. In effect, would it not have been *ultra vires* on the footing that the denial of compensation was not 'necessary for the safety of the realm'? He drew an analogy with the ruling of Mr Justice Salter in the *Newcastle Breweries* case that the denial to the citizen of access to the courts in the event of disagreement over the value of goods requisitioned was *ultra vires* the enabling act.[25]

The second point is that, given the admission of the legality of the take-over, the Law Lords were not required to determine as a question of fact whether, in the circumstances, the prerogative power could properly be exercised to justify taking over the hotel. A connected factual question had been addressed

24. [1920] A.C. 508, at pp. 526, 528. That statement was not itself a confirmation that compensation accompanied any lawful acquisition by prerogative.
25. See below, chapter 8

in the High Court but revolved around the wartime statutory provisions. Only the briefest reference to whether the prerogative could have justified the hotel's take-over, had that legal basis not been 'abridged' by the requisitioning legislation, was made in the House of Lords. Lord Moulton doubted whether prerogative powers, *simpliciter*, 'ever did exist in such a form as would cover the proposed acquisition [of the hotel], a matter which is far from clear in such a case as the present'.[26]

Finally, it is to be observed that the Law Lords refrained, in general, from commenting on the wider political issue of the balance between public and private interests and rights during wartime. Only Lord Moulton appears to have raised this aspect in his speech. In his opinion, the Defence Act 1842 (and its predecessors), 'has indicated unmistakably that it is the intention of the nation that the powers of the Crown in these respects should be exercised in the equitable manner set forth in the statute, so that the burden shall not fall on the individual, but shall be borne by the community'.[27] Whether Moulton's previous experience as director-general of explosives supply in the Ministry of Munitions made him more receptive to non-legal considerations and to advancing a policy-based interpretation of the law is open to speculation.[28]

Once the litigation had been concluded and Whinney's stance vindicated, the department had to attend to the business of meeting the hotel's claim. Three months after the House of Lords ruling of 10 May 1920, the Office of Works put to the Treasury for its approval the terms of the settlement.[29] Sir Lionel Earle informed the Treasury that the hotel had recently been sold by Whinney and that part of the bargain was that the purchasers should have the benefit of the hotel company's claim against the government. That claim was for rent at £17,500 per annum for four years and the assessment of dilapidations (necessary repairs at the end of the tenancy) at approximately £35,900 calculated by the company's surveyors. They also sought interest on the outstanding rent on the footing that it should have been paid quarterly, and finally they claimed that the furniture and similar items should be reinstated in the hotel in their original condition.

The department offered a total of £85,000, which the purchasers, Alexander Lawson Ormrod and James White, accepted after considerable demur, as they were reselling the premises and wished to avoid lengthy arbitration proceedings. Conditions attached to acceptance were that the costs of litigation be paid by the government, as the House of Lords had directed; that furniture, linen, crockery and glass stored in government warehouses be delivered to the hotel within two months from July 29, 1920; and that breakages were to be paid for, though no polishing was required. Delivery would be to the largest rooms so that the items might be displayed for sale. Finally, the fees

26. [1920] A.C. 508, at p. 553. Cf. his remarks about the 'debatable proposition' at ibid., p. 549, quoted in chapter 2, above.
27. Ibid., p. 553
28. See above, chapter 2.
29. PRO, T 161/39/S2532 for this and following information.

of the surveyors and assessors of the dilapidations were to be paid for by the government.

The figure of £85,000 had been reached by taking into account 'fair allowances' for the rent, for reinstating the premises and furniture and for the possibility of interest payments on the rent. The Office of Works had obtained the services of two surveyors, Howard Martin and Andrew Young, who had valued the property at £14,267 per annum and £12,800 per annum respectively. It was believed that any arbitration award would be at least as high as Martin's valuation. On that basis, four years rent would be £57,000.

The department's architect calculated dilapidations at £21,000 as against the hotel company's claim of £35,900. On the basis of other hotel reinstatements, the cost of reinstating De Keyser's Hotel was put at £6,000 while, in respect to interest on the rent, counsel for the Office of Works advised that such a claim was unsustainable. However, if the matter went to arbitration, the arbitrator would be free to take into account interest on outstanding rent.

Earle concluded by advising against arbitration and indicated that £20,000 had already been paid on account. Apart from seeking assurance that the recipients could make out a good title to receive the sum in settlement, the Treasury approved the proposal of the Office of Works.

About eighteen months later, the hotel company submitted a further claim for £1,227 representing discrepancies between the items listed in the inventories on the take-over in 1916 and those returned on reinstatement. The Office of Works explained to the Treasury that at the time of the requisition, the department had been 'unable to obtain the services of competent inventory clerks', with the result that furniture porters were doubling as clerks, while also engaged in furniture removal. Some breakages had occurred in transit and it was probable that a certain amount of pilfering had taken place. Although the Treasury considered it a 'most unsatisfactory position', authorisation of payment was granted, and De Keyser's Royal Hotel Ltd passed into every textbook on British constitutional law.

The hotel itself was purchased in early 1921 by Lever Bros who moved their administrative headquarters from Port Sunlight and renamed the building Lever House.[30] It finally disappeared from the London landscape when the company decided in 1930 to build a large new headquarters. The site of De Keyser's Royal Hotel is now occupied by the Unilever Building.[31]

30. Charles Wilson, *The History of Unilever: A Study in Economic Growth and Social Change*, i (London, 1954), p. 272.
31. Ibid., ii, p. 310.

7

The Cannon Brewery Explodes

At first glance, government requisition of public houses in order to facilitate the war effort seems a remote idea. On closer inspection, a strong case could be made, not only for the regulation of the trade under the defence of the realm legislation (DORA), but even for outright state purchase and management of licensed premises.

Efforts to demonstrate a link between drink and the conduct of the war were made in the early months of the conflict, as restrictions began to be imposed on alcohol consumption. An Intoxicating Liquor (Temporary Restrictions) Act was passed in late August 1914, while DORA regulations enabled the military authorities to request the police to close down or limit drinking hours in pubs in military areas. The claim was being heard that as a result of alcohol consumption, soldiers were missing their troop trains or were falling asleep on duty.[1]

In early 1915 munitions workers became the targets of accusations that absenteeism was the result of drink, Lloyd George complaining that 'Drink is doing more damage than all the German submarines put together'.[2] This was political hyperbole, sustained by unsubstantiated allegations by shipbuilding employers and intended to show a preference, on the part of shipyard employees, for working half a week and drinking the rest of the week. Figures for lost time at work, which the Board of Trade had adopted uncritically from employers, were published on 1 May 1915 and the climate was ripe for further controls over liquor.[3]

The Defence of the Realm (Amendment) (No. 3) Act was passed during that month and restrictions were placed on pub opening hours, a legacy, until recently, of the First World War. The strength of alcohol was reduced and the practice of 'treating' fellow-customers to a drink was

---

1. John Turner, 'State Purchase of the Liquor Trade in the First World War', *Historical Journal*, 23 (1980), pp. 589–615, at pp. 593–94.
2. Cited in Ian Donnachie, 'World War I and the Drink Question: State Control of the Drink Trade', *Scottish Labour History Society Journal*, 17 (1982), pp. 19–26, at p. 26.
3. For the employers' campaign, see Gerry R. Rubin, *War, Law, and Labour: The Munitions Acts, State Regulation, and the Unions, 1915–1921* (Oxford, 1987), p. 181. The Board of Trade's report was the *Report and Statistics of Bad Time Keeping in Shipbuilding, Munitions and Transport Areas*, P.P. 1914–16 (220), 1v, 947.

outlawed.[4] A differential tax on heavier gravity beers was proposed but was not implemented, following Irish objections to this threat to Guinness. Total prohibition was firmly advocated by the temperance movement, but an alternative proposal was floated, the nationalisation of the liquor trade. Though scarcely attractive to the brewery lobby in peacetime, the proposal held some attractions for the industry during the war, as its economic position became increasingly insecure. The new Chancellor of the Exchequer, Lloyd George, set up advisory committees in the spring of 1915 to explore the possibility of state purchase. The cost of purchasing the trade in England and Wales was put at around £250 million and in Scotland at around £10 million. Payment would be by government stocks redeemable at the government's option after seven years, and would reflect the high profits earned by the trade during the favourable years of 1910–13.

The Asquith Cabinet, perhaps still not convinced that *laissez-faire* was now outdated, refused to sanction wholesale nationalisation of the trade. Instead, the more modest proposals cited earlier were implemented. Additionally, authority was granted to permit the take-over of pubs and breweries in selected areas. New machinery was established both for this purpose and for other activities, such as promoting industrial canteens, which also reflected a social reformist perspective on the perceived problem. The new machinery was the Central Control Board (Liquor Traffic), set up under DORA (No. 3) on 10 June 1915, not only to control the sale and consumption of alcohol in any scheduled area, but also to purchase breweries and pubs.[5] Among its membership were Lord D'Abernon (chairman), who was a banker, Major Waldorf Astor, chairman of the *Observer* and Conservative M.P., Sir William Lever, the soap manufacturer, John Hodge, the Labour M.P. and later wartime Minister of Labour, Philip Snowden, the Independent Labour Party M.P., and Neville Chamberlain, the Conservative M.P. and later wartime Minister for National Service. How was it that the expedient of nationalising the pubs in certain parts of the country came about? Three areas were selected as suitable for this initiative. They were the border region between Scotland and England, the area around Woolwich Arsenal, and the Cromarty Firth's Invergordon naval area.

Gretna had been chosen as the site for the construction of an immense national explosives factory, employing 10,000 workers to be brought in from outside the district, as well as the building workers required for its construction.[6] The plan included the development of both temporary housing

4. Though the legality of the regulation in question was challenged before Edinburgh Sheriff Court only for the Crown to appeal successfully to the Justiciary Appeal Court. See the *Scotsman*, 23 November 1915.

5. For an overview of its activities, see M. E. Rose, 'The Success of Social Reform? The Central Control Board (Liquor Traffic), 1915–1921', in M. R. D. Foot (ed.), *War and Society: Historical Essays in Honour and Memory of J. R. Western, 1928–1971* (London, 1973), ch. 5.

6. For this and subsequent information, see Donnachie, 'World War I and the Drink Question'.

and facilities to feed and entertain the new arrivals to the district. The whole area from Penrith to Annan absorbed the influx, with the pubs patronised to bursting point. Between October 1915 and June 1916 about 15,000 new arrivals moved into the area and figures for drunkenness convictions rose accordingly. Parallel increases occurred in other districts. Restrictions on drinking hours, as well as on treating, on allowing credit or on hawking, were imposed throughout the country, but the problems of the Border area, the Cromarty Firth and around Enfield Lock were acute.

In the case of Gretna, nationalisation was virtually effected between January and the summer of 1916, while in Carlisle, the board took over local breweries and 120 public houses between July and October. Other premises in West Cumbria were also acquired so that direct control extended over 500 square miles and a population of 140,000. In the wake of take-over, the board terminated redundant or 'undesirable' licences; further restricted, or even prohibited, the sale of spirits; banned the sale of most alcohols to under-eighteens; removed liquor advertisements; and extended Sunday closing. On the positive side, it reconstructed pubs and provided canteens and recreation centres, transforming pubs into social and leisure institutes. A leisure centre was opened in Annan, complete with bowling green and cinema: it was named Gracies's Banking Tavern. Parallel developments, though on a lesser scale, occurred at Invergordon and Enfield Lock. In the latter district, where the Cannon Brewery Company's Ordnance Arms was located, the government's munitions works, the Royal Small Arms Factory, had been rapidly enlarged and the numbers employed increased enormously.[7] A new thousand-seater canteen had already proved inadequate, so that at mealtimes the men made for the four pubs in the district, or else ate their meals on the roadside, or beside outbuildings or hedges. Even in inclement weather, the same pattern occurred. It was evidently not conducive to adequate relaxation during their break periods. After the board issued a restriction order on drinking in the London area on 24 September 1915, it was approached by a deputation of munitions workers who recounted the unsatisfactory state of the local facilities. The board was mobilised into action and for the first time in modern history, the state became a liquor retailer by buying up the four public houses in the area and, later on, the one off-licence in the district.

After the acquisitions which, in the case of the Ordnance Arms, was to lead to the legal complications eventually resolved in the House of Lords in 1919, the board sought to limit the sale of alcohol to mealtimes and to build new dining halls. Two of the four pubs, the Greyhound and the Royal Small Arms, were extensively reconstructed, Edwin Montagu, the Minister of Munitions, attending the reopening of the former in November 1916. It was soon supplying a thousand meals a day in an airy and comfortable environment. Despite the nearly five-fold increase in the numbers of employees

7. Henry Carter, *The Control of the Drink Trade* (London, 1918), pp. 172–74.

at the factory, liquor receipts only doubled in the first half year. By contrast, food sales had shot up nearly sevenfold.

The Royal Small Arms Tavern was reopened in June 1917 after extensive reconstruction. Previously, hundreds of men from each shift had crowded into eight small rooms, into a small temporary outbuilding, into the passages and onto the stairs. There were few places to sit down, as men competed for any available space to rest against the walls. Now, instead of those 'indescribable' conditions, there was the new dining hall with 600 seats, enabling between 2,000 and 3,000 men to use the building each day, with beneficial effects on the men's morale, health and efficiency. Here was an instance of social reform being prompted by the more immediate exigencies of war.

The interest in the scheme, for our purposes, is the legal basis for the acquisition of licensed premises and breweries undertaken by the Central Control Board. The primary statute, as noted earlier, was the Defence of the Realm (Amendment) (No. 3) Act, passed on 19 May 1915. This provided in section 1 (1) that the government had power to issue regulations by order in council with a view to control the sale and supply of intoxicating liquor in any area where it appeared expedient for the successful prosecution of the war. The area had to be one where war material was being made, loaded or unloaded, or dealt with in transit, or was one where naval or military personnel were assembled. By July 1917, virtually the whole country fell into one or more of those categories, and orders were issued accordingly. Under section 1(2), the government could issue regulations conferring, *inter alia*, exclusive power on the 'prescribed Government authority', that is, the board, to sell or supply, or control the selling or supplying of alcohol in the area; to acquire compulsorily or by agreement, temporarily or permanently, any licensed or other premises in the area, or any interest therein, if it appeared necessary or expedient for liquor control; and, generally, to give effect to the transfer of control of liquor traffic in the area. Thus, while a scheme of national state purchase of the liquor trade had been ruled out as politically inadmissible, area purchase was permissible and could theoretically apply to most of the country, though, in the event, it remained a geographically limited experiment.

The detailed regulations themselves, the Defence of the Realm (Liquor Control) Regulations, were issued on 10 June 1915. After repeating in Regulation 6 the board's power to acquire premises compulsorily or by agreement, temporarily or permanently, Regulation 7 declared,

> 7. Where the Board determine to acquire compulsorily any premises or any interest therein, they shall serve on the occupier of the premises and, if any person other than the occupier will be affected by the acquisition of the interest proposed to be acquired, also on any person who appears to the Board to be so affected, notice of their intention to acquire the premises, or such interest therein as may be specified in the notice, and where such a notice is served, the fee simple in possession of the premises or such interest in the premises as aforesaid shall, at the expiry of ten days from the service of the notice on the occupier, by virtue of these Regulations, vest in the trustees for the Board,

subject to or free from any mortgages, rights, and interests affecting the same as the Board may by order direct.

The board also received power simply to take possession of any premises and also to acquire any business, including stock in trade, carried on in any premises in the area, whether or not they took possession of, or acquired, the premises in which the business was being carried on.

Thus a distinction could be drawn between merely taking possession of premises and acquiring premises. The latter would indeed be a state purchase but the former would simply be a state user of the premises, with no permanency attached. In either case, the regulations were silent as to compensation to the owners. Lloyd George's advisory committee of early 1915, in contemplating nationalisation of the whole trade, had recommended, it will be recalled, 'that the property which is to be acquired should be bought by the exchange of £100 of Government 4 per cent stock for every ascertained £100 worth of liquor-trade securities properties . . .',[8] which would amount in total to about £250 million. With the demise of the scheme and its replacement by the more limited proposals in DORA (No. 3), the compensation arrangement was that claims should be referred to the Defence of the Realm Losses Commission (DRLC). 'The only instruction we shall give to them', Lloyd George declared, 'is that they should pay fairly the trade and all who lose by our action.'[9]

Of course, 'fair' payment was to be confined to direct and substantial loss, those terms of reference being retained when a separate commission, the Defence of the Realm (Licensed Trade Claims) Commission, was set up on 2 August 1915, to deal separately with liquor traffic claims. The usual practice of the board was to agree provisionally the amount of compensation subject to and conditional upon such parties applying to the commission formally to issue an award. Treasury sanction was also required, but was always granted where such awards had been made. While in Scotland the commission tended to award what had been agreed between the parties, the Southern division of the commission awarded less than the agreed sums in seven cases. The total amount agreed had been £10,000 and the total of awards was £1,205 less than the amount, a reduction of 11.9 per cent. However, some of the claimants refused to accept the lower amounts awarded, though it is not clear how matters were resolved. The three other pubs taken over at Enfield Lock, the Greyhound, the Royal Small Arms and one other, were the subjects of contested claims before the commission.

In June 1918 a local official of the board based in Carlisle described the terms of purchase applied in his area. He observed that the regulations offered no guidance, though he did not refer to the Licensed Trade Claims

8. Ibid., p. 59.
9. Ibid., p. 74

Commission (LTCC), presumably on the footing that its guidelines were themselves insufficiently precise for his purposes. He also added that the proceedings in the Cannon Brewery case were throwing considerable doubt as to the proper approach.[10] Nonetheless, the board's view, since it began the procedures of negotiation in September 1915, had been that owners should receive the fair market value on pre-war conditions. No addition would be made for a compulsory sale (for which an additional 10 per cent was habitually permitted under the Lands Clauses Act), nor for improved trade due to the establishment of the large munitions complex at Gretna. Nor was notice taken of the general upward movement of prices during the war which might have benefited an owner disposed to sell without compulsion. The official reported that the board had succeeded so far in acquiring public houses and breweries at prices which compared approximately with the recommendations of Lord Sumner's Committee on State Purchase. That committee had been reexamining the issue of state purchase in the summer of 1917 and its report was published the following year.[11] Sumner had recommended that the purchase of breweries would normally be based on fifteen years' purchase of the pre-war profits reduced in proportion to the depreciation of the capital asset, the property itself, at the time of purchase. This would represent, it was pointed out, a much smaller number of years' purchase. The procedure for compensation thus proposed did in fact reflect the tension existing between rival approaches to brewery valuations. The companies tended historically to favour a barrelage basis, essentially an internal valuation, and the Sumner committee's proposal to take account of the fifteen year pre-war profit levels was probably a genuflection towards the brewery interest. In contrast, the regard paid to the depreciation of capital value corresponded more closely to the view that breweries were essentially property companies.[12] The rights of debenture and priority holders with whom the Central Control Board had no power to deal separately, were to be abrogated, the amounts payable on the various classes of stock apportioned on a sliding scale. Debenture holders would receive less than par value, although the income on the reduced capital at a higher rate per cent would substantially prevent any real loss: income flows backed by government would be more secure.

In the case of free houses, compensation would be based on similar principles, and fixed by the LTCC. The general basis was to capitalise the true rack rent, what the tenant might fairly expect to pay by the year in the open market, by a multiplier appropriate to pre-war conditions. The amounts

---

10. PRO, HO 190/491, 'J.D.W., Notes on Terms of Purchase Under the Land Clauses Acts, Acquisition of Land Act etc.', 25 June 1918.

11. See *State Purchase of the Liquor Trade: Reports of the English, Scotch and Irish Committees*, P.P. 1918, Cd. 9042, xi, 145. The English committee calculated that nationalisation of the whole trade would cost more than £400 million. That scheme, like its predecessor in 1915, was also dropped. See Turner, 'State Purchase', at pp. 608–13.

12. The present author is grateful to his colleague, Mike Murphy, for advice on accounting matters.

so arrived at would then be scaled down proportionately to the depreciation of capital values between the outbreak of the war and the completion of purchase.

In the light of these guidelines, the Central Control Board in Carlisle paid four brewery companies about £360,000 in respect of pre-war profits of £28,000 a year, or about thirteen years' purchase on average. In respect to free houses, concern was expressed about the possible controversial effect of writing down pre-war values, given the reduced purchasing power of the war years.

Two other compensation schemes could be employed, those under the Lands Clauses Act 1845 and those under the Defence of the Realm (Acquisition of Land) Act 1916 in respect to permanent acquisition. While it remained a matter of voluntary resort, the Lands Clauses Act 1845 was unlikely to be favoured by the board, given the relative generosity of the terms to owners, as well as the relative expense of its procedures compared with, say, the 1916 Act. Under the 1845 Act, the basis of compensation, as outlined already in chapter two, was the value to the owner at the date of the notice to treat, plus compensation for injurious affection, severance and damage or injury sustained. Compensation for dormant or prospective value could also be claimed though, in respect to trades or businesses, the basis was loss. An additional 10 per cent was also payable for compulsory purchase.

The board expressed the view that,

> The general principles of compensation under the Lands Clauses Act (subject to criticism as to the 10 per cent) are fair and reasonable. Nothing could be fairer than the broad principle that the landowner should be compensated for the loss he sustains by the taking of his property.

However, the act's procedures were unattractive. Owners could choose either arbitration or jury reference. The awards of the latter were unpredictable, while the arbitration procedure was costly, the costs for counsel, experts and arbitrators sometimes exceeding the award. The whole of the costs of both sides were payable by the promoters (in this case, the board) unless an offer had previously been made equal to or exceeding the actual award. But such an offer could be risky: if the umpire learned of it, he would be tempted to make a higher award, 'rather than saddle the claimant with costs'. Finding an impartial umpire was difficult. Therefore, to avoid resort to arbitration, promoters were disposed to offering generous terms to reach agreement. In sum, Lands Clauses Act compensation was reckoned to be 20 per cent above the price obtainable between a willing buyer and a willing seller.

If the procedures under the 1916 Act were to be used, however, compensation would be payable on the value at the date of the notice to treat, without regard to any enhancement or depreciation as a result of works or improvements carried out by the state for purposes in connection with the war. No compulsory purchase premium was payable, a single arbitrator was appointed and no juries. The Lord Chancellor could fix a scale of costs and the arbitrator had discretion to fix or disallow or allocate costs. There was no doubt, that in agreeing the level of compensation payable to breweries or to licensed premise owners, the provisions of the Lands Clauses Act were to be avoided. The corollary was that it might be in the best interests of the owners to insist on using those provisions. The Cannon Brewery Company at Enfield Lock certainly thought so.

On 22 December 1915, the board served a notice on the Cannon Brewery Company and on the landlord of the Ordnance Arms, George William Platt, that they intended to acquire the premises. The premises comprised the following accommodation.[13] On the first floor were four rooms and a garret. On the ground floor was a bar with four entrances, a tap room, a public parlour and three other rooms. There was also a brick-built mess room, water closet and urinal. At the other side of the bar was a small room, kitchen, store room, scullery and two larders built of timber. At the rear of the premises was a small piece of ground with a gateway entrance from the road, and an old timber and tiled range of outbuildings. Finally, the basement contained a cellar prone to flooding. Thirteen days after the notice was issued possession was actually taken, on 4 January 1916, and George Platt received payment for his stock. Negotiations then ensued between the board and the company as to the compensation payable to the latter, but broke down over the same principle which divided the parties in the Shoreham Aerodrome and *De Keyser* cases, that is, whether the owners were entitled, *ex lege*, to compensation on the favourable terms laid down in the Lands Clauses Act and imported from the Defence Act 1842, or whether they had to make do with the less generous payments offered as an act of grace by the commission set up under the prerogative.

The company had presented an application for compensation to the LTCC on 16 March 1916, that is, two and a half months after the take-over. That application stated that the company reserved all their rights. This was unacceptable to the commission whose warrant only allowed them to entertain claims 'not otherwise provided for'. The commission therefore wrote back to the company on 3 April on these lines, following which, the company withdrew its application. For the next three months, the company did nothing further. Then, on 5 July, it wrote to the board's solicitors, Travers Smith & Braithwaite of Throgmorton Street in the City of London, demanding Lands Clauses Act compensation. The solicitors wrote back, disputing the claim and citing the Court of Appeal judgment in the Shoreham Aerodrome case. The brewery's response was to serve a claim under section 68 of the 1845 Act on 21 July. Under that provision, the company insisted that arbitration be arranged or that a jury be empanelled within twenty-one days to consider its claim for

13.   PRO, HO 190/491, Marks & Barley, valuers, to Sir John Sykes, Central Control Board, 6 August 1919.

compensation, failing which the amount sought would be claimed through the courts. That amount was £13,638, plus 5 per cent interest, from the previous January until payment. The board resisted the claim on the ground that it was 'grossly excessive',[14] and resigned itself to facing a challenge to the validity of its regulations (which did not in fact materialise) and to the company's claim that the Lands Clauses Act provisions for compensation applied.

Was that amount 'grossly excessive'? The figures appear to have been provided by the company's valuers, Messrs Motion & Son of Bloomsbury Square, London. They had provided the board's own valuers, Messrs Marks & Barley of High Holborn, with returns for the three years, 1913 to 1915, showing the net barrelage with net cash value, a statement of the bottled beer trade for 1915 (the only complete year obtainable), and the gallons of wines and spirits together with the net cash value, also for the years 1913 to 1915.[15] The brewery's valuers stated that for 1913 and 1914 an inclusive rent of £150 was received, including licence duty of £90 and rates and taxes of just under £60 paid by the tenant. For 1915, the total inclusive rent of £560 was paid by the tenant, the licence duty and outgoings element amounting to £166. The company's assessment of takings for 1914 was £2,917, which the valuers believed would justify a rent of £150, though only £100 was in fact allocated in their valuation statement.

Whether these figures were an exaggeration must remain a strong possibility. According to Lord Justice Bankes in the Court of Appeal hearing in May 1918, the yearly takings for 1913 to 1915 were £1,215, £2,018 and £4,653 respectively.[16] In August 1919 the board's valuers criticised the company's figures after perusing the books. As to rent, whereas the company had stated a figure of £560 per annum in 1915, it had ignored the fact that the net rent actually received in 1913 and 1914 was only £20 per annum. The company also claimed £1,350 for 'separation from the brewery at the rate of 3s per barrel on 919 barrels = £1,378. 10s. 0d., say, £1350'. This item, claimed Marks & Barley, was simply untenable.

Instead, the board's valuers divided the trading into two parts; first, the average pre-war trade and, second, the average war trade. They capitalised the net average profits of the pre-war trade from 1911 to 1913 by ten years purchase, which they claimed as the normal number of years, which was also the number of years purchase actually claimed. To this capital value, they added two years of the additional annual profits made during the three years the board had been in possession, from 1916 to 1918. They explained that they now believed that the claimants were entitled to those two years, although, had an adjudication been done in January 1916, they would have suggested just one year.

14. PRO, TS 27/46, Travers Smith & Braithwaite, solicitors to the board, to Treasury Solicitor, 20 October 1916.

15. PRO, HO 190/491, James Motion & Son to Messrs. Marks & Barley, 17 October 1916.

16. *Cannon Brewery Company Ltd* v. *Central Control Board (Liquor Traffic)* [1918] 2 Ch.101, at p. 126.

That advice was proferred in August 1919, after the House of Lords had upheld the company's claim for Lands Clauses Act compensation.[17] Interestingly, the enhanced profit figure for 1915 does not seem to have been taken into account. In that year the Ordnance Arms, as a licensed premises, was full beyond capacity, catering to the drink requirements of thousands of new munitions workers drafted into the area, who were not yet weaned on the less alcoholic and presumably cheaper fare which the canteens programme of the board was soon to offer with considerable success.

Instead of the Sumner Committee guidelines of capitalisation on the basis of fifteen years pre-war profits, reduced by dilapidations, the board's valuers sought to strike the best bargain on the basis of (selected) wartime conditions. As to dilapidations, even after the board had been in occupation for a few years, the valuers considered in 1919 that: 'The premises appear to be very old, are in a dilapidated condition and nearly worn out.'[18] As mentioned previously, the cellar in the basement was mostly flooded and required the use of a pump, located in the public bar, to clear it out. No doubt the nature of the property brought down the offer price from a significantly higher figure representing the profits of the business.

As legal proceedings were now in train, the Law Officers, Sir Frederick Smith and George Cave, were soon consulted by the board. They transmitted an opinion on 3 August 1916.[19] Their opinion was not encouraging for the government. It could no longer be assumed to be clear, they argued, that there was no legal right to compensation. The 'greatest possible doubt' had been thrown on the Court of Appeal ruling in the Shoreham Aerodrome case by the Law Lords in that prematurely terminated hearing, and it was unlikely that that Court of Appeal decision case would be approved by the House of Lords in proceedings involving the Cannon Brewery, 'if it is constituted in anything like the same way'. Moreover, the wording of Reg. 7 of the Liquor Regulations differed from that in Reg. 2 of the Defence Regulations, making the right to compensation more probable. The wording of acquisition by 'agreement' reinforced that view. Consequently,

> we think that the Board should endeavour (without waiving any rights) to agree the compensation or to get it referred to some tribunal acceptable to both sides. If the claimants are wholly unreasonable and will not listen to any fair settlement, the best course would perhaps be to let them develop their claim and realise the considerable difficulties which they too will have to face. It would probably be two years before the matter would reach the Lords.[20]

17. *Central Control Board (Liquor Traffic)* v. *Cannon Brewery Co. Ltd.* [1919] A.C. 744 (H.L.).
18. PRO, HO 190/491, Marks & Barley to Sir John Sykes, 6 August 1919.
19. Copy in PRO, MUN 5/95/346.1/8.
20. Ibid. See also chapter 5, above.

Thus, a temporising approach was favoured in the hope that the law's delays would be a discouragement to the company. As we noted in chapter five, the Law Officers were concerned not to disrupt the existing arrangements for compensation payments by the DRLC (and by implication, by the LTCC) and to secure that the Shoreham Aerodrome decision in the Court of Appeal remain intact. If, in the fullness of time, the House of Lords were to take a different view, the new situation could be tackled, 'when the executive is less busily engaged'.

The pessimistic legal prognosis was soon having its effect on the board's negotiating strategy vis-á-vis firms other than Cannon Brewery. In Carlisle, several licensees had claimed that notices under Reg. 7 were *ultra vires* by virtue of the absence of compensation provisions.[21] On 3 August 1916, the same date as the Law Officers' opinion, a notice had been served on Edward Greenhow, the occupier of the Great Central Hotel, Carlisle. He refused to give up possession until compensation had been paid. On 10 October 1916, he raised an action against the board for a declaration that the latter had no statutory right to enter upon or take possession of the premises, except on terms laid down in the Lands Clauses Act. In view of the Law Officers' opinion, the board agreed compensation with Greenhow rather than face litigation, but was concerned that pressure would be placed on it to settle other cases in Carlisle on disadvantageous terms.

The board was in some doubt as to the legal competency of its settling by voluntary agreement cases in which a compulsory notice under Reg. 7 had been served. The Treasury refused to authorise any agreement fixing the amount to be paid or fixed by reference to arbitration unless the LTCC had confirmed the settlement. Since some claimants were now refusing to accept this condition, it was impossible to reach settlements in some cases. Once again the opinion of the Law Officers was sought to enquire, in particular, whether the issue of a Reg. 7 notice by the board conferred on it a good and indefeasible title, and whether it was competent for the board, after issuing a notice, to settle compensation without reference to the commission.

The Law Officers replied on October 26 and conveyed a second unpromising reply. On the argument, which they appeared to accept, that the Lands Clauses Act was implicitly incorporated into the DORA No. 3 Act of 1915 and that the regulations were silent as to compensation, there was a 'considerable risk in relying on them in their present form', in order to confer a good and indefeasible title. The advice was that legal proceedings should be avoided until the regulations could be amended. It was at least possible, they advised, for the board to agree compensation subject to Treasury sanction, without the necessity for confirmation by the LTCC. In order to assess compensation, they advised, a simple amendment to incorporate the Lands Clauses Act, failing which, the LTCC, would be required, though it was not desirable to insert any directions as to the principles on which compensation should be assessed. Once the regulations were amended, fresh notices ought to be served in respect to those properties in dispute, though it was inadvisable at that point to propose that the titles to those properties already acquired by the board should be confirmed by legislation. Presumably the Law Officers estimated that this would generate not only more resentment, but perhaps more litigation against the board.

The opinion was quite blunt in advising that the regulations required to be amended. It was a straightforward admission that the legal arguments favoured the brewery company and that the government's compensation strategy was gravely vulnerable. Moreover, it implied some doubt by the Law Officers whether the board could take the premises compulsorily at all. Yet the government chose to lodge a defence to the Cannon Brewery's legal action which was eventually set down for hearing before Mr Justice Younger in the High Court on 16 May 1917. Perhaps the only rationale for the government's stance was to delay the day of reckoning for as long as possible, preferably till after the war was over. By then the increased economic burden implied by Lands Clauses Act compensation would at least pose no threat to the defence of the realm, as its struggle to defeat Germany would by then have reached an assumedly happy conclusion. Playing for time seemed to be the guideline for the immediate future, though the possibility of amendments to the regulations had, of course, been floated by the Law Officers.

In drawing up whatever legal defences could be mustered, Treasury counsel, H.M.Giveen, advised on 22 January 1917, that if the court were to hold the brewery entitled to compensation in principle, but not to the liquidated amount which the company were seeking, the board should argue that arbitration should fix the level of compensation. He also advised that if the board proposed, as an alternative to its claim that the company were free to apply to the commission, that the company had a right to apply *only* to the commission, then that might expose the commission to judicial review of its activities, which Giveen clearly felt was unacceptable. As with most legal propositions, it was the subtlety of the wording which mattered.[22]

When the case was finally heard in the Chancery Division in May and July 1917, the outcome would scarcely have been a surprise to the board; while Mr Justice Younger's approval of the statement of an Irish judge in *R. v. Abbott* [1897] 2 I.R. 362, at p. 405, that: 'No doubt the Defence Act is of national importance, and *salus populi suprema lex*. But the safety of the State is best secured by a general average contribution, and not by making jettison of individual interests', would have been exceedingly unpalatable to the parsimonious Treasury.

---

22. See also ibid., A. H. Dennis, Treasury Solicitor to Sir John Mellor, Treasury, 29 January 1917. Dennis, too, found unconvincing the defences drawn up.

The outcome of the case bears comparison with the views of the Law Lords in the Shoreham Aerodrome and *De Keyser* cases. The principles expounded were basically common to all three. There were, however, some points of difference between the brewery case and the other two. The wording of the Liquor Control Regulations 1915 and of the DORA No. 3 Act of 1915, conferring a power to 'acquire compulsorily or by agreement' (which Mr. Justice Younger held to be 'almost terms of art' and which thus incorporated the 1845 Lands Clauses Act) were distinct from a power merely to 'take possession', which was the wording of Regulation 2 under the 1914 DORA Consolidation Act. The judge in *Cannon Brewery* was impressed by the argument of counsel for the company, led by P.O. Lawrence KC (who also appeared in the Shoreham Aerodrome and *De Keyser* cases), that 'acquire' meant to acquire by purchase, and that that was so whether the acquisition were 'compulsory or by agreement'. As Mr Justice Younger insisted, in delivering his judgment on 31 July 1917, that is, eighteen months after the board took possession of the Ordnance Arms:

> If payment on compulsory taking is not also involved in that phrase, what a mockery the privilege of selling by agreement becomes! What sort of price will be offered under agreement if the property in default of agreement can be taken for nothing?[23]

Moreover, Reg. 7 stated that the fee simple in the property should vest 'subject to or freed from any mortgages'. As the judge pointed out:

> That seems clearly to show that the mortgage must either be discharged by the Board or assumed by the Board. They would never be required to assume it if they were entitled to get rid of it for nothing. Is it then to be contended, on the fair construction of that regulation, that the Board may take a man's property for nothing and yet leave him to discharge the incumbrances upon it? In my opinion, it cannot be necessary to have recourse to any special canon of construction to escape from such a result. I feel no doubt that the power to take 'compulsorily or by agreement', whether subject to mortgage or free from mortgage, necessarily involves payment for what is taken.[24]

The authority of the prerogative power to justify the acquisition was raised by the Solicitor-General, Sir Gordon Hewart, 'but only faintly', in the words of Mr Justice Younger, who found no difficulty in dismissing its relevance. For,

23. [1918] 2 Ch. 101, at p. 112. There were a number of technical arguments in the case, such as whether, for Lands Clauses Act purposes, the board were the 'promoter' of a scheme, what was the nature of the 'undertaking', whether the 1915 Act and the Liquor Control Regulations constituted the 'special act' required for the purposes of land acquisition, and whether the board were in the position of the Crown, and thus not bound by statute (and so requiring procedure by petition of right). The court found in favour of the company on these points.
24. Ibid.

'the king is not entitled under his prerogative to take a man's fee simple estate', as distinct, of course, from taking possession for the duration of the emergency. Perhaps incautiously approving Lord Justice Warrington's somewhat broad affirmation of the prerogative power in the Shoreham Aerodrome case as, 'the right to take and use the lands for so long and in such manner as may be necessary for securing the public safety and the defence of the realm during the present war', Mr Justice Younger averred that: 'It cannot, I think, go further if Magna Carta is to remain unrepealed.'[25] In any case, as the board could acquire permanently, even assuming that it was invested with prerogative powers which probably was doubtful, the Attorney-General in the Shoreham Aerodrome case, Sir Frederick Smith, had conceded that compensation was payable in such instances.

The decision inevitably had repercussions on negotiations with other breweries. From the date of the judgment, that is, from the beginning of August 1917, the reference of claims to the LTCC was suspended and outstanding claims, as far as possible, settled by direct agreement. Balance sheets for the Carlisle and Enfield Lock districts, showing the board's capital expenditure upon property acquisition, could not be prepared for publication in the uncertain climate.[26]

Particular problems arising from the decision included one involving the acquisition of the Maryport Brewery Co. The board had agreed to purchase the brewery business and premises and some 180 public houses compulsorily under Reg. 7. The agreement fixed the amount of compensation payable to the company for the acquisition of its interests. But some of its properties were held on leasehold tenure and the board had resolved to acquire the fee simple by serving Reg. 7 notices on the occupier and on other interested parties. Moreover, some of the premises were let to tenants upon a yearly tenancy. But neither the lessors nor the tenants were affected by the agreement, and in the light of the *Cannon Brewery* judgment, 'it would appear to be open to them to raise contentious claims for compensation or to dispute the validity of the notices'.[27]

Apart from the case of Edward Greenhow, the occupier of the Great Central Hotel in Carlisle, at least two other legal proceedings were commenced against the board by local interests. On 16 April 1917 the Carlisle Old Brewery Company raised an action in King's Bench, claiming a declaration of entitlement to compensation, though proceedings were at a standstill. On 4 July 1917 the Victoria Hotel in the same town served a notice for compensation under the 1845 Act and apparently was declining to leave the matter in abeyance pending the hearing of the *Cannon Brewery* appeal. But

25.   Ibid., p. 115.
26.   Central Control Board, *Fourth Report*, P.P. 1918 (Cd.9055), xi, 117.
27.   PRO, TS 27/46, '*Cannon Brewery* v. *The Central Control Board (Liquor Traffic)*: Case for the Opinion of the Law Officers of the Crown', p. 5.

the onus lay on the hotel to take the next step and to move for arbitration or for a jury settlement. This, at least, relieved the board of the need for an immediate response.

In addition to these proceedings, the board understood from correspondence and from information received from its general manager in Carlisle that proceedings were imminent in other cases. This added to its uncertain position both as to future acquisitions and as to those already concluded. In the case of the latter, the Law Officers reassured the board on 6 September 1917 that awards by the commission had resulted in concluded contracts which neither party had the right to reopen. Where, however, the commission had awarded an amount less than that provisionally agreed, there remained the possibility of reopening the agreement where the claimant had refused to accept the lower amount or had accepted it only under protest, unless he had foresworn making any other claim. Smith and Hewart also advised that it was not possible to stay proceedings by other claimants, pending the outcome of the *Cannon Brewery* appeal, except with the consent of the parties, thereby underlining the board's precarious legal position in respect to compensation claims.[28]

The board was not to be pleasantly surprised by the outcome of the proceedings either in the Court of Appeal or in the House of Lords, except that, as predicted by the Law Officers in 1916, it was at least two years before the case reached the Law Lords. By the time of their judgment, in May 1919, the war had been over for six months and the climate very different from that at the time of the acquisitions.

---

28. The Chancery Division ruling in *Cannon Brewery* also prompted the board to seek an opinion from the Law Officers whether to proceed with the sale of surplus land which was acquired together with Deakin's Vaults in Carlisle. The board's solicitors doubted whether it had in fact any powers of sale. But if the Law Officers advised that such powers were implied (as they subsequently did), then certain provisions of the Lands Clauses Act would apply to the sale, if the *Cannon Brewery* decision were correct. The Act would possibly require the board's trustees to incur personal responsibility which the board could not indemnify after its cessation. Thus the Law Officers advised that it would not be prudent to make sales while awaiting the final decision in the *Cannon Brewery* case, though they did suggest that provisional sales, pending the decision, could be made. The board, pleased with the opinion that it possessed powers of sale, was happy to postpone any further sales until final decision in the courts. A legal problem of a different kind arose in the wake of the acquisition of Nanson's Vaults, also in Carlisle, where the Law Officers apparently advised that the procedure under Reg. 7 applied only to compulsory acquisition and not to acquisition by agreement. In the case of the latter, a deed of conveyance of title was essential, rather than a notice, whether under the regulations or under the Lands Clauses Act. The advice posed a serious difficulty for the board which had always treated purchases as compulsory in form, even in agreed cases. Indeed, agreement came first as with the Maryport Brewery Co. The implication was that in those cases the board would not have obtained a legal title to the properties in the absence of deeds of conveyance of title. The board's officials charitably concluded that the Law Officers were not addressing that particular issue when drafting their opinion. As one official, R. Sutton, minuted to his colleague, A. S. Cane, in 13 August 1918: 'As you know, I have always rather been against the fiction of using compulsory powers when in fact we were proceeding by agreement; but I do not think that the Law Officers had that point before them – I think what they mean is you need not worry about any notices if there is an Agreement, you can get the conveyance and none of these questions then arise.' On both the Deakin's and Nanson's Vaults cases, see PRO, HO 190/491.

The Master of the Rolls, Sir Charles Swinfen-Eady, had characterised the board's claim that the company had no right to compensation as a 'startling' one and had asked whether Parliament had 'really sanctioned confiscation' of property, while acknowledging that the Solicitor-General had 'repudiated the idea of confiscation' by offering resort to the commission. As Lord Justice Bankes pointed out, the commission technically could only report to the Treasury 'what sums ought in reason and fairness to be paid out of public funds to applicants'. The commission itself had no power to award of its own initiative. As Bankes vividly put it:

> The respondents claimed a recognition of their legal and statutory right. They were offered the opportunity of applying for an ex gratia payment. They claimed a decision which they could enforce in a Court of law; they were offered a report to His Majesty's Treasury. Well might the respondents say that they asked for bread and were given a stone.[29]

As a matter of strict construction of what was an undertaking 'authorized by any Act' (in the words of the 1845 Act), Bankes L.J. disagreed with Swinfen-Eady and with the third judge in the Court of Appeal, Mr Justice Eve, as to whether the Lands Clauses Act was incorporated into the DORA No. 3 Act 1915 and its regulations. He thought it was not, but saw no obstacle to the company enforcing its right to payment through court action without reference to the statutory scheme of compensation.

Neither judge could resist a tilt at encroaching executive powers which appeared to threaten the liberties of the individual property-owner. Swinfen-Eady, for example, did not want it to be assumed, simply because the brewery company did not challenge the *vires* of Reg. 7, that DORA authorised the making of regulations to deprive an owner, by mere notice, of his fee simple without payment or conveyance and free from any subsisting mortgage. Bankes echoed these sentiments in somewhat more general terms when he cautioned that:

> attention is necessarily directed to the disadvantage attending a system of legislation under which the main outlines only of some proposal before Parliament are settled by the Legislature, and it is left to the Executive to set up the machinery by which the proposal as outlined is to be carried into effect. The times, no doubt, are abnormal. Emergency legislation in time of war cannot be expected to proceed on exactly the same lines as legislation in times of peace. I venture to doubt, however, whether the extent to which private rights and the rights of property are endangered by the system of legislation to which I have referred is sufficiently appreciated.[30]

29. [1918] 2 Ch. 101, at p. 129.
30. Ibid., p. 124.

The House of Lords, without, for the most part, resorting to the highly charged rhetoric of property rights which would not be out of place in the particular context of the case, systematically found in favour of the company, rejecting not only the board's contentions but also Lord Justice Bankes' deviation. Only Lord Parmoor was spurred to oratory:

> I desire, however, to enter an emphatic protest against the argument that the private opinion of certain Commissioners, however eminent may be their qualifications, should be regarded as equivalent for claims made as a matter of right, under the protection of a rule of law, and in accordance with well-established legal principles. It is not necessary in a case of this character to base the decision on any presumption in favour of construing an Act of Parliament so as to give compensation where property is acquired for public purposes, but the presumption is too well established to be open to doubt or questions. The prerogative of the Crown was referred to in argument, but it is contrary to a principle enshrined in our law, at least since the date of Magna Carta, to suggest that an executive body, such as the Central Control Board, can claim, under the prerogative, to confiscate for the benefit of the Crown, the private property of subjects.[31]

Viscount Finlay and Lords Atkinson and Wrenbury were content with a clinical demolition of the board's claims. With the war already over, the consequences of the judgment would be only economic or political, rather than, to some extent, military.

The immediate consequences were that an arbitrator was appointed to fix the purchase price of the Ordnance Arms, as agreement could not be reached. The board's valuers, Marks & Barley, had in August 1919 advised a sealed offer of £6,500.[32] It is not clear whether this was in fact delivered but, on 23 April 1920, the arbitrator, J. H. Townsend Green, a surveyor with offices in Chancery Lane, awarded £6,335, with his own costs fixed at £84 10s. 6d.[33]

Apart from that case, the board's solicitors wrote to their clients, arguing that the judgment established that the commission 'has no jurisdiction whatever even to consider cases of claims to compensation in respect of lands'.[34] This drastic conclusion followed from a combination of the remit of the commission to cases 'not otherwise provided for', and of the applicability of the Lands Clauses Act to compensation claims. In other words, land acquisition claims were now very much 'provided for'. As the commission itself noted in its summary report of its proceedings, 'Our labours have been

31. [1919] A.C. 744, at p. 760.
32. PRO, HO 190/491, Marks & Barley to Sir John Sykes, 6 August 1919.
33. PRO, TS 27/46, 'In the Matter of an Arbitration Between the Central Control Board (Liquor Traffic) and the Cannon Brewery Limited', 19 January 1920.
34. Ibid., 'J.S.E. Questions Concerning Future Action and Policy Arising from the Lords' Judgment in the Cannon Brewery Case', 2 June 1919.

materially reduced owing to' the *Cannon Brewery* ruling.[35] In consequence, the board's solicitors advised the Central Control Board to reopen negotiations in all cases not yet settled and to endeavour to reach an agreement. Very considerable increases should be offered, since in the event of arbitration or a jury assessment, the whole costs would be payable by the board unless the sum awarded was the same or less than the offer. In those circumstances each party bore his own costs, with both parties sharing the arbitrators' costs. Another difficulty concerned the firm of Messrs Worthington's. They had responded to the board's notices to acquire the freehold of the company's Golden Lion and the lease of its Gaol Vaults by instituting proceedings seeking a declaration of a right to compensation. The board had intended to defend the action but, in view of the Lords' rulings, it doubted whether any defence was now possible. However, the amount demanded by Worthington's had been high and the practical possibilities now open to the board were to reopen negotiations with the company on the basis of a much larger offer from the board, or to invite Worthington's to agree to arbitration on the basis that compensation was due as of right.

In the few cases where Reg. 7 notices had been served but where the owners had not retaliated by serving a writ, informal agreement or compensation had been reached, though difficulties arose with respect to other interested parties, such as tenants or lessees. Here, the board endeavoured to, 'concede all that can possibly be conceded on the minor points which may arise in order that the original settlement may be sustained and a formal agreement concluded'.[36]

In Scotland, a number of practical difficulties arose. The owner of the Buck Hotel, Annan, had applied to the commission for £8,738 after abortive negotiations. The board had offered £3,000, though its valuer had informed the hotel's owner that he might be willing to recommend £3,500 to the commission, subject to certain conditions. The offer was unacceptable, however, and all previous offers withdrawn, with the licensee and proprietor, Mr Cruickshank, still managing the hotel for the board. Eventually, the commission awarded £3,200, which the owner refused to accept. Following the *Cannon Brewery* case, he wrote to the board, asking whether the latter now had any fresh proposals to make. The board proposed to reply to the effect that, while it was unclear as to the grounds on which he claimed to reopen the matter, the board would nonetheless after first submitting it to the commission, be prepared to discuss the possibility of reaching an amicable settlement.[37] Meanwhile, the board also sought the opinion of

35. PRO, T 80/5, Defence of the Realm (Licensed Trade Claims) Commission, *Report*, 20 March 1921, para.7.

36. PRO, HO 190/491, Travers Smith & Braithwaite to Central Control Board, June 2, 1919.

37. Ibid., 'J.S.E. Outstanding Compensation Cases in Scotland – Legal Effects of Cannon Brewery Judgment', 12 August 1919.

the Lord Advocate, James Clyde, as to whether claimants were entitled to have compensation assessed on a Lands Clauses Act basis where, first, the amount payable was agreed between the parties, subject to the ratification of the commission and, second, where the amount was agreed unconditionally without reference to the commission. In both circumstances, the opinion was that the owner could not reopen a case under the Lands Clauses Act where agreement, with or without the commission's ratification, had been reached, and whether or not any money had been paid over. If there was no agreement, the owner was entitled to reopen, even where he accepted payment of an amount by the commission.[38] Such appeared to be the case with the Buck Hotel.

Two other problem cases existed, also in Annan. The first was the Central Hotel. The owners had claimed £7,000 whereas the board's valuer, Wallis, had made a provisional offer of £2,000. When it was refused, the offer was formally withdrawn. The owners and the board then went before the commission as a contested case, the commission awarding £2,000 which the owners refused to accept. The final case was that of the Globe Hotel, which had not in fact been before the commission at all. The owners had first claimed £1,800, coming down to £1,425. They were offered £1,250 and then £1,350. On 4 May 1916 Wallis advised that the case should go before the commission but, on 20 May, he reported the owners' acceptance of his offer of £1,350. This provisional agreement was, in the light of the practice of the board, subject to confirmation by the commission. But the owners' solicitors had refused to proceed any further, prompting the board to conclude they were simply waiting for a favourable outcome in the *Cannon Brewery* case, in order to obtain better terms.

In all three cases, the next move, in the board's opinion, had to come from the owners, after which the board's invitation to reach an amicable settlement would be issued. In making that offer, the board was advised to point out that the trade in Annan had now dwindled, which it took as proof that the owners would not have enjoyed any protracted period of war profits.

By the date of this advice, August 1919, the wartime rationale for state purchase had ceased and the Treasury, in December 1918, had already reminded the Central Control Board of the need for financial stringency. The social rationale of reducing drunkenness and of improving the quality of life by extending canteen facilities did not impress the guardians of economic asceticism, even where the board was making annual profits of £139,000 in 1919–20, which represented a return of $16\frac{1}{2}$ per cent on capital.[39] Support for the schemes among local opinion was strong, and representations were made to the government not to sell off the state licensed trade. The Gretna local advisory committee, for example, felt keenly that a return to a system

38. Ibid., 'J. A. Clyde, Legal Opinion', 31 July 1919.
39. Rose, 'The Success of Social Reform?' pp. 79, 82.

'controlled by the desire for private profit' would result in a reappearance of all the vices surrounding alcohol which the state scheme had successfully eradicated.[40]

In the event, the board was wound up in 1921 on the passing of the Licensing Act that year, its powers vesting in the Home Secretary and the Secretary for Scotland. Yet the purchase programme was not quite over. It was contemplated in January 1922 that the Home Office should acquire the remaining licensed premises in the Carlisle area, about fifty in all, which had not been obtained during the war.[41] Such a purchase would complete the monopoly of state ownership in the area and, as Rose points out, the schemes, for the most part, survived (until 1971 in fact), 'partly no doubt because the government was unwilling to face the problem of unscrambling them and also, in the case of Carlisle at least, because of strong local pressure for their continuance'.[42] Not so, sadly, in the case of Enfield Lock, where four pubs, including the Ordnance Arms, whose particular features preoccupied civil servants and judges alike, were sold off to private buyers in 1923.

40.   Scottish Record Office, Edinburgh [SRO], HH 31/7, 'Central Control Board: Gretna-without-the-Township Local Committee', 20 July 1921.
41.   PRO, HO 190/491, 'Licensing Act 1921: Powers of the Home Secretary as Successor to the Liquor Control Board'.
42.   Rose, 'The Success of Social Reform?', p. 83. See chapter 14, below.

8

Newcastle Rum

In 1740 Admiral Edward Vernon informed General Charles Cathcart that rum drinking among sailors at Port Royal, Jamaica, 'might cost us as great a loss of Men, As a Generall Action'.[1] At the conclusion of the Napoleonic Wars in 1815, Sir Gilbert Blane, the naval surgeon, investigated the high rate of insanity in the Navy in comparison with the population as a whole. He concluded that naval madness was the second greatest occupational hazard in the service (ruptures were the first), and was mainly due to crewmen striking their heads on low beams aboard ship while in a state of inebriation. What brought about that drunkenness was the deliberately excessive quantity of rum, half a pint a day, issued to the men:[2]

> It was . . . their only solace. They drank it when they were thirsty. They drank it when they were hungry. They drank it when they were afraid. They drank it to celebrate victory. They drank it to drown defeat. They drank it before they were flogged. They drank it, through bitten lips, after a flogging. They drank it to drown the stench of the mess-decks. They drank it so they could join in the orgies. They drank it to forget them. Above all, they drank rum to make the Navy bearable, so they could forget the Navy and their torturing thoughts of women and children, parents and friends they had not seen for years and whom they might not see again.[3]

All this, notwithstanding that in the eighteenth century Navy there was no official issue of spirits.[4]

By the time of the First World War, conditions on board ship had improved beyond recognition. Yet the soothing properties of rum were still appreciated by the Royal Navy. On 6 October 1917, acting under Reg. 2B of the Defence

---

1. Quoted in Daniel Baugh, *British Naval Administration in the Age of Walpole* (Princeton, NJ, 1965), p. 216n. Vernon's nickname was 'Grogram'. It was he who first had grog (a mix of spirits and water) served to sailors instead of neat rum.
2. Stanley Bonnett, *The Price of Admiralty: An Indictment of the Royal Navy, 1805–1966* (London, 1968), p. 35; see also Michael Lewis, *A Social History of the Navy, 1793–1815* (London, 1960), pp. 400–1.
3. Bonnett, *The Price of Admiralty*, p. 36.
4. N.A.M. Rodger, *The Wooden World: An Anatomy of the Georgian Navy* (London, 1986), p. 73.

Regulations, the Admiralty gave notice to Newcastle Breweries Ltd of their intention to take possession of a quantity of rum belonging to the company. On 20 November they took possession of 239 puncheons. Their reason for requisitioning was that, for some months previously, the market price of rum had been rising steadily, partly as a result of restriction on imports: in August 1917, the Admiralty found it no longer possible to obtain adequate supplies through the normal trade channels.[5] After consulting the War Office, they decided to issue an order on 6 October, calling for returns of stocks in bonded warehouses in the United Kingdom, in order to ascertain who were the owners.

The figures in Table 1 for rum imports between 1910 and 1921 show a dramatic rise and fall during the war years. They emphasise the effect of the import restriction which prompted the Admiralty to resort to requisitioning.

Table 1

Rum Imports, 1910–21

Year	Thousands of Proof Gallons	Year	Thousands of Proof Gallons
1910	4,714	1916	9,958
1911	4,834	1917	4,562
1912	3,991	1918	2,808
1913	4,709	1919	9,266
1914	5,672	1920	3,882
1915	10,484	1921	4,429

Source: G. P. Williams and G. T. Brake, *Drink in Great Britain, 1900 to 1979* (London, 1980), table I.14.

Even though the figure for 1917 was comparable to those for the immediate pre-war period, the increase in the size of the Royal Navy put pressure on the available stocks, helping to force up the price of the commodity in a non-regulated market. Evidence given by the manager of Messrs Southard & Co., a firm of spirit brokers, to the High Court hearing of Newcastle Breweries' petition of right, indicated the scale of the price increases which prompted the Admiralty to requisition under Reg. 2B.[6] The witness, J.G. Simmonds, informed the court that on 28 September 1917, the date of an auction which the firm had organised, the price per proof gallon of Demerara was between 16s. and 17s. 6d. and that of Jamaica was 16s. 6d. (or 23s. per liquid gallon). The next rum sale was the following December, with the Demerara realising from 44s. to 47s. and the Jamaica between 36s. and 53s. per proof gallon according

5.   PRO, HO 45/10895/362392, Admiralty to Under Secretary of State, Home Office, 19 June 1918.
6.   PRO, LCO 2/441, 'Indemnity Bill Memorandum: Newcastle Breweries Case'.

to age. In other words, the price of rum had risen in about two months from around 16s. to around 50s. These figures also compared with the price of 4s. 8d. for Demerara in October 1916 and 1s. 7d. in November 1914, the last figure being a quoted circular price as distinct from what was realised at subsequent sales. As Simmonds explained, prices began to fluctuate so dramatically from November 1914 that the company ceased quotations thereafter. Shipping shortages and general transport difficulties were inevitably identified as the causes of the dramatic increases.

By the time the Admiralty came to requisition from Newcastle Breweries, the department had come to the conclusion that, 'in effect there was no real market value in 1917',[7] and therefore it was reasonable to invoke Reg. 2B which made provision for a 'fair profit'. The additional cost to the Exchequer if the compensation provision in the regulation were held *ultra vires*, was calculated, in the case of rum alone, at £750,000.

On 6 October 1917, the Newcastle Breweries Ltd, a firm of brewers and wholesale and retail wine and spirit merchants, based in Haymarket, Newcastle-upon-Tyne, had stocks of rum, amounting in total to 658 puncheons, 91 hogsheads and one octave (a puncheon is a large cask holding from 72 to 120 gallons; a hogshead is about 50 gallons and an octave is usually 105 gallons).[8] There was Cuba, Demerara, Jamaica, Mauritius, Natal, Trinidad and Vatted rum in store, all of which had been purchased by the company over the previous three to four years.

On 16 October the company submitted its return to the Admiralty Director of Contracts and on 20 November, it was informed that the Admiralty were taking over certain quantities of the company's rum supply, requiring average samples to be sent to the Admiralty's brokers. The particulars of the rum requisitioned were 172 puncheons of Demerara, 30 of Cuba, 20 of Natal and 17 of Trinidad, a total of 239 puncheons. The Admiralty stated that they had not yet definitely fixed what amount of profit should be allowed to the company. In the first instance, the company would receive only what it itself had paid for the rum, plus incidental charges for carriage, rent and insurance to 31 December 1917 plus interest at 5 per cent. A further communication would be sent.

This arrived on 8 February 1918 when the Admiralty, claiming that the acquisition was made under Reg. 2B, offered payment on the basis previously stated, plus an additional element. This was either 6d. or 1s. 6d. per proof gallon, as the case might be, in respect of every parcel of rum which could have earned a customs rebate under the Immature Spirits (Restriction) Act 1915 (which required that all spirits should be three years old before consumption) if it had been cleared for duty not later than 21 January 1918 (some of the rum had been purchased – presumably imported – in 1917), and also 1s. per

7. Ibid.
8. PRO, HO 45/10895/362392, 'The Newcastle Breweries Ltd. Petition of Right', 23 May 1918, for this and subsequent information.

proof gallon as a consolidated allowance to cover appreciation in value due to maturing in the rum itself, and overhead profit on the transaction. If the offer were not accepted, stated the Admiralty, then the company could apply to the Defence of the Realm Losses Commission (DRLC).

The company scorned both proposals and demanded the market price for the rum. It was calculated that the Admiralty's offer was around £10,774 9s. 3d., or about 6s. per proof gallon, which would leave the company with a profit significantly below that which, in the ordinary course of business before the war, they were making. It was also far below the market value of the rum, even below the price at which the company would have to replace the requisitioned rum for their business. According to Newcastle Breweries, the 'fair and reasonable price' at the time of both notice and acquisition in late 1917 was from 15s. to 17s. per proof gallon in bond, which would have produced a further £18,000 for the company. The maximum price of wholesale rum was fixed subsequently by the Spirits (Prices and Description) Order of 22 April, 1918, with the result that rum sold in bond to a licensed trader was priced at 20s. a gallon, and if sold to a person buying for resale to a licensed trader, at the same price less a minimum discount of 15 per cent. Prior to the order of April 1918, no maximum price had been fixed. As can be seen from the figures, the Admiralty's offer was just over one-third of the market value demanded by the company and was claimed to be justified by the provisions in respect to compensation contained in Reg. 2B.

Reg. 2B had first been made on 15 January 1916 and was expanded a number of times over the next year.[9] It was divided logically into two sections: the power to requisition and the provision for compensation, the latter provision being added on 23 February 1917, presumably in acknowledgment of the possibilities of litigation opened up by the legal challenges in other areas of government requisition in 1916.

The requisitioning provision declared:

> It shall be lawful for the Admiralty or Army Council or the Minister of Munitions to take possession of any war material, food, forage and stores of any description and of any articles required for or in connection with the production thereof. If, after the Admiralty etc. have issued a notice that they have taken or intend to take possession of any war material, food, forage, stores or articles in pursuance of this Regulation, any person having control of any such material, food, forage, stores or article, sells, removes or secretes it, without the consent of the Admiralty etc., he shall be guilty of an offence against these Regulations.

Until the addition of 23 February 1917, noted above, nothing was stipulated in the regulation about compensation, nor about how it ought to be calculated. From that date, Reg. 2B provided that,

---

9. See the judgment of Mr Justice Salter in *Newcastle Breweries Ltd.* v. *The King* [1920] 1 K.B. 854 for this and subsequent information.

In determining [compensation] regard need not be had to the market price, but shall be had: (a) If the goods are acquired from the grower or producer thereof, to the cost of production and to the rate of profit usually earned by him in respect of similar goods before the war and to whether such rate of profit was unreasonable or excessive, and to any other circumstances of the case; (b) if the goods are acquired from any person other than the grower or producer thereof, to the price paid by such person for the goods and to whether such price was unreasonable or excessive, and to the rate of profit usually earned in respect of the sale of similar goods before the war, and to whether such rate of profit was unreasonable or excessive, and to any other circumstances of the case; so, however, that if the person from whom the goods are acquired himself acquired the goods otherwise than in the usual course of his business, no allowance or an allowance at a reduced rate, on account of profit shall be made. Provided that where, by virtue of these regulations or any order made thereunder the sale of the goods at a price above any price fixed thereunder is prohibited, the price assessed under this regulation shall not exceed the price so fixed.

If the parties agreed on the level of compensation, then the regulation's guidelines to the relevant tribunal, the DRLC, need not be invoked. But, inevitably, the DRLC would follow those laid down.

The inelegantly drafted regulation drew a distinction between goods in the possession of a grower or producer and those held by a middleman. In respect to the former, the cost of producing the food, forage or other material, as well as the level of pre-war 'reasonable' profits, were to be taken into consideration. In the case of merchants, the regulation was 'designed on the one hand to discourage mischievous speculation and hoarding, and on the other hand to safeguard the *bona fide* trader against loss'.[10] The price paid by the merchant was relevant in assessing compensation, so long as that price itself was not considered unreasonable or excessive. Also relevant was the rate of 'reasonable' profit normally earned by the merchant prior to the war. The regulation sought to offer no comfort to those speculating in commodities outside their normal course of business. In their case the tribunal would offer either no compensation for lost profits or a reduced amount. Where a fixed maximum price had been set, the Admiralty could requisition at a price which it itself had predetermined. There had been no maximum price in force at the time of the requisition of Newcastle Brewery's rum.

Given the company's refusal to accept the level of compensation offered by the naval department, the legality of that part of Reg. 2B dealing with compensation came under the scrutiny of Mr Justice Salter in the High Court at the end of December 1919. By that date the Armistice had been signed, though the country was still, legally, in a state of war. Moreover, Reg. 2B had been the principal instrument of control used by the War Office as well as by the Admiralty, and under its aegis, vast quantities of wool tops, hides, leather and other commodities had been requisitioned. An adverse ruling

10. Lloyd, *Experiments in State Control*, p.54.

on the *vires* of its compensation provisions would have wide implications, possibly involving the Treasury in extra outlays amounting to tens of millions of pounds, even if the military struggle had come to an end.

The government therefore were prepared to defend the *vires* of the regulation, even though at least one of their own officials had cast doubt on the legality of its compensation provisions. Newcastle Breweries' petition of right had been submitted in May 1918, but it had been received with such alarm at the time that the War Office had made application to the War Cabinet for legislative protection.[11] At the end of 1918, the matter was referred by the Cabinet to Lord Cave's Committee on Emergency Legislation, but since, as far as the War Office knew, no litigation was then pending (presumably because Newcastle Breweries were waiting to settle out of court), the need for express validation of the regulation by statute did not immediately arise.

It was decided to recommend the inclusion of Reg. 2B in the War Emergency Laws (Continuance) Bill for the purpose of extending its operation for twelve months after the legal termination of the war. Philip Guedalla (1889–1944), a legal adviser to the Contracts departments of the War Office and of the Ministry of Munitions, believed that this would remove doubts as to the validity of the regulation during the period of the operation of the Bill, and that, 'the position of the previous operation of the regulation might be somewhat strengthened by its prolongation after consideration by Parliament'.[12] Whether the regulation would thereby be legally or merely morally strengthened was not spelt out.

The Treasury Solicitor's department was consulted on the Ministry of Munitions' 'simple and unobtrusive' amendment to the War Emergency Laws (Continuance) Bill, but in a reply to the War Office on 27 February 1919, Dr A.W. Brown, one of the department's four chief clerks, advised that the proposal, 'appeared to be open to serious objection in point of legal policy and propriety'. Since it affected the subject matter of pending litigation, the brewery presumably having lost patience with the Admiralty, the Law Officers ought, he thought, to be consulted. Brown added that:

> If he rightly understood the matter, it was suggested under the guise of an extension of the operation of Emergency Laws, a Regulation (which it was assumed for that purpose was not law or was doubtful law) should not only be extended, but retrospectively validated, and that that should be done 'unobtrusively' with the object of affecting ex post facto rights of persons who had already appealed to the Courts of Law. The Law Officers might

---

11.   PRO, LCO 2/440, 'Interdepartmental Committee on Indemnity Bill and Statute of Limitations.   Memorandum no. 9.   On the question of the validity of Defence of the Realm Regulation 2B', for this and subsequent information.

12.   Ibid.   Guedalla had been admitted to the bar (Inner Temple) in 1913, but retired from legal practice in 1923.   He was secretary to, and effective organiser of, the Flax Control Board, 1917–1920.   He contested a number of parliamentary seats as a Liberal between 1922 and 1931.   A prolific writer, he joined the RAF in World War Two.   See also below, Chapter 14.

consider that any such legislation should only be secured with the conscious assent of Parliament, and under such safeguards as it might require, and not under cover of an apparently innocent provision, ostensibly designed merely to secure continuance of existing powers.[13]

He added that there were many legally trained Members of Parliament who were quite aware of the questions raised about the validity of defence regulations and, since there was now a greater disposition to question extensions of the regulations, he warned against any step 'which might savour of want of candour in this connection'.[14]

The Law Officers' opinion of 14 April 1919, signed by Gordon Hewart and Ernest Pollock, cautioned against a special amendment and validation of Reg. 2B in the Continuance Bill (the Bill itself simply declared that scheduled regulations were to be continued for a further period, 'and as so continued shall have effect as though communicated in this Act'). They advised that the issue raised in the petition of right be decided by the court, as they did not anticipate an adverse judgment. If they were wrong in that assessment, the matter could then be pursued further.

In the event, their legal opinion was faulty. On 20 February 1920, Mr Justice Salter found in favour of the petitioner, and declared *ultra vires* that part of Reg. 2B dealing with compensation. The market value of the rum therefore had to be paid. His reasoning was as follows. First, he reviewed the legislative basis for the requisitioning of the rum and concluded that statutory power existed independently of the Defence of the Realm Act. For the Army Act 1881, s. 115, as amended by the Army (Supply of Food, Forage and Stores) Act 1914, by the Naval Billeting etc. Act 1914, by the Army (Amendment) Act 1915 and by the Army (Amendment) (No. 2) Act 1915, conferred powers of requisition of 'articles' on the naval and military authorities. Subsection four of s. 115 of the 1881 Act, as subsequently amended, provided that the Army Council or Admiralty were to cause due payment to be made for goods requisitioned, any difference as to amount to be determined by a county court judge in accordance with a schedule. That schedule provided that the amount of payment should be such as appeared to the county court judge to be the fair market value of the article requisitioned, as between a willing buyer and a willing seller on the day on which it was required to be furnished. The Army (Amendment) Act had received the Royal Assent on 16 March 1915 and in the opinion of Mr Justice Salter:

13. Ibid.
14. Guedalla, whose proposal for amendment drew this fierce criticism from Brown, vigorously refuted the imputation that he was seeking to slip legislation through without adequate parliamentary scrutiny. In the event, Reg. 2B was extended for a further twelve months after the legal termination of the war (which occurred at midnight on 31 August 1921) by the War Emergency Laws (Continuance) Act 1920 without its provisions being modified. See chapter 14, below.

> At that time, therefore, the Legislature is showing the plainest intention that persons whose goods are requisitioned in emergency by the naval and military officers of the Crown shall be paid in full, and that the amount payable shall, if disputed, be determined by a Court of Law.

But the rum in question was requisitioned after Reg. 2B had been issued, and expressly in the name of that regulation. In the government's view, this made a world of difference. As noted previously, the regulation was in two parts, the first dealing with requisition, the second, added on 23 February 1917, dealing with compensation and enjoining the relevant tribunal, 'that regard need not be had to the market price.'

As the petitioner challenged the *vires* of the compensation provision, the judge turned his attention to the relation between DORA and Reg. 2B. He noted that DORA conferred temporary power on the Crown to issue regulations for securing the public safety and the defence of the realm: for a general scheme for which the regulations were 'designed', where the word 'designed' was taken to mean 'framed' rather than 'intended'. Was the circumscribed compensation provision in Reg. 2B 'reasonably capable of being a Regulation for securing the public safety and the defence of the realm'? Was it appropriate to the general scheme? If it was, then the provision was valid and it was for the Crown to determine the expediency of applying the regulation. He also noted that subsections (a) to (e) of section 1 of DORA 1914 listed more specific objectives of defence regulations. One subsection contemplated regulations 'designed, (e) otherwise to prevent . . . the successful prosecution of the war being endangered'. Thus if Reg. 2B *in toto* was reasonably capable of achieving this objective, irrespective of the general objectives of public safety and the defence of the realm, then it would be valid. The decision in *Lipton* v. *Ford* [1917] 2 K.B. 647 had upheld the validity of the requisitioning provision of Reg. 2B, but that case had arisen prior to the expansion of the regulation which included provision for fair, as distinct from market-level, compensation.

The question was reduced, in its essentials, to whether the provision in Reg. 2B, which stated that, 'the price to be paid in respect of [goods requisitioned] shall in default of agreement be determined by the [DRLC]'. was 'for the purpose of securing the public safety and the defence of the realm' in general, or more specifically and in the alternative, 'designed, (e) otherwise to prevent . . . the successful prosecution of the war being endangered'.

The judge's approach to this question was somewhat cursory. He observed that the DRLC's jurisdiction applied where no other statutory or contractual right to payment or compensation existed or was alleged. If the whole regulation were valid, the subject would be deprived of his statutory right to market level compensation as prescribed by the Army Act 1881 as amended, and he would only be permitted to seek an *ex gratia* payment from the DRLC. This was a proposition with which the judge could not agree:

I do not think that a Regulation which takes away the subject's right to a judicial decision [that is, under the 1881 Act, as amended], or transfers the adjudication of his claim, without his consent, from a Court of Law to named arbitrators, could fairly be held to be a Regulation for securing the public safety and the defence of the realm, or a Regulation designed to prevent the successful prosecution of the war being endangered within the meaning of these words in the Defence of the Realm Consolidation Act 1914.

Such was his argument. But what of the reasoning behind his argument? There were two strands to this exercise. The first was a further repetition of the well-rehearsed doctrine that a statute could not be read as authorising the taking of a subject's property without payment, unless the words of the statute clearly imported such an intention: 'This rule must apply no less to partial than to total confiscation, and it must apply *a fortiori* to the construction of a statute delegating legislative powers.' Given that parliament in 1915 had legislated for the payment of fair market value for goods requisitioned under the Army (Amendment) (No. 2) Act, and given that DORA 1914 did not contain precise language to the contrary (from which the validity of a regulation removing market value might be derived), the compensation provision of Reg. 2B was held to be *ultra vires*. Anticipating the Food Controller's unlawful action in 1919 in imposing a milk levy by regulation,[15] the judge added: 'A power to take the goods of a particular subject, or class of subjects, without payment of the then cash value, is a power of taxation by the Executive'. Though he did not say as such, such power was contrary to the Bill of Rights 1689 which reserved revenue-raising powers to Parliament.

The second strand was to adopt the reasoning employed by the judges in *Chester* v. *Bateson* [1920] 1 K.B. 829, decided shortly before the *Newcastle Breweries* hearing, a reasoning which seemed to challenge the reductionist approach that almost any municipal restriction on a subject's freedom of action could contribute, however remotely, to public safety and the defence of the realm. In *Chester* v. *Bateson*, the validity of Reg. 2A(2) had been challenged. It provided that in any area where munitions work was being performed, the Minister of Munitions could schedule that area, with the result that it would be unlawful for a landlord, without the consent of the minister, to take legal proceedings to recover possession of his premises or to eject any munitions worker who was a tenant in the landlord's premises and who was paying rent and observing the other conditions of the tenancy. The aim was to prevent the disruption to munitions work caused by the tenants being made homeless. Any landlord breaching the regulation was guilty of a summary offence.

When a landlord in Barrow-in-Furness took proceedings before the magistrates to recover possession of his dwelling-house from a munitions worker employed at Vickers shipyard, the worker claimed that the proceedings were invalid, as the prior consent of the minister had not been obtained before

---

15. *Attorney-General* v. *Wilts United Dairies* (1921) 37 T.L.R. 884 (C.A.); (1922) 38 T.L.R. 781 (H.L.).

legal action began. The landlord's response was to argue that the regulation was *ultra vires* DORA 1914. Mr. Justice Darling's test of its validity was tersely put:

> I ask myself whether it is a necessary, or even reasonable, way to aid in securing the public safety and the defence of the realm to give power to a Minister to forbid any person to institute any proceedings to recover possession of a house so long as a war worker is living in it.

His initial answer did not, in fact, address that question. Instead, he relied on a more traditional approach:

> This might, of course, legally be done by Act of Parliament; but I think this extreme disability can be inflicted only by direct enactment of the Legislature itself, and that so grave an invasion of rights of all subjects was not intended by the Legislature to be accomplished by a departmental order such as this one of the Minister of Munitions.

This reasoning was a matter of statutory construction, that is, what did or did not DORA specifically provide. As denial of access to the courts of law in wartime ('so grave an invasion of rights of all subjects' – at least once the Armistice had been signed) had not been expressly authorised by DORA, it was a straightforward matter to infer its unlawfulness when stipulated in an executive regulation.

The approach to testing the *vires* of the regulation to which Mr Justice Darling more specifically adverted was what we may call a 'plausible empirical' one. Was it a reasonable argument, let alone an irresistible one, that the war effort would be assisted by restricting landlords' rights of access to the courts, in order to rid themselves of unwelcome tenants undertaking munitions work? Or was the argument spurious, in that such restrictions imposed on landlords could not conceivably further public safety and the defence of the realm?

It will readily be appreciated that the landlord was not required to establish by, for example, the use of statistical findings, that the housing position of munitions workers would not be rendered less secure were the need removed for the minister's consent to proceedings to evict. Nor, for that matter, did the minister require to establish that the existence of such a provision reassured munitions workers living in temporary private accommodation that their tenure would be more secure than if such consent were not required. The issue was not one of empirical verifiability *tout court*. It was one of empirical plausibility which positive circumstantial evidence might support, though the absence of such circumstantial evidence would not necessarily render the provision in the regulation *ultra vires*. If the judge thought the connection between the regulation and both the public safety and defence of the realm was so remote that no scenario could remotely be envisaged where the former might promote, albeit tenuously, the latter, only then would the regulation be *ultra vires*.

Although Mr Justice Darling seemed to promise an investigation along these lines by asking, 'whether it is a necessary, or even reasonable way to aid in securing the public safety and the defence of the realm' that such power be conferred on the Minister of Munitions in Reg. 2A(2), he failed to answer his own question and reverted to high principle and narrow statutory construction:

> I allow that in stress of war we may rightly be obliged, as we should be ready, to forgo much of our liberty, but I hold that this elemental right of the subjects of the British Crown cannot be thus easily taken from them. Should we hold that the permit of a departmental official is a necessary condition precedent for a subject of the realm who would demand justice at the seat of judgment, the people would be in that unhappy condition indicated, but not anticipated, by Montesquieu in *De l'Esprit des Lois*, where he writes: 'Les Anglais pour favoriser la liberté ont ôté toutes les puissances intermédiaires qui formoient leur monarchie. Ils ont bien raison de conserver cette liberté; s'ils venoient à la perdre, ils seroient un des peuples, les plus esclaves, de la terre.'

For Mr Justice Salter in *Newcastle Breweries*, such reasoning was compelling:

> In *Chester* v. *Bateson*, it was decided that Regulation 2A(2) of these Regulations is invalid. The judgments in that case are, in substance, applicable here. The Regulation deprived a class of subjects, in certain circumstances, of their common law right of access to the Courts. This Regulation takes away a right of access to a particular court given in express terms by a recent statute.

The question which he did not pose directly but which was central to the government's thinking was what effect would it have (or, to be more precise, have had at the time of the hearing) on the conduct of the war if the regulation were declared *ultra vires*. We have already noted the concern of the requisitioning departments that a heavy additional financial burden would be incurred were the departments compelled to pay the market value for the goods requisitioned. Sums running to tens of millions of pounds were thought to be at stake. There is no indication that during the period of the fighting itself, that is up to November 1918, the government believed the country would be bankrupted into defeat. Needless to say, a regulation issued under DORA, which had as its immediate consequence a saving to the Treasury, could plausibly be said to be for the public safety and the defence of the realm, if only because the savings arising from one compensation payment at DRLC-approved, rather than at market, rates, could be applied to the payment for further material requisitioned for war purposes. To that extent, a regulation prescribing 'fair' compensation payments could be held to be *intra vires*. The card played by the judges which trumped this argument was, as we have seen, the 'high principle – statutory construction' card, that the fundamental rights to full compensation for requisitioned goods or property and to free access to the courts could only be denied by express words in a statute passed by

Parliament. Executive command was not enough and Newcastle Breweries were on their way to reaping their full reward.

The goalposts were then moved. The compensation provision in Reg. 2B may have been declared *ultra vires*. Some months later, Parliament passed the Indemnity Act 1920 which gave statutory confirmation not only to regulations made under DORA, but also to regulations 'purporting to be made' under the authority of DORA. The Indemnity Act also replaced the DRLC with the War Compensation Court whose remit was similar to that of its predecessor, with the important qualification that awards would now be *ex lege*.

Far from being able to expect compensation on the basis of the (inflated) market value of the requisitioned rum, Newcastle Breweries Ltd now found that the discredited compensation provisions were far from buried. Since no voluntary payment by the Admiralty seems to have been made after the delivery of Mr Justice Salter's ruling, the claim of the company went before the War Compensation Court,[16] when it was clear that no appeal to the Court of Appeal would be undertaken. The War Compensation Court, to the chagrin of the company, considered itself bound by that part of a regulation which only months earlier had been declared *ultra vires* by the High Court. That provision had, of course, stated that, in respect to compensation, 'regard need not be had to the market price' but to the pre-war rate of profit earned in respect to the sale of similar goods; while any unreasonable or excessive profit or any other circumstances of the case were to be taken into consideration.

The court, having concluded that there was no market price at the time of the Admiralty's requisition, held that the price paid by the company for the rum should be assessed at 4s. 2d. per proof gallon, and that the pre-war rate of profit for such goods should be assessed at 4s. 7d. The total price per gallon for compensation purposes was therefore fixed at 8s. 9d. which compared with the Admiralty's offer of around 6s. per gallon and the company's claim of between 15s. and 17s. per gallon, as noted earlier in this chapter. The total amount of compensation was therefore fixed at £15,624. 11s. 4½d., the sum of £10,774 9s. 3d., representing the Admiralty's initial offer, having already been paid in advance. This compared with the company's claim for just under £29,000, a figure which included an element representing the fall in the value of money which took place after the company had purchased the rum which the Admiralty subsequently requisitioned. The cost to the company of replacing its stocks was consequently increased. In the submission of the brewery, this constituted 'other circumstances of the case'. But the submission was bound to fail. The inflation was not due to the Admiralty's action but was a general consequence of war conditions. As such, the court was bound to ignore it as a factor.

The case of *Newcastle Breweries Ltd* fits neatly into the general picture of compensation struggles during the First World War. For those individuals and

16. War Compensation Court, *Second Report* (London, 1923), pp. 31–34. See chapter 13, below.

companies prepared for a lengthy battle with the authorities, the promise of something more than compensation for direct loss was held out. But success in the courts, which held out the prospect of compensation levels reflecting inflated market values, proved to be a false omen. Parliament, albeit with bad grace, agreed to move the goalposts with the Indemnity Act 1920, and Regulation 2B was back in business.

9

The Pulses of the Nation

It is surely a paradox that the military victory achieved by British forces over their German adversaries in November 1918 can be attributed to a substantial degree to British success in feeding its civilian population adequately. For it was not superior British military strength but the failure of German morale, due in part to starvation at home, which reduced their military resistance and prompted the enemy to lay down their arms.[1]

The British success was the more astonishing in that the United Kingdom had a limited agricultural sector and was more dependent on imported foodstuffs (amounting to 60 per cent of its total food supply and 80 per cent of its wheat) than was Germany which, relatively speaking, was self-sufficient in food production.[2] Moreover, the belated shift in Britain towards central control by the Ministry of Food, set up in December 1916 under the direction of a Food Controller, demonstrates how much ground was made up. The food question and the controversy over government intervention were major contributory factors in the downfall of the Asquith coalition, in which responsibility for the matters pertaining to food had lain with the Board of Trade under Sir Walter Runciman, noted for his aversion to state interference.

With the onset of unrestricted German submarine warfare in February 1917, British shipping losses, and of course, food cargo losses, became so serious that Admiral Jellicoe informed an American naval colleague in April that, 'it is impossible for us to go on with the war if losses like this continue'.[3] Shipping losses continued but much of the credit for the eventual British success lay

---

1. It is acknowledged that this is an oversimplified explanation but it reflects one of the principal factors in Germany's defeat. See L. Margaret Barnett, *British Food Policy during the First World War* (London, 1985), p. xiii; P.E. Dewey, *British Agriculture in the First World War* (London, 1989); Avner Offer, *The First World War: An Agrarian Interpretation* (Oxford, 1989).

2. For this and subsequent information, I have relied on the following sources: Barnett, ibid.; Mancur Olson Jr, *The Economics of the Wartime Shortage* (Durham, NC, 1963), ch. 4; Sir William H. Beveridge, *British Food Control* (Oxford, 1928); José Harris, *William Beveridge: A Biography* (Oxford, 1977), ch. 10; ibid., 'Bureaucrats and Businessmen in British Food Control, 1916–19', in Kathleen Burk (ed.), *War and the State: the Transformation of British Government, 1914–1919* (London, 1982), ch. 6; F.H. Coller, *A State Trading Adventure* (Oxford, 1925).

3. Olson, *The Economics of the Wartime Shortage*, p. 84.

with the new ministries set up by Lloyd George's government which had replaced the Asquith coalition in December 1916.

The Ministries of Shipping and Food were endowed with extensive powers under the Defence of the Realm Acts (DORA) to such an extent that 90 per cent of the United Kingdom's imports were eventually controlled by the government, while the Ministry of Food, together with two royal commissions (on the supply of sugar and wheat) became, in effect, a 'state trading adventure' with turnover exceeding £1,400,000,000. The central devices used by the Ministry of Food to secure equitable food distribution were price controls and rationing between 1916 and 1919. These were made more urgent by the conjunction of, on the one hand, a home demand as unemployment fell and wages rose, and on the other, the increasing shortages of shipping and cargo space.

Rising food prices had prompted speculators to move into the market and some hoarding occurred, while industrial discontents began to manifest themselves, only partially appeased by inflationary wage settlements. The pressures proved too much for Runciman and his *laissez-faire* approach. A month prior to the fall of the Asquith coalition, the Board of Trade were granted certain powers under DORA over the production, price and distribution of food, a strategy which William Beveridge, within the Board, was instrumental in formulating. With the arrival of Lloyd George at 10 Downing Street, a Food Controller was appointed and the Ministry of Food set up. The first Food Controller, Lord Devonport, a Liberal businessman, was by most accounts a failure. He failed to delegate or to appreciate the consumer point of view and introduced schemes of control of peripheral significance. Most damningly, his schemes were not grounded in economic commonsense. While he imposed price controls, for example, on potatoes, he failed to control the wholesale supply, prompting producers and wholesalers to withhold supplies from the market.

Meanwhile, continued shortages of commodities inevitably fanned further discontent which was given expression both in Parliament and in the newspapers. Devonport resigned in May 1917 to be replaced by D.A. Thomas, Lord Rhondda, another Liberal businessman, whose approach was the opposite to that of Devonport: fellow-businessmen were retained by the ministry, but in the capacity of technical advisers rather than policy makers. He ensured that retailers' accounts were publicly audited. Regional food commissioners and local food control committees were established, so that local interests might be represented. A national Consumers' Council was set up to represent the perspective of the consumer, particularly the working-class consumer, in the formulation of policy. The council itself was also asked to scrutinise food control orders as they were being drafted. The new regime also sought to corner the market in commodities by bulk purchases both from overseas and from home. Retail price controls would be effective, while supplies and proper distribution would be maintained. The mistakes of the Devonport era were not to be repeated. It was in this way that the state trading adventure, mentioned previously, was organised, with 85 per cent of civilian food supplies being controlled by the Ministry of Food, even yielding a small profit of 0.05 per cent at the end of it all. General food rationing was introduced in February 1918 and covered most basic commodities. Food queues became rare thereafter as the moral message was reinforced by over 70,000 prosecutions and the imposition of fines amounting to over £400,000 for breaches of the Food Controller's orders.

The controls over Britain's food supplies emerged in three phases. The first period to December 1916 was characterised by a slow shift from virtual absence of controls (except in the case of the royal commission covering sugar, most of which before the war had been imported from Austria and Germany) to the first attempts at direct controls. Weak DORA powers to control production, prices and distribution were conferred on the Board of Trade, while the government established the Royal Commission on Wheat Supplies, an executive body which bought in bulk from abroad. The second phase involved the establishment of a Ministry of Food and the appointment of a Food Controller. Ad hoc controls were imposed, including a defective power to regulate the prices of beans, peas and pulse. Inchoate controls only fuelled demands for more rigorous food regulation and for a more competent ministry. That arrived in the third phase with the appointment of Lord Rhondda in June 1917, until his death a year later. As William Beveridge remarked, this period:

> witnesses the establishment of complete control over nearly everything eaten and drunk by 40,000,000 persons. The civilian population is catered for like an army; nothing is left to chance or private enterprise. The whole of the essential supplies imported or homegrown are bought or requisitioned by the Food Controller at fixed prices; the manufacturers, importers and distributors become in various ways his agents on commission; they handle and distribute at fixed prices or fixed margins of profit under his direction.[4]

The Ministry of Food continued until 1921, being preoccupied after July 1918 with international food import programmes, initial decontrol pressures after the Armistice and the reimposition of further controls in 1919 and 1920, giving rise, in the case of the Milk Prices Order of April 1919, to the controversy resulting in the House of Lords ruling in *Attorney-General* v. *Wilts Utd. Dairies* (1921). In that case the Food Controller's 2d a pint levy on certain milk producers was held to be disguised executive taxation, and therefore unlawful.[5]

The orders pouring out from the Food Controller filled 700 pages of the *Food Supply Manual*. As Beveridge wryly commented,

4. Beveridge, *British Food Control*, pp. 2–3.
5. *Attorney-General* v. *Wilts United Dairies* (1921) 37 T.L.R. 884(C.A.); (1922) 38 T.L.R. 781(H.L.).

One member of Parliament declared that, in despair of reading or counting the orders of the Ministry he had taken to weighing them and found that on one day in February [1918] he had received nearly half a pound's weight.[6]

There were almost five hundred food control orders by the end of 1918, omitting all the general licences, authorisations, directions and notices issued under the orders themselves. According to Beveridge, only two or three orders were found to be legally defective. Apart from the Beans and Milk Orders already mentioned, the Food Hoarding Order of 1917 sought to include tea within its ambit, only for King's Bench in April 1918 to rule that the commodity was not a 'food' at all, apparently because it was not so defined in the Sale of Food and Drugs Act 1899. Moreover, a scientific analysis would likewise exclude it from the category of foodstuffs, as it produced no calories.[7] Nonetheless, the hoarding of tea could not be tolerated by Lord Rhondda, so an amending order was issued a week after the High Court ruling.

Turning to the controversy surrounding the Beans, Peas, and Pulses Order and its impact on government decision-making, it is appropriate to spell out the legal powers granted to the Food Controller under DORA. By Regulation 2F of the Defence of the Realm Regulations, he was given powers, from January 10 1917, of intervention in the food market. Under paragraph one of Reg. 2F, he could make orders regulating, or giving directions with respect to, the production, manufacture, treatment, use, storage, distribution, supply, sale or purchase of, or other dealing in, or measures to be taken in relation to any article (including orders as to maximum and minimum price),[8] where deemed expedient to safeguard the country's food supply. Such provision did not, however, confer ownership or possession of articles of food on the Food Controller. That was governed by paragraph two which provided that:

> The Food Controller may by order require all or any persons owning or having power to sell or dispose of any article, or any stocks thereof, to place at the disposal of the Controller, the article, or the whole or any part of the stocks thereof, as may be directed by the Controller on such terms as he may direct, and to deliver to the Controller or to any person or persons named by him the article or stocks in such quantities and at such times as the Controller may require, where it appears to him necessary or expedient to make any such order for the purpose of encouraging or maintaining the food supply of the country.

Compensation for requisition would be payable either by agreement or by arbitration. In the case of the latter, the arbitrator was to have regard to the cost of production and to the allowance of a reasonable profit, without

6. Beveridge, *British Food Control*, p. 69.
7. The case, which was not identified by Beveridge, was *Hinde* v. *Allmond* (1918) 34 T.L.R. 403.
8. For the view that the Food Controller lacked effective price controls, see Barnett, *British Food Policy*, p. 100. Yet as he had powers to fix maximum and minimum prices, there seems no reason why he could not requisition commodities after having fixed maximum prices.

necessarily taking into account the market price of the article at the time. Clearly, the government wished to offer little encouragement to producers or wholesalers who might seek to play the markets by withholding goods in order to raise prices, with a view to obtaining speculative profits from government requisition.

Paragraph three declared that any order under Reg. 2F could apply generally or particularly, and any such order could direct that all contracts, or any class of contracts, or any special contract, affected by the order, were to be abrogated or remain in force absolutely or subject to modification.

In the spring of 1917, as wheat supplies to the United Kingdom fell in volume, the Food Controller, Lord Devonport, appealed to the population to reduce their intake of bread. Substitute foods were recommended to those who could afford the cost, and beans, peas and lentils were identified as suitable alternatives. With increasing demand prices rose, and very soon the commodities became the object of intense speculation, 'in which consignments afloat changed hands time after time'.[9]

Galvanised into remedial action, Lord Devonport issued an order under Reg. 2F on 1 May 1917, requisitioning all imported Burmah beans and peas which had arrived in the United Kingdom by then, all those which were then in transit and all those which would arrive in the future. The price to be paid to the 'original consignees', that is, to the importers, was £37 a ton, which compared with the then current market price of £78 and the pre-war price of £22. A fortnight later, a similar order was issued, requisitioning all other beans, peas and pulse, at a price to be fixed subsequently by the Food Controller.

As this second order, the Beans, Peas and Pulse (Requisition) Order 1917 was to give rise to litigation, we may quote its relevant provisions.[10] By virtue of paragraph one, the Food Controller ordered:

(1) All persons owning or having power to sell or dispose of any beans, peas or pulse suitable for human food which have arrived in the United Kingdom or which shall hereafter arrive (except beans, peas, and pulse arrived which have been sold by the original consignees and paid for by the purchasers) shall place and hold such beans, peas and pulse at the disposal of the Food Controller;

(2) The beans, peas and pulse are taken over by the Food Controller from the original consignees and the Food Controller will subsequently communicate to them the prices which he will be prepared to pay for the same;

(3) ... all contracts made by the original consignees or any persons claiming under them for the sale of any beans, peas and pulse taken over under this Order are cancelled and sellers and/or buyers are to stand released from all liability as to brokerage.

9. Beveridge, *British Food Control*, pp. 36–37; Barnett, *British Food Policy*, p. 119; Coller, *State Trading Adventure*, pp. 45–46.
10. S.R. & O., No. 457, 16 May 1917.

By 23 August 1917, about 60 per cent of the goods covered by the orders, amounting to 580,000 tons under the first order, and 120,000 tons under the second order, had been requisitioned.[11] The traders affected had cooperated with the provisions to enable the goods, on arrival at the docks, to be taken by the Wheat Commission on behalf of the Food Controller. The original consignees received payment as stipulated in the orders, the produce then passing to wholesalers at a price which enabled subsequent retailers to sell in the shops at prices fixed by the Food Controller. In no single case, according to the ministry, had the original consignees, who had actually imported the goods, complained of the government's action. The departmental view was that the orders had worked in practice and had wrought no injustice.

Difficulties for the government were soon posed by those 'claiming under the original consignees', that is, those who had entered into contracts with the importers while the goods were still afloat and who now claimed that ownership in the goods had already passed to them. Those purchasers were middlemen, at one or more removes from the importers who were the 'original consignees'. On each resale, the price would go up. In an inflationary wartime climate it would rise dramatically, bearing harshly upon the consumer, particularly the working-class consumer for whom the rise in food prices operated like regressive taxation.

The encroachment of middlemen was seen by Beveridge as an illustration of pure profiteering. There had been extensive dealings in the commodities and prices had risen to an 'extraordinary figure'. The dealers were particularly unwelcome as men having had no previous connection with the trade, who now saw an opportunity to make vast profits. It had been estimated that Burmah beans had been resold from seven to ten times over.

In one case, involving butter beans, twenty-five tons had been bought at £36 a ton on 16 November 1916. They were sold on December 13 at £44 a ton and then resold on 30 March 1917 at £89 a ton. But the beans only arrived in the United Kingdom at the end of May 1917. Thus, on the basis of the order, the original consignees would be paid £37 a ton, generating for them a small profit of £25 on the consignment, while the two subsequent sales would be cancelled. If, however, such sales went through, the first seller, after the original consignee, would earn £200 that is, 25 times (£44–£36), and the second seller £1,125, that is, 25 times (£89–£44). Two other examples were given. In the first case,[12] 315 bags of Madagascar butter beans aboard the *Sidon* and the

---

11. PRO, MAF 60/131, 'Memorandum on Beans, Peas and Pulse Requisition Order', unsigned and undated, though probably drafted by Beveridge as the Cabinet memorandum submitted by Lord Rhondda.   See PRO, CAB 24/27, G.T.2133, 26 September 1917.

12. This was presumably 1917.   J.R. Clynes, Rhondda's parliamentary secretary (and shortly thereafter his successor), in citing this example in Parliament on 6 May 1918, gave the date as 22 January. *Hansard* did not state the year of the transaction.   But Clynes followed, almost to the letter, the memorandum drafted in 1917 (note 11, above).   Only the briefest mention of the affair appears in Clynes' autobiography.   See J.R. Clynes, *Memoirs, 1869–1924* (London, 1937), p. 218.   For the Commons debate on 6 May 1918, see H.C. Deb., 5th series, 105, cols. 1899–1933.

Warrior were bought by Amis, Swain & Co. on 21 January at £43 a ton c.i.f. and sold on 9 March at £70, plus one-half per cent c.i.f. This represented a profit of just over £400 or 64 per cent. In the second case, 515 bags of the same goods, arriving on the same vessels, were bought by Amis, Swain & Co. on 17 November at £36 a ton c.i.f. and sold to Gaskain, Barker & David Ltd. on 13 December at £44 a ton c.i.f. Gaskains then resold the consignment on 30 March at £90 per ton landed terms (equal to £89 per ton c.i.f.) The total profit on those two transactions was £1,311 14s. 0d., or about 147 per cent on the original purchase price of £36 per ton c.i.f. Of this profit, Amis, Swain & Co. claimed 22 per cent, and Gaskains 125 per cent. Under the terms of the order, the Wheat Commission would purchase the consignment from Amis, Swain & Co. at £37 a ton, giving the latter a profit of £515, while the subsequent contracts would be cancelled.

Early indications of legal problems over the implementation of the orders emerged in July 1917, when an enquiry was put to the Wheat Supplies Commission in connection with one particular transaction. Here, 3,000 bags of Brazilian beans were being imported by Messrs Methuen & Sons to London and 2,000 had been off-loaded to a firm in Mincing Lane, Wimble, Sons & Co., which passed them on to a neighbouring firm, W.T. Sargant & Sons.[13] The latter then sold 1,000 bags to a Mr C.P. Johnson, further up Mincing Lane. The beans arrived in London aboard the SS *Manchuria* on 13 May 1917 and on 16 May the three subsequent purchasers paid the sums due under their respective contracts. The Beans, Peas and Pulse (Requisition) Order now intervened, and the third purchaser, Johnson, possibly fearing a financial loss on the introduction of price controls, raised an action against the second purchaser, Messrs W.T. Sargant & Sons, claiming the contract was cancelled, that as a result of the new order the bags were now at the disposal of the Food Controller, and demanding the return of his money. The order, as we saw, did not requisition all supplies, whether arrived or in transit. It contained an exception in paragraph one for beans, peas and pulse which had already arrived and which had been sold by the original consignees, and also paid for by the purchasers before the order took effect. As stated above, the beans had arrived on 13 May, had been sold earlier, and the purchasers had settled their contracts on 16 May itself, the date of the order, but not the date of publication of the order, which only appeared in the press the next day. The ministry were informed by the Wheat Supplies Commission that the latter body had not excepted from requisition commodities sold and paid for on May 16. If a different approach had been taken,

> endless confusion would have arisen in view of the fact that through the extensive speculation in these articles, the documents passed through many hands. It would therefore be a physical impossibility either to get back documents already passed

13. PRO, MAF 60/131, 'Re the Beans, Peas & Pulse (Requisition) Order 1917', c. 18 July 1917; *Johnson* v. *Sargant & Sons* [1918] 1 K.B. 101.

from the shippers into other possession, or to trace the goods to which they referred.[14]

The next day, the ministry's legal adviser, A. Andrewes-Uthwatt (later, as Lord Uthwatt, a judicial member of the House of Lords between 1946 and 1949) wrote to Sir John Beale, the secretary of the Wheat Commission, suggesting that if the commission simply reimbursed Johnson in exchange for the beans, 'His cause of action against Sargeant [sic] would go – but I don't know'.[15] The remark perhaps signified the weakness of Johnson's claim against Sargant, as well, of course, as the doubtful legality of the commission's decision to requisition supplies sold and paid for on May 16. As Mr Justice Bailhache concluded:

> While I agree that the rule is that a statute takes effect on the earliest moment of the day on which it is passed or on which it is declared to come into operation, there is about statutes a publicity even before they come into operation which is absent in the case of many Orders such as that with which we are now dealing; indeed, if certain Orders are to be effective at all, it is essential that they should not be known until they are actually published.

He therefore held that the order only came into effect when it became known. Therefore the sale to Sargant had been concluded and paid for by that day, and Johnson's action failed.[16]

Uthwatt had more deep-seated doubts about the order than mere transitional complications. As he informed Beale:

> For your information – and I know you will treat this as confidential – I advised Devonport when he made his requisitioning Order for Burmah Peas and Beans, that it was probable that the clause cancelling contracts was ultra vires, – and certainly the case if the documents had passed.[17]

Uthwatt added that he had heard that 'some sportsman' had just commenced an action to have the order declared *ultra vires*.

Whether 'sportsman' was a literal description or signified a party prepared to gamble in the courts of law was not clarified. What is beyond dispute is that, with the backing of other traders, the firm of J. Hindhaugh & Co., a subsequent purchaser of beans from an original consignee, raised an action in King's Bench against the Food Controller some days later. The Attorney-General's assessment of the claim was that where the consignee had, before

14. Ibid., A.W. Hurst, Royal Commission on Wheat Supplies, to Ulick H. Wintour, Ministry of Food, 19 July 1917.
15. Ibid., Andrewes-Uthwatt, Ministry of Food, to Sir John Beale, Royal Commission on Wheat Supplies, 20 July 1917.
16. *Johnson v. Sargant & Sons* [1918] 1 K.B.101, at p. 103.
17. PRO, MAF 60/131, Andrewes-Uthwatt to Sir John Beale, 20 July 1917.

the date of the order, parted with the documents of ownership, then the order could not require him to retrieve the documents from the purchaser or otherwise affect him. Presumably, also, the subsequent purchasers would be unaffected by the order, and could not be compelled to disgorge their gains. The commission was advised to settle with the persons who actually held the documents at the date of the order, even though they were not the original consignees.[18]

The challenge to the order of 16 May by Messrs J. Hindhaugh & Co. and their collaborators came before Mr Justice Rowlatt on 30 July. The plaintiffs, who were the original consignees, did not seek to challenge the legality of Reg. 2F nor of the first paragraph of the order which requisitioned the goods. What they argued was that in the circumstances of a particular transaction, they were not persons 'owning or having power to sell or dispose of any beans, peas or pulse . . .' in the words of paragraph one, and consequently could not be affected by the order. At the date of the order, the goods were still at sea, although the shipping documents had not only reached the plaintiffs but had, in turn, been transferred by them to the consignees' purchasers. The contracts for sale had been completed at the date of the order and therefore the plaintiffs no longer owned nor had any power to sell or dispose of the goods. The regulation was not retrospective and did not authorise any order to have retrospective effect. Insofar as the order purported to impose any duty on the plaintiffs, it was, the argument ran, *ultra vires*.

The decision in favour of the plaintiffs only applied to goods afloat at the date of the order, the importers of which had completed their sale contracts. It did not prevent the Food Controller from obtaining the goods in question, though he was required to do so from those who had an interest in them at the date of the order. Any uncompleted contracts at that date could then be annulled, but while the difficulty of completed deals was a transitional one which would disappear eventually, the cost to the Exchequer was bound to be hefty if the Wheat Commission requisitioned the beans.

In the light of the decision, Beveridge put forward the alternatives to his department. The first was to accept the High Court's decision, which meant that the Wheat Commission would have to pay over to each of the persons who speculated in the beans the profits of such speculation. The other possibility was to introduce a Bill in Parliament, validating the May 1917 orders. Beveridge believed that the moral arguments in favour of legislating were powerful. He also considered the possibility that, since the traders were acting together in the matter, the mere threat of a bill might induce them to agree to comply with the spirit of the orders.[19]

The proposal was not welcomed by Sir John Beale, who thought it would

18. Ibid., W.H. Beveridge, Ministry of Food, to E.R. Holland, Royal Commission on Wheat Supplies, 27 July 1917.
19. Ibid., W.H.B, 'Decision of High Court as to Beans, Peas and Pulse Order', 23 August 1917.

be both undesirable and unsuccessful.[20] The danger lay, particularly, in the presentation of a bill. As it would affect individual subjects, it would have to be referred to a select committee. They, in turn, would examine Ministry of Food witnesses who would then have to admit that the scheme of control in the orders differed from that adopted in the case of other foodstuffs; that the control of other foodstuffs had been conducted equitably; and that the orders would have caused grave hardship to a large number of traders who had been carrying on their businesses in a legitimate manner to the advantage of the country.

He recognised Beveridge's point about profiteering but questioned whether the select committee would be willing to adopt the principle, 'that the innocent and the guilty should be equally punished'. Either the committee would refuse to pass the preamble to the Bill, or they would insert such amendments or protection clauses as to make it valueless. He pointed out that while the order served a useful purpose by putting a 'dead stop to a notorious speculation in the articles covered' by them, the ministry's advisers had expressed some misgivings about the provisions. Therefore, 'there would be little gain from legalising them now'.

What seemed especially to concern Beale was the need to 'secure the confidence and esteem of the Commercial Community', as well as consumers: 'Traders rightly look to the Law Courts as guardians of fair dealing and in my opinion they would be seriously alarmed if Parliament was asked to reverse the only important decision of the Courts adverse to the Ministry'.[21] He therefore advised that the ministry seek negotiations to settle with the trade, which had been more or less united in bringing proceedings, and considered that a lump sum payment of £1,000,000 or £1,500,000 might be required. The trade might not prove difficult to deal with, as many of them were also earning income as government agents for the sale and distribution of other commodities. They were therefore 'hardly likely to contemplate pushing their advantage to undue lengths'. Were the legal ruling to stand, the cost to the Treasury could reach £4,500,000, which represented the total amount involved in transactions in the goods.

Lord Rhondda put the case for legislating to a Cabinet meeting on 2 October advising that the government should immediately announce their intention to legislate in the next parliamentary session.[22] The War Cabinet, however, wanted a broader picture painted of the legal problems confronting not just the Food Controller, but also other departments. It therefore asked the Law Officers for their views regarding more general legislation to regularise those government actions of 'doubtful legality', past or future.[23]

---

20. Ibid., J.F.B., 'Beans, Peas & Pulse Orders', 4 September 1917.
21. Ibid.
22. PRO, CAB 24/27, G.T.2133, 26 September 1917.
23. PRO, CAB 23/4, W.C.244(1), 2 October 1917. The following week, the Secretary of State for War, Lord Derby, presented his bill to neutralise the outcome of the Shoreham Aerodrome hearing in the House of Lords, and to require owners to resort to the Defence

The Law Officers' memorandum was necessarily wide-ranging, as required, while at the same time spelling out the legal intricacies of the *Hindhaugh* decision.[24] Looking also at the compensation issues arising from the Shoreham Aerodrome case and at some difficulties relating to a number of other defence regulations, their pessimistic conclusion was that:

> if the Prerogative or the Regulations do not permit the acquisition or the use of land without a legal right of compensation, they cannot authorize the taking of ships, food, forage or coal without a like right arising, and consequently if compensation in the case of land is to be measured by actual value, as distinguished from the actual loss of the person dispossessed, the same rule must apply to goods and chattels, and, as pointed out above, the provisions which direct the assessment of compensation upon any less favourable basis are all *ultra vires*.

The War Cabinet discussed the memorandum on 7 November, but deferred taking any action until the Law Officers themselves could be present.[25] Meanwhile, the ministry undertook the drafting of a bill to rectify the *Hindhaugh* decision, and the Defence of the Realm (Peas, Beans and Pulse (Orders) Bill was presented to the Cabinet on 28 November.[26] At that meeting, Christopher Addison, the Minister of Munitions, expressed the view that the main object of the Bill, to penalise speculative dealings in necessaries during war, was one which would have widespread support both in the House of Commons and in the country as a whole. The Solicitor-General, Sir Gordon Hewart, however, pointed out that the draft would not prevent an original consignee from applying to the DRLC for compensation. This was incompatible with the provisions in the orders themselves for payment of compensation to the original consignee at £36 a ton or at a price to be fixed subsequently. Therefore some redrafting would be required. This took longer than anticipated and it was early March 1918 before Lord Rhondda could resubmit the Bill to the War Cabinet, after the Solicitor-General had approved it.[27] In the Commons, the Bill had its second reading on 6 May 1918, during which J.R. Clynes, the parliamentary secretary, faced some determined opposition to the measure.[28] He recounted the history of the orders, the speculative dealings and the legal challenge upheld by Mr. Justice

---

of the Realm Losses Commission (DRLC) to recover for direct loss. Again, the War Cabinet indicated a preference for a more general bill of indemnity. See PRO, CAB 23/4, W.C.247(6), 9 October 1917.

24. PRO, CAB 24/4, G.165, October 1917, 'Legality of Certain Acts Done Under the Defence of the Realm Regulations'. Sir Edward Carson, Minister Without Portfolio and former Law Officer, also advised that the defect in the Beans, Peas, and Pulse Order be rectified by legislation. See CAB 23/4, W.C.253(5), 19 October 1917. See above, chapter 5.

25. PRO, CAB 23/4, W.C.267(18), 7 November 1917.

26. PRO, CAB 23/4, W.C.285(14), 28 November 1917.

27. PRO, MAF 60/54, 'Defence of the Realm (Beans, Peas & Pulse Orders) Bill. Memorandum by the Food Controller', 9 March 1918.

28. H.C. Deb., 5th series, 105, 6 May 1918, col.1930.

Rowlatt, and added that if the Bill were not passed, then 'persons who were not legitimately entitled to be engaged in this process', would be entitled to large sums from the ministry or the commission. The figure which he had heard was £600,000 (considerably less than previous departmental estimates), though that figure was inexact.

He believed that opposition to the measure was because it constituted an unprecedented interference with the sanctity of contract. His reply was that such transactions as those should not be regarded as contracts that ought to be observed in such abnormal circumstances. The contractors were making inordinate profits to which, morally, they were not entitled.

Debate was joined on matters of high principle. Sir Frederick Banbury did not disappoint: 'I look on this Bill as one of the most tyrannical attempts of the Ministry of Food to get over a legal decision. If a king had done that sort of thing he might have lost his head.'[29] Banbury proclaimed that he preferred to locate justice in a court of law rather than within a government department. Moreover, the Bill was to be retrospective in its effect, legalising orders of the ministry which the court had declared illegal. With a rhetorical flourish, he foresaw the end of sanctity of contracts, which was the foundation of all business transactions and of the liberty of the subject.

Another M.P., Thomas Lough, claimed that the ministry itself had been responsible for some of the profiteering which had occurred, 'for when commodities had been bought at a certain sum, they had required dealers to sell at a greatly enhanced price'. The ministry's policy had led to the cancellation of import orders, which resulted in higher prices and scarcity. More constructive opposition came from those who advocated that some settlement be reached with the traders involved, rather than strip them of their profits by means of the Bill. Clynes offered to consider possible safeguards for those to be affected. But as the Bill would go forward if approved on its second reading, it was not clear what room for manoeuvre remained. After a division, it was in fact given a majority of over one hundred. Nonetheless, the spirited opposition in Parliament prompted the Food Controller to approach the Treasury shortly before the committee stage of the Bill, to secure funds to compensate *bona fide* traders as distinct from speculators.[30] The Food Controller believed that unless some concession were made, the passage of the Bill might be endangered. The sum in mind was now down to around £250,000. Treasury sanction was given and Clynes was able to announce in Parliament on 17 June that, as soon as the Bill became law, the Food Controller would investigate transactions affected by it, and would consider making allowance to legitimate, that is, to regular traders.[31] Allowances would be 'limited to a proper profit to such persons on the normal turnover in these articles'. A proper profit was not that which

29. Ibid., col.1903.
30. PRO, MAF 60/131, W.H. Peat, Financial Secretary, Ministry of Food, to Treasury, 12 June 1918.
31. H.C. Deb., 5th series, 107, 17 June 1918, col.134.

would have been made if the transactions had stood, but was one related to the usual pre-war rate of profit in that class of transaction and to the other relevant circumstances of the case (comparable to Reg. 2B in the *Newcastle Breweries* case). On 10 August, a press notice announced that Mr A.A. Patterson, former president of the London Corn Trade Association, and deputy chairman of the London Court of Arbitration, would investigate and decide upon transactions affected by the act, which had become law on June 27.[32]

In respect to the Beans, Peas and Pulse Order 1917, the crisis of legality during the war was now over, having provided only fleeting glimpses of clashes over matters of high principle. It was not so much the claim of the sanctity of private property against the extravagant requisitioning claims of the executive, but of sanctity of contract which was raised as a bulwark against the over-mighty executive. In this case, the executive did not prolong its fudging or bluffing in order to await the welcome relief of military victory, but quickly resorted to Parliament after Mr Justice Rowlatt's adverse ruling. No doubt Clynes calculated that a measure designed to restrain the excesses of profiteering middlemen would hardly prove to be unpopular, especially where food controls were concerned. The voluble eccentricities of characters like Sir Frederick Banbury, whose voices represented lost causes, could be ignored where the executive enjoyed, during the years of battle, the overwhelming support of an obedient Parliament, among the bulk of whose members the instinct to preserve fundamental liberties was submerged in the *mentalité* of war measures. An additional feature of the reality of the times was the prescience of the Food Controller that his orders when issued were, at the least, of doubtful legality. His own legal adviser had told him so. Yet rather than seek new powers from Parliament at the outset, the Food Controller was content to proceed regardless, hoping that none would be so unpatriotic as to challenge his actions. No doubt, *bona fide* traders would resent the accusation that to litigate against the government was to behave unpatriotically, though there is no indication that the plaintiffs had directed their mind to such question. Perhaps they were motivated solely by financial considerations of a selfish nature. Arguably, they were performing a public duty in going to law.

The saga of the Beans, Peas, and Pulse Order continued for some years after the war. Two of the firms affected by the order, claiming to be original consignees, Messrs Meulemeester & Co. and Messrs Amis, Swain & Co., had been awarded £9,000 and £15,178 respectively under arbitration.[33] In the case of the former, the Wheat Commission had appealed from the arbitration under the Arbitration Act 1889, but the judge, Mr Justice Bailhache, had upheld the award.

In the Amis, Swain case, the arbitrator was appointed in pursuance of Reg. 2F and of the order of 16 May 1917. Again, the commission appealed,

32. Copy in PRO, MAF 60/131.
33. PRO, MAF 60/131, J.W. Tetley to F.H. Coller, 6 April 1922.

this time direct to the Court of Appeal, which also considered a further appeal by the Wheat Commission in the Meulemeester case at the same time. The Court of Appeal allowed the appeal in the latter case, so that nothing would be payable to the claimant, but the Amis, Swain case was more complex. There had been eleven separate transactions, in only two of which the Court of Appeal held the claimants to be the original consignees. Both the legal costs and the costs of arbitration relating to the nine cases won by the department were to be paid by the company. Three years later, the matter of costs had still not been resolved. In 1924 the President of the Board of Trade, Sidney Webb, had agreed that the arbitrator's fee should be paid by the department. But that had not been welcomed by F.H. Coller, a subsequent Permanent Secretary to the Ministry of Food and historian of the *State Trading Adventure*.

Coller was of the opinion that 'if any concession were made, it would satisfy no one and give us endless trouble'.[34] With the fall of the minority Labour government, the question could be reconsidered, and was raised again in May 1925, presumably at the instigation of Amis, Swain & Co., whose financial position was insecure. Coller doubted whether any favourable treatment for the company would be beneficial. In a comment with unsavoury undertones, he remarked:

> If it were a question of helping Amis, Swain & Co., I should be glad to recommend an ex gratia payment, merely on the grounds of their utility to us in the disposal of dried fruits. But, whatever happens, Amis, Swain & Co. will get nothing, any additional money would go first to their Hebrew [sic] solicitors and ultimately perhaps to their creditors.

Coller, it seems, had the knack of justifying principle by reference to the unwelcome consequences which would flow from any departure from that principle. Whether Amis, Swain & Co., as distinct from Meulemeester, deserved to be abandoned by the ministry to their post-war fate after the events of 1917 is open to debate.

34. PRO, MAF 60/131, Frank H. Coller to J.W. Tetley, 11 May, 1925.

10

HMT 39BBB

The requisitioning of ships and cargo space by the Crown was yet another area of government's wartime activities which gave rise to doubts and uncertainties as to compensation.[1] As with other kinds of property, the Crown's legal claims to requisition shipping for national defence were grounded in both prerogative and statute, but whether those legal bases imported a legal right to compensation was a matter of dispute.

The right to requisition ships per se by virtue of the royal prerogative and for the purpose of the defence of the realm seemed in no doubt.[2] Precedents could be traced from the time of the Plantagenet kings to the close of the seventeenth century. While the prerogative was not invoked in the eighteenth century in order to requisition vessels, this was because the necessity to resort to this method did not arise. The legal power itself still existed.

In the medieval period, trading vessels were recruited for naval purposes by the royal warrant of 'stay and arrest', as there was no distinction between commercial and fighting ships. During the Tudor period, such a differentiation began to occur and by the time of the Commonwealth, merchantmen were no longer used as fighting vessels, although they were requisitioned as troopships and storeships. Gradually the expansion of the mercantile marine led to a change of policy away from requisitioning under the prerogative and towards the practice of chartering at reasonable rates on the open market. There is no trace of requisitioning during the Revolutionary and Napoleonic wars, though the prerogative power itself was confirmed by the courts in 1743 in *R. v. Broadfoot* (1743) Foster's Cr. Cas. 154.

The eminent legal historian, Sir William Holdsworth, writing in the *Law Quarterly Review* in 1919,[3] had concluded that the Crown retained a prerogative to requisition all British ships wherever they might be situated: whether

1. For general consideration of shipping during the war, see, apart from sources cited below, J.A. Salter, *Allied Shipping Control* (Oxford, 1921); S.J. Hurwitz, *State Intervention in Great Britain: A Study of Economic Control and Social Response, 1914–1919* (New York, 1949), ch. xi; and Martin Doughty, *Merchant Shipping and War* (London, 1982), passim.
2. For this and subsequent historical detail, see C. Ernest Fayle, *War and the Shipping Industry* (Oxford, 1927), ch. v.
3. W.S. Holdsworth, 'The Power of the Crown to Requisition British Ships in a National Emergency', *Law Quarterly Review*, 35 (1919), pp. 12–42.

the ships were in territorial waters, on the high seas or in a foreign port was not relevant to the existence of the common law right. He observed that this conclusion appeared to conflict with a recent High Court decision in *Russian Bank of Foreign Trade* v. *Excess Insurance Company* [1919] 1 K.B. 39, but suggested that the judge in that case had lacked the exhaustive historical enquiries of the kind undertaken by Holdsworth and which underpinned the latter's conclusion. Moreover, the decision in *China Mutual Steam Navigation Co. Ltd.* v. *Maclay* [1918] 1 K.B. 33, referred to elsewhere in this study, which dealt with the question of requisitioning the services of shipowners (as distinct from ships themselves) seemed to proceed on the assumption of the existence of prerogative power to requisition ships. During the Boer War, the chartering of troop transports had led to a rapid rise in freights but the transportation of the British Expeditionary Force to France in 1914 was an operation of an altogether different magnitude. Six divisions were sent over (a division being about 30,000 men), together with artillery, horses, stores and other equipment. The Navy was also to play a prominent role for which the South African War offered no precedent. The demand for colliers and other supply vessels was potentially great. But as the historian of shipping during the war, C. Ernest Fayle, pointed out: 'It was, however, the question of time that was the decisive factor.' No matter how accommodating shipowners might be, the negotiation of individual charters could be a protracted business, whereas it was vital from the military point of view that the Admiralty should be able to obtain vessels at a moment's notice and without quibble. For this purpose the prerogative was available. Consequently, on 3 August 1914, on the outbreak of the war, the Crown issued a proclamation stating that it intended to exercise its power of requisitioning over British ships in territorial waters. A proclamation, per se, has no legal authority. The authority to requisition exists independently of a proclamation. Thus it was possible, during the 'precautionary period' before the declaration of war and before the issue of the proclamation, for the Crown to invoke the prerogative (assuming that a precautionary period is one when the defence of the realm is in danger) to requisition a tug, the *Simla*, by telegram on 30 July 1914.[4]

The requisitioning at common law had been undertaken by the Admiralty but, in December 1916, the Ministry of Shipping was established. The ministry was a statutory body and the powers of the Shipping Controller were exercised under statute (though arguably common law powers were available to all components of the Crown). Under section 6 of the New Ministries and Secretaries Act 1916, the Shipping Controller, Sir Joseph Maclay, was granted, inter alia, those powers as might be conferred on him by regulations under

---

4. See *The Sarpen* [1916] P.306. In *The Broadmayne* [1916] P. 64, at pp. 67–68, the Court of Appeal upheld the 'validity' of the proclamation of 3 August, though it is not clear what this confirmation signified. For departmental consideration of the *Broadmayne* case, see PRO, MT 25/22/61774/1918, 'Powers of Shipping Controller. Memorandum to War Cabinet 60, Appendix D', 9 February 1917.

the Defence of the Realm Acts (DORA). The regulation in question was Reg. 39BBB issued on 28 June 1917. It provided that:

> (5) The Shipping Controller may by order requisition or require to be placed at his disposal, in order that they may be used in the manner best suited for the needs of the country, any ships, or any cargo space or passenger accommodation in any ships, or any rights under any charter, freight engagement, or similar contract affecting any ship, and require ships so requisitioned to be delivered to the Controller or any person or persons named by him at such times and at such places as the Controller may require, where it appears to the Controller necessary or expedient to make any such order for the purpose of making shipping available for the needs of the country in such manner as to make the best use thereof having regard to the circumstances of the time.

The background to the promulgation of Reg. 39BBB can be traced to two factors. The first was the doubt whether requisitioning of vessels early in the war under the prerogative by the Admiralty for the purpose of carrying commercial rather than military cargo was lawful, when the underlying motive was to avoid paying market rates. Was national economy an aspect of the defence of the realm? No litigation on that question took place in respect to shipping requisition by the Admiralty although the matter was later analysed in respect to Reg. 2B in the *Newcastle Breweries* case. But the statutory power conferred on the Shipping Controller by Reg. 39BBB, 'to control and regulate any shipping available for the needs of the country in such manner as to make the best use thereof', was later judicially interpreted in *Hudson's Bay Co. v. Maclay* (1920) 36 T.L.R. 469 as empowering the Controller to carry particular cargoes between named ports at fixed rates of freight. This was effectively requisitioning for commercial employment.[5]

The second factor was the extended scheme of requisitioning ordered by the War Cabinet as the unrestricted German submarine campaign commenced from 1 February, 1917. Under the Liner Requisitioning Scheme, for example, whole shipping lines were being taken over by a general letter of requisition. Vessels would be allocated to trades where, for the time being, they were most required, such as the North Atlantic trade, with only a minimum number of vessels being left to maintain the original peacetime connections of the line.[6] However, doubts existed within the Ministry of Shipping as to whether there was at the time (February 1917) power to requisition in that manner. Shipowners had been lodging protests and questions had been raised in the House of Commons. In addition, there were a number of other areas where it was felt that the more specific provisions in a regulation would be preferable to reliance on prerogative powers, especially since all requisitioning was now

---

5. Fayle, *War and the Shipping Industry*, p. 72. See also, below, note 7 and, above, chapter 8.
6. On the scheme, see ibid., ch.xiv.

being effected through the ministry and not the Admiralty. The difficult areas which would be better dealt with by regulation included the conferral of power on the ministry to relet a requisitioned vessel, if she were not at any specific point in time being employed on government service; power to requisition space in cargo vessels and passenger accommodation in passenger vessels; and power to take over from a charterer the benefit of any charterparty into which he had entered without the state requisitioning the ship herself from her owners. The purpose of such latter power was primarily to secure control of neutral vessels chartered to British charterers (which could not be achieved *via* prerogative powers).[7] Reg. 39BBB was thought to cover those areas.

These were the legal bases for shipping requisition as a genre of government activity. As will be seen, more gaps as to the scope of requisitioning were identified by government departments as the war progressed, prompting proposals for amendments and additions to the legal armoury. Moreover, in one significant instance, the scope of the power of requisitioning itself was successfully challenged. In this case, the China Mutual Steam Navigation Company sought to test in the courts the validity of the Liner Requisitioning Scheme. According to Fayle, the judgment of Mr Justice Bailhache, 'shattered at one blow the whole legal basis of the elaborate structure that had been so carefully raised'.[8] The company claimed that the requisitioning letter purported to requisition not only vessels but also the services of owners and crews and that this exceeded the Controller's powers in Reg. 39BBB. The Crown did not, in fact, argue that such a power of requisitioning services existed. It argued merely that the requisitioning letter contained only an aspiration that owners would cooperate in working the scheme. The judge rejected this contention: the letter did propose to requisition services, this was *ultra vires* the regulation and the scheme was null and void. If the company had chosen to press their claim for the release of their vessels, then only retroactive legislation would have protected the government. However, the firm did not embark on this course. Instead, they immediately intimated their intention to waive their rights under the ruling and the other shipping companies affected followed suit. For the shipowners merely wanted, and soon obtained, recognition from

---

7.   Another possible justification for the promulgation of regulations was put forward by a Ministry of Shipping official to J.A. Salter, head of the Requisitioning Branch. He pointed out that the prerogative enabled the Crown to take all necessary steps for the safety and defence of the realm. He observed that the extended scheme of requisitioning ordered by the War Cabinet was no doubt aimed at the proper organisation of the entire shipping resources of the country. But this correspondent understood, also, that, 'the directions of the War Cabinet have been given primarily for financial reasons', which might not justify the exercise of prerogative powers. He concluded: 'It is a sound rule not to rely on the prerogative when it is possible to effect the same object by means of statutory powers'. This memorandum is undated and unsigned. It was possibly written by M.L. Gwyer and was drafted in early 1917. See PRO, MT 25/23/62103/1918.

8.   Fayle, *War and the Shipping Industry*, p. 237. The case was *China Mutual Steam Navigation Company Ltd* v. *Maclay* [1918] 1 K.B. 33.

the government that their cooperation was achieved by volition not coercion. Fayle suggested that by raising their action, the company had:

> performed an important public service, for while there was no desire to scrutinise too closely measures taken for the public safety, the tendency to over-ride constitutional principles by departmental decree had become a serious menace to the liberties of the subject.[9]

More pertinent was the question of compensation for requisitioning. The government fondly comforted itself in the belief that no compensation as of right was due to owners whose properties had been requisitioned under the prerogative for the defence of the realm. Indeed, in *The Zamora*, a decision in April 1916 of the Judicial Committee of the Privy Council on the interpretation of prize law, Lord Parker of Waddington had remarked *obiter*: 'The municipal law of this country does not give compensation to a subject whose land or goods are requisitioned by the Crown.'[10] This corresponded to the Court of Appeal ruling in the Shoreham Aerodrome case the previous year, and was also claimed by the Crown to be the underlying premise for the provision of *ex gratia* compensation to British shipowners whose vessels had been requisitioned under the proclamation of August 1914. That proclamation stated that owners of requisitioned vessels, 'shall receive payment for their use and for services rendered during their employment in the Government Service and compensation for loss or damage thereby occasioned'.

Such payment or compensation was such as might be mutually agreed between the owners and the Admiralty, 'or failing such agreement by the Award of a Board of Arbitration to be constituted and arranged by Us [the Crown] for this purpose'.

Thus an arbitration procedure was introduced to settle disputed cases (the Defence of the Realm Losses Commission (DRLC), by contrast, was never described as an arbitration body). In respect to requisitioning by the Shipping Controller under Reg. 39BBB from June 1917, it was provided in paragraph three of the regulation that:

> Such compensation shall be paid in respect of the use of a ship so requisitioned and for services rendered during the use thereof and for loss and damage thereby occasioned as in default of agreement may be determined by the Board of Arbitration . . .

Thus while the arbitration panel envisaged under the proclamation was assumed to grant awards *ex gratia* and not *ex lege* (on the view that Crown requisitioning under the prerogative conferred no legal right to compensation), the compensation awarded by that same tribunal under the regulation was

9. Fayle, *War and the Shipping Industry*, pp. 237–38.
10. [1916] 2 A.C.77, at p. 100. For the subsequent fate of the *Zamora*, see PRO, MT 23/798/T47401/17.

payable as of right. A further difference between the two schemes was that the proclamation confined requisitioning by the Admiralty to vessels within the British Isles and waters adjacent thereto, while the powers of the Shipping Controller extended to British vessels wherever they might be.

The arbitration body which was established was the Admiralty Transport Arbitration Board consisting of Lord Mersey, president, William Walton, vice-president, and a panel of seventy-two members representing shipping and allied interests. Eleven were government nominees, twenty-six were shipowners, six were bankers and cargo owners, twenty-three represented marine insurance, and the remaining six represented deck officers, engineers and seamen, firemen and stewards. They were nearly all appointed by their representative associations.[11] Mersey (1840–1929) was the son of John Bigham, a Liverpool merchant and shipowner. A barrister and Conservative member of parliament for Liverpool Exchange (1895–97), he became, as Sir J. Bigham, a King's Bench judge (1897–1909), president of the Railway and Canal Commission (1904–9) and of the Probate, Divorce and Admiralty division in 1909–10, and Wreck Commissioner in 1912. He also presided over the *Lusitania* enquiry in 1915. Walton (1844–1929) was a Berkshire magistrate and honorary member of Lloyds.

When cases came before the board, the president would nominate Walton and two other arbitrators from the panel.[12] Written cases would be exchanged between the parties in the first instance and submitted to the arbitrators. They would also hear oral arguments and such evidence as they thought necessary. Most disputes concerned the rate of hire to be paid for requisitioned vessels. But the numbers of such cases were limited by the fact that the president in the early months of the war appointed a number of sub-committees from the panel of arbitrators for the purpose of recommending rates of hire for different categories of vessels. These rates, the 'Blue Book' rates, were based on the principle that shipowners should receive a rate of hire affording a fair commercial profit on the pre-war capital value of their vessels irrespective of the freight market.[13] An internal report observed that at the time when these rates were fixed, they were somewhat in excess of the then current market rates of freight. However, in the light of the upward surge of market rates during the war, reliance on the Blue Book rates had eventually saved the government £300 million.[14] It was also felt within the Admiralty that these rates had generally been accepted by shipowners as affording a fair and reasonable commercial profit,[15] irrespective of the market rates ruling from time to

11.   Fayle, *War and the Shipping Industry*, p. 72.

12.   For this and subsequent details unless otherwise indicated, see PRO, LCO 2/369, 'Requisitioning of Ships Bill, 1917'.

13.   PRO, LCO 2/440, 'Claims Against the Crown in Respect of Requisitioning of Ships', n.d. (1919?).

14.   Details of the fixing of these rates and their relation to market rates are in Fayle, *War and the Shipping Industry*, pp. 79–83.

15.   PRO, LCO 2/369, 'Requisitioning of Ships Bill'.

time.[16] Where disputes had arisen, they had principally been concerned with exceptional cases to which it was contended that the Blue Book rates could not be held to apply. In no case, however, did the board admit the claim of a shipowner to be paid market rates or even rates approximating to market rates. A 'reasonable commercial profit' was all that was conceded.

It may be recalled that a preoccupation of the DRLC was to award compensation only for direct loss. The arbitration board, likewise, admitted only such applications. Claims were of two kinds, those by shipowners and charterers, and secondly, those by third parties, such as cargo owners, whose interests had been prejudiced by the requisitioning. The board ruled, however, that only owners, or charterers for the time being in the position of owners, were entitled to claim under the proclamation. Third parties who experienced interference with their business or loss of profits as a result of requisitioning suffered only indirect loss and therefore could not recover. Charterers not in the position of owners, such as the Elliott Steamship Co., would receive no joy from approaching the DRLC instead. It had, indeed, been proposed by the Lord Chancellor that the DRLC should take over all the functions of the board which would then be abolished. This was resolutely opposed by the Admiralty which believed that the machinery of the board had proved very convenient and effective, that it was now familiar to shipowners and that the particular problems of shipowners justified a special tribunal to handle them. Nagging doubts about the legal position, however, were never absent from the thought of officials. For example, in discussions on a proposed measure dealing with the permanent acquisition of ships, it was observed that the Admiralty were not seeking stronger legal powers in respect to hirings under the proclamation, but nonetheless were, 'hoping that they will be able to stave off Petitions of Right in respect of indirect loss'.[17]

The requisitioning which occurred was not usually a full-blooded taking over of a vessel involving the expulsion of its crew and the installation of Crown servants in their place. The Blue Book rates were based upon an ordinary time charter of vessels by the government. Owners, either expressly or by implication upon receiving a requisitioning notice, were deemed to have entered into such a charter, which at least permitted them to retain a certain amount of control. Requisitioning in the fullest sense applied only in those cases where the owner refused to time charter his vessel to the government or where the nature of the service for which the vessel was required dictated that ownership be transferred, even temporarily. Ships to be used as block ships would be such an instance. Lord Mersey's Board of Arbitration had, however, decided that, by their terms of reference, they were precluded from determining questions of compensation where ships had been permanently acquired. At the same time as the government were considering

---

16. See also Fayle, *War and the Shipping Industry*, ch. xviii.
17. PRO, LCO 2/369, 'Interview with V.W. Baddeley', 6 June 1917. See also chapter 12 below and pp. 197–98.

a legislative response to the Shoreham Aerodrome proceedings in the House of Lords, this lacuna was also considered in February 1917 for inclusion in the proposed Defence of the Realm (Compensation for Loss) Bill.[18] The proposal was that the determination of compensation in such cases should remain with the Arbitration Board, and that the principles of compensation should prevent shipowners from obtaining the enhanced value of a ship where that enhancement had been to a large extent due to government requisitioning during the war. Where, however, the owner had himself paid an enhanced price for the vessel, he would be permitted to recover that amount.

That general measure was not proceeded with. But consideration of the shipping requisition question did not cease. A separate Acquisition of Ships Bill, dealing solely with that latter matter, was prepared in June 1917, following discussions between Sir Claud Schuster in the Lord Chancellor's Office and Sir Vincent Baddeley, the Admiralty Controller. Clause one of the proposed Bill would confirm the exclusive role of Lord Mersey's board in settling compensation for permanently acquired vessels and would cut off resort to the courts. In respect to compensation, it declared:

> Provided that the compensation payable shall, at the option of the owner, be assessed on the basis of the cost to the owner of the acquisition of the ship or vessel, or on the basis of the market value thereof as between a willing buyer and a willing seller after deducting any part of that value which is attributable to the increase in the value of shipping since the commencement of the present war.[19]

The first alternative thus repeated the provision in the general Compensation for Loss Bill. But in respect to the second alternative,[20] which seemed to contain provisions partially cancelling each other out (by allowing market value but deducting wartime enhancement), the Admiralty (deviating from the normal departmental attitude) were unhappy that the whole of the enhancement value of a ship caused by wartime shortages should be denied

18. PRO, LCO 2/367, 'Defence of the Realm (Compensation for Loss) Bill: Memorandum'. In fact, there is some doubt as to whether permanent acquisition of ships, either under the prerogative or under Reg. 39BBB, did occur at all. According to Sir A.H. Dennis of the Treasury Solicitor's department, 'No attempt has been made to acquire ships under the prerogative or D.R.R. since the Law Officers advised, early in the war, that there was no power to do so'. See LCO 2/440, Dennis to Sir Frederick Liddell, 6 November 1919.

19. PRO, LCO 2/369, typescript of draft Acquisition of Ships Bill. The printed draft version was the Defence of the Realm (Requisitioning of Ships) Bill 1917.

20. The phrase 'between a willing buyer and a willing seller' was contained in various statutes conferring a power of requisition of commodities by the military authorities. The measures included the Army (Supply of Food, Forage and Stores) Act 1914, the Naval Billeting Act 1914, the Army (Amendment) Act 1915 and the Army (Amendment) (No. 2) Act 1915. According to the Federation of British Industries in a memorandum to the Select Committee on the Indemnity Bill 1920 (see below), 'The provision that the price was to be determined as *between a willing buyer and a willing seller* was no doubt inserted with the view of preventing anything in the nature of profiteering, and at the same time with the view of protecting the honest trader'. See P.P.1920 (136), vii, p. 497.

to shipowners, 'as this would be to impose a penalty upon the shipowner whose ship is taken as against the shipowner who is left in possession of his ship with freedom to sell in the market'.[21]

Instead, market value compensation should be allowed though that value would be calculated upon the basis that the ship, if retained by the owner, would have earned rates of hire not in excess of those which would be earned by similar ships temporarily requisitioned under the 1914 proclamation. This acknowledged that, in spite of the government's requisitioning activities, freights had continued to rise in price. It would be unfair to penalise shipowners whose vessels had been requisitioned by paying compensation which totally ignored wartime price rises.

The problem for the government was double-edged. On the one hand, there was now a pervading feeling within the requisitioning ministries that legal challenges could be mounted at any time in respect to the exercise of government powers. In the case of the Admiralty taking over shipyards or the forced disgorgement on Treasury instructions of foreign securities held by individual investors (to give two examples cited by the ministry), there were fears that defence regulations which authorised such actions could not compel the owners to be content with an arbitrary figure as compensation. On the other hand, if primary legislation were proposed in order to legalise the payment of other than market value compensation, then parliamentary opposition, especially in the House of Lords, would be strong. As Schuster wrote to Baddeley's legal adviser, A.J. Clauson, K.C. (later Lord Justice of Appeal, 1938–42):

I must admit that the whole matter causes me the very gravest apprehension. The Law Officers have wavered from time to time both as to the powers and as to the measure of damages. On the other hand, I believe that the House of Lords are unlikely to pass any statute giving further powers or transferring powers [in respect to ships and shipyards] unless at the same time the measure of damage is provided for . . . What I mostly fear is that the Law Officers will advise that action should proceed without legislation, and that subsequently when Parliament has risen, some bold spirit may successfully withstand your attempts to take over the yard . . .[22]

But the Defence of the Realm (Requisitioning of Ships) Bill suffered the same fate as the Compensation for Loss Bill and was not proceeded with during the war. The political prospects for its enactment were not encouraging, with questions in the House of Commons from time to time putting the government on the defensive. Bonar Law, the Chancellor of the Exchequer, wondered, 'whether it might not have the effect of stirring up the whole issue of the doubtful position of the Crown's prerogative'.[23] It was not surprising

---

21. PRO, LCO 2/369, 'Interview with V.W.Baddeley', 6 June 1917.
22. Ibid., Schuster to Clauson, 9 July 1917.
23. Ibid., cited by Baddeley to Schuster, 20 July 1917.

therefore that Baddeley's Requisitioning of Ships Bill was 'definitely killed by the War Cabinet'.[24] However, the following year, the Ministry of Shipping put up more modest proposals dealing with a number of loose ends. For example, where unseaworthy ships were requisitioned on hire and repaired at the government's expense for government service, there had existed no legal means whereby the cost of such repairs could be recovered from the owners. The timing of the proposals, and the impending 'Coupon' Election in the last quarter of 1918, meant that no substantive progress had been reached by the time of the Armistice.[25]

So the position up to that point was that Lord Mersey's Board of Arbitration awarded *ex gratia* payments for direct loss incurred by shipowners and charterers but refused to award for indirect loss. Neither charterers not standing in the position of shipowners, nor any other third parties, whether shippers or shipyards or agents, were offered compensation by the board. Moreover, the board determined compensation in respect to what were equivalent to hirings, rather than for permanent acquisitions. The other compensation provision was contained in Reg. 39BBB /promulgated by the Shipping Controller in June 1917. It also provided that, in the absence of agreement, the Board of Arbitration would determine the compensation payable. Unlike the proclamation of August 1914, the regulation was an example of delegated legislation. At least it purported to be a valid regulation. Assuming it was *intra vires*, then a legal right to compensation (as distinct from a claim to an *ex gratia* payment) was not in dispute. It would, however, remain a matter of statutory interpretation as to whether compensation was payable only for direct loss, as the terminology of the regulation eschewed the words 'direct' and 'indirect'.

Major questions remained unresolved, for example, the matter of permanent acquisition of vessels; while, more ominously, the vulnerability of government departments to legal challenges to the basis on which they offered compensation to owners remained a concern of senior civil servants.

The problem became more serious when a majority in the Court of Appeal in April 1919 rejected the Crown's reliance on the prerogative as the basis for denying compensation *ex lege* to De Keyser's Royal Hotel (chapter six, supra). The way was now open, if the House of Lords were to confirm the ruling, for vast numbers of property owners to demand more generous levels of compensation than those currently offered by the Arbitration Board. As an interdepartmental committee reported to the War Cabinet:

> Shipowners as a whole have not been unwilling to submit cases of dispute to the Mersey Board, but it is by no means clear, since the De Keyser's Hotel case, whether they would not have a legal right to claim compensation from the Crown through the machinery of a Petition of Right, if they desire to do so. Some shipowners have, in fact, while accepting Blue Book rates, reserved

24. Ibid., 'Extract from Letter Received from Mr W.H. Graham-Harrison'. Graham-Harrison was with the Parliamentary Counsel's Office.
25. PRO, MT 25/23/62103/1918, 'Memorandum on Proposed New Bill'.

all their rights against the Crown, and the De Keyser's case will no doubt encourage them to proceed by Petition of Right.[26]

Additionally, the continuing doubts as to whether Admiralty requisitioning under prerogative powers extended to permanent acquisition, given the abortive efforts to introduce legislation in 1917, meant that a large number of claims by shipowners remained outstanding. The interdepartmental committee felt that these claims, which, following *De Keyser*, could also include claims for 'indirect and consequential loss' (admittedly a confusing choice of phrase) would run into millions of pounds. To save the Exchequer, such claims should either be barred or the basis for compensation clearly settled, while the exclusive right of the Board of Arbitration to assess compensation should be confirmed by law.

Similarly, so far as it affected requisitioning by the Ministry of Shipping, the decision of 20 February 1920 in the *Newcastle Breweries* case threatened to undermine the compensation policy hitherto adopted. A memorandum by the ministry attempted to assess the damage to the department if the *Newcastle Breweries* decision in respect to Reg. 2B were followed in cases of requisition under Reg. 39BBB.[27] It contemplated (a) the possibility of hirings of requisitioned vessels at market rates in lieu of the Blue Book rates; (b) that compensation for the loss of requisitioned vessels covered by government-backed war risk insurance might have to be awarded on the footing that the vessels were free from requisition, that is, that they were capable of earning market rates of hire; (c) that claims for indirect loss by third parties due to the requisition of a vessel might have to be met, contrary to the Arbitration Board's principles; and (d) that claims for compensation for interference with the general business of the applicant by reason of the requisition of his vessel might have to be entertained. If, in the cases of (a) and (b) above, there was found to be a contract between the department and the shipowners, this, it was thought, might preclude the owner from seeking further remuneration or compensation than that already awarded. However, shipowners who reserved their rights at the time of requisitioning might not be so barred. Moreover, worried the ministry, the moral claim of shipowners who had contracted with the ministry, to receive equal treatment with those who reserved their legal rights, 'would create a very difficult administrative position for the Government'. Practical illustrations of what a shift to market rates would entail were cited. The Blue Book rate for ocean-going tramp tonnage for the greater period of the war was about 8s. per deadweight ton per month. From about 1916, British tonnage which was free from requisition but subject to various forms of control could obtain without difficulty 25s. to 30s. per deadweight ton (neutral tonnage was as much as 45s. per deadweight ton). On *Newcastle Breweries* principles, the amount paid for the hire of

26. PRO, LCO 2/440, *First Interim Report of the Interdepartmental Committee on the Indemnity Bill and Statute of Limitations*, July 1919, para. 13.
27. PRO, LCO 2/441, 'Memorandum by the Ministry of Shipping', n.d. (early 1920?).

requisitioned British ships could rise from about £8 million a month to about £24 million. In the case of requisitioned vessels lost under war risk insurance, an extra 25 per cent more than was actually paid might have to be set aside. The additional amount of £28 million was cited. On third party claims, a suggestion put the possible outlay at £400 million, while no figure was quoted for general interference with the owner's business as a result of requisitioning his vessel, though such claims would certainly involve substantial sums.

In view of such potential financial demands, the interdepartmental committee advised that legislation should confirm that the Arbitration Board possessed exclusive jurisdiction to assess compensation on the limited bases laid down by Reg. 39BBB (the ministry did not requisition for acquisition, no doubt due to the strong shipowning influence within the department, whose head from 1916 to 1921, Sir Joseph Maclay (1857–1951), was a Glasgow shipping magnate. He was, nonetheless, no toady of the industry).[28]

The committee offered the War Cabinet two alternatives. The first was to preclude by an Indemnity Act any legal proceedings arising out of the exercise of prerogative or statutory powers (or purported powers) for the defence of the realm. Thus any payments made by the Crown would remain *ex gratia*. The second was to enshrine in statute a legal right to compensation, based on the principles adopted by the Board of Arbitration and, in respect to permanent acquisition, on the assumption that the ship was not, during the war, capable of earning freight at rates higher than the Blue Book rates. The strongly expressed views of Lord Mersey to the committee, rejecting any right to compensation for indirect loss or damage due to the existence of the war, reinforced the recommendation:

> The interference with trade and business caused by the requisition of vessels is an ordinary and necessary result of war. The consequences to individuals must vary according to the nature of their business and affairs, and it appears to me that the only proper course is to leave each individual to bear the loss which happens to fall on him.[29]

When an early draft of the Indemnity Bill was produced, embodying substantially the second alternative, it also permitted claims for alleged breach of contract to be instituted by petition of right (though not claims for compensation or damages for loss). As the vice-president of the Arbitration Board, Sir William Walton, pointed out,[30] and as has already been noted, a

---

28. See S.M.H.Armitage, *The Politics of Decontrol of Industry: Britain and the United States* (London, 1969), pp. 28–30.

29. Copy in PRO, LCO 2/440, Lord Mersey to G.H.Drury, War Office, 10 September 1919; also reproduced in *Report and Special Report from the Select Committee on the Indemnity Bill*, P.P.1920 (136), vii, pp. 393–94.

30. PRO, LCO 2/440, 'Memorandum no. 42. Interdepartmental Committee on the Indemnity Bill and Statute of Limitations. Memorandum by Sir Wiliam Walton relating to shipping cases and the work of the Admiralty Arbitration Transport Board'; ibid., Memorandum no. 44, Interdepartmental Committee. Minutes of the 7th Meeting, 2 December 1919. See below, chapter 13.

large proportion of the cases which came before his board were based on contract. In some cases, there was an express contract. In others, it was partly expressed and partly implied. In many cases it would be very difficult to say whether the case was one of contract or simply the exercise of the Crown's prerogative. If a contractual relationship were held to exist, then shipowners could resort to the courts which might award compensation on principles different from those applied by the board. A number of instances were offered by Walton. For example, there was a large and complicated claim by the Atlantic Transport Company for extra allowances and expenses of running and repairing a number of vessels, which were outside the agreed rates of hire, but which the company had alleged were due under the Blue Book rates. In another case, a Scottish company submitted a large claim for lost vessels.

The bases of valuation in case of loss were disputed as was whether the owner could take into account in assessing loss the cost of a replacement. All these matters, if a contractual basis were established, could be taken to the courts instead of to the Arbitration Board. Thus a divergence might be created between the board and the courts, which could only cause dissatisfaction and uncertainty. It might even tend to increase litigation, contrary to the objects of the Indemnity Bill. Claimants might wish to reopen cases in the courts,[31] and this would be an intolerable situation for the board. M.L. Gwyer from the Ministry of Shipping added that 95 per cent of all so-called requisitions by his department under Reg. 39BBB were in fact contractual, whether express or implied. The committee therefore advised the Parliamentary Counsel, Sir Frederick Liddell, to make the necessary amendments to ensure that the Arbitration Board had exclusive jurisdiction in such cases.

This was done and the intention of the government to oust the jurisdiction of the courts and to confine compensation to direct loss or damage became public knowledge on the publication of the Indemnity Bill. As with the cases of land, buildings and other commodities, the motivation of the government was primarily financial and secondarily to ensure equitable treatment between those who had accepted the Arbitration Board's awards and those who had 'reserved their legal rights'.

In presenting the Bill to Parliament on 3 May 1920, the Solicitor-General, Sir Ernest Pollock, admitted that while large numbers of shipowners had settled their claims to compensation by accepting the Arbitration Board's awards, which were, of course, the Blue Book rates, nonetheless, 'Certain persons have reserved their legal rights.'[32] In view of this, the choice was either to reopen all decided cases or to confirm the principles of compensation accepted by the vast majority. Apart from the administrative problems attaching to the first alternative, there were the financial implications for the country

---

31. It was not acknowledged that the courts might refuse to hear cases which they concluded had already been settled.
32. H.C. Deb., 5th series, 128, 3 May 1920, col.1756.

in so doing. Pollock explained that £331 million had already been paid out at Blue Book rates for requisitioning. If market rates were to be paid, he pointed out, that would entail a further £350 million. Moreover, in the case of vessels sunk by submarines, compensation had been paid by the government on the footing that the vessels, being requisitioned, were not free to ply their trade in the market place. If market rates were to apply here also, then the Exchequer would be obliged to find another £28 million for the owners.[33] In one court hearing, the *Longbenton* case, it was held that the value of the sunk vessel in question was £27,500 as a requisitioned ship and £45,000 as a free ship. As she was under requisition at the time of the sinking, the government were held liable under the war risks scheme only for £27,500. If the government were called upon to pay market value which ignored the fact of requisitioning, then the economic consequence, as shown above, would be significant.[34]

Was there a major threat to the financial health of the nation posed by shipowners prepared to launch legal proceedings for market value compensation, or even to seek compensation for indirect loss? During the debate on the second reading of the Indemnity Bill, Leslie Scott M.P., the co-author of *The Case of Requisition*, challenged the assumption underlying the justification for legislation:

> I will make a definite statement as to the majority of the shipowners of this country. I say deliberately that if this Bill is not passed there will be no claim such as is indicated of £350,000,000 sterling for the differences between Blue Book rates and the theoretical measure of damages which the Common Law might have given them.[35]

He had been in close touch with the parliamentary committee of the Chamber of Shipping and was satisfied that if the legislation were not passed, then, 'there will be practically nothing heard of any claim to have more than the Blue Book rates for the ordinary requisitioning of either the steam or sail tonnage of this country during the War'.[36]

One of the many shipowners in the Commons, Sir William Raeburn, concurred in this assessment. He knew of very few cases where shipowners had not willingly accepted the Blue Book rates. If any individual shipowner did resort to the courts to obtain market rates, Raeburn would attribute this to the exceptional circumstances of the particular case rather than treat it as a precedent for all shipowners to invoke. He believed that the number of pending cases must be very few and the amounts involved very small: 'The fabulous sum [£378 million] mentioned in the Memorandum [to the Bill] is a

---

33. Ibid., col.1758.

34. *Select Committee on the Indemnity Bill*, q. 655 (Sir William Walton); PRO, LCO 2/441, 'Select Committee on the Indemnity Bill 1920. Estimate of Additional Cost to the Exchequer if the Bill is not Passed', 8 June 1920.

35. H.C. Deb., 128, col.1773.

36. Ibid., col.1774.

mere bogey to frighten Members of the House who know nothing about the subject.'[37] What Raeburn desired was not the reopening of cases settled on Blue Book rates but that where there were special circumstances, the parties should have liberty to resort to the courts. A hypothetical example was offered by Leslie Scott in his speech. Under the ordinary charter to which the Blue Book rates applied, the government accepted liability as insurer when a vessel was lost as a result of war risk. But what constituted a war risk as distinct from an ordinary marine risk? When two vessels, sailing at night, collided because on Admiralty instructions they were sailing without lights, was that a war risk or a marine risk (in which case the marine insurer would be liable according to the marine insurance contract)? The matter had been the subject of litigation in the courts, and critics of the bill felt strongly that to deny the judicial House of Lords the power to adjudicate on such a question would be a constitutional outrage.[38]

There were many other instances cited by Raeburn where damage caused to ships under requisition had not be compensated by the Arbitration Board. For example, where cargo was discharged by heavy grabs, damage was invariably caused by these instruments to the structures of vessels. Yet the cost of repairing the damage and the loss of hire while the repairs were being carried out were not recoverable. Of course, it might be the case that were such claims to have gone to court, damages might not have been forthcoming from that source either, as the requisite standard of proof of negligence or of breach of contract might not have been demonstrated. For critics of the measure, that was not the point. It was not that the courts would compensate them adequately, whereas the Arbitration Board would not: it was that the courts represented a bastion of liberty:

> I think it would be a very great hardship indeed, after all we have done and submitted to, and willingly submitted to because of the needs of the country, that the one defence we have against autocratic injustice, namely, appeal to the Courts, should be denied us.[39]

When the bill was sent for scrutiny by a House of Commons select committee, it was admitted by Sir William Walton of the Arbitration Board that, contrary to Sir Ernest Pollock's statement in Parliament, the board had not received any formal reservation of legal rights by owners who had accepted Blue Book rates.[40] However, Sir Henry Bunbury, Accountant-General to the Ministry

37. Ibid., col.1777.
38. The case was *Ard Coasters* v. *The Crown* in which the Court of Appeal upheld the decision of Mr Justice Bailhache that the Crown were liable as war risk insurers to pay for the loss of the S.S. *Ardgantock* on the ground that she had been sunk in collision with H.M.S. *Tartar*, a patrol vessel, when both ships were sailing at night without lights. According to Leslie Scott, the Indemnity Bill would nullify the decision of the Court of Appeal and compel the owners to reopen the case before the Arbitration Board. See *Select Committee on the Indemnity Bill*, qq. 921, 943.
39. H.C. Deb., 128, col.1779.
40. *Select Committee on the Indemnity Bill*, q. 555.

of Shipping, pointed out that the charterparty T. 99 sent to all owners after requisition was signed and returned by some owners; was not signed by others; was returned, signed, by yet others who accepted it under protest while reserving their rights; and in yet other cases, was ignored by shipowners who merely wrote back reserving their rights.[41] On the more critical question of shipowners who intended to reopen claims for market rates by going to law (in the event that the Indemnity Bill were not passed), Bunbury could only cite a couple of cases, and those involved small shipowners. Admittedly, there were a very great number of outstanding matters involving larger firms which had not yet been settled, and these might well concern claims for market rates rather than Blue Book rates. Bunbury cited a recent attempt in this respect. A petition of right had been brought against the ministry by a shipping line, in which one of the points at issue had been whether the vessel had received a fair rate of remuneration. The ministry were prepared to argue the point in court. At the last moment, the case was dropped by the company, perhaps in the belief that the court would not interpret a fair rate of remuneration differently from the Blue Book rates. As one member of the select committee, Thomas Inskip (later, as Viscount Caldecote, to become Lord Chancellor, 1939–1940 and then Lord Chief Justice, 1940–1946), remarked: 'It had gone so far that he thought bluff was exhausted, and abandoned his claim.'[42]

It seems likely that the case concerned the *Snowdon*, a steel screw steamship of 3,189 gross tons.[43] She was requisitioned from the Port of London on 17 October 1916 and was taken into service at Dunkirk by the Admiralty following receipt of a telegram by the owners, the Snowdon Steamship Company Ltd of Cardiff. The telegram was confirmed by a letter of 20 October from the Admiralty, enclosing a letter of requisition and copies of charterparty T. 99. The correspondence stated that the rates of hire were those fixed by the Arbitration Board, and that payments on account on that basis would be made by the Admiralty and Ministry of Shipping. Though such payments were made, the owners at no time agreed or were invited by charterparty or otherwise to agree to accept these payments as final or as representing the full hire of the vessel.

On 20 May 1918, the ship was lost through enemy action while still on government service. The owners valued her at the time of loss at £133,750 and claimed that, if she had not been requisitioned, she would have earned under a commercial charterparty covering the period May 1916 to May 1917 the sum of £50,183. Between May 1917 and the date of her sinking, the owners calculated that she could have earned a further £91,877 6s. 8d. Her net earnings between 17 October 1916 and 20 May 1918, according to the company, would have amounted to £76,623 12s. 0d. Therefore a total claim (including insurance payments) was submitted for £188,414 5s. 7d. As the ministry were refusing

---

41. Ibid., q. 668.
42. Ibid., qq. 694,696.
43. PRO, LCO 2/441, '"Snowdon" Petition of Right', 13 February 1920.

to pay the 'reasonable rate of remuneration', that is, the sum of £76,623 less £26,497 3s. 9d. paid on account, and as it did not accept the market value approach of the company to the value of the lost vessel, a petition of right was lodged by the company's London solicitors on 13 February 1920. No further information about the progress of the claim is available, highly suggestive of the eventual withdrawal of the proceedings, corresponding to the account given by Bunbury.

It would be a mistake to accept uncritically the claim of those who bemoaned the inaccessibility of the courts. The Arbitration Board remained subject to the provisions of the Arbitration Act 1889, section 19, which enabled parties to state a case for the courts. This was a procedure, albeit protracted, designed to allow the courts to pronounce on a question of legal construction of the reference, that is, whether the board had misdirected itself as to the scope of its powers. It was a rare procedure designed to test questions of law, not of fact, and did not address the merits of any claims.[44] The solicitor to the Ministry of Shipping, Thomas Barnes (who later became Treasury Solicitor in 1934), noted that two such cases had occurred, one involving the *El Zorro* or the *Ariadne Christine* (Barnes could not remember which) and the other involving the firm of Cory Brothers. In addition, two cases (presumably one of them the *Snowdon* case) were taken direct to the courts, and one of these was still pending during the select committee hearing in June 1920.

In his evidence to the select committee, Leslie Scott pointed out the kinds of cases suitable for the courts which the bill would prevent being heard there. These included 'reconditioning' cases after vessels were released from requisitioning; secondly, cases such as the *Helmsmuir* where, in October 1914, at the request of the Admiralty, the shipowner diverted his ship from a Dutch port to which, under a pre-war charter, he had contracted to send her, thereby incurring a liability to the charterer of £25,000. The board refused compensation and the owner was now claiming by petition of right. Thirdly, there was damage to vessels due to a variety of causes, such as faulty loading or faulty berths or unsuitable cargoes or coaling large warships in rough seas. Finally, there were claims arising out of obedience to orders, such as those by the Shipping Controller ordering tea ships away from London to ease congestion at the docks. The direct result was a total loss of freight. Scott ended his evidence with a strong principled plea:

> In cases like these and similar cases generally, whether the subject-matter be ships or not, there is no satisfactory reason for taking away the jurisdiction of the Courts, or depriving the subject of his legal rights. Indeed, having in mind the pertinacity and adroitness of the Executive throughout the War in resisting the rights of the subject, and the persevering arguments of the law officers in

---

44. Walton did not attach much importance to the question of expressly excluding the operation of section 19. In the bill, he desired to leave the possibility of reference to the courts of a case stated to the discretion of the board. See PRO, LCO 2/440, 'Memorandum no. 44', para. 8.

support of the view taken by the Executive, I submit that it is essential to retain the ordinary procedure of the King's Courts.[45]

Scott's emotive appeal made only limited impression on the government, which, in respect to the Arbitration Board, made provision for appeals (as distinct from case stated) on questions of law to the Court of Appeal, thence to the House of Lords.[46] On the continued application of Blue Book rates by the Arbitration Board, the government refused to budge: the principles of compensation followed by the board, whether in the case of requisitioning under the proclamation of August 1914 or under Reg. 39BBB, continued to apply. Thus section 2, subsection 1 of the Indemnity Act 1920 provided that a person:

(a)   being the owner of a ship or vessel which or any cargo space or passenger accommodation in which has been requisitioned at any time during the war in exercise or purported exercise of any prerogative right of His Majesty or of any power under any enactment relating to the defence of the realm, or any regulation or order made or purporting to be made thereunder, shall be entitled to payment or compensation for the use of the same and for services rendered during the employment of the same in Government service, and compensation for loss or damage thereby occasioned.

The section went on:

(ii) Where the payment or compensation is claimed under paragraph (a) of subsection (1) of this section [supra], it shall be assessed in accordance with the principles upon which the Board of Arbitration constituted under the proclamation issued on the third day of August nineteen hundred and fourteen has hitherto acted, which principles are set forth in Part I of the Schedule to this Act.[47]

The government therefore got their way and constitutional principles gave way to expediency.

45.   *Select Committee on the Indemnity Bill*, q.946.
46.   See below, chapter 13.
47.   The explicit insertion of the principles of compensation was conceded by the government during the Bill's parliamentary passage.

11

Lord Rosebery and a Gang of Inefficient Swankers

In November 1919, following a stroke, the former Liberal Prime Minister, Lord Rosebery, was recovering at his estate near Edinburgh. His son, Dalmeny, read out to him the main items from each day's newspapers. 'I see that Turnhouse Aerodrome is up for sale', he announced. 'But that's my property', Rosebery replied immediately.[1] From that point on, a flurry of sharply worded correspondence flew between Edinburgh and the office of the Director-General of Lands at the Ministry of Munitions, Sir Howard Frank.[2]

To set the scene on the controversy, we must go back three years to the night of 2–3 April 1916, when three German naval airships, L14, L16 and L22, set out to raid the Rosyth Naval Dockyard and to attack the Forth Bridge. The captain of L14, Kapitänleutnant Bocker, failed to locate his targets, and bombed Edinburgh and Leith instead around midnight. L22 was further south, and dropped bombs in fields near Berwick-upon-Tweed, though her captain, Kapitänleutnant Martin Dietrich, claimed he had raided factories in Newcastle. Travelling northwards along the coast, L22 eventually dropped her remaining bombs on Edinburgh around the same time as the attack by L14. L16, however, appears not to have crossed into Scotland, but dropped her bombs near and on Cramlington aerodrome. The casualties caused by the airships were thirteen dead and twenty-four injured, with damage to the value of £73,113. Air defence was minimal. Two Wright seaplanes were based at Dundee; it is not clear whether they in fact got airborne. At Cramlington, two BE 2cs went up, one of which crashed on landing and then blew up when its bombs exploded.[3]

The British military authorities had already determined to locate an air defence base in the Forth area, to counter further Zeppelin threats. For on 2 March 1916, 123 acres at Turnhouse Farm to the west of Edinburgh were requisitioned by the War Office from the then owner, Mr Hope Vere,[4] on whose Craigiehall Estate the farm was located. The sitting tenants, Messrs J.

---

1. Robert Rhodes James, *Rosebery* (London, 1963), p.460.
2. Rhodes James reproduces a small selection of the correspondence in ibid., pp. 481–83. Rosebery himself privately printed the full published correspondence in a pamphlet, *Turnhouse: An Object Lesson* (n.d., c. 1920).
3. Cole and Cheesman, *The Air Defence of Britain*, pp. 122–23.
4. PRO, AIR 2/29/SCOTTISH/1960, 'Turnhouse Aerodrome: Memoranda, 1920–1923'.

& W. Young, were similarly required to vacate land, as were neighbouring farmers and tenants on the Barnton Estate, the owner of which was Lady Mary Steel-Maitland,[5] wife of the Conservative politician, Sir Arthur Steel-Maitland. As is clear from the above, Lord Rosebery did not, in fact, own any of the farmland at Turnhouse when it was requisitioned. He purchased from the owner only after the War Office occupation had begun.

Following the occupation, a flight of No. 36 Squadron at Cramlington was temporarily attached to Turnhouse and a new Royal Flying Corps (RFC) aerodrome became operational.[6] The War Office also began to put into effect changes to the site, to render it suitable to receive and maintain aircraft and personnel. In so doing, it decided on 29 April 1916 to relinquish about thirty-four acres of the Barnton estate as unsuitable for its purposes, and restored them to Mrs Steel-Maitland's tenants. However, on 28 August 1916, a further tract of eight acres of land at Turnhouse Farm was requisitioned for a hutment camp,[7] though the construction work later led to a dispute between the ministry and the builders which had to be resolved by arbitration.[8] Together with two further land requisitions in October 1916 and January 1917, the land in government hands was now 190 acres. The first unit duly arrived in May 1916. This was a training squadron, No. 26 Reserve Aeroplane Squadron, whose pilots, after training, went on to newly formed squadrons or were sent as replacements to France.[9] The following year, the headquarters of No. 77 Home Defence Squadron were moved from premises in Edinburgh to Turnhouse, after the War Office had decided against disbanding the squadron following the blunting of the Zeppelin challenge.[10] There was provision for eighteen aircraft at landing sites at Whiteburn, New Haggerston and Penston, while Turnhouse itself became a flight station for 'A' Flight of No. 77 (Home Defence) Squadron.[11] Nonetheless, only five aircraft were on the strength, with four available, and just seven pilots on duty.[12]

In mid 1917, No. 26 Training Squadron (as it was now renamed) departed, and was replaced by No. 73 Training Squadron, which arrived from Thetford

---

5. Part of her property, known as Craigleith Quarry, had been leased privately to a quarrying company, John Best & Sons Ltd, until the Ministry of Munitions took over her land in April 1916. See *John Best & Sons Ltd* v. *Lord Advocate* 1918, 2 S.L.T.220; SRO, GD 193/48/6, 'Craigleith Quarry: War Department, 1909–1919' (Steel-Maitland Papers); GD 193/959, 'Correspondence relating to military occupation of Gogar Mains and Meadowfield, Turnhouse Airport, 1916–18'.

6. (Anon.) 'RAF Turnhouse', *Aeromilitaria: The Air-Britain Military Aviation Historical Quarterly*, 1 (1986), p. 15.

7. PRO, AIR 2/29/SCOTTISH/1960, 'Turnhouse Aerodrome'.

8. For a dispute over payment to contractors on the site, see SRO, GD 283/6/130, 'Arbitration between Secretary of State and Messrs Watson's, Perth, in respect to Turnhouse Aerodrome, 1918–1919'.

9. (Anon.) 'RAF Turnhouse'.

10. Cole and Cheesman, *Air Defence of Britain*, pp. 189–90.

11. David J. Smith, *Action Stations 7: Military Airfields of Scotland, the North-East and Northern Ireland* (Cambridge, 1983), p. 210.

12. Cole and Cheesman, *Air Defence of Britain*, p. 190.

with Sopwith Camels. It remained till February 1918 when it transferred to Beaulieu. Turnhouse now became a Fleet Practice Station and Fleet Aircraft Repair Depot.[13]

The naval dimension was the need to find a location for the disembarked aircraft of the battlecruiser squadron based in the Forth. The proximity to the naval dockyard at Rosyth was also relevant. Donibristle on the northern shore of the Forth had been chosen as the venue, but the site was not yet completed. Consequently, Turnhouse fulfilled a naval air station role until the Armistice. The aircraft which occupied the aerodrome at this time included Camels and Sopwith $1\frac{1}{2}$ strutters which had flown off the platforms of battleships and battlecruisers based in the Forth.

After the Armistice, the aerodrome continued to be used by the Air Ministry until November 1919, when it was transferred to the Disposal and Liquidation Board of the Ministry of Munitions. It was then advertised in the press as being available for disposal and interested parties were invited to contact the board for further particulars.[14] The area in question covered about 178 acres and the board contemplated selling the buildings and land either with or without the aerodrome itself. The buildings comprised three wooden hangars, vehicle shed, workshops and offices. There were also an electric light plant, water supply, drainage and permanent roads, with an adjoining railway station.

The property was advertised as being suitable, not only as an aerodrome, but as a factory, storage depot, sanatorium or training institution and, stated the advertisement, 'can, if necessary, be purchased under and subject to the provisions of the Defence of the Realm (Acquisition of Land) Act 1916.'

Since the Air Council were not the owners of Turnhouse at the time, but only the occupiers under Defence of the Realm Act (DORA) powers, their claim to sell the property could only derive from the provisions of the 1916 Act. In the first instance, the Air Council actually purchased the land in autumn 1916 after the War Office occupation began the previous April. As Lord Rosebery was unwilling to sell by agreement, the government were forced to the expedient of compulsory purchase under the 1916 Act, before subsequently selling to a third party. That party was Edinburgh Corporation which, as we shall see, envisaged Turnhouse as the new municipal aerodrome for the city.

The legal difficulty which had to be addressed was whether the Defence of the Realm (Acquisition of Land) Act 1916 covered the contemplated situation. The 1916 Act made provision, in respect to property, for the continuance in possession by any government department for a limited period after the termination of the war, and for the permanent acquisition of land of which possession had been taken, subject to payment of compensation fixed, in the case of dispute, by the Railway and Canal Commission whose consent to the

13. Smith, *Action Stations 7*.
14. See, for example, the *Scotsman*, 26 November 1919.

exercise of compulsory powers in any particular case was required.[15] One of
the motives behind the measure was to enable the government to purchase
land upon which buildings and works had been erected wholly or partly at
government expense, rather than spending more public money on restoring
the property to its previous condition prior to returning it to the owners.
Though the phrase 'Defence of the Realm' appeared in the title of the act, the
object of retaining the property was primarily financial or social. If defence
purposes were identified, then the provisions of the Defence Act 1842 or the
Military Lands Act 1892 could still be invoked to purchase compulsorily.

At the time the Act was passed, in 1916, the government had in mind
the possibility of retaining the land on which the various national factories
had been or were being constructed.[16] Moreover, the government had given
financial assistance to companies to expand their works by erecting more
buildings and costly plant. That assistance was often by way of straightforward
capital payment as distinct from, say, a mortgage of the property to the
government, as in the case of the expansion of the Grahame-White Aviation
Co. to enable it to produce more aircraft.[17]

While the Bill was proceeding through Parliament, one firm of solicitors
was particularly anxious to ensure the inclusion of certain statutory safeguards
for a certain class of landowners, that is, those on whose property an
aviation business had been conducted. The solicitors were (one might have
guessed) Wingfield, Blew & Kenward, the agents for the Brighton-Shoreham
Aerodrome Company. What most concerned George Wingfield was that the
Bill should include a right of pre-emption for the owner in respect of any
building erected by the government on the aerodrome. Without such a prior
right, he feared, the government could compel the owner to pay an extravagant
sum for the buildings, under the threat of compulsory purchase. Moreover,
if priced out of his own property as a result of government improvements,
the modest pre-war entrepreneur, whose land was taken over, would also be
denied the opportunity of selling out to a larger aviation company at a profit
which reflected his own aviation initiative and enterprise prior to the war. In
short, complained Wingfield;

The Government are in touch with all the Aeronautical Manufacturers, and the
owners have been put out of touch with them by the Government during the

15. It appears that Edward Coles of the War Office Lands Department was not too keen
on the commission being accorded this role. The Lord Advocate, Robert Munro, by contrast,
'cannot conceive a body more fitted to deal with the questions which are likely to arise and
to deal with them with due regard for public and private interests'. See SRO, AD 52/18,
p. 112. Perhaps the sensitivity of the politician was greater than that of the civil servant. See
below, chapter 14.
16. For a dispute between the Ministry of Munitions and the Sheffield steel firm of
Hadfields, on whose land a national projectile factory had been constructed, see PRO,
MUN 4/645. This file deals with other similar cases in London, Leeds and Glasgow.
17. For the Grahame-White case, see A.D. George, 'Aviation and the State: the Grahame-
White Aviation Company, 1912–23', *Journal of Transport History*, 9 (1988), pp. 209–14.

war. These Aeronautical Manufacturers reading this Bill can see that they could acquire this Aerodrome cheaper through the Government officials by buying from the Government than they could by buying from the owner.[18]

The issue at stake was whether imaginative and industrious private landowners should reap the benefit of the enhanced value of their own property, even though the culmination of the improvement was brought about by government expenditure or by a newly-emergent social need (like a municipal aerodrome). Or should the fact that the enhancement was due to external causes mean that the public interest should benefit at the expense of the private interest?

In the case of the Defence of the Realm (Acquisition of Land) Act 1916, the civil servants dealing with the Turnhouse case were in no doubt that their manoeuvrings were designed to secure the disposal of the aerodrome on the most favourable financial terms obtainable to the government as representing the public interest.

About fifty acres had already been relinquished on 28 February 1918 and another fifty were restored on 9 March 1920 for cultivation. But 141 acres were still in government hands at that date, including land from Lady Steel-Maitland's Barnton Estate. While it was proposed to restore part of that land including the site of the camp, the government's intention was to purchase 117 acres which it occupied, seventy-two of which were owned by Lord Rosebery, and forty-five acres by a Mr John E.B. Couper (or Cowper) of Gogar Mains, Corstorphine, Edinburgh (who, like Rosebery, bought his interest after the DORA requisition).

The government's reasons for wishing to purchase the land for subsequent resale were stated as being in the interests of civil aviation and in the interests of financial exigency. As regards the first claim, the government's argument to the Railway and Canal Commissioners, who were the statutory authority which could authorise the purchase, was that Turnhouse Aerodrome was required to meet the necessities of the City of Edinburgh for civil aviation facilities. This was at a time, after the war, when Sir Frederick Sykes, following successful wartime service as Chief of the Air Staff in the RFC and Royal Air Force (RAF), was vigorously promoting, in his subsequent official capacity as Controller of Civil Aviation, the expansion of municipal aerodromes.[19] Turnhouse was preferable to the only other alternative site, Saughton Mains Aerodrome. If the latter were chosen, heavy expenditure on buildings would be incurred and the land value was also greater. With the support of the Air Ministry, the city authorities in Edinburgh were keen to establish a municipal aerodrome which would be to the benefit of the city.

18. PRO, MUN 4/6921, letter from Wingfield, Blew & Kenward, 30 June 1916, and probably circulated to all Members of Parliament. See above, chapter 4.

19. John Myerscough, 'Airport Provision in the Inter-War Years', *Journal of Contemporary History*, 20 (1985), pp. 41–70, at pp. 43–44. See also chapter 14, below.

In respect to the financial argument for purchase, the government had already spent £40,000, divided into buildings (£30,000), land works and drainage etc (£5,000) and DORA compensation (£5,000). If the land were not purchased but reinstated, the government would only recoup £2,000, that is, the balance between the scrap value of the buildings (£6,000) and the cost of reinstatement (£4,000). If, however, the government acquired the land, Edinburgh Corporation would purchase it from the government at whatever price the government would pay to Lord Rosebery (as fixed by the commissioners), and it would also pay £10,000 for the buildings. In other words, the Exchequer would gain at least £8,000 if the land were purchased compulsorily from Lord Rosebery and then resold to the corporation (the land itself being valued at £13,000 by the government). Indeed, in the opinion of Sir Howard Frank, in a note on 18 May 1920 to Sir Sigmund Dannreuther, the assistant permanent secretary to the Air Ministry, purchase was preferable to reinstatement and sale of the buildings as scrap, even if Edinburgh Corporation were unable to obtain power to purchase the property (because of statutory restrictions on its scope of powers), and even if no other buyers could be found. But the corporation's keenness was undiminished at the time and Parliament was proposing to include powers in section nine of the Aerial Navigation Act 1920 to permit municipalities to purchase land for use as airports.

What was Lord Rosebery's opinion of these governmental aims? It appears that when the RAF no longer had need of Turnhouse in November 1919, the Air Ministry informed him that the aerodrome, 'will neither be required as a civil or service aerodrome and that the land will be evacuated as soon as possible'.[20]

The ground was then handed over to the Disposal and Liquidation Board and shortly thereafter, as we have seen, the property was advertised for 'disposal', inducing apoplexy on the part of Lord Rosebery. It seems evident that in the three weeks or so between the Air Ministry's intimation to Lord Rosebery that the property was no longer required for government service, and the appearance of the advertisement in the *Scotsman* on 26 November 1919, the Disposal Board had been doing its sums on the comparative costs of reinstatement on the one hand and purchase and resale on the other. The fortuitous conjunction of the relinquishment of the aerodrome by the RAF and the adoption by Edinburgh Corporation of a policy in favour of the establishment of a municipal aerodrome provided cost-conscious civil servants with an opportunity to kill two birds with one stone.

Lord Rosebery, for his part, saw things quite differently. There is little evidence that he had his own development plans for the site. The purchase would inevitably diminish the value of the remaining portions of Turnhouse and Gogar Mains Farms, and that might itself have justified Rosebery's opposition to the government's plans. But compensation for such loss was

___

20.   PRO, T 161/117/59364, memorandum by S.H. Wright, Treasury, 20 April 1921.

available through the Defence of the Realm Losses Commission (DRLC) or its successor, the War Compensation Court. The tenants of Turnhouse Farm, Messrs J. & W. Young, were at that very time presenting their compensation claims to the DRLC.[21] The speculation within the Disposal Board, however, was that Rosebery's action, 'was simply due to a desire to embarrass the schemes of a Department of the Government'.[22]

As the 'arch-enemy of State interference',[23] and a politician of immense experience, he opted for sarcasm in his battle of wits with the department. In his opening salvo to the *Scotsman*, written on 28 November, he took great delight in exposing the ministry as a seller with no title to sell. Sir Howard Frank's reply on December 1 rehearsed the formal legal position whereby, under the 1916 Act, the government was entitled to purchase the property and to recover for the taxpayer whatever recoupment for war expenditure might be obtained. On 3 December Rosebery replied, complaining that while legislation oppressive of the rights of individuals might be tolerated in wartime, it had no place at a time of 'profound peace'. As for compensating the taxpayer, why not compensate the owner, turfed out of a productive farm at a time of acute food shortages to make way for an aerodrome, 'which, I understand, owing to pockets of wind, was a failure'?

By this time, Sir Howard Frank was being ruffled at the adverse publicity which the affair was attracting. An official communication was issued by the Ministry of Munitions which attempted to explain the government's position under the 1916 Act. It pointed to the huge expenditure carried out on requisitioned land during the war and emphasised that such capital construction work was undertaken at a time when it was not possible to know whether outright purchase of the land would be necessary or desirable after the war. The 1916 Act enabled the government, after the war, to give careful thought to the question of permanent acquisition within three years of the termination of the conflict (which, legally speaking, ended as late as midnight on 31 August 1921), thus permitting the exercise of purchase powers until 1924 for purposes not connected with the defence of the realm. A further provision, explained the communication, was to permit the government to sell any land so acquired subject to rights of preemption on the part of the original owner where no permanent buildings had been erected at government expense, a matter which held the attention of those involved in the Turnhouse affair.

To explain the apparently peculiar device of advertising for sale property which it did not own, the government argued that it now possessed an option to purchase a large number of properties but that in the case of some, such as aerodromes, it was impossible to know whether there was likely to be a market for them. The expedient of advertising that they were available for 'disposal' was adopted. If interested parties came forward, the communication

21. *Glasgow Herald*, 17 December 1919.
22. PRO, T 161/117/59364, memorandum by S.H. Wright.
23. Rhodes James, *Rosebery*, p.480.

added, the government 'can then ascertain the owner's views as to selling', and if necessary, seek the approval of the Railway and Canal Commission for compulsory purchase. If there were no response to the adverts, then the land would have to be reinstated prior to restoration to the owner. The essence of the advert was made out to be a testing of market interest, rather than an offer to sell; a negative response would lead to restoration of the property to the owner.

This was not what the government intended in respect to Turnhouse. For even if the deal with Edinburgh Corporation fell through, for one reason or another, the board was still intent on acquiring the property from Rosebery, even in the absence of a resale on the horizon. The reason was simple. It would be more economical to purchase, and then hold the land for an indefinite period, than to incur expenditure on reinstatement and restoration to Lord Rosebery. Since the 1916 Act granted a right of preemption, if Lord Rosebery wished to exercise this after the government had already bought the land from him, he would have to pay the value *in situ* of the buildings, in addition to the price for the land. This, also, would be more financially advantageous to the Exchequer than selling the buildings for scrap and restoring the property to Lord Rosebery.

These manoeuvrings were tortuous and it is not surprising that Rosebery was unimpressed by the government's case. For him, the issue was crystal-clear. He owned the property, yet the government laid claim to sell it. The two sides were 'as far apart as the poles, or as honesty from dishonesty', and to Rosebery, 'it is a matter of indifference, if I am robbed, whether it is by a pickpocket or a burglar.'[24]

Such unscrupulous actions should be a matter of shame. Instead, the government 'seem to glory in them. Times are changed ...' In vain did Sir Howard Frank protest that he was acting under statutory authority which also made provision for compensation. Rosebery's riposte on December 16 was still vigorous and animated:

> You resent being compared to a burglar or a pickpocket, but when anyone attempts to rob me of my land, I regard him as a thief. What is the case? You built a few huts at an insane cost on the edge of a fine farm, and now you claim to confiscate the farm to conceal the shameless waste of public money perpetrated by your department.
>
> You claim without a blush to protect the taxpayer. It is from you, however, that he needs protection, you who have spent £68,000 on these squalid huts. No wonder you wish to hide this extravagance. What I complain of is that you wish to hide it at my expense.
>
> That is the whole story. I cannot go on repeating it, or continuing a futile discussion. Your position, if sinister, is manifest; so is mine. You propose to sell a rich farm of mine against my will. It is unnecessary to repeat what honest men think of such conduct. The public must decide and I think it has.'[25]

24. Rosebery to Frank, 12 December 1919, copy in *Turnhouse: An Object Lesson.*
25. Ibid., 16 December 1919.

Perhaps the colourful comments of *Flight* magazine exemplify one strand of thinking on the affair sympathetic to the former Prime Minister:

It may be carelessness or deliberate annexation, but Lord Rosebery will be fortunate if he reaps any benefit from the transaction in any case, judging by other cases of 'grace' which have been so dis'grace'fully prevalent under bureaucracy. This object lesson ... should once more focus attention on the absolute necessity for the immediate abolition of the temporary power placed – or misplaced – in the hands of a gang of inefficient swankers [sic].[26]

Inevitably, the matter was soon raised in Parliament. On 16 December the Coalition Liberal member, Major H. Barnes, questioned Churchill, the Secretary for War, as to whether the government's cost-saving exercise involving Turnhouse Aerodrome:

ought to be done under the Defence of the Realm Act. He did not think it was intended by anybody that the Act should be passed in order to enable the Government to make a profit. There had been no idea that the Government would go in for business and trading in land.[27]

Perhaps more memorable was the contribution of an Irish member of the House, Joseph Devlin, who complained:

Things had come to a pretty pass when an Irish nationalist member had to stand up to defend Lord Rosebery against the Bolshevism of the Government [Laughter]. So low had the morale of this country fallen that the most eloquent Bolshevist orators were now to be found on the Ministerial benches. They could seize a former Prime Minister's farm with the same ability as they could suppress an Irish newspaper [Ironical cheers].[28]

The same day, the Parliamentary and Financial Secretary to the Ministry of Munitions, Frank Kellaway, spoke at Crewe on the controversy. He insisted that the issue went beyond the taking of Lord Rosebery's farm and embraced the relationship between the public and the private interest. In particular, the power of the private landowner to render virtually worthless government buildings constructed on his property, merely by refusing to part with his land at a fair price, was unreasonable. The legislation of 1916 which could prevent this was 'essential' in the public interest. Lord Rosebery could not see this as 'he had allowed his personal interest and convenience to colour his judgment', and had refused to purchase the buildings *in situ*. Kellaway particularly regretted the personal attack on Sir Howard Frank, who had worked for the government throughout the war for no remuneration (Frank

26. *Flight*, 4 December 1919.
27. H.C. Deb., 5th series, 123, 16 December 1919, col.304.
28. Ibid., col.306.

was a partner in the distinguished property agency, Knight, Frank & Rutley).
He also observed that, unlike the vast majority of landowners who had made
sacrifices without complaint:

> It was left to Lord Rosebery, from whom better things might have been
> expected, to secure for himself the unenviable isolation of complaining of
> sacrifices which other classes of the community had patiently borne.[29]

A cutting reply by Rosebery was delivered the next day:

> The Department have let loose one of their understrappers to deliver an invective
> against me. He says that he knows my record. I cannot reciprocate. He comes
> from the Ministry of Munitions, but I do not know whether he is a Minister
> or a Munition.
>   I rejoice in the violence of his language, because that is always the sign of a
> weak case, which it is intended to obscure. His invective lacks point, but that
> will improve with age and experience, and Mr Kellaway may yet live to annoy
> somebody . . . Mr Kellaway mouths a good deal about patriotism. Patriotism is
> a sacred word and should not be prostituted to perorations. I am not afraid of
> my record of patriotism, though no doubt it does not equal Mr Kellaway's.[30]

According to Robert Rhodes James,[31] a government minister indirectly involved
in the affair approached Rosebery's son a number of years later and apologised
for Rosebery's treatment at the hands of Sir Howard Frank. His son dismissed
the need for an apology. The controversy had given the old man a new lease of
life for another ten years.

Rhodes James also remarked that government ministers, alarmed at the
adverse publicity they were receiving, instructed the department to concede
Rosebery's wishes.[32] This may well have been prompted by motives not
only to avoid offence to a former Prime Minister with whose position the
general public might sympathise. It may also have arisen from policy doubts
concerning the need for civil aviation facilities in general and, in particular,
the involvement of local authorities in that activity. The Department of Civil
Aviation attached to the Air Ministry had been set up under Sir Frederick
Sykes in early 1919 and Sykes had identified the Edinburgh area as the
location for one of eleven 'key aerodromes' in the country.[33] He also
favoured the municipalisation of such aerodromes in preference both to
private ownership and management and to government ownership. However,
in September 1919, Churchill approved a more modest scheme for only
four aerodromes, with Edinburgh not eliminated from the scheme. Both
the Treasury and Sir Hugh Trenchard, Chief of Staff at the Air Ministry,

29. *Glasgow Herald*, 17 December 1919.
30. *The Times*, 19 December 1919.
31. Rhodes James, *Rosebery*, p. 483.
32. Ibid., p. 482.
33. Myerscough, 'Airport Provision', pp. 43–45 for this and subsequent information.

registered their hostility to the idea. In the case of Trenchard, he apparently disapproved of civil aviation in principle, while the Treasury made clear its preference for private initiatives and for the prioritisation of housing and educational schemes on the sites of redundant aerodromes, for which limited government financial assistance was available. Nonetheless, the Treasury did not expressly refuse to sanction the sale of aerodromes to municipal authorities: its penny-pinching approach towards the Turnhouse property simply reflected either its distaste for the application of public funds to such ventures or the concern of Treasury officials to demonstrate their economic soundness to the most senior departmental officials.

While the municipalisation of aerodromes did not meet with the universal support of government departments, and while Rosebery's campaign un-doubtedly attracted much sympathy (which could well have frightened govern-ment ministers into calling for a capitulation), the plan to purchase his property went ahead.

On 2 June 1920 the Disposal Board applied to the Treasury for authority to purchase.[34] Sanction was refused at this stage, though it appears that technical-legal reasons rather than a policy reconsideration were the cause. The legal powers of a local authority did not clearly embrace airport management and a change to the Aerial Navigation Act was awaited. In addition, doubts were being cast on the existence of compulsory powers in the Defence of the Realm (Acquisition of Land) Act 1916, which would enable the purchase of Turnhouse to proceed. This arose in the wake of a decision of Mr Justice Lush in *Minister of Munitions* v. *Mackrill* [1920] 3 K.B. 513, which had decided that the government could not purchase 'occupied' property with a view to resale for financial gains. As just such a resale was being envisaged in the Turnhouse case (and in many other instances), the government was forced to reassess the position.

The following month, 2 July 1920, Sir Howard Frank minuted his irritation to Churchill, Secretary for Air, and to his financial secretary, Sir Sigmund Dannreuther: 'It is all very well,' he complained, 'for the Treasury to sit tight, but in the meantime Lord Rosebery is working up an agitation for the return of his land, not because he wants it, but because it affords him an opportunity to attack the Government.'[35] Frank understood that Rosebery was arranging to have the fierce correspondence between the two parties privately published. It eventually appeared in a limited edition of one hundred copies as *Turnhouse: An Object Lesson*. Frank was also concerned that Rosebery's campaign would imprint in the public mind 'the wrong idea', which would in turn 'have a certain influence on the bench, especially when the question of hardship is the deciding factor, and not a question of law'. As the government were neither returning the land nor instituting compulsory purchase procedures

<hr />

34. PRO, T 161/117/59364, memorandum by S.H. Wright.
35. PRO, AIR 2/29/SCOTTISH/1960, Frank to Churchill and Dannreuther, 2 July 1920. For *Minister of Munitions* v. *Mackrill*, see below, chapter 14.

for the moment, Frank felt distinctly uncomfortable, even though Rosebery's position was not identical to that of Mackrill's, whose 'business' was being damaged by the continued government occupation.

The Scottish Law Officers, Thomas Morison and C.D. Murray, were consulted, and advised that the *Mackrill* decision would indeed prevent the Air Council acquiring Turnhouse with a view to a resale.[36] However, they confirmed that the Air Navigation Bill, then proceeding through Parliament, made provision for such acquisition without the need for the consent of the Railway and Canal Commission, though the Air Council would have to pay not only for the land but also for the buildings erected thereon. Yet a later opinion by Morison, dated 9 November 1920, repeated the fears that a resale was not contemplated by the terms of the Bill.[37] Prompted by the Mackrill and Rosebery cases, the government therefore decided to present a short bill to amend the Defence of the Realm (Acquisition of Land) Act 1916. That Bill became law on 23 December 1920 as the Defence of the Realm (Acquisition of Land) Act 1920. It provided that the power of acquiring land conferred by the 1916 Act should be deemed to have authorised acquisition for the purpose of resale, in those cases where such resale was required for the best realisation of buildings and works erected on the site by the occupying department, or where, for any other reason, it appeared expedient in the financial interests of the state to resell. A safeguard for the owner, however, was the retention of his right of pre-emption, as contained in section five, subsection three of the 1916 Act, provided that the buildings erected on the property were not permanent. As previously noted, however, this would require Rosebery to purchase those buildings *in situ* which he had previously described in derogatory terms, on the further understanding that they were, in fact, temporary.

With the necessary legislation now in place by the end of 1920, the Disposal Board sought further reassurance from the Scottish Law Officers that there would be no further embarrassing hiccups caused by inadequate legal powers. In particular, the Law Officers were asked whether the case was one in which the Railway and Canal Commission would be likely to authorise the use of compulsory powers. Secondly, the department raised anew the issue of a binding, preceding contract for sale between the department and Edinburgh Corporation. The Law Officers' opinion was delivered on 17 February 1921. The first question posed by the department was 'not a question of law', and so the Law Officers could only express their belief in an affirmative answer. On the second question, they again advised against such a contract and also warned of Rosebery's right of pre-emption if the buildings in question were temporary.[38]

36. SRO, AD 54/67, 'Power of Air Council to Acquire Turnhouse Airport Compulsorily under Acquisition of Land Act 1916 for Purpose of Resale to Edinburgh Corporation', opinion of Scottish Law Officers, 4 August 1920.

37. Ibid., 9 November 1920.

38. ibid., draft opinion, 17 February 1921. A clean copy of the opinion is in PRO, T 161/117/59364, memorandum by S.H. Wright.

If Rosebery desired to scupper the government's plan, he was at liberty to do so, so long as the department could not establish the permanent character of the buildings. The department had, indeed, originally acknowledged their temporary character. In the event, some departmental disagreement arose when a later inspection was carried out. According to the War Office's surveyor, Lt-Col. Archibald Thompson, the following brick buildings on the site, that is, Women's Royal Air Force (WRAF) rest house, water tower, tower house, two transport sheds, shower baths and machine gun range, while possibly termed of a permanent nature, were not 'any more permanent than those which are now being removed on the Horse Guards Parade'.[39] Frank, however, disagreed. On a visit on 14 March 1921 he concluded that, since the Turnhouse buildings had foundations while those on Horse Guards Parade did not, they were, in his opinion, permanent.[40] Such a finding would prevent Lord Rosebery exercising his right of pre-emption, were he so inclined to do so. As if to mock the advocates of a science of law, the Scottish Law Officers, in turn, doubted whether the buildings were indeed permanent for statutory purposes.[41] Thus the right of pre-emption remained, though payment for the value of the buildings *in situ* would be a deterrent to its exercise.

Negotiations with the owner of Turnhouse Farm, Lord Rosebery, and with the owner of Gogar Mains Farm, John Cowper, recommenced, with a view to reaching an agreed settlement. The effect was in vain. Rosebery remained adamant that only compulsory purchase would deprive him of ownership, while Cowper, likewise, informed Edward Coles at the Lands Directorate that he desired to continue to farm the land.[42] Cowper had already submitted a claim to the War Compensation Court, reflecting the previous occupation of his land and, faced with compulsory powers, realistically proposed to include this claim with the price for the sale of his property, which he intended to submit to the arbiter, James Davidson of Saughton Mains, Edinburgh. The department's Scottish agent, Campbell Smith, was himself alive to the bargaining ploys which could save on costs. Thus he sought authority from the Treasury Solicitor to make substantial unconditional offers to the sellers so that, if such offers were declined and the arbiter awarded less than offered, the Air Council would save on costs under the terms of the Acquisition of Land (Assessment of Compensation) Act 1919, section five (chapter fourteen, infra).[43] But Rosebery was proving stubborn and dilatory, partly due to outstanding negotiations on compensation for land which the ministry had previously willingly relinquished to him.[44] By February 1922 the Air Ministry

39. Ibid., Thompson to Frank, n.d. (*c.* 1 March 1921).
40. Ibid., Frank to Coles, 14 March 1921.
41. Ibid., Opinion of Scottish Law Officers, 24 March 1921.
42. PRO, AIR 2/29/SCOTTISH/1960, Cowper to Coles, 18 July 1921.
43. Ibid., Campbell Smith to Air Council, 15 September 1921.
44. War Compensation Court, *Second Report*, appendix, notes a payment to Lord Rosebery of £1,455 19s. 3d. (See appendix, no. 8491). No information is given concerning this award.

were faced with two options. The first was to restore the property to him and to agree a payment in lieu of reinstatement. A figure of £1,050 in full settlement was reached with his solicitors, an outlay which the ministry felt was a fair one in the light of the capital agricultural value of the land. The alternative was to purchase after arbitration, though in the view of the Air Ministry, this would leave the department 'with a parcel of useless land'. Nonetheless, Treasury sanction to purchase the land was given within a week.[45] The arbitration was conducted some weeks later, and a cheque for £5,958 13s. 2d. wended its way to Messrs Tod, Murray & Jamieson, solicitors to the Rt Hon. Archibald Philip Primrose, Earl of Rosebery and Midlothian, K.G., K.T.

There is one mystery to be cleared up. *Did* the ministry acquire a parcel of useless land rather than a viable aerodrome which was immediately thereafter to be sold to Edinburgh Corporation? As Myerscough has noted: 'Perhaps the most notable omission from the 1939 map of airport provision was Edinburgh . . .'[46] He observed that no agreement could be reached between the corporation and the Air Ministry for the civilian use of RAF Turnhouse and this prompted the corporation to explore further sites from 1928 onwards. Indeed, after the war, the aerodrome was used infrequently until squadrons of the Auxiliary Air Force and Special Reserve began to form up in the mid 1920s.[47] They included No. 603 (City of Edinburgh) Squadron, which was formed in October 1925 and flew DH9A day bombers.

In the late 1930s the RAF expansion scheme led to a 'station headquarters' being set up at Turnhouse and the airfield became host to further squadrons. Following the outbreak of the Second World War, construction work on a hard runway was commenced, as flooding from the Gogar Burn in rainy weather was proving troublesome. Turnhouse's importance during the early period of the Second World War was due to the fact that the east of Scotland was easily accessible to German aircraft, whereas the Low Countries formed an obstacle to their reaching Southern England. Consequently, much aerial activity occurred in the skies above Edinburgh at this time. For the rest of the war, a variety of fighter squadrons and army cooperation units spent time at Turnhouse. After 1945 runway extensions enabled British European Airways Viscounts and Vanguards to use the aerodrome until they were latterly replaced by shuttle jets on the London route. In April 1971, the British Airports Authority took over Turnhouse and built an entirely new runway which obviated the threat of dangerous cross-winds, which even Lord Rosebery had suggested would prove problematic more than fifty years previously.[48] A municipal airport of high quality had now been completed, with the earlier controversy merely a memory in the mists of time.

45. PRO, T 161/117/59364, Air Ministry to Treasury, 17 February 1922; ibid., Treasury to Air Ministry, 25 February 1922.
46. Myerscough, 'Airport Provision', p. 53.
47. (Anon.) 'RAF Turnhouse', p. 15.
48. Smith, *Action Stations 7*, p. 213.

Why had the scheme of municipalisation not gone ahead in the early 1920s? A number of false starts occurred throughout the country, with short-lived developments at Manchester (Alexandra Park), Birmingham (Castle Bromwich) and Glasgow (Renfrew).[49] Only at Croydon did a post-war municipal aerodrome successfully take root, while private aerodromes had little significance for passenger services. Government policy towards civil aviation was extremely lukewarm, so perhaps this attitude fed through to some municipalities. Even when Sefton Brancker replaced Sykes as head of civil aviation in 1922, little movement in the promotion of municipal aerodromes occurred till near the end of the decade, by which time the impetus behind Edinburgh Corporation's enthusiasm for Turnhouse had to be cranked up again. Brancker circularised the town clerks of all cities with populations of at least 10,000 to promote municipal aerodromes. He was now backed by the Air Council, alarmed at the progress attained in this sphere overseas. National pride, as well as strategic considerations, played their parts in the revitalisation of the campaign. By 1939 all the large cities, bar Edinburgh and Sheffield, had built municipal aerodromes, though the former had been actively looking for an alternative site to Turnhouse since 1928, after failing to reach an agreement with the RAF over the use of Turnhouse. It was more than twenty-five years after Sir Frederick Sykes, the Controller-General of Civil Aviation and former Chief of the Air Staff, had identified Turnhouse as one of ten 'key aerodromes' which ought to be retained in public hands in the interests of civil aviation, that the municipal aerodrome era arrived in Edinburgh.[50]

49. Myerscough, 'Airport Provision', pp. 45–47, for this and subsequent information.
50. Ibid., p. 61; PRO, T 161/117/59364, memorandum by S.H. Wright; PRO, AIR 2/29/SCOTTISH/1960, Frank to Dannreuther, 18 May 1920. For Sykes' own views, see Sir F.H. Sykes, *Aviation in Peace and War* (London, 1922). Cooper has recently described him as a visionary who was isolated from his colleagues in the wartime air service. See Malcolm Cooper, *The Birth of Independent Air Power: British Air Policy in the First World War* (London, 1986), pp. 129–30.

12

Compensation as Usual?

When the House of Commons was debating the Defence of the Realm (Amendment) (No. 2) Bill in March 1915, which conferred power on government departments to compel factories to undertake munitions work and otherwise to regulate or restrict their activities, anxious M.P.s expressed concern about the financial sacrifices this might entail for firms. In reply, the Chancellor of the Exchequer, Lloyd George, reassured them that compensation would be available for the:

> conduct of naval or military operations; for assisting the food supply; and promoting the continuance of trade, industry, business and communications, whether by means of insurance or indemnity against risk; the financing of the purchase and re-sale of foodstuffs and materials, or otherwise; for relief of distress, and generally for all expenses arising out of a state of war.[1]

A war risks shipping insurance scheme, underwritten by the state, had been hastily introduced on the outbreak of the war, to reassure the owners of the merchant fleets, while a compensation scheme for those suffering direct loss by enemy action, as in the case of the Zeppelin raids which had commenced on 19 January 1915, was also introduced.

The interruption and cessation of business contracts for non-essential products and their superimposition by munitions contracts, the very negation of 'business as usual', was likely to have wider economic ramifications. Would these wider consequences be taken into account, queried a back-bench Member of Parliament, Edward A. Goulding, when it was announced that a commission would be established to hear applications for compensation? He instanced the hypothetical case of a firm forced to decline a contract for a client with whom it had dealt for many years, as it was now obliged to undertake munitions work. That client would turn to an American firm to fulfil its requirements. If the new supplier proved satisfactory then the English firm would probably lose its valued customer for the future. Would that future loss be compensated, in addition to that incurred as a result of the interrupted contract? Lloyd George's response was unequivocal:

---

1. H. C. Deb., 5th series, 70, 10 March 1915, col. 1459.

> I think the speech of the hon. Gentleman opposite is an illustration of the way in which compensation ought most distinctly not to be given. The hon. Gentleman is demanding compensation in a spirit of exacting the uttermost prospective damage ... He wants not merely compensation for the actual loss in respect of the particular contract involved, but compensation in respect of possible loss of business. That is an impossible demand ... Every business is suffering.[2]

Moreover, it was urged by many that 'business' ought to be broadly interpreted, to permit claims also to be submitted by parties other than factory owners. Lloyd George himself identified the case of the person whose buildings may have been damaged or destroyed for the purpose of the defence of the realm. He also instanced the case of the farmer whose land had been rendered useless for agricultural purposes for the foreseeable future as a result of the construction of trenches or from other military operations. What was to be the basis for calculating compensation in those cases? While insisting that the proposed commission 'should sit down first of all and invite claims, and then themselves consider the principles upon which they should proceed', the Chancellor of the Exchequer had already put down markers. Prospective loss, as we saw above, was excluded. Instead compensation would be payable only for the actual loss and damage: for the direct loss suffered as a result of official requisitioning. It was thus implicit, and indeed soon made explicit, that generous compensation on Lands Clauses Act terms would not be permitted.

This pronouncement had two aspects though the first one was not spelt out in the parliamentary debate. The first dimension was that the compensation scheme was to be non-statutory. In other words, a Defence of the Realm (Losses) Commission (DRLC) was to be established under the royal prerogative to disburse compensation as appropriate on an *ex gratia* basis. No legal obligation to make such payments, apart from contractual agreement, was admitted. Indeed, the Treasury was adamant that the Crown's take-over of of private property under the Defence of the Realm Acts (DORA) and the relevant regulations was 'without any assurance of compensation to the owners or occupiers',[3] a proposition extended to requisitioning under the prerogative power, following the High Court and Court of Appeal rulings in the Shoreham Aerodrome case in 1915.

The idea for a non-legally enforceable claim to compensation seems to have derived from Henry Duke KC (1855–1939), the Conservative M.P. for Exeter. Duke became first chairman of the DRLC before his appointment to

---

2. Ibid., col. 1483. See also, chapter 2 above.
3. PRO, T 24/50, Treasury to War Office, 22 December 1914. The establishment of the DRLC was possibly a set-back for the Treasury inasmuch as it believed that the 'sacrifices required will in the majority of cases be only such as patriotic citizens can reasonably be asked to submit to, without compensation, and while the Treasury are prepared that exceptional cases of special hardship be considered on their merits as a matter of grace, the Treasury are opposed to any general scheme of compensation'. See ibid.

Asquith's and Lloyd George's Cabinets as Chief Secretary for Ireland from July 1916 to May 1918. His elevation direct to the Court of Appeal bench, from where he delivered a dissenting judgment in the *De Keyser* case in favour of the Attorney-General, followed thereafter and his career culminated in his appointment, as Lord Merrivale, to the presidency of the Probate, Divorce and Admiralty Division of the High Court (1919–33). In his speech in the Commons debate on the DORA (No. 2) Bill 1915, Duke made reference to the principle of 'eminent domain' (chapter two, supra), and suggested that heavy legal expenses could be avoided by establishing a compensation scheme under the royal prerogative which could make *ex gratia* payments. The idea was seized upon both by the Commons and by the government, despite the criticism, noted earlier, of the restricted scope of compensation.[4]

Prior to the Shoreham Aerodrome ruling and to the establishment of the DRLC in early 1915, the language employed in correspondence between the War Office and property owners was sometimes ambiguous where the specific authority of the defence regulations was not invoked. For example, on 5 October 1914, the commanding officer of the Royal Engineers in the Cardiff district wrote to the clerk of Barry Urban District Council in the following terms:

Dear Sir,

It may be found necessary to erect a number of huts for troops in the neighbourhood of Barry, and a site has to be selected.

Will you please ask your Council if they would be prepared to let the War Office have the use of the Recreation Ground near the County School for this purpose.

Yours faithfully,

(sgd.) Arthur R. Evans
Major C.R.E.,
Cardiff District.[5]

This letter apparently did not differ in kind from similar letters which commonly heralded the military occupation of premises,[6] and as the successor

---

4. H. C. Deb., 70, cols. 1490–93; D. DuBois Davidson, 'The Defence of the Realm Losses Commission and the War Compensation Court', *Journal of Comparative Legislation*, 3rd series, 5 (1923), pp. 234–52, at p. 235. Davidson was secretary, in turn, of the DRLC and the War Compensation Court.

5. War Compensation Court, *Second Report*, pp. 59–62, at p. 60.

6. One solicitor complained in 1916 that: 'Military authorities have been actively engaged of late in commandeering premises for various purposes, usually for billeting soldiers. The form of notice used in this locality states peremptorily that the premises are required under the Defence of the Realm Act and must be vacated by a certain date, usually within a week; but does not state the purpose for which the premises are required, and implies that the owner has no option in the matter'. He complained that DORA should only apply if there existed a 'well-grounded fear of imminent invasion or civil riot'. See *Solicitors' Journal*, 61, 21 October 1916, p. 7.

to the DRLC, the War Compensation Court (WCC), noted after the war, it could not be construed as a request for a free loan or gift of council property. In the case in question, the council intimated that they would be prepared to 'let' to the War Office the particular site. The next day, the Army moved in and stayed for five-and-a-half years, without negotiating over the suggested letting. The council for its part confirmed at a later meeting that 'the military authorities be allowed the use' of the land but made no reference to lease, loan or gift. As the WCC recognised in 1921–22: 'In 1914, there was no very clear understanding of the rights of owners of property to compensation for the use and occupation of requisitioned land . . .'[7] a situation remaining until the *De Keyser* decision in 1920. Nonetheless, the WCC concluded that the Crown had entered into occupation of the ground in 1914 in the purported exercise of the prerogative, while the question of compensation was left open. Such an interpretation is not inconsistent with the Treasury view expressed above, though it does not confirm that the War Office, for its part, believed that no compensation need be paid. The purpose of the establishment of the DRLC was at minimum to meet a moral obligation on the part of the government to property owners without conceding a legal obligation.

The second significant feature of Lloyd George's Commons statement was the basis for calculation of loss. He stressed that the principles of compensation in the Lands Clauses (Consolidation) Act 1845 were not to be applicable to the DRLC. The compensation provisions of the 1845 Act, passed in the age of railway expansion when the landed interest had not yet yielded to the power of industrial wealth, 'left the landowner with real opportunity to enhance his price upon a compulsory acquisition',[8] and the courts tended not to criticise ample awards by juries or by private arbitrators. The calculation might include an element for prospective use, even where the landowner was hardly likely to embark upon such a development. Additional recoveries might be obtained where adjoining land was diminished in some way, whether physically or not, while the sensitivities of the age of *laissez-faire* dictated that the pain of compulsory acquisition be soothed by liberal doses of financial consolation.

Such generous compensation provisions, also reflected in the Defence Act 1842, applied to land which was purchased outright, albeit compulsorily. The remit of the DRLC, by contrast, covered the case of interference with property or business rather than with permanent land acquisition. That latter contingency might also be subject to the separate compensation provisions of the Defence of the Realm (Acquisition of Land) Act 1916, in the case of those properties requisitioned during the war which the government determined to retain for social or economic reasons after the cessation of hostilities. The DRLC could also award *ex gratia* compensation in the event that goods, as

---

7. War Compensation Court, *Second Report*.
8. Cornish and Clark, *Law and Society in England, 1750–1950*, p. 153. See above, chapter 2.

distinct from land or buildings, were requisitioned for the defence of the realm. Here, also, the aim, conscious or unconscious, was to outflank the existing statutory provisions such as the Army Act 1881, section 115, which required market value compensation to be paid, rather than the direct loss incurred. As if self-conscious of the legal tightrope represented by the DRLC, the government amended Regulation 2B of the Defence Regulations in February 1916, to enable departments to requisition food, war *matériel* and 'any articles required for or in connection with the production thereof', without reference to price. In due course, even this subterfuge was exposed, the government consenting to specify the basis for compensation in revised regulations a year later (though arguably all regulations stipulating compensation at less than market value were *ultra vires* in the absence of legislative authority in the relevant Defence of the Realm Act itself).[9]

The terms of reference of the Royal Commission on the Defence of the Realm (Losses), when it was announced on 31 March 1915, were:

> to enquire into and determine, and to report what sums (in cases not otherwise provided for) ought in reason and fairness to be paid out of public funds to applicants who (not being subjects of an enemy state) are resident or carrying on business in the United Kingdom, through the exercise by the Crown of its rights and duties in the defence of the realm.

Apart from Henry Duke as chairman, the commission was initially composed of Sir Matthew Wallace (1854–1940), formerly president of the Scottish Chamber of Agriculture, and Sir James Woodhouse (1852–1921), later Lord Terrington, formerly Liberal M.P. for Huddersfield (1895–1906) and subsequently a member of the Railway and Canal Commission. Subsequent appointments, which enabled the DRLC to hold simultaneous hearings, thereby speeding up the proceedings, included Edward Shortt K.C., M.P. (1862–1935), Chief Secretary for Ireland from May 1918 to January 1919 and Home Secretary from January 1919 to October 1922. Further appointees were Laurence Hardy (1854–1933), Conservative M.P. for Ashford, Kent (1892–1918) and deputy chairman of the Commons' Ways and Means Committee (1905–6), William F. Hamilton LL.D., K.C. (1848–1922), bencher of the Middle Temple and author of *Company Law* (1910) and *Compulsory Arbitration in Industrial Disputes* (1913), and William Watson K.C., M.P. Leading surveyors such as Sir John Oakley (1867–1946), president of the Surveyors' Institution, and agricultural land inspectors such as Ernest Savill O.B.E. and J. M. Clark were also appointed, as were architects from the Office of Works. They sat in London with occasional hearings in Edinburgh. As the remit attempted to make clear, in the absence of contractual agreement for the rent of property,

9. Hurwitz, *State Intervention in Great Britain*, pp. 152–53. See above, chapter 8 and below, chapter 14.

claims would only be entertained if applicants renounced all other legal claims and thereby conceded the Crown's right under the prerogative or the defence regulations to requisition property without any legal duty to pay compensation. It was assumed, perhaps in anticipation as much as in hope, that patriotic zeal would inspire the good citizen to banish any thoughts that more rewarding legal redress might be available in preference to the offer of such *ex gratia* payments as 'ought in reason and fairness to be paid out of public funds to applicants'. The *Second Report* of the DRLC, issued in 1917, did indeed observe that claimants had 'cheerfully' acquiesced in the awards of the commission. It added:

> We regard this as the more noteworthy tribute to the general sense of patriotism because the complexity of the problems arising out of the present emergency has necessitated the application of State interference in a number of fields which had previously been left to the unrestricted effort of private enterprise, and where such interference would previously have been regarded as arbitrary unless it had been accompanied by liberal or even lavish compensation.[10]

Hurwitz points out that such patriotic acquiescence could be explained by the lack of alternative means of obtaining redress, with claimants under the impression that no legal right to secure market value compensation was available.[11] It was not only the Shoreham Aerodrome rulings in 1915 but a more prevalent hesitation on the part of the ordinary citizen to involve himself or herself in legal proceedings, especially against the Crown, which severely limited the number of legal challenges. The determined professional men, George Wingfield and Arthur Whinney, were not so easily bluffed.

How did the system of requisition, followed by reference to the DRLC, operate? We have already noted that nineteenth-century legislation, including the Army Act 1881, section 115 and the provisions for billeting in Section 106 of that act, assumed that the market principle would operate. There is some indication (despite the strong opinion of the Treasury that no compensation for requisitioned land, buildings or goods was due as of right once war had broken out) that the Army was busy settling claims with property owners. Whether market value compensation was being paid in those cases, rather than compensation for direct loss, is not, however, clear. We have already noted the tortuous early negotiations over compensation between the Office of Works and Arthur Whinney, the receiver of De Keyser's Royal Hotel Ltd. before the dispute moved on to a different plane. The memoirs of a country lawyer, Tilney Barton,[12] reveal that following Barton's recruitment on an unpaid

---

10. DRLC, *Second Report*, P.P.1917–1918, x, Cd. 8751, 1917, p. 3.
11. Hurwitz, *State Intervention in Great Britain*, p. 152.
12. Tilney Barton, *The Life of a Country Lawyer in Peace and War-Time* (Oxford, n.d., *c.* 1931), ch. vi for this and subsequent information. See above, chapter 6.

part-time basis on to the staff of the War Office land agent on Salisbury Plain, soon after war was declared, he was heavily occupied investigating local claims for compensation. In one case he travelled to a large remount camp to settle compensation with a small farmer who had been compelled to sell off dairy cows, hay and marigolds following the commandeering of part of his land. The claim was for more than £1,200, which was stated to represent a loss of 50 per cent on the forced sale of those items. In the event, all the subjects of the sale were found to be still *in situ*, the farmer eventually admitting that the stock had been bought by sympathetic friends who had allowed him to repurchase them. A fictitious sale, the active participation of friends and of a local auctioneer and valuer hardly squared with the commission's later praise for patriotic restraint.

Following the establishment of the DRLC at the end of March 1915, Barton was given paid employment at Southern Command headquarters. He was advised that all claims against the War Office would have to be approved by the DRLC and that he in turn would have to scrutinise the reports of the War Office land agents within his command. A colleague at the War Office Lands Branch wrote:

> Both you and the Agent directly concerned will have to be prepared to give evidence before the Commission when the particular claim comes up. They are pretty certain not to award more than we assess, but if our assessments are modest, and well thought out, I think they may generally adopt them.[13]

Barton was not wholly complimentary about the command land agents who were serving officers. He illustrated his point by demonstrating how a shooting tenant, claiming compensation for loss sustained by him by virtue of his shoot being surrounded by Army camps, had doctored the figures by describing all kills as birds, whereas the majority were rabbits and hares.

Another appointment soon followed for Barton, this time as Chief Compensation Officer and Captain at Southern Command, taking over from the Royal Engineers all matters relating to land acquisition within the command. Despite an overlap with the work of the Officer-in-Charge Barracks and of the Assistant Quartermaster-General, he also dealt with matters arising from the acquisition and occupation of buildings. Eventually, a more comprehensive arrangement took root when a distinct Lands Branch, Southern Command, was established with Barton as Lands Branch Officer. The following list gives an indication of the scope and geographical breadth of his work:

Golf course at Falmouth (camp)
Rifle range at St Budeaux, Plymouth
Pendennis Hotel, Falmouth, used for hospital
Buildings at Weston-Super-Mare (quarters)

---

13. Ibid., p. 45.

The Colston Hall, Bristol (recruiting station)
University Buildings, Bristol (Cadet Corps)
Aerodromes at Fitton, Cirencester, Salisbury Plain, etc
Houses at Swanage, Bath, Cheltenham, Winchester, Boscombe, Milford-on-Sea, Weymouth
Colleges at Oxford, used for hospitals, Training Corps and Flying Corps
Houses at Leamington
Halls, buildings, schools etc. at Birmingham
Buildings at Coventry, Frome, Warwick, Worcester
Golf Club, Malvern (camp)
Race Course, Portsmouth (camp)[14]

He was highly critical of the Ministry of Munitions and of the Office of Works, which, he complained, secured property within his area without regard to cost, for the use of different government departments. The former department used its requisitioning powers in respect to land, while the latter rented buildings at what Barton considered were extravagant rents. By contrast, the War Office strictly instructed its lands branches to rent buildings and leave the question of compensation to the DRLC. The ploy proposed by the War Office that tenancy contracts be terminated and be replaced by requisitioning without compensation in the period prior to the establishment of the DRLC seems not to have been adopted in Southern Command.

Interdepartmental rivalries over the hiring of premises sometimes surfaced. In Birmingham, for example, Barton pointed out that the Ministry of Munitions had installed numerous inspectors in 'fine suites of offices at extravagant rents'.[15] A large building called Lincoln's Inn then became available to the War Office free of rent and authority was granted to Barton to take over the building if existing government departments could be persuaded to transfer their offices to Lincoln's Inn and thus save on existing rentals. Not only did the Ministry of Munitions refuse to transfer their inspectors to the spacious accommodation in Lincoln's Inn, they installed their Inspecting Office, Mechanical Transport, in a new suite of offices at a high rental. This doubly affected the War Office. If Lincoln's Inn could not be filled, the condition for requisitioning it could not be met. Secondly, the activities of the Ministry of Munitions in the rented property market might push up the level of rents for the War Office. Whether the awards of the DRLC reacted against this upward push was not explored by Barton.

The administrative duties involved in quartering troops in empty premises were daunting to Barton and to the department land agents. In the early days of the war, scores of houses were commandeered in Southern Command and filled with troops who were not too conscientious in respecting their

14.   Ibid., p. 62.
15.   Ibid. See above chapter 5.

physical surroundings. Mantelpieces, banisters, skirting boards, stair-treads were all vulnerable to damage, resulting in the payment of considerable sums for dilapidations. In the winter of 1914, £10,000 in compensation was paid over. Marching-in and marching-out inspections had to be undertaken in the presence of the land agents, while regimental officers were under command instructions to carry out daily and weekly inspections, instructions which were sometimes ignored. When the 72nd Division and the South Midland Brigade were transferred to the Midlands in January 1917, 860 houses had to be vacated and inspected by the land agents checking for dilapidations.

A further complaint voiced by Barton was the failure of the War Office to employ the resources of the Inland Revenue Land Valuation Department in assessing compensation. For example, in one case a claim for £1,500 had been submitted for damage to a block of disused and virtually derelict farm buildings. The War Office land agent had supported the claim but Barton ascertained from the local valuer that the buildings had been valued for the purposes of probate at £400 two years previously. It is arguable, of course, that some property values had risen significantly in the interim period. In addition, there are some doubts as to the reliability of the Land Valuation Department's assessments, which were for the purposes of death duties calculation. But as Offer has indicated, 'Valuations other than actual sales were bound to be more or less arbitrary due to the imperfection of the property market . . .'[16]

By the end of 1917 Barton's appointment at Southern Command HQ had come to an end. This followed major reorganisation initiated by Sir Howard Frank when he assumed the post of Director of Lands at the War Office (in addition to his appointment at the Ministry of Munitions) some months earlier. All work in respect to lands and to quartering was now transferred to London, leaving local management in the hands of the land agent, with no further need for Barton's expertise in this sphere of administration.

Turning to the DRLC itself, it will be recalled that Lloyd George announced in the Commons that the commissioners, charged with determining what sums 'ought in reason and fairness' to be paid as compensation, would themselves work out the principles guiding their awards. These principles were gradually revealed in the introductions to the five reports issued by the DRLC between 1916 and 1920. However, the most important principle was, as we have seen, contained in the royal warrant itself and not evolved by the commission. That was that the DRLC would not entertain claims 'otherwise provided for', that is, where the applicant had, or claimed to have, a right enforceable at law. This provision was designed to prevent individuals or businesses from submitting claims to the DRLC and then, perhaps disappointed with the level of award, subsequently going to law with the same claim. As we shall see, this did not deter some applicants from applying to the DRLC and then subsequently

---

16. Avner Offer, *Property and Politics, 1870–1914: Landownership, Law, Ideology and Urban Development in England* (Cambridge, 1981), p. 109.

seeking a remedy through the courts, as De Keyser's Royal Hotel in fact attempted.

The provision was also intended to exclude from consideration by the commission claims which did not arise from the exercise of prerogative powers or from defence of the realm regulations. Thus in one case, an applicant sought compensation from the DRLC because the Ministry of Munitions erected a factory on land adjoining the applicant's.[17] The latter had built his house surrounded by green fields and now found that his pleasant view of the countryside had been removed. While the DRLC sympathised with the applicant's predicament, they confessed that any remedy for the detriment suffered would lie with an action in the courts for nuisance. Such an interpretation might have been an unduly restrictive view of the commission's remit, though it may be noted that no actual financial loss appeared to have been suffered while the applicant continued in ownership of his property.

In contrast was the situation where claimants acknowledged that they possessed no right to compensation in peacetime but nonetheless argued that on the basis of 'reason and fairness', the DRLC ought to award them some compensation. An example might be a 'golden handshake' or some other *ex gratia* payment awarded in peacetime. Such a claim would be dismissed by the DRLC. So, also, would be one where the Crown took steps on defence grounds arising out of the conduct of an individual. This might apply to an individual who perhaps trespassed onto Admiralty or War Office property and was deported to a different part of the kingdom under Reg. 14B, rather than prosecuted under the Official Secrets Act 1911, section 1. The leaders of the Clyde Workers' Committee, deported from Glasgow to Edinburgh in March 1916,[18] would thus not have qualified for compensation, in the unlikely event that they had been disposed to apply to the DRLC.

Such a scenario might be contrasted with the case of H. L. Suhr, listed in the *First Report* of the DRLC covering the period March 1915 to August 1916.[19] The applicant was a middle-aged tailor, born in England but of German parentage. For six years he had lived with his wife and children in an area now proclaimed as subject to restrictions on aliens and those of alien background. Suhr was a British subject but the Army deported him under Reg. 14 on the ground that his 'sympathies might naturally be with the Germans'. Nonetheless, as his own conduct was not the cause of his removal (the military authorities seem to have over-reacted), his case fell within the scope of the DRLC: compensation was awarded for the 'interference' suffered.

Two other broad principles were established. One, cited previously, was that compensation was for actual loss suffered, not for the market value loss, unless

---

17.   PRO, MUN 4/6912, 'Claims and Losses: Disposal of Surplus Government Property'.

18.   Rubin, *War, Law, and Labour*, p. 96. See also War Compensation Court, *Third Report* (London, 1923), pp. 18–22 (case of Samuel Maddick). See comments on Maddick in PRO, HO 45/13350/419253/4.

19.   DRLC, *First Report*, P.P.1916, vii (Cd. 8359), 1916, appendix, no. 9.

the two happened to coincide. A case listed in the *Third Report* concerned a dynamo built by the Electric Construction Company and requisitioned by the Ministry of Munitions. The equipment had been earmarked for a customer at £567. The ministry later asked the company to tender for an exactly similar dynamo. It offered one for £816, which the ministry accepted. In determining the compensation payable for the requisitioned item, the DRLC decided that the actual loss was £816, the price accepted by the ministry for the commissioned dynamo. Here the direct loss was the fair market value of the equipment as reflected in the accepted tender price.

Having rejected claims for loss of anticipated profits, the commission also expressly ruled against the payment of compensation for consequential damage (notwithstanding that the two heads of loss might overlap). In its *Second Report*, it cited claims for the requisitioning by the Army of a motor chassis and wagon. In these cases, the legal authority invoked was section 115 of the Army Act which provided for compensation fixed by a county court judge with reference to fair market value. The owners found that their business activities thereafter were more confined than previously, as a result of the requisitioning, and sought compensation for the 'consequential damage' incurred. The DRLC noted that as the Army Act was silent as to whether consequential damage was recoverable, it assumed that no such provision existed in the act although it declined to hold that the legislation specifically forbade such payment. Since the commission's remit was in respect to 'cases not otherwise provided for', and as 'cases' referred to 'cases of interference' rather than to categories of loss or damage not otherwise provided for, it concluded that it possessed no jurisdiction to award for consequential damage.[20]

In summing up the cases of loss or damage, the *First Report* asserted:

> Except in an exceedingly small minority of cases, applicants have cheerfully acquiesced in the view that payment for the actual loss caused to a subject in the course of the operations of public defence is a reasonable and sufficient discharge of his claim upon the State and that to forgo the commercial profit which might have been gained upon like transactions in time of peace or between subject and subject is a reasonable and patriotic sacrifice.[21]

Thus, when agricultural land was commandeered, farmers' claims based on the estimates of future crops were disallowed. Only the value of crops then in existence or the value of land then in occupation was allowed.[22] A farmer whose fallow field was taken over by the military would obtain no compensation, on the ground that he was suffering no loss. The same

---

20. For the later rehabilitation of 'consequential damage', see below.
21. DRLC, *First Report*, para. 9.
22. J. A. Fairlie, *British War Administration* (New York, 1919), p. 153.

would apply in the case of an unoccupied house, though a reservation would exist in respect to a possible change of circumstances where continued Crown occupation would lead to a loss incurred by the property owner. Moreover, if occupation led to the suspension of a business which was being carried out at a loss at the date of occupation, and which was capable only of being so carried on during the relevant period, no award would be made, unless the occupation were to cause additional loss. The DRLC had in mind the cases of municipal undertakings and charitable organisations but it may be recalled that at the time of its requisitioning by the War Office, most of the facilities of De Keyser's Royal Hotel were also being run at a loss which, from the government's point of view at the time, justified the denial of any compensation for its occupation. Finally, it was laid down that compensation would not be payable merely for loss of amenity or of pleasure. The case cited previously, of the applicant whose view of green fields surrounding his house had been rudely disturbed by the building of a government factory would be such an instance, as was the case (listed in the *First Report*) of the diminution of shooting rights on a country estate caused by the establishment of a military firing range over part of the shoot. As the rights were admitted to be only for pleasure, the owners did not suffer the requisite damage to 'property or business'.

The fourth significant principle was that compensation was payable only to those directly affected by the exercise of Crown powers and would not be available to those affected by the general operation of a legal power for the defence of the realm. If produce was requisitioned by government order, the compensation was available to the owner. If, however, a producer was no longer permitted to export to enemy countries by virtue of the general applicability of the Trading With the Enemy Acts, then he fell outwith the scope of the DRLC. Other similar illustrations from the reports include the photographer whose business was disrupted following the general prohibition on photographing certain areas and sites, the hirer of pleasure boats who could no longer ply his trade after the Admiralty imposed general restrictions on sailing in prescribed waters, and the onion exporter whose business suffered when a general order banned onion exports and caused a dramatic fall in the price of the produce.

A variant on this theme was that only the person or business directly affected by the exercise of a Crown power, and not the persons or businesses who themselves dealt directly with the first category, could seek compensation. In one example quoted in the *First Report*, the Ministry of Munitions requisitioned a factory owned by suppliers of spelter. This had the effect of depriving a firm of metal merchants, who were the applicants to the DRLC, of the delivery of a quantity of spelter which the factory had agreed to supply. The merchants suffered financial loss as a result but were awarded no compensation. Similarly, when the Admiralty exclusively occupied some docks, a stevedoring firm formerly employed there by a shipping company lost business, for which it also received no compensation. Finally, in a more complex set of transactions, a firm of meat retailers had contracted for 40,000 carcasses of frozen New Zealand meat. Following discussions between the New Zealand and British governments, the former prohibited the export of all meat to anywhere except the United Kingdom. They followed this up by purchasing the whole stock of New Zealand meat which they then sold to the British government. The latter sold part of it to wholesalers, who in turn sold a quantity to the applicant at a higher price than it had agreed to pay on the original contract for the 40,000 carcasses. The DRLC ruled that the applicant was affected by the operation of general regulations and could not therefore recover for the increased costs incurred.

It may be noted that the DRLC was directed to pronounce on 'substantial' claims, but the seriousness with which it pursued this aim may be gauged from the case of Mrs E. A. Ireland who claimed for occupation of a house. She sought just £1 and was awarded the same.[23]

In looking somewhat randomly at a few more of the claims, some odd results can be shown. To accommodate all the prisoners of war and interned aliens, to store vast quantities of munitions and to provide training spaces, the authorities took over racecourses and football grounds. Yet while York racecourse received all the £1,600 it asked for, and while Carlisle racecourse (near the huge Gretna munitions village) received £700 as against the £1,300 it sought, Sandown racecourse claimed £14,000 and obtained nothing.[24] The stewards of the course, as the *Second Report* recounts, had cancelled nearly all race meetings following representations by Sir Walter Runciman, President of the Board of Trade. There then occurred the military occupation of the land and buildings followed by an application by the stewards for compensation for loss of profits, due to the cancellation of six days flat racing and six days steeplechasing. The Crown replied by admitting the occupation but denying that that had caused the loss of business, as racing had already been suspended at the time of the occupation. The stewards' response was to argue that were it not for the occupation, they could obtain a licence to resume racing. They pointed to submissions to Runciman by the Association of Racehorse Owners, Breeders and Trainers in October 1915 of a scheme for

---

23. DRLC, *Schedule to First Report*, P.P.1918, viii (Cd.9048), 1, appendix B.

24. The clerk of the course at Sandown, T. A. Hwfa Williams, later submitted a claim, reported in the *Fourth Report*, for loss of fees. The award was refused as no 'interference with business' could be established. The DRLC held the clerk was in no different position to that in which he might find himself were the stewards to have sold the racecourse to a third party which then declined to continue using it for this purpose. Nor did the stewards themselves fare much better during the period August 1921–August 1922 when they submitted a claim for £5,245 14s. 0d. and were awarded just £31 10s. 0d. See War Compensation Court, *Second Report*, p. 97. Under Reg. 9B, the minister had power to ban race meetings if he had reason to apprehend that the holding of such meetings would impede the production of war material. Such a power was exercised in October 1916 in respect to future meetings at the Carntyne Trotting Grounds in Glasgow (except for a meeting held on New Year's Day, 1917). The owner was able to secure compensation from the commission for his loss of profits on ten proposed meetings which were cancelled under Reg. 9B. See PRO, MUN 4/6912. The position in respect to Sandown Racecourse was wholly different.

race meetings at a number of courses. This would not necessitate the running of trains, there would be small attendances and any profits could go to the Red Cross or similar. Of fifty-seven courses listed in two submissions, only six, including Lingfield and Newbury but not Sandown, were approved, as they were not then under military occupation. The Sandown stewards took this as confirming that the refusal of a race licence was due to the military occupation of their course and that therefore their business suffered interference by the Crown. Just so, admitted the DRLC, but as the profits were to be handed over to charity, no loss of profits was incurred by the occupation and therefore the only compensation awardable was for the minimal outgoings on the property and for the occupation thereof (where the latter caused actual loss, perhaps by way of dilapidations).

In respect to the occupation of rooms, perhaps for the recuperation of injured officers or for clerical use, King's College, Cambridge, sought £946 and received £896 and an annual payment of £122. Selwyn College obtained £890 instead of the £1,000 claimed. St John's was awarded £115, just under £100 less than it claimed, while Corpus Christi College, Oxford, was given £42, precisely what it sought. The more intriguing claims included the Central Unemployed Body for London, seeking compensation for occupation of a labour colony; the rejected claim of Mr S. Salter for interference with his bathing-machine business (he was perhaps the innocent victim of an order of general application declaring part of the coastline a closed area); the Reigate Constitutional Club sought compensation for the occupation of caves; the Anglo-Continental (formerly Ohlendorff's) Guano Works was awarded nothing (because at the date of 'interference' it was, in fact, a German company, even though later acquired by a British firm); the Bank of Scotland increased its considerable balances by five pounds, the amount it had been seeking, while (a presumably different) W. Owen sought compensation for occupation of a distillery.

The activities of the DRLC between its establishment on 31 March 1915 and its expiry on 20 August 1920, when it was renamed as the (statutory) War Compensation Court can be summarised in Table 2. The commission clearly felt pride in educating the spending departments of government to appreciate more clearly the actual cost basis for settling with those whose property claims had been considered. The principles of compensation thus enunciated had enabled the DRLC 'to reduce misconceived and/or inflated claims to moderate and just proportions', in the words of the *Third Report*. More than half of the amounts claimed, whether as lump sums or as annual payments, were allowed, but claims amounting in total to £3,427,921 were rejected, a significant saving to the Treasury. There is a consistent pattern of upwardly increasing awards over the five year period in respect to annual payments, which may reflect inflationary trends. In the case of lump sum payments, the increased generosity of the DRLC (especially in the year 1917–18) is dramatically reversed for 1918–19 before reverting to an upward course. One would, perhaps, expect an increase in successful applications over time, as the more speculative claims were eliminated and as wider knowledge of the principles of compensation,

Table 2

Defence of the Realm (Losses) Commission
31 March 1915 to 20 August 1920

1	2		3	4	5	6	7	8	9
Year	Hearings		Applications	Lump Sum Claims (in £s)	Lump Sum Awards (in £s)	Proportion of (5) to (4)	Annual Claims (in £s)	Annual Awards (in £s)	Proportion of (8) to (7)
	London	Edinburgh							
31 March 1915 to 31 August 1916	130	13[1]	1,094	652,779	276,965	42.4%	355,694	191,857	53.9%
1 September 1916 to 31 August 1917	129	5	1,128	1,011,496	439,177	43.4%	273,507	154,630	56.5%
1 September 1917 to 31 August 1918	206	8	1,232	2,707,460	2,038,288	75.2%	336,107	213,341	63.4%
1 September 1918 to 31 August 1919	220	17	1,362	1,101,061	331,397	30.0%	567,991	383,978	67.6%
1 September 1919 to 20 August 1920	190	4	1,163	1,082,992	677,429	62.5%	194,936	145,437	74.6%
Total	–888[2]	–	5,979	6,554,809	3,763,256	57.4%	1,728,235	1,091,827	63.1%

Notes:　1　Includes one hearing in Dublin.
　　　　　2　386 applications withdrawn.

Sources:　DRLC, *First Report*, P.P. 1916, vii, Cd. 8359, 1916, p. 1; ibid., *Schedule to First Report*, P.P. 1918 vii, Cd. 9048, 1918, p. 1; ibid., *Second Report*, P.P. 1917–18, x, Cd. 8751, 1917, p. 485; ibid., *Third Report*, P.P. 1918, viii, Cd. 9181, 1918, p. 35; ibid., *Fourth Report*, P.P. 1919, xiii, Cmd. 404, 1919, p. 905; ibid., *Fifth Report*, P.P. 1920, xiii, Cmd. 1044, 1920, p. 861.

and indeed of the scheme itself, was disseminated. But such an explanation does not fully match the figures in the returns.

The DRLC felt obliged to express its regret at the substitution of other bases for compensation under particular DORA regulations. It observed that Regulation 2B which authorised the requisition of goods (such as Newcastle Breweries' rum) on the basis of cost, plus an allowance for profit at the rate usually earned prior to the war, might not be objectionable as it covered permanent expropriation, whereas the DRLC was more commonly concerned with temporary interference with business. However, it considered that the recently enacted Corn Production (Amendment) Act 1918, substituting for the DRLC a large number of scattered and unconnected paid arbitrators without any definite or clear basis for compensation for requisitions by the Food Production Department of the Board of Agriculture was unwelcome. No doubt it feared the reintroduction of extravagant claims for loss of profits and a generous accommodating response by some arbitrators.

With the enactment of the Indemnity Act 1920, the DRLC became the War Compensation Court, presided over by the High Court judge, Sir Alfred T. Lawrence (later Lord Trevithin and appointed Lord Chief Justice in 1921 until replaced by Gordon Hewart the following year), and by the Court of Session judge, Lord Hunter. Wallace and Hamilton retained their posts from the DRLC and two further appointments were made. They were Sir Dunbar Plunket Barton K.C. (1853–1937) and Sir Francis Taylor, the judge of the Liverpool Court of Passage. Barton had been Conservative member of parliament for Mid Armagh, and a bencher of Gray's Inn as well as Solicitor-General for Ireland (1898–1900) and a judge of the Irish High Court (1900–18).

The terms of reference of the court under the Indemnity Act were to assess compensation under three heads.[25] First, the specific directions in this regard contained in defence regulations were to apply in relevant cases. This appeared to be so even where such compensation provisions had previously been declared *ultra vires*, for example, Reg. 2B in the *Newcastle Breweries* ruling. This may be inferred from the wording of section two, subsection two, paragraph one of the Indemnity Act which referred to 'any Regulation or order made or *purporting* to be made' under DORA (my italics).

Second, the principles enshrined in the Admiralty Transport and Arbitration Board scheme would apply in respect to shipowners' claims. Third, and more significantly,

(a) If the claimant would, apart from this Act, have had a legal right to compensation, the tribunal shall give effect to that right, but in assessing the compensation shall have regard to the amount of compensation to which, apart from this Act, the claimant would have been legally entitled, and to

25. This section is based, in part, on Scott and Hildesley, *The Case of Requisition*, pp. 161–66.

the existence of a state of war and to all other circumstances relevant to a just assessment of compensation:

Provided that this subsection shall not give any right to payment or compensation for indirect loss [section 2(2) (iii) (a)].[26]

To what types of claim did this provision apply? It appears to have applied to those cases where the claimant could in principle establish a legal right which had been infringed by actions by the Crown or by Crown servants but in respect of which the 1920 Act itself declared could only be pursued through the War Compensation Court. A proviso to this restriction preserved the right to sue the Crown under the petition of right procedure for breach of contract, so long as proceedings were instituted within one year of the legal termination of the war or the date when the cause of action arose, whichever was the later. Thus the 'legal right' envisaged might be a claim for compensation for occupation of land which, as the *De Keyser* decision in the House of Lords had shortly before confirmed, was guaranteed by the provisions of the Defence Act which in turn overrode any purported prerogative power to take without compensation. It might also be a claim for compensation for requisitioned goods taken under a defence regulation which did not prescribe the method of calculating compensation; the validity of which regulation might be impugned so as to confer on the claimant a legal right which the Crown had infringed. That the court was now directed to have regard 'to the existence of a state of war and to all other circumstances relevant to a just assessment of compensation', was an invitation to it to evolve its own principles of compensation, though whether the injunction to refuse compensation for 'indirect loss' signified any change of legal principle would depend on whether it was taken to mean that the court should ignore remote damages or whether it was required to apply the 'direct' loss principle of the DRLC. That latter instruction was contained, by reference to Part II of the schedule to the act, in section 2(2) (iii) (b) which governed the claims of those who 'would not have had any such legal right' to compensation, irrespective of the Act. Part II of the schedule read:

Principles on which the Defence of the Realm Losses Commission has hitherto acted. The compensation to be awarded shall be assessed by taking into account only the direct loss and damage suffered by the claimant by reason of direct and particular interference with his property or business, and nothing shall be included in respect of any loss or damage due simply and solely to the existence of a state of war, or to the general conditions prevailing in the locality, or to action taken upon grounds arising out of the conduct of the claimant himself rendering it necessary for public security that his legal rights should be infringed, or in respect of loss of mere pleasure or amenity.

26. 'Except' seems more appropriate than 'apart'. See PRO, T 161/88/56659/1, C. L. Fielder, Admiralty, 'Memorandum relating to the War Compensation Court', December 1920. For the Admiralty Transport and Arbitration Board scheme, see above, chapter 10.

The assumption was that legal powers to interfere with business or to requisition without payment of compensation were available to the Crown in circumstances other than those in which litigation or statute had established that this was not so. It was the lodestar by which the departments had guided themselves in regulating the economy during the war, even where it was recognised that such an assumption was fantasy.

Did the War Compensation Court pursue a path similar to that trodden by the DRLC, or was the lifting of the restrictions of the command economy reflected in the adjudications of the court? One major event may have haunted the deliberations of the court. That was the effect of the *De Keyser* decision on public awareness of the fragility of the government's legal powers in respect to compensation. Virtually the whole point in enacting these provisions of the Indemnity Act was to rescue the government from the financially crippling prospect of having to pay out nearly £700 million in compensation if the act were not passed.[27] Given that *De Keyser* implied that claimants such as hoteliers and landowners now possessed an independent right to compensation, rather than to a mere *ex gratia* claim, those who had already been before the wartime DRLC might now feel they had grounds for the reopening of their wartime awards. For these had been calculated on an actual loss basis, whereas *De Keyser* upheld the more favourable Defence Act basis. The Indemnity Act endeavoured to plug this gap by providing in section two, subsection three, that where any claims had been made, disposed of, or rejected before 15 April 1920, that is, the date of the first reading of the Bill in the Commons (and one month before the House of Lords decision in *De Keyser*), then no further claims arising from the same requisition could be brought without leave of the court. The court, in turn, emphasised that such leave would be granted only on proof of a material change of circumstances relating to the applicant or of new evidence not previously available.

Was the *De Keyser* ruling such a material change of circumstances or new evidence not previously available? The question very quickly came before the War Compensation Court, in an application for payments or compensation additional to those awarded by the DRLC.[28] The company involved, the Newfield Sanitary Pipe Co., had been taken over by the Ministry of Munitions in April 1917. Their claim for reimbursement of the rent paid on the property leased by them for their business had been rejected by the DRLC, but compensation for extra insurance premiums paid by the company had been allowed. The War Compensation Court, having considered that the claim had thus been disposed of or rejected by the DRLC, now had to consider whether, under section two, subsection three of the Indemnity Act, there had been a material change of circumstances, so as to enable the company to apply for further payments or compensation, that is, for reimbursement of the rent actually paid.

27. Hurwitz, *State Intervention in Great Britain*, p. 153. See below, chapter 13.
28. War Compensation Court, *First Report* (London, 1921), pp. 16, 20.

The company's view was straightforward. The House of Lords decision in *De Keyser*, confirming a legal right to compensation and not merely a liberty to apply for an *ex gratia* award, constituted just such a material change. But it was never likely that such a claim would be admitted, given that it would undermine the very purpose of the Indemnity Act in saving the Treasury from financial catastrophe. The court approved the Attorney-General, Gordon Hewart's, submission that: 'the judgment in the De Keyser case had not changed the law but had explained and expounded the law appropriate to the case and that the law was the same before and after such decision and that it was open to the claimants in 1917 to pursue, if they so elected, their legal claim'.[29]

The court therefore rejected the claimant's proposition that *De Keyser* constituted a material change to the circumstances of the company (or indeed that the Indemnity Act itself was a material change). 'Proof' of such a material change, it was stressed, required the existence of 'facts in the case itself' and not merely a change in judicial opinion. Indeed, there was clear authority that the courts in the pre-war period had refused to allow a past transaction or proceeding to be reopened, merely because of a change of judicial opinion. The decision was plainly a critical one which, if it had been decided in favour of the claimants, could have sparked off a large spate of applications to reopen previous determinations.

The failure to establish that *De Keyser* constituted a material change of circumstances did not establish what could be such a change. The Northern Brick Company Ltd sought to base its claim to reopen the award of the DRLC on this ground.[30] The government had occupied its premises on 28 June 1916 for the storage of munitions. This had not interfered with its brick-making business, which had been in abeyance while it concentrated on other activities. The DRLC had granted an award in July 1917 for occupation of the premises and the company now wished to reopen that settlement. It claimed that from the spring of 1917 a demand for bricks for the construction of munitions factories had begun; that in August 1917 the Army Council requisitioned the output of brick works in its district; that contractors were anxiously seeking further supplies of bricks; and that brick works were now making healthy profits. The applicants claimed for the loss of profits they would have earned had they been able to reopen their brick works and that the increased demand for bricks was a material change of circumstances. The court held that the loss of the hypothetical profits was due solely and merely to the existence of a state of war and that such a general factor was excluded by Part II of the schedule to the Indemnity Act as a ground for awarding compensation. If the profits actually earned by other firms were to be held to be a material change of circumstances, there was no evidence that any such profits would have been

29. Ibid., p. 19.
30. Ibid., *Second Report*, pp. 57–59.

made by the claimant. 'Material change of circumstances' thus remained a very elusive concept.

What of the further development by the War Compensation Court of the principles expounded by the DRLC or indeed the establishment of new principles by which to assess compensation claims? A number of examples will illustrate the point. Take, first, the issue whether there had been direct interference with the claimant's business or whether the claimant merely suffered as a result of the general application of emergency powers. In one case, an Army Council order of July 1917 was issued declaring that the council was taking possession of all raw horse hides in the United Kingdom and instructing all owners to furnish particulars of their holdings to the Director of Army Contracts.[31] The claimants, who were American, had wanted to export the hides to the United States, but an embargo on such exports had already been imposed and an export licence refused. The claimants made the return of their holdings as required by the order. Between July and October 1917, the hides remained in store, the army eventually deciding, after inspecting the goods, that it did not wish to acquire them and releasing them for sale. An export licence was at last granted but the quality of the hides had suffered by being kept in store over the summer and autumn: the claimants sought compensation for the depreciation in their value.

In its judgment, the War Compensation Court held first that the Army Council order, taking possession of all horse hides in the country, was not a requisition of the particular goods of the claimants and was therefore not a direct or particular interference with the claimants' property. Any loss sustained by them arose either from the operation of the original embargo on export, from the general order of July 1917, from the refusal to grant an export licence, or from the abortive negotiations in respect to the proposed sale. Compensation for loss was therefore refused. One can see how a narrow conception of property was employed by the court: merely the physical ownership of the goods, not extending to any right freely to dispose of them. If the latter had been recognised as a property right, direct interference with that right could have been established when the export licence had been refused.

In a similar case, the owner of an office site at the junction of King William Street and Cannon Street in London was refused a building licence to develop the site by the Director-General of National Service under Reg. 8E.[32] He sought compensation for two years' ground rent to August 1919, when building eventually commenced, and for loss of interest on borrowed money. The court interpreted Reg. 8E as a general order of 'interference' prohibiting all such building work unless a licence were granted; the refusal to relax a general interference did not amount to a direct and particular interference with

31. Ibid., *First Report*, pp. 9–11 (Case of Messrs L. Beebe and Sons).
32. Ibid., *Third Report*, pp. 22–25 (Case of R. Stafford Charles).

the claimant's property or business. Otherwise, it cautioned, anyone wishing to build would be entitled to compensation for loss simply by having a licence refused in accordance with the general restriction.

In October 1914 cloth was seized by the police from a Swiss carrying on business as a cotton exporter. The legal authority for the seizure was the proclamation of war of 3 August 1914 and section eight of the Customs and Inland Revenue Act 1879, which the WCC held was properly regarded as an enactment relating to the defence of the realm.[33] The allegation against the exporter was that he was proposing to export component parts of aeroplanes, airships and balloons, but the magistrate dismissed the subsequent prosecution, not being satisfied that the goods in question were in fact such components. The police nonetheless held on to the goods for some time before the trader was able to sell them to Vickers Ltd in March 1915. He now sought compensation for their detention and the direct interference with his business. As in the cases above, his claim failed on the grounds that the interference was by virtue of the operation of an order of general application.

The case also gave rise to a different issue, one which addresses the historical judgment advanced by Hurwitz that the cheerful acquiescence of the subject in sacrificing his property rights disguised the reality of the lack of choice available to him. Six other parcels of goods of the claimant were 'transferred' to the Crown in 1918, for which he claimed £9,000, the sum of the difference between the amounts paid by the Crown and the alleged market value or reasonable prices for them. The Crown replied by arguing that there had been no requisition and that the goods had been purchased by agreement and payment accepted before 15 April 1920. The Court reviewed the evidence and concluded:

> while it is clear that the department intended to have these goods, and used some expressions indicating that the goods were to be reserved for them, and also would no doubt have requisitioned them if necessary, the claimant, in consequence of the large quantities which he held and the impossibility of selling to any of the allied governments, did, in fact, sell the goods to the Crown at the prices of which he now complains.[34]

Payments were made and receipts given. It could not be sustained that the claimant entered into the transactions under the threat of requisition. 'From the exigencies of the situation, it was the best he could do, and he did it, though reluctantly.'

In another case, where premises were occupied,[35] it was alleged that written signed agreements had been obtained by duress. The court, however, concluded that the claimants or their agents 'fully understood' the agreements

---

33. Ibid., *Seventh Report* (London, 1928), pp. 45–53 (Case of William Gschwind and W. Gschwind & Co.). See comments on Gschwind in PRO, HO 45/13350/419253/4.
34. War Compensation Court, *Seventh Report*, p. 45.
35. ibid., *First Report*, pp. 15–16 (claim of W. Bracey).

they signed, and signed them in order to have an agreement for a fixed amount rather than face a requisitioning order and a later claim for compensation. 'We think it very probable that the claimants were told by the Military Authorities that if they did not agree the premises would be taken. This was an accurate statement of the position.' No doubt the potential contractor weighs up the opportunity costs of failing to enter into an agreement in a free market situation. Whether the concept of opportunity costs can apply to *force majeure* situations seems distinctly unlikely in classical theory. The notion of 'agreement' recognised by the court seems somewhat strained. One can understand, perhaps, why a number of businesses and individuals would feel compelled to join together to form an 'Association for the Protection of Owners and Occupiers of Commandeered Premises', an organisation which does not seem to have made any significant impact on events.[36]

The concept of the general effect of war, explored in the Northern Brick Company Limited case, was reconsidered in a claim for compensation for structural damage to properties in Clapton.[37] The damage was alleged to have been caused in 1917 by vibration generated by the firing of an anti-aircraft gun placed on Clapton Orient football ground. Such damage, it was claimed, was by reason of interference with private property through the exercise of a prerogative power or under Reg. 2, clause (f), which enabled the Crown 'to do any other act involving interference with private rights or property' necessary for the defence of the realm. The Crown denied that the above legal powers applied to the case here, alleging that the doctrine of necessity operated. If the firing of the gun were held to be an exercise of the prerogative, any loss or damage was due solely to the existence of a state of war and that compensation therefore was excluded by the act. The court refused to be drawn into the possible legal basis for the firing of the weapon, holding only that there was no direct and particular interference with the claimant's property. The firing was not aimed at the property even though the resulting damage was particular. The disturbance of the atmosphere was general and likely to cause general loss, a consequence due simply and solely to the existence of war.

The situation was distinguished from that in a Scottish case, *Monypenny* v *Lords Commissioners of the Admiralty*, where a British mine in a dangerous condition had drifted onto the coast on the claimant's property. As a safety measure the mine was blown up, causing damage to Monypenny's house. The Inner House of the Court of Session held that direct interference by virtue of Reg. 2F had occurred, entitling the owner to compensation. Whereas the arrival of the mine from the sea on the claimant's property might be due simply and solely to the existence of a state of war, it was impossible to say that its destruction was entirely due to the same cause.[38]

36.   *Solicitors' Journal*, 62, 5 January 1918, p. 187.
37.   War Compensation Court, *Third Report*, pp. 92–94 (claim of Misses Stevens).
38.   *Monypenny* v. *Lords Commissioners of the Admiralty* 1922 S.C. 706; see also War Compensation Court, *Third Report*, pp. 62–67.

Perhaps the most significant aspect of the War Compensation Court's jurisprudence was its detailed analysis of what fell within the scope of direct loss. In particular, how were claims for loss of profits resolved? It will be recalled that under the DRLC, claims for speculative profits were not allowed but only for loss of profits on items then in existence which could not subsequently be sold. This might be because of requisition or because the land or premises on which the goods or product were being grown or produced before sale had been occupied by the Crown. While the calculation of loss of profits in the case of marketable commodities for sale might not be problematic from the standpoint of actual loss, the calculation of direct loss might be more complicated in respect to certain goods, such as ships available for charter, or of land or buildings (apart from questions of payment for mere occupation). Two major cases, both eventually reported in the official law reports, as well as in the periodical reports of the War Compensation Court, analysed these questions in detail.

The first case concerned the Elliott Steam Tug Company Limited, which in November 1914 chartered the tug *Frank* from her owners.[39] The company could retain her as long as they pleased, with a right to determine the hiring on fourteen days notice in writing. The rate of hiring was £155 per calendar month. On 19 May 1917, the Admiralty requisitioned the tug, retaining her till November 1919, but the company decided not to determine the charter as they desired to re-employ her after derequisitioning by the Admiralty. The compensation claim submitted was for the amount of hire which they continued to pay to the owners during the period of the requisition and for the loss of profit they would have made during that period by the use of the tug. They were willing to allow credit for all sums paid by the Admiralty to the owners, which the latter had passed on to them.

The War Compensation Court, confirmed by the Court of Appeal, held that, to minimise loss, the company ought to have terminated the hire (though the court allowed the company one month's hire representing a reasonable period in which to decide upon a course of action). As to the loss of profits, 'or expressed more accurately, the loss of what would be the average and ordinary net earnings of the tug during the period of requisition', the War Compensation Court had similarly allowed thirty days' loss of profits rather than loss of profits for the period of May 1917 to November 1919. The Court of Appeal first upheld the claim for loss of profits (ignoring for the moment the period covered) as DRLC-based direct loss within the meaning of section 2(2)(iii)(b) of the Indemnity Act, where the company, as a charterer rather

39. Ibid., *First Report*, pp. 13–15; ibid., *Second Report*, pp. 8–25; *Elliott Steam Tug Company Limited* v. *Shipping Controller* [1922] 1 K.B. 127 (C.A.). Cf. War Compensation Court, *Second Report*, pp. 44–51 (claim of the Moss Steamship Company); *Moss Steamship Company* v. *Shipping Controller* [1923] 1 K.B. 447; War Compensation Court, *Fourth Report* (London, 1924), pp. 73–75 (claim of W. A. Jenkins & Co.).

than owner of the tug, would not have had any legal right to compensation apart from the act. To the objection of Crown counsel that the DRLC (which included the War Compensation Court) had never employed the practice of awarding compensation for loss of profits, the Court of Appeal had no judicial notice of this point. In any case the Court of Appeal were dealing with the 1920 Act and interpreting it accordingly. In regard to whether loss of profits for two years or only for thirty days should be recoverable, the Court of Appeal were prepared to call for further evidence on the matter. The company themselves pointed out their inability to obtain another tug on reasonable terms at the time. Either their continued payment of the hire of the *Frank* would be seen as a direct (that is, consequential) loss following the requisitioning, and should therefore be recoverable, or the unavailability of another tug was due solely and simply to the existence of a state of war, in which case the hiring costs were not recoverable. On the reference back to the War Compensation Court, this latter proposition was held to be factually correct.

The second major case was a claim by a firm of taxi and garage proprietors in Dublin whose premises had been requisitioned by the Royal Air Force in September 1918.[40] The claimants argued that they could only preserve their business by purchasing other premises which they were obliged to equip and adapt to their own purposes. The adaptation of the substituted premises was to be completed as quickly as possible. This meant heavy labour costs with much overtime working, while the equipping of the new premises proved an expensive task. They were forced to this expedient, having failed to rent suitable alternative premises in the locality while awaiting the derequisitioning of their original property. When this latter occurred, in March 1920, they sold the alternative premises at a loss. The central question was whether the expenditure on the substituted premises should be compensated as a 'direct loss'. The War Compensation Court originally disallowed this claim but was overruled by the Court of Appeal. That latter court agreed that the finding of fresh premises and any loss occasioned by that undertaking could be, as both a question of fact and a question of law, a direct loss caused by government interference with the claimants' business. So long as the steps taken by the firm were reasonable in the circumstances, compensation for the net losses incurred in purchasing and adapting the substituted premises, as well as for the cost of reinstatement of the requisitioned premises (after deducting the proceeds of sale of the substituted site), was recoverable. The Court of Appeal rejected the finding of the War Compensation Court that the expenditure on the substituted premises was an indirect result of the requisition of the original premises. It was, the Court of Appeal held, a direct result of requisitioning. As such, the applicants suffered direct loss for which they were entitled to recover compensation.

40. Ibid., *Second Report*, pp. 67–83; *A. & B. Taxis Limited* v. *Secretary of State for Air* [1922] 2 K.B. 328.

Where, apparently, the War Compensation Court had been in error was in holding that the Indemnity Act, by referring to 'direct loss' in the schedule, had excluded compensation for 'consequential' damage, which it took to be, inter alia, the expenditure made on adapting the new premises to the needs of the company's business. In an ordinary common law action, argued Lord Hewart, the Lord Chief Justice and president of the War Compensation Court, 'you can get consequential damage which is direct. Here consequential damage is cut off by the statute'. The Court of Appeal disagreed. As Lord Justice Atkin replied:

> Now that appears to me to be precisely the point – the difference between the view taken by the Court below and the view taken by this Court. In my view it is impossible to say that consequential damage is cut off by the Statute. The learned President himself says that it may be direct, and if it is direct it appears to me that it may give rise to a direct loss by reason of the interference with the property. The President goes on to say, 'But is it ever made direct by it being a reasonable thing for somebody else to do? There you get the intervention of another doing something which he thinks reasonable [here, the claimants purchasing and adapting the new premises after the government's interference with the original premises]. That at once cuts off the direct [loss] and makes it consequential'. From what I have said I think it follows, at any rate within my view, that that is a mistaken view of what is meant by 'direct'. Indeed the word appears to me to connote no more than the rule for determining the measure of damages arising from any breach of duty, whether in contract or in tort, which gives rise to a claim for damages ... It may be that up to the passing of the Indemnity Act the Defence of the Realm (Losses) Commission had not always proceeded upon that view, and instead of giving all the direct loss it gave something less than the direct loss. That I do not know'.[41]

Thus 'direct loss' in the act had to be construed according to its plain and ordinary meaning (which would include consequential loss), and it was quite impossible to construe it by reference to any suggestion that the principles of the DRLC fell short of that plain statutory meaning.[42] It may be that the distinctive facts of the case, whereby the taxi company with a large fleet of cars and garage facilities had to obtain equivalent, spacious, local accommodation to that requisitioned, explains the broad approach to direct loss. It is perhaps also significant that the absence of suitable alternative premises for rental was not attributed, as was done in the *Elliott Steam Tug* case, to the general factor of the existence of a state of war which otherwise would have prejudiced the company's full claim.[43]

41. War Compensation Court, *Second Report*, pp. 80–81.
42. The judges cited *Weld-Blundell* v. *Stephens* [1920] A.C. 983 (H.L.) in support of their reasoning.
43. The case was remitted to the War Compensation Court to settle the compensation for direct (including consequential) loss. See War Compensation Court, *Second Report*, pp. 82–83.

Table 3

War Compensation Court
20 August, 1920 to 31 March 1929

	1	2	3	4	5	6	7	8	9
	Year	Hearings	Applications	Lump Sum Claims (in £s)	Lump Sum Awards (in £s)	Proportion of (5) to (4)	Annual Claims (in £s)	Annual Awards (in £s)	Proportion of (8) to (7)
1)	20 August 1920 to 16 August 1921	234	1203	1,973,972	1,246,678	63.1%	65,458	38,940	59.4%
2)	16 August 1921 to 16 August 1922	219	856	2,490,060	1,311,114	52.6%	13,198	12,314	93.3%
3)	16 August 1922 to 16 August 1923	176	656	2,122,956	866,147	40.7%	4,982	3,674	73.7%
4)	16 August 1923 to 16 August 1924	155	422	1,660,429	761,018	45.8%	4,928	3,629	73.6%
5)	16 August 1924 to 16 August 1925	100	189	733,239	363,618	49.5%	NA	NA	NA
6)	16 August 1925 to 16 August 1926	74	139	855,684	373,556	43.6%	NA	NA	NA
7)	16 August 1926 to 16 August 1927	84	92	1,473,085	266,505	18.0%	NA	NA	NA

Table 3 (cont.)

War Compensation Court
20 August, 1920 to 31 March 1929

1	2	3	4	5	6	7	8	9
Year	Hearings	Applications	Lump Sum Claims (in £s)	Lump Sum Awards (in £s)	Proportion of (5) to (4)	Annual Claims (in £s)	Annual Awards (in £s)	Proportion of (8) to (7)
8) 16 August 1927 31 March 1929	2[1]	—	—	—	—	—	—	—
Total	1044[2]	3557[3]	11,309,425	5,188,636	45.1%	88,616	63,696	71.6%

Sources: War Compensation Court, *First* to *Eighth Reports* (inclusive), 1921–29.

Notes:
1. Presumably relating to applications lodged in the previous period.
2. A combined figure for London and Edinburgh, the latter hearing 67 applications between August 1920 and August 1926.
3. 295 claims were withdrawn or otherwise disposed of, including 39 during the final period of 16 August 1927 to 31 March 1929.

In one respect, the War Compensation Court may be seen as a worthy successor to the DRLC, inasmuch as it consciously aimed to minimise the financial burden on the government. That it went too far for the Court of Appeal's liking in this regard can be inferred from the latter's criticism of the War Compensation Court's approach to direct loss. The additional speculation that the DRLC might likewise have been unjustifiably tight-fisted would not, one might think, unduly have worried the Treasury. In January 1927 Sir David Neylan, the secretary of the Surplus Stores and Liquidation Department at the Treasury which had responsibility for the remaining wartime munitions stores still in government hands, wrote to his Treasury colleague, J. T. Davies.[44] He had been informed by another colleague, G. L. Barstow, that the Treasury wished to close down the War Compensation Court on 30 July 1927 and would not be asking parliament to vote more money for compensation. It was therefore essential that government departments should make every effort to bring their outstanding cases before the court at the earliest possible date. Neylan, however, advised Davies that the court had 'behaved very reasonably from a Governmental point of view', and that, if it were to close down prematurely, there was a risk of losing more in awards than in the expense of maintaining the court in existence. Perhaps this meant that the repeal of section two of the Indemnity Act which made provision for the war compensation scheme might lead to common law proceedings for interference with property under the *De Keyser* principle, with potentially heavier awards than those issued by the War Compensation Court. Some of the outstanding claimants might prove stubborn. The Port of London Authority, for example, which had eleven claims against the War Office still unsettled, had proved 'difficult people to deal with'. In the end, the curtain fell on 31 March 1929. The vital statistics of the court are shown in Table 3, the most significant finding being that the court awarded less than half the lump sum payments sought, saving the Treasury £6,120,789. The court's judgments in just two cases, which went eventually to the House of Lords for resolution, led to a net saving on other claims of £813,000.[45] Inasmuch as from the very outset the DRLC saw its task as to work in harmony with the Treasury,[46] the latter cannot have been too displeased with either that body or its successor, the War Compensation Court.

44. PRO, MUN 4/6311, Surplus Stores and Liquidation Department, Treasury, 'Reports on Position of Land Compensation Cases', 12 April 1927.
45. War Compensation Court, *Eighth Report* (London, 1929), n.p.
46. PRO, T 80/1, 'Defence of the Realm (Losses) Commission, Minutes of 1st Meeting', 31 March 1915.

13

The Scrapping of English Constitutional Law since the War?

The Indemnity Act 1920 made provision for the continuation of payment of compensation to those whose properties or businesses had suffered interference as a result of war measures taken by the Crown. Behind the verbose provisions of the statute, with its tortuous guidelines on the bases for compensation, lay a delicate preparation of the ground before eventual enactment. It was perceived by the officials presenting it as a highly controversial measure which would attract intense parliamentary opposition unless the merits of what was being proposed could be justified to its harshest critics.

The very title of the proposal, the Indemnity Bill, hinted strongly at what might be considered highly distasteful in the provision. For Indemnity Acts had graced, some might say disgraced, the statute book in the past, and were designed to relieve the executive of legal liability for their own intentional or unintentional wrongdoings during some crisis or other. As A. V. Dicey, the celebrated constitutional lawyer, then or now, remarked, 'An Act of Indemnity is a statute, the object of which is to make legal transactions which when they took place were illegal, or to free individuals to whom the Statute applies from liability for having broken the law.'[1] This was parliamentary sovereignty *in extremis*, at its most suspect and disreputable, where the canons of the rule of law, subjecting individuals or the Crown to legal accountability for their own illegalities, could be blatantly suppressed or, more charitably, where the goalposts were moved. For Dicey, there were always pragmatic justifications for such measures which:

> afford the practical solution of the problem which perplexed the statesmanship of the sixteenth and seventeenth centuries, how to combine the maintenance of law and the authority of the Houses of Parliament with the free exercise of that kind of discretionary power or prerogative which under some shape or other, must at critical junctures be wielded by the executive government of every civilized country.[2]

---

1. A. V. Dicey, *Law of the Constitution* (6th edn, London, 1902), p. 547. His opinion was cited in the House of Commons debate on the second reading of the Indemnity Bill. See H. C. Deb., 5th series, 128, 3 May 1920, col. 1796 (A. Shaw).

2. Dicey, *Law of the Constitution*, p. 408.

No hint here of Parliament as an elective dictatorship, in Lord Hailsham's phrase in 1977, nor as the chamber into which, as Sir George Trevelyan once suggested, a score or two of members would rush 'between two mouthfuls of soup', anxiously demanding, 'Are we Ayes or Noes?', and then being directed accordingly into the appropriate division lobby. Dicey evidently failed to conceive of the possibility of Parliament as a mere tool of a ruthless executive, compliantly doling out retrospective legalities for illegal executive conduct. For Dicey, 'critical junctures' would always test the capacity of governments to act in the public interest within the law; if they were to step over the boundary of legality occasionally, then outright condemnation would be unfair and legalisation justified.

A glance through the statute book, especially for years immediately following the cessation of hostilities, points to a succession of Indemnity Acts in the past. They would invariably neutralise the legal consequences of suspending habeas corpus, whose suspension would be accompanied by the executive detention of suspects without trial. Such action was technically a trespass giving the detainee a right to legal redress unless an Indemnity Act denied him his remedy. The Indemnity Act passed after the Boer War did precisely this. The 1920 Act went further.[3] It provided first, in section one, subsection one, an indemnity against personal liability for Crown servants, whether they be civil servants, government ministers or military personnel, who acted illegally or exceeded their powers. This was subject to the proviso that the action complained of was done in good faith and in the execution of duty or for the defence of the realm or the public safety or for the enforcement of discipline, 'or otherwise in the public interest'. A government department itself could certify that authority for the impugned action existed, while good faith was presumed to exist unless the complainant could demonstrate otherwise. The section also barred, subject to exceptions, all legal proceedings of whatever kind against the Crown, in respect of anything done during the war. Indeed a petition of right, the device by which De Keyser's Royal Hotel, Newcastle Breweries and many others commenced their proceedings, was a 'legal proceeding'. The exceptions were important. First, a petition of right for breach of contract, but not for any other remedy such as illegal occupation of property, was preserved.[4] The Act also made elaborate provision for the payment of compensation by the Crown in a number of other circumstances. The most important were those matters, discussed in the previous chapter, falling within the scope of the War Compensation Court. Provision was also made for receipt of compensation for shipowners whose cargo or passenger

---

3. For this and the following section, see Scott and Hildesley, *The Case of Requisition*, pp. 158–61.

4. It will be recalled (chapter 6, above) that the petitioners in *De Keyser's Royal Hotel* did not allege a trespass by the Crown. Otherwise, their claim would be barred on the basis of Crown immunity from proceedings in tort. They admitted a legal right of occupation by the Crown, thus permitting the employment of the petition of right procedure in order to seek compensation.

space or vessel had been requisitioned during the war and who prior to the Act sought *ex gratia* payments from the Admiralty Transport Arbitration Board.

While, at first sight, an Act which made provision for payment of compensation could hardly be controversial *per se*, the circumstances of its enactment, coinciding with the climax of legal proceedings in both the *De Keyser* and *Newcastle Breweries* cases, injected a strong note of opposition to the measure among certain politicians. The government's principal advisers were aware both of the suspicions harboured against any measure which retrospectively whitewashed official wrongdoings, albeit committed in the 'public interest', and of the incoming tide of legal rulings which might further embarrass, both financially and otherwise, the government and the legitimacy of its domestic emergency measures.

How was the question of an Indemnity Act handled by government departments and what reasons were advanced to ministers to justify confronting Parliament with such a controversial measure? The origins of the measure were to be found in a recommendation by Lord Cave's Committee on the Continuance of Emergency Legislation after the Termination of the War. The committee's first report of 5 February 1919, after considering the recommendations of a War Office emergency legislation committee, advised that an Act of Indemnity be passed, and that it should provide *inter alia* that all claims arising out of or in connection with the war be barred unless presented within twelve months after the termination of the war or within twelve months after the date on which such claims arose, whichever was the later.[5] Lord Peel, Under-Secretary of State for War, suggested to the War Cabinet in May 1919 that given the 'possible early termination of the war' (in the strictly legal sense of signing peace treaties as a prerogative act), a Bill should be immediately prepared by an interdepartmental committee.[6]

The committee, which first met on 6 June 1919, had in front of it a draft Bill,[7] which only partially addressed the compensation issue while focusing primarily on the scope of the indemnity to be granted to those acting in a governmental executive capacity.[8] Reference to the practical difficulties the

5. PRO, CAB 24/5, G.233, 'War Cabinet. Committee of Home Affairs. Continuance of Emergency Legislation After the Termination of the War', 5 February 1919. See below, chapter 14.

6. PRO, CAB 24/78, GT.7297, 21 May 1919. The Home Affairs Committee of the Cabinet approved Peel's proposal two days later. See CAB 26/1, H.A.C. 29(2), 23 May 1919.

7. PRO, LCO 2/440, 'Memorandum no. 4. Interdepartmental Committee on Indemnity Bill and Statute of Limitations'.

8. One major concern was the potential personal liability of Board of Trade Controllers and their superiors in illegally winding up a business under the Trading With the Enemy Acts and in unlawfully prohibiting the importation of goods other than arms, ammunition and gunpowder under the Customs (Consolidation) Act 1876, section 46. See PRO, BT 103/32 and chapter 3, above. In respect to the prohibition on legal proceedings (which were conceptually distinct from compensation claims before the War Compensation Court) exceptions would be permitted (a) on behalf of the Crown (suing its own officials); (b) for breach of contract, subject to a limitation of twelve months; (c) for negligence; (d) for damage to persons or property in a foreign country, subject to the *fiat* of the Attorney-General; or (e) in respect to the validity or infringement of a patent.

government would have to confront on the question of compensation was soon made by the Ministry of Munitions representative on the committee, E. D. Chetham Strode.[9] He pointed out that the Defence of the Realm Losses Commission (DRLC) would only award compensation where the claimant renounced the option of going to court. He added that in a large number of cases, parties actually signed documents to this effect. Yet it was not certain that such an undertaking would be binding in law and he considered that there was a very considerable risk of large claims being made against the government as soon as the Defence of the Realm Acts ceased to operate. Chetham Strode was aware of pending proceedings which might destroy the legal basis on which limited compensation was payable and was presumably aware of the compromise outcome of the Shoreham Aerodrome proceedings in the House of Lords. Finally, he must have known that the termination of hostilities would have lessened the commitment of property owners to acquiesce 'cheerfully' in short-changed requisitioning.

At the next meeting of the committee, on 20 June 1919, it was decided to validate the institution of civil proceedings in respect to property requisition where a statutory right to compensation already existed. This decision was clearly prompted by the Court of Appeal ruling which had been delivered on April 9 in favour of the suppliants in the *De Keyser* case. The committee felt that by this stage a denial of the *De Keyser* principle was not feasible, though this still left open the possibility of barring the reopening of cases already decided by the DRLC. The Law Officers had already advised against the validation by legislation of the DRLC principles whilst these principles were still *sub judice*. At the meeting on 20 June the Solicitor-General, Sir Ernest Pollock, reiterated his objection to immunity in dealing with clause one, paragraph (b) of the Bill, which was designed to prevent ordinary civil proceedings for damage or for requisitioning under the authority or purported authority of defence regulations (thereby forcing recourse to the DRLC, *faute de mieux*). The Law Officers' advice was not pleasing to other government departments. J. A. Corcoran from the War Office pointed out that vast sums of money were involved and that the 'present state of uncertainty' as to the basis on which compensation was to be assessed was causing 'almost insuperable' administrative difficulties. Edward Coles from the Lands Branch commented that as far as land was concerned, owing to the decision in the *De Keyser* case, the department did not know how to deal with claims, as no one would go to the DRLC, and it was invidious for the department to refuse all compensation. From the Ministry of Munitions, Phillip Guedalla expressed concern about the status of Reg. 2B's provisions for compensation for requisitioned commodities, that is, the cost price plus pre-war rate of profit basis, as against the current market price. (The *Newcastle Breweries* case was still pending, the petition of

9. | PRO, LCO 2/440, 'Memorandum no. 6. Minutes of Proceedings of the First Meeting', 6 June 1919.

right having been submitted in May 1918 but with the court hearing before Mr Justice Salter not yet arranged.)

The Solicitor-General responded by stressing the effect that the forthcoming Acquisition of Land (Assessment of Compensation) Act 1919 would have.[10] This measure was intended to overcome the delays and extravagances of the Lands Clauses Act of 1845; would apply to all cases of land compulsorily applied to public purposes under any statute; and would have retrospective effect, though not to the extent of reopening decided issues. It might therefore provide a model for payment of compensation for wartime requisition, even though the latter covered mere temporary occupation. Coles, however, reminded the committee that the principle of compensation in the Land Acquisition Bill, based on what would be agreed between a willing buyer and a willing seller (that is, in effect the market value of the property) would not meet the requirements of his branch, which desired to limit compensation to actual loss. The adoption of any other basis would simply invite the reopening of an enormous number of claims. Given the committee's lack of consensus, the matter was sent back to the Law Officers, though the committee agreed that the question of validation of compensation in the case of land ought to be (but was not) dealt with in a separately drafted bill. In the event, the Law Officers acknowledged the point of view of the departments and, at the next meeting of the committee on 11 July,[11] the Solicitor-General conceded that it might, after all, be necessary to insert a clause to prevent claims to enforce statutory compensation rights, 'notwithstanding that it would have the effect of disposing of the de Keyser case before it was come to the House of Lords [sic]'. This was a policy question for which the War Cabinet's determination was required (it was never contended that the government should renege on every obligation to compensate. Indeed, a few more categories of claims were identified, for example, compensation for damage during the Easter Rebellion in Dublin.[12] The question, as always, was what was the basis for calculating compensation, statutory compensation under the Lands Clauses scheme being recognised as the most generous and therefore financially most onerous scheme). The next stage, therefore, was to report to the War Cabinet as to which policy options were available. Sir Frederick Liddell, Parliamentary Counsel, was to draft the alternative statutory provisions.

The first interim report of the interdepartmental committee was delivered

---

10.　Discussion of the post-war Acquisition of Land Bill obviously overlaps with our analysis of wartime compensation issues. But it is concerned with conceptually distinct matters of post-war land and housing reform. For limited discussion, see chapter 14, below.

11.　PRO, LCO 2/440, 'Memorandum no. 22. Minutes of Proceedings of the Third Meeting', 11 July 1919.

12.　Some shipping requisition fell outwith the remit of the Admiralty Transport Arbitration Board (the Woodhouse Commission) and provision for this was also recommended. For shipping questions raised during the preparation of the Indemnity Bill, see chapter 10, above.

on 31 July 1919.[13] The report rehearsed the history of wartime compensation, pointing out the *ex gratia* basis for payments and the doubts first sown in the Shoreham Aerodrome settlement in the House of Lords. The possible adverse House of Lords ruling in *De Keyser*, the *Cannon Brewery* decision and the *Newcastle Breweries* litigation were all adding to the problem of the possible reopening all the DRLC awards, while the Law Officers' reluctance to validate retrospectively any suspect regulations awarding compensation was also explained. Where the DRLC had for one reason or another rejected claims, the interdepartmental committee anticipated that claimants would commence legal proceedings in a number of these cases. The War Cabinet were therefore asked to decide whether a legal right to compensation was to be recognised (or, it might have added, denied) by statute for interference with property or goods on the authority or purported authority of prerogative powers or defence regulations. The committee believed that the direct loss principle was not unreasonable, since the loss or damage or interference was for the general good in a time of national emergency and there was no logical basis for payment of compensation on a profiteering basis, as under the Lands Clauses Acts. 'On the other hand,' it added, 'the fact must not be overlooked that owners who were fortunate enough not to have their property requisitioned were able to take advantage of the enhanced prices prevailing.'[14]

While appreciating the strength of the opposition to any validating legislation which would nullify existing (and, presumably, potential) court decisions, the committee did not consider that claimants who refused compensation on the DRLC basis, which had been accepted in the majority of cases, should benefit by such action. Appendix B to the report listed the two alternative clauses for the War Cabinet to select, in the event that it accepted the principle of barring absolutely all proceedings in the regular courts for actions arising out of the exercise of emergency powers. Both clauses, if enacted, would render void all actions already commenced, including the *De Keyser* and *Newcastle Breweries* cases. The first clause denied a legal right to compensation, merely offering *ex gratia* payments without specifying the tribunals by which compensation was to be assessed. The substantive effect would be to confer a wider jurisdiction on the DRLC which hitherto did not consider claims 'otherwise provided for', for example, by the courts or by the Licensed Trade Claims Commission.[15] There would, thenceforth, be

---

13. PRO, LCO 2/440, *First Interim Report of the Interdepartmental Committee on the Indemnity Bill and Statute of Limitations*, 31 July 1919 (copy also in LCO 2/441). Cf., CAB 24/89, G.T.8203, letters from Lords Terrington and Mersey, 22 September 1919.

14. PRO, LCO 2/440, *First Interim Report*, para. 19.

15. Sir Frederick Sykes of the Central Control Board (Liquor Traffic) felt that compensation under the Acquisition of Land (Assessment of Compensation) Act 1919 would be more appropriate given the permanency of the board's acquisitions. See PRO, LCO 2/440, 'Memorandum no. 34. Note by Sir F. C. J. Sykes (Central Control Board (Liquor Traffic)) on effect of Bill on cases in which the Board are interested', 3 November 1919. He got his wish the following month. See ibid., 'Memorandum no. 44. Minutes of the Seventh Meeting', 2 December 1919, para. 7; chapter 14, below. See also, chapter 7 above.

no cases 'otherwise provided for'. The second alternative (eventually adopted in the Act), conferred a specific right to compensation, but only from the specified tribunals and on definite principles. It received the support of Winston Churchill, Secretary of State for War.[16] At the Home Affairs Committee meeting on 18 August, Sir Frederick Liddell pointed out that while either alternative, 'would arouse tremendous opposition in the country and in Parliament, as they would overrule pending cases', the government nonetheless had to grasp the nettle.[17] Otherwise hundreds of millions of pounds might have to be paid as compensation. Of the two alternatives, he added, the second was the better, but presented a larger target for attack. The Lord Advocate took a similar view but a decision on which clause to endorse was postponed until the views of Lord Terrington, at the time chairman of the DRLC, had been solicited. He had no hesitation in supporting the second alternative, adding that, 'the present uncertainty owing to the *De Keyser* judgment is proving very embarrassing' to the DRLC, and advising speedy legislation. On 9 October, the War Cabinet formally approved the second alternative.[18]

Apart from a decision of the Home Affairs Committee of the Cabinet on 9 October 1919, approving the barring of claims for 'indirect and consequential loss', no further progress on the Bill took place over the next few months.[19] But on 20 February 1920, the decision in the Newcastle Breweries case was delivered, declaring the compensation provisions of Reg. 2B ultra vires. The Ministry of Munitions believed that, as drafted, the Bill would still protect the department (and, indeed, other departments such as the Board of Trade which had been requisitioning Irish flax at cost price plus pre-war profit) from having to pay market price compensation. Additional protection could be achieved by inserting the words 'or purported to be made' after the words 'any regulation or order made'. It was, however, conceded by W. H. Salter, a senior ministry official, that such an insertion, 'might draw too much attention to the fact that we are seeking to upset the recent decision of the Courts, and attract further opposition to the Bill'.[20] Indeed, Philip Guedalla, in writing to Sir Claud Schuster on February 18, conveyed Liddell's feeling that 'our

16. PRO, CAB 24/85, G.T.7877, 'Bill of Indemnity and Statute of Limitations, Memorandum by Secretary of State for War, W. S. Churchill', 2 August 1919. See above, chapter 12.

17. PRO, CAB 26/1, H.A.C. 39(2), 18 August 1919.

18. PRO, LCO 2/440, 'Memorandum no. 26' for these points. The assistant Treasury Solicitor, Sir A. H. Dennis, later wrote to Liddell suggesting that the right of recourse to the courts for compensation under the Army Act 1881, section 115 should be retained. This section offered market price compensation for requisitioned commodities, as Newcastle Breweries endeavoured to show.

19. PRO, CAB 26/1, H.A.C. 41(3), 9 October 1919. The War Cabinet itself later confirmed the decision on 15 April 1920. See CAB 23/21, W.C.20(20), 15 April 1920. Cf., the *Elliott Steamship* and *A & B Taxis* cases in chapter 12, above.

20. PRO, MUN 4/6356, W. H. Salter to Sir W. Graham Greene, secretary to the Ministry of Munitions, 1 April 1920. Cf. LCO 2/440, Philip Guedalla to Sir Claud Schuster, 13 February 1920.

masters will never have the courage to introduce the Indemnity Bill even as it stands!'[21]

Meanwhile, the interdepartmental committee had to take stock of the new position after Mr Justice Salter's ruling. A *Second and Final Report* of the committee was prepared for the War Cabinet following the issue of the *Newcastle Breweries* decision. The report declared that the committee were 'not unmindful' that the general effect of clause two of the Bill would be to override the judgments in *De Keyser* (in the Court of Appeal) and in *Newcastle Breweries*. The justification for the issue of Reg. 2B in order to outflank section 115 of the Army Act was outlined:

> As the war progressed, it was found almost impossible to ascertain fair market value [under section 115], since the requisition of articles in large quantities by the Government for the troops automatically forced up the price out of all proportion to the cost thereof to the sellers.[22]

Since Mr Justice Salter invalidated the substituted basis for compensation in Reg. 2B, the claimants could now receive an additional £18,000, while the total surplus payment on all rum requisitioned could be, the report continued, about £750,000, 'which represents excess profit pure and simple'. Indeed, the report continued: 'The extra charge to the Exchequer in respect of all classes of goods would possibly run into several hundred millions of pounds or almost as much as the total national debt prior to the war.' While legislation affecting pending disputes could be justified only in exceptional circumstances, the 'evil to which the clause is directed' would not be averted, as the claims which it was desired to confine within a reasonable limit had already arisen. In other words, the committee envisaged that the thousands of claimants who had already settled with the DRLC, on the basis of direct loss or of Reg. 2B compensation prior to the *Newcastle Breweries* ruling, would be clamouring on the doors of the courts demanding market value compensation. Such a scenario had to be avoided. It concluded:

> Notwithstanding that the clause may possibly meet with strong opposition from vested interests, the Committee feel that when the matter is fully explained, there should be no difficulty in securing its acceptance by Parliament, especially as the desired object of the opposition is to secure to the owners of stocks requisitioned for the purposes of the war, not only the actual cost plus a reasonable rate of profit but also the abnormal increases in price due to the requisitioning and to other circumstances of the war.

---

21. Ibid., 18 February 1920.
22. PRO, LCO 2/441, *Second and Final Report of the Interdepartmental Committee on the Indemnity Bill and Statute of Limitations*, 27 February 1920, para. 16. The draft of this report, prepared just prior to the judgment, is in LCO 2/440. See also ibid., 'Memorandum no. 51. Indemnity Bill Report. Proposed New Paragraph 16'.

To paint the 'opposition' as those hard-faced men who seemed to have done well out of the war was ironic for a government allegedly composed of just such men. Of course, this was too simplistic an analysis as motives in favour or against the proposal proved complex. Churchill, the Secretary of State for War, did not feel inclined to mince his words and believed that the public would sympathise with the government:

> The Executive's interference with the rights of property would appear to have scandalised the Courts, but I am of opinion that any concession to the ex post-facto demands of war profiteers would far more deeply scandalise public opinion.[23]

When the Cabinet Home Affairs Committee next met on 14 April 1920,[24] the Solicitor-General, Sir Ernest Pollock, advised the urgent necessity of introducing the Bill. Judgment would shortly be given in the House of Lords in the *De Keyser* case, and he believed that it would uphold the Court of Appeal's decision against the Crown. Market-value compensation at the time of requisition would then be applicable and a number of similar cases were in the pipeline, awaiting the grant of Sir Gordon Hewart, the Attorney-General's, *fiat* which he was holding up pending the outcome in the House of Lords. Immediate legislation would then be necessary to avoid creating two classes of recipients for compensation for identical interference or loss. In anticipation, Pollock asked for detailed information on the fortuitous and exorbitant profits which would be made if the market value principle were to apply universally. The Bill was to be introduced in the Commons the next day, 15 April 1920.

In response to the call for financial information, the Ministry of Munitions were able to supply instances. For example, the Home Affairs Committee were told that in the case of Lewis guns, a saving of between 400 and 500 per cent on the cost was effected.[25] Deep in the recesses of the ministry, the exercise was not so straightforward. Guedalla had asked the departmental finance section to provide approximate data showing the amount expended in purchases of commodities where the purchase price had been reduced by requisitioning or by prices fixed under the defence regulations; also the differences which the government would have been bound to pay if it were necessary to pay for those articles at the price which would have prevailed in the open market at the time of acquisition. The official concerned, A. E. Watson, pointed out that price

---

23. PRO, CAB 24/100, C.P. 845, 'Bill of Indemnity and Statute of Limitations. Memorandum by Secretary of State for War', 12 March 1920. Copy also in PRO, BT 103/32, 'Memorandum *re* Indemnity Bill', 4 October 1919. The phrasing was possibly Philip Guedalla's who had been working in both the War Office and the Ministry of Munitions. Churchill had been head of both departments in his time. See PRO, MUN 4/6496, Guedalla to J. A. Corcoran, 26 February 1920.
24. PRO, CAB 26/2, H.A.C. 54(3), 14 April 1920.
25. PRO, MUN 4/6496, Sir W. Graham Greene to H. A. L. Fisher, chairman, Home Affairs Committee, 24 April 1920.

controls were a principal device in keeping down costs of materials such as pig iron, steel, copper, spelter, lead and glycerine, though additional expenditure was incurred in providing subsidies to the manufacturers. He explained that, from the outset of price controls, the ministry spent approximately £1,800 million on finished munitions, 90 per cent of whose raw materials were controlled. As 40 per cent of the price of finished munitions was represented by materials, there was therefore a total expenditure on materials at controlled prices of £720 million. In the absence of controls, excess payments of between 10 and 50 per cent would have been required, somewhere between £72 million and £360 million. Perhaps an additional £200 million would be approximate, half of which would have been for iron and steel.

But these were contractual payments, not payments following requisition, though this was recognised as a distinction without a difference: 'The powers were held by the Ministry as a threat over the heads of contractors in case they refused what the Ministry considered to be a reasonable price for their output . . .'[26] Any resistance would be met with requisitioning under defence regulations. In fact requisitioning by the ministry, though not of course by the military departments, was a rare occurrence and the amount thereby saved was considered by Watson to be 'negligible' as compared to the figures mentioned above.

Perhaps the 'immorality' of reaping unearned profits from a national emergency was excused by the 'immorality' of executive legal blackmail directed against government 'contractors'. What is certain is that the mood of the Commons on the second reading of the bill on 3 May forced the interdepartmental committee into a further flurry of activity.[27] The bill received a hostile reception even from government supporters, with only one sympathetic back-bencher prepared to endorse the measure from the floor of the Commons. For other government supporters, their loyalties were being sorely tested. The Solicitor-General opened the debate, stressing the financial problems which would flow from the failure to tackle the *De Keyser* and *Newcastle Breweries* rulings. Attached to the Bill was a memorandum detailing the additional costs, in relation to different categories of property, which would be incurred by the application of the market value principle of compensation. Shipowners would be entitled to a further £350,000,000 and to £28,000,000 for lost vessels. For munitions, an additional £200,000,000 would be required. For the raw materials used in those munitions, another £200,000,000. For leather, £22,500,000; for wool, £2,500,000; for hospital supplies, £4,000,000; for flax, £9,000,000; for meat, £40,000,000; and for imported timber, £12 million: a total of £850,000,000, while the memorandum quoted the more conservative figure of £700,000,000. Even canned salmon requisitions would require the additional payment of £2,000,000.

26. Ibid., A. Watson to Guedalla, 19 April 1920.
27. H. C. Deb., 5th series, 128, 3 May 1920, cols. 1741–1856.

There was also the question of indirect loss which would 'undoubtedly' be reopened in the courts were the Bill to be rejected:

> Brokers, insurers in shipping, etc., have all lost money in consequence of ships being requisitioned and taken from their control. The Port of Southampton was closed for commercial shipping and that caused a great deal of loss to those who were accustomed to use it. The indirect loss has been enormous . . . We can rely upon Magna Charta and our rights to go to a court of law, and nobody would wish in any way to suggest that that is not one of our great privileges as part of our liberties; but when we go to a court of law we must go there on the understanding that the standard of compensation must have the interests of the community in sight, and must not be one which asks for something which is, beyond all question, outside the range of all practical claims that can be made.[28]

The portrayal of this part of the Bill as an urgent measure to save the Exchequer from crippling obligations towards war profiteers, impressed few speakers in the debate. The principal adversary of the Bill was Leslie Scott, the co-author of *The Case of Requisition*, and chairman of the Ministry of Reconstruction's Acquisition of Land Committee in 1917, whose deliberations resulted in the passing of the Acquisition of Land (Assessment of Compensation) Act 1919, an Act which proved only slightly less generous to the landed interest than did the Lands Clauses Act 1845. Scott was sceptical of the huge figures bandied about in the memorandum (as was Sir Edward Carson, later in the debate), and demanded, 'full information, because as it stands, it [the Bill] is an attempt to tax individuals chosen by accident in regard to the war, and not to distribute the burden of those individuals evenly over the community'.[29] Repeating the allegations that the Bill legalised bureaucratic tyranny by ousting the courts and that its scope was unprecedented in the annals of Indemnity Acts, he at least offered a constructive suggestion. The DRLC could be retained for those who wished to use it while leaving open the doors of the courts for those who did not, although in the latter case, directions might be given to the courts that compensation at something less than the ordinary measures at common law might be appropriate.

For many speakers the ogre was not the bloated capitalist war profiteer, typically the shipowner and the brewer, who might earn windfall gains simply because the government, in its hour of need, had to enter and dominate the market, drastically reducing supply in relation to demand and forcing up the price. In many instances businessmen had themselves been victims of price rises, inasmuch as they had entered future contracts to provide commodities when the negotiated price was lower, and had found that to obtain supplies to fulfil their future commitments, they were trading at a loss. Indeed, this was

28. Ibid., cols. 1765–66.
29. Ibid., col. 1768. See below, chapter 14.

precisely the case with many owners who had had their rum requisitioned by the government. As Leslie Scott pointed out:

> In order to fulfil these [future] contracts they had to go into the market and buy at the market price, while the Government took from them their stocks at the DORA price. The result was that although they could sell to the Government at only 5s., if the Government were right, they would have to replace their stock at 15s. or thereabouts.[30]

But for other speakers, forgotten specimens of the 'poor property owner', the elderly spinster with few possessions who had taken in boarders in her now requisitioned rooms or the genteel retired folk, parts of whose unoccupied mansions were taken over by the military, were being denied their due entitlement to compensation.[31] The Indemnity Bill would simply reaffirm this if it endorsed the actual loss principle of the DRLC (which it would do if it simply overturned the *De Keyser* ruling).

It was always likely that emotional arguments about the wealthy interests on the one hand and the cheated gentlefolk on the other would be paraded. Apart from members of the government, only one back-bencher spoke in support of the measure, castigating as he went along even the critical voice of Labour represented by the Railwaymen's leader, J. H. Thomas: 'Let us make no error about it; all the speeches . . . had as their main burden the rights of property', declared Lt -Col. John Ward, M.P.:

> Everybody who has listened to the discussion knows that it is purely a question of pounds, shillings and pence from beginning to end . . . I am surprised at Labour Members being brought into the swim, and I am astounded that they have also taken the side of the propertied people who want, like Shylock, to get their last pound of flesh out of the State.[32]

The fierceness of the attack on the Bill succeeded in drawing concessions from the government. A more formalised tribunal, the War Compensation Court, presided over by a High Court judge, with provision for witnesses to give evidence on oath for a 'case stated' (effectively an appeal on grounds of law), all attested to the sensitivity of the government to the charge that the DRLC and similar tribunals had been unregulated by legal authority and that to exclude judicial authority was politically dangerous.

---

30. Ibid., col. 1772. One member of Parliament later told the Commons that a quantity of his hay had been requisitioned at the 'controlled' price of £5 10s. 0d. per ton. But as he still had to feed his cattle, he later had to enter the open market and pay £7 15s. 0d. per ton. See ibid., 132, 20 July 1920, col. 374 (Col. J. Gretton). Presumably the requisitioning was under the Army Acts 1881 and 1914 with market value compensation, and the market price later rose significantly by £2 5s. 0d. Otherwise, one would have expected his own purchase price to have been controlled.

31. Ibid., col. 1820 (H. Maddocks).

32. Ibid., col. 1814.

One further important amendment was also accepted. It had been pointed out by a number of speakers that the requisitioning of unutilised or unprofitable property, for example, in Felixstowe, where the military occupation of the whole area precluded the commercial renting out of rooms by seaside landladies, did not attract compensation from the DRLC (indeed, theoretically, the Crown might have claimed it proper for the DRLC to award De Keyser's Royal Hotel Ltd no compensation at all for occupation (with the exception of the profitable restaurant) as the company were running at a loss).[33] Given the strong views condemning this practice, the government considered it prudent to rectify the position and to make provision for compensation even if no loss had been suffered. What this meant, in effect, was that the Court of Appeal decision in *De Keyser* (and, indeed, the subsequent House of Lords ruling) would *not* be overruled in the Bill. The redraft would provide that if a claimant, apart from the Bill, possessed a legal right to compensation, then the tribunal should take that into account and, in calculating compensation, should have regard to the amount of compensation to which, apart from the Act, the claimant would have been legally entitled (though the existence of a state of war was also to be considered). Therefore, since the Defence Act basis of compensation which was held to apply in *De Keyser* offered more than mere actual loss payment, such basis would, subject to the proviso as to the existence of a state of war, now apply under the Indemnity Bill.[34]

More than recovery for mere actual loss, certainly. But Lord Justice Warrington in the Court of Appeal in *De Keyser* had stressed that the Defence Act introduced, in the case of temporary use, 'the same measure as that resorted to in actions for use and occupation, that is to say, what the occupation is worth, and I do not think the Suppliants are entitled, in addition, to compensation for loss arising from their being prevented from carrying on their business'.[35] So a reasonable rental would be recoverable,

---

33. One illustration, offered during the later committee stage of the Bill, concerned the Ravensbourne Club, belonging to the late Sir Frederick Cook, Bt. He had erected the building in 1913 at a cost of £20,000, to be used as a residential club for the younger members of the staff of Messrs Cook, Sons & Co., at a nominal cost to them. The authorities requisitioned the premises but as the owner had not derived any profits from the building, compensation was refused. It was suggested, by contrast, that the DRLC was adopting a less rigid attitude to compensation claims in similar circumstances in the period prior to the introduction of the Indemnity Bill. On the other hand, it was alleged that the 'settlement' of the Ravensbourne Club case was being held up, 'pending . . . an Indemnity Bill, in which the protection given by the De Keyser case will be nullified'. This one example illustrates the existence of a number of cross-currents in the events recounted here. See ibid., col. 318 (C. H. Cautley); ibid, col. 327 (Sir Frederick Banbury); ibid., col. 334 (H. N. Rae).

34. Ibid., col. 1851 (Sir Gordon Hewart, Attorney-General); *Indemnity Bill: Proposed Amendments to the Indemnity Bill*, P.P. 1920 (Cmd. 567), xl, 631. The following was later added, 'and to all other circumstances relevant to a just assessment of compensation'. Minor House of Lords amendments were also accepted.

35. [1919] 2 Ch. 197, at p. 238. See also PRO, LCO 2/440, D. DuBois Davidson, secretary to the DRLC to G. H. Drury, secretary to the Interdepartmental Commmittee on the Indemnity Bill, 11 May 1920.

but not consequential loss of profits.[36] On this matter, the House of Lords in *De Keyser* did not interfere. Sir Ernest Pollock told a meeting of the Interdepartmental Committee on the Indemnity Bill that he had been in conversation with one of the law lords sitting on the case who had informed him that the court 'did not intend that compensation should be based on the inflated market prices'. It was for that reason that the Solicitor-General had proposed inserting references to the fact of the existence of a state of war and to all other circumstances relevant to the case. The committee learned from Edward Coles of the War Office Lands Branch that disputed and undisputed cases of payment for occupation and use of property would amount to about £8,000,000 (Admiralty occupation would cost only £500,000). Presumably these figures were not so daunting as to justify incurring political costs by overturning *De Keyser* by legislation. As to the possible reopening of cases already determined by the DRLC on the erroneous basis that no legal rights to compensation existed, that matter remained unsettled for the moment.[37]

While future claimants could now rely on the *De Keyser* principle that compensation existed as of right,[38] the Indemnity Bill did not pay the same amount of respect to the *Newcastle Breweries* ruling. The government refused to permit that the basis for compensation for requisitioned commodities, as laid down in Reg. 2B (and, indeed, in Reg. 2F and Reg. 7), should succumb to the market value basis contained in the Army Act 1881, section 115 and in its accompanying 1914 act. Other judges chose not to accept the proposition of Mr Justice Salter in *Newcastle Breweries* that government departments could not issue regulations authorising the acquisition of private property at below current market prices or at prices set by arbitrators who took account of the owner's costs plus a reasonable amount for profit. Mr Justice Greer in *Hudson's Bay Co.* v. *Maclay*,[39] Mr Justice Darling in *Robinson & Co. Ltd* v.

36. Douglas Davidson, the secretary to the DRLC, actually described the measure of compensation recognised by the *De Keyser* rulings as being 'direct loss', that is, the limited class of compensation awardable by the DRLC. But clearly he was drawing an unspoken distinction between direct loss and 'actual loss'. See PRO, LCO 2/440, 'Memorandum no. 56. Minutes of the 9th Meeting', 13 May 1920.

37. On these points, see ibid. The Ministry of Munitions representative on the committee, Philip Guedalla, suggested that persons whose businesses had been interfered with by orders of general application, and who consequently received no compensation from the DRLC, would, apart from the Bill, probably have had a legal right to compensation. Therefore, to incorporate the *De Keyser* ruling in the Bill might also be to confer compensation rights in respect to loss caused by an order of general application, unless the wording of the amendment were carefully drawn. The exclusion of compensation for indirect loss was not thought by his department to be a sufficient safeguard here. While both Pollock and Liddell thought otherwise, the final drafting did make the position watertight. See PRO, MUN 4/6356, W. H. Salter to Sir W. Graham Greene, 29 May, 5 August 1920.

38. The Bill, after scrutiny by a select committee, also protected the claims of the De Keyser Company itself and those of other claimants who had obtained final judgment prior to enactment. See section one, subsection four of the Act.

39. (1920) 36 T.L.R. 469, at p. 476.

The King,[40] and Mr Justice Bailhache in *Commercial & Estates Co. of Egypt v. J. E. B. Ball*,[41] all refused to hold as invalid regulations making provision for compensation at less than current market value. Such rulings would undoubtedly reinforce the government's determination to outface its critics. They might even appease its critics. Similarly, the reliance of the Admiralty Transport and Arbitration Board, that is, the Woodhouse tribunal, on the Blue Book rates would not be set aside in favour of market principles in the case of shipping requisition.[42] For as already noted, at stake here was a sum calculated as being somewhere between £300 million and £400 million.

In the wake of the Commons' debate of 3 May and of the House of Lords decision in *De Keyser* on 10 May, the Home Affairs Committee of the Cabinet met on 17 May. The proposed changes to the Bill were outlined, but one outstanding matter was reserved for the Commons' select committee to which the revised Bill was now referred.[43] That concerned the matter left open by the interdepartmental committee meeting on 13 May: whether decided cases could be reopened in the light of the *De Keyser* ruling. At that earlier meeting, Edward Coles had argued that as many as 120,000 cases could theoretically be reopened, since 'agreements' had been reached under duress. Another member of the committee, Sir Reginald Acland, Judge Advocate of the Fleet, had also observed that some property-owners were receiving yearly rental compensation for occupied land, but were protesting against the insufficiency of payments on each occasion. The Home Affairs Committee had two options. The first was to identify the prevention of the reopening of adjudicated claims as an organic element of, and a condition for, the amendments which the government had agreed to insert in the Bill. A second option was preferred: this was to give the select committee a free hand and for the government to explain to its members the difficulties which would arise if the necessary words were not inserted in the Bill. It was confidently believed that, 'The Select Committee would no doubt be influenced by the very heavy expenditure which would otherwise arise'.[44] That view substantially prevailed, and the reopening of cases was restricted to those where proof of material change of circumstances or of new evidence not previously available could be marshalled. *De Keyser* was not expressly mentioned, and one had to await one of the early adjudications of the War Compensation Court, in the Newfield Sanitary Pipe Company case for final confirmation.

The Select Committee on the Indemnity Bill received submissions from various individuals and organisations. As in the Commons debate, one of

40. (1920) 36 T.L.R. 773.
41. (1920) 36 T.L.R. 526.
42. PRO, LCO 2/440, 'Memorandum no. 53. Note of the Criticisms on the Bill during the 2nd Reading Debate', 11 May 1920.
43. PRO, CAB 26/2, H.A.C. 60 (3), 17 May 1920.
44. PRO, LCO 2/440, 'Memorandum No. 56. Minutes of the 9th Meeting', 13 May 1920. See above, chapter 12.

the shrewdest critics was Leslie Scott. Without reiterating the points he had made in the past, Scott submitted a memorandum to the committee in which he conceded that an Indemnity Bill was necessary (but not this one); that with one exception, claims already decided should not be reopened; and that generally speaking it was proper to exclude from state compensation, in some cases at any rate, sums reflecting 'war' or 'monopoly' values which were attributable directly to the special shortage of, or special demand for, any articles required for war purposes. The Solicitor-General, Sir Ernest Pollock, responded by indicating the unique character of the Great War in contrast to previous wars, on the conclusion of which Indemnity Acts had been passed. There had been nothing comparable in previous conflicts to the submarine menace in the recent war; and it was that factor which had caused market rates to become illusory, thereby justifying Reg. 2B's compensation principle and the general principles of the DRLC.

As to the question of reopening cases, Scott had argued this should be permitted, 'where the applicant can show that he was induced by the misrepresentation of the Executive that he had no legal rights to settle his claim on the lines dictated by the Executive'.[45] However, Pollock rejected this proposal both on administrative grounds and on the ground that Scott was unable to substantiate his allegations.[46] In the event, the select committee itself concluded: 'That it would be impracticable, and undesirable, to reopen past, decided and agreed cases extending over the last five years.'[47] This was somewhat harsh on property owners who the DRLC had already ruled had not incurred actual loss, even though they had suffered interference by virtue of Crown occupation of their properties. For identical occupations of property not hitherto the subject of claims for compensation would now be compensated under the Bill. The numbers of cases heard by the DRLC where property had been taken over without it causing actual loss, because the property in question had been unprofitable or unutilised, was never specifically calculated. The following extract (overleaf) from a longer table may perhaps cast some light on this matter.

We can see that 363 cases of agricultural and non-agricultural occupation attracted virtually no compensation. Averaged out, the amounts actually awarded here were about £6 9s. 9d. per claim which is suggestive of the award of expenses and not of compensation. We do not know how many of these 363 cases received 'nil' awards because there had been no actual loss. The claimants might have been the indirect victims of general orders, or they might otherwise have incurred only indirect loss or they might have been enemy aliens. But if we were to assume that all these claimants would

45.   Ibid., 'Memorandum no. 53. Note of the Criticisms on the Bill during the 2nd Reading Debate', 11 May 1920.
46.   Ibid.
47.   *Report and Special Report from the Select Committee on the Indemnity Bill*, P.P. 1920 (136), vii, 397, para. 1.

Table 4

Defence of the Realm (Losses) Commission:
Applications Determined by the Commission
to 30 April 1920

	Number of Cases	Amount Claimed		Amount Awarded	
		Lump Sum £	Annual Payment £	Lump Sum £	Annual Payment £
A. Occupation cases					
I. other than agricultural					
(a) determined on rental basis					
(i) "nil" awards	353	63,145	43,883	2,333	19
(ii) others	1,993	535,406	787,561	293,782	576,060
Total (a)	2,346	598,551	831,444	296,115	576,079
II. Agricultural					
(a) determined on rental basis					
(i) "nil" awards	10	901	1,143	13	–
(ii) others	364	91,178	28,239	57,543	24,981
Total (a)	374	92,079	29,382	57,556	24,981

Source: LCO2/440, D. DuB. Davidson to G. H. Drury, 11 May 1920.

have qualified for compensation under the *De Keyser* principle, then we can see that the amount saved by the Exchequer by not reopening these cases was the relatively inconsiderable sum of £109,072. If this is approximately accurate (and the issue here was not the difference between actual loss and market value of the property on the assumption that there had been no actual loss incurred) then the refusal to reopen cases such as these would hardly seem worth defending. One can only surmise that these specific cases were subsumed within the broader class of cases where compensation only for actual loss (including, after *De Keyser*, reasonable rental in the case of properties likely to be so utilised) was for policy reasons to be upheld against claims for market value compensation.

The Bill was to be reconsidered by the House after the report of the select committee, accepting the compensation principle of the measure, had been issued.[48] For those interests which still felt threatened, anxious lobbying continued to take place, for instance, by the Brewers' Society in respect to the denial of market value compensation for requisitioned commodities,[49]

48. PRO, LCO 2/441, 'Select Committee on the Indemnity Bill 1920. Precis of Evidence by Solicitor-General', 22 June 1920.
49. Ibid., 'Memorandum by the Brewers' Society'.

by the Liverpool Law Society in respect to the breadth of the immunities to be conferred on government officials,[50] and by the good burghers of genteel seaside resorts, still harbouring grievances against tyrannous military occupation.[51] But the broad principles of compensation desired by the government survived virtually unscathed during the remaining prolonged stages of the Bill through Parliament. Yet many of its own supporters remained dissatisfied, and even during the third reading debate there were levelled sharp accusations of government deception and double-dealing,

> towards hundreds and thousands of little people who were not so well advised and who took the advice of my right hon. Friend [The Attorney-General] – that the only remedy [for requisitioning] was the Defence of the Realm Losses Commission; and when the Commission decided against them they had nothing more to do.[52]

The DRLC by any other name would not suffice. Only the king's courts would do. In short, proclaimed one speaker:

> The name of the Bill is a misnomer; it is not an Indemnity Bill at all. It is a Bill to alter the law of England, and a bad one at that. If my Right Hon. and Learned Friend wanted an Indemnity Bill in the proper sense of the word he could have got such a Bill passed through all its stages in an afternoon. That is not what we have got here. We have got here a Bill of very much wider scope; a Bill which touches English rights and liberties, and which ought not to be allowed to go through without a protest.[53]

For this speaker, property, the courts and the constitution were inseparable.

50. H. C. Deb., 5th series, 130, 16 June 1920, cols. 1297–98 (written answer).

51. Aeneas Henderson, *The Indemnity Bill: A Case of Compensation for War Loss* (Southport, privately printed, 31 July 1920). His complaint on behalf of his wife was raised in Parliament. According to one Commons member, 'there is not one Member of the House who has not had brought to his notice numbers of cases of most justifiable complaint of their [i.e. the DRLC's] action'. See ibid, 20 July 1920, cols. 384–85 (Mr R. McNeill). Henderson's grievance, above, was primarily directed at the military authorities. For criticisms of the War Office in May 1919 when properties were being occupied for demobilisation purposes, see *Solicitors' Journal*, 63, 31 May 1919, p. 560.

52. H. C. Deb., 5th series, 132, 29 July 1920, col. 1836 (Major R. W. Barnett).

53. Ibid., cols. 1834–35.

14

'What Did You Salvage from the Great War, Daddy?'

The end of the war inevitably brought about a major change of direction in respect to the public acquisition of private property. Although many of the defence regulations authorising the requisitioning of private property continued in force for a period after the Armistice, much energy was now directed towards divesting the government of land and buildings no longer required for state purposes.

As late as 1922 the War Office still held 28,500 acres of land for war emergency purposes which had not yet been relinquished. The Air Ministry was still temporarily occupying 14,000 acres. The Office of Works retained, inter alia, about 10,000 houses erected either in connection with the Woolwich Arsenal housing scheme, or by the Ministry of Munitions and other departments to provide accommodation for employees at factories and plants occupied during the war. Finally, a body known as the Disposal and Liquidation Board still held properties covering an area of approximately 24,000 acres. These properties were available for immediate sale or were no longer required for storage purposes.[1] In addition, the board was in possession, after the war, of £500 million worth of stores, comprising 350,000 different types of articles.[2]

In order to dispose of the large portfolio of buildings in government hands which had been occupied in order to house the vast army of civil servants, both permanent and temporary, Sir Auckland Geddes, the President of the Board of Trade, informed the War Cabinet on 19 June 1919, that a board of liquidation should be established as a government department. This would be empowered to take over and wind up all work transferred to it by any other government department engaged on war work.[3] That board eventually became the Disposal and Liquidation Board (DLB) attached to the Ministry of Munitions. On

---

1. See *Committee on Crown and Government Lands: Interim and Final Reports*, P.P. 1922, vii (Cmd. 1689), 225, pp. 7–8. The chairman was Sir Howard Frank, the Director of Lands at the War Office and Ministry of Munitions.

2. R. M. Jackson, *The Chief: The Biography of Gordon Hewart, Lord Chief Justice of England, 1922–40* (London, 1959), p. 112. For a parliamentary controversy over the sale of government vehicles to the Leyland Motor Company rather than to Lever Bros., see ibid., pp. 112–13.

3. Copy in PRO, MAF 60/102, 'Liquidation of War Work of Government Departments. Memorandum by Sir Auckland Geddes', 19 June 1919.

the winding-up of the latter ministry in September 1921, responsibility for the DLB passed to the Surplus Stores and Liquidation Department of the Treasury.

Even before the DLB was set up, the staff engaged on liquidation work at the Board of Trade and at the Ministries of Munitions, National Service and Reconstruction were concentrated at Alexandra Palace in London to facilitate the coordination of such work, while the DLB staffs were transferred to the Earl's Court Exhibition Buildings. It may be noted in passing that a result of such relocation in London was to permit the return of a number of private buildings to their owners. They included the following hotels, the Grand, the York, most of the Metropole and De Keyser's Royal Hotel itself, also known, due to its Royal Air Force (RAF) connections, as Adastral House.

The business of restoration of private properties to their owners was proving prolonged and burdensome. As a joint memorandum to the Cabinet, presented by Winston Churchill, Secretary of State for War and Air, and by Lord Inverforth, Minister of Munitions, pointed out in November 1920,[4] there remained much outstanding work to complete in this area. The two main tasks were the payment of compensation for government occupations for war purposes, and the disposal of factories and other buildings erected at public expense for war purposes, with the purchase, where necessary, of the sites of such factories and buildings with a view to their subsequent disposal.

The backlog of work was attributed, in respect to compensation claims, to the doubts existing as to the legal position while the final decision in the *De Keyser* case was awaited, to the unavoidable suspension of compensation work between the date of that decision and the passing of the Indemnity Act 1920, and to the readjustment of machinery and procedures necessitated by the provisions of the Act. In the case of the disposal of government factories and buildings, delays were caused by the complicated nature of the transactions themselves. In addition, the assumed legislative authority for the government purchase and subsequent resale of property contained in the Defence of the Realm (Acquisition of Land) Act 1916 had revealed some flaws which required remedying in a Bill subsequently introduced in the House of Lords. This revision of the 1916 Act was necessitated by the decision in the *Mackrill* case. In this incident (chapter 11, above), a piece of land had been used by Mackrill, a builder, as a storage yard. In 1916, the Ministry of Munitions took possession of the land and erected permanent buildings at a cost of £2,500. In 1919, the ministry decided to sell to the Hammersmith Distillery Co. both the land and the buildings thereon. The latter, having suffered fire damage, were valued at £500.

Mackrill objected to the proposed sale as he required the yard for his own business, which he claimed would otherwise suffer. The ministry applied under sections three and thirteen of the 1916 Act for the consent of the

---

4.   Copy in PRO, TS 27/149, 'Concentration of Government Land Valuation. Memorandum by the Secretary of State for War and Air, and the Minister of Munitions', November 1920.

Railway and Canal Commission (RCC), the authorising body in such cases, for the compulsory purchase of the land. Section three enabled the Crown to acquire by agreement or compulsorily any land or interest in land occupied by a government department, or any land on, over or under which any buildings had been erected by the state for war purposes. Section thirteen, however, stipulated that the consent of the RCC was required where the purposes of acquisition under section three were purposes other than those for which land could be acquired under the Defence Acts or the Military Lands Act, that is, for purposes other than military purposes. The ministry argued that as £2,500 of public funds had already been spent on erecting the factory, most of that amount could be recouped if, on purchase of the land by the department, the land and buildings were subsequently resold to the distillery. If, however, the land were to be returned to Mackrill, the latter would pay only the diminished value of the buildings and the public purse would consequently suffer. In effect, here was a case, in the post-war period, where public and private interests clashed sharply. Reflecting the retreat from wartime collectivism, the commission under Mr Justice Lush decided that as its remit was, 'to protect the subject against any undue exercise of the power of the Crown to deprive [Mackrill] permanently of his property . . .',[5] it ought to ensure, before granting its consent to compulsory purchase, that the minister's application 'was, on its merits, a proper one to which to accede'. Second, it held that compulsory purchase powers were not intended to be exercised simply to avoid a substantial financial loss to the state. Finally, the public interest had to be balanced against any hardship and injustice caused to property owners where consent for a compulsory purchase was sought. Unlike other sections of the 1916 Act, the relevant provisions in *Mackrill* made no reference to 'national importance' or to 'national interest' in determining whether consent ought to be granted, and which might tend to weight judgments in favour of the department.[6]

5. *Minister of Munitions* v. *Mackrill* [1920] 3 K.B. 513, at p. 523.
6. The commission were more amenable to the ministry's petition in respect to the purchase of land from St Bartholomew's Hospital to resell to Handley Page Ltd, which proposed to operate it as Cricklewood Aerodrome. The ministry had acquired the land from the hospital in 1917 and had erected an aeroplane factory costing £250,000 on the site. In its petition to the RCC, the ministry stated that if consent for the land purchase were not granted and if the buildings and machinery were removed, only a very small fraction of their value would be recovered by the state. Reinstatement costs or compensation in lieu of reinstatement would also require to be paid. Finally, a subsequent sale to Handley Page was in the national interest in securing the continued employment of those in the factory. See PRO, TS 27/286, 'Land Acquisition for Aerodrome. St Bartholomew's Hospital: Petition for the Release of Money etc., 1926–33, 1967'. In another case, the RCC by a majority refused the Air Ministry permission to close a public right of way between Hillingdon and Uxbridge in West London which intersected an aerodrome (presumably Hounslow). The court stated, 'The legal maxim, "Once a highway, always a highway" was as old as the common law itself, and power to close highways was only granted in times of war and when the country was threatened with invasion'. See *Secretary of State for War* v. *Middlesex County Council* (1923) 39 T.L.R. 357, at p. 358. The imperatives of the military were by now a distant memory, and *public* property, in the literal sense of the word, was accorded proper respect.

To overcome the barrier erected by the *Mackrill* ruling to a more cost-conscious process of government divestment, the government sought a reform of the law which eventually became the Defence of the Realm (Acquisition of Land) Act 1920, passed on December 23 that year and which added to the delay in reducing its portfolio of temporarily occupied premises. In addition to the problems posed by hostile judicial interpretations, occasional difficulties were caused by the division of labour within government departments. Compensation work was being undertaken by the Lands Directorate under Sir Howard Frank for four separate departments, the War Office, the Air Ministry, the Ministry of Munitions and Ministry of Labour. The Inland Revenue Valuation Department was carrying out similar work for the Admiralty, while the Office of Works was acting in cases where premises had been occupied in order to accommodate the staffs of government departments. As to the disposal of factories and buildings, this fell within the scope of the Lands Directorate, acting on behalf of the DLB.

In anticipation of the work continuing for a number of years, the Chancellor of the Exchequer, Austen Chamberlain, suggested in 1920 the establishment of a single department responsible for all purchases, sales and valuations on behalf of all other government departments. He envisaged that the Inland Revenue's valuers would be suitable. Both Churchill, the War Secretary, and Lord Inverforth, the Minister of Munitions, argued, however, that the Lands Directorate, with its negotiating, administrative and property disposal experience, would be more suited to the task than a department whose expertise was limited to valuations.[7] The rival proposals prompted the Treasury to establish a committee under the chairmanship of Sir Howard Frank to enquire into the question of concentrating in one department all government purchases and sales of land and buildings and the management of Crown estates and government property. The committee reported in favour of setting up a Central Lands Department,[8] but little more was heard of the proposal in spite of the numerous examples offered to the committee by Sir Alexander Lawrence, assistant Treasury Solicitor, in which the purchasing or disposal activities of one government department came into accidental conflict with the interests of other government departments due to the absence of a central coordinating department.[9] Indeed, in one 'fiasco', a government department bought at an auction a property put up for sale by the Disposal Board. The purchasing department had bid through an agent not known to the board. The latter assumed he was an outside purchaser and forced up the price to a figure above the reserve price. The identity of interest was only discovered when the Lands Directorate which conducted the sale were asked whether the price paid by the purchasing department was too high.

7. PRO, TS 27/149, 'Concentration of Government Land Valuation'.
8. *Committee on Crown and Government Lands*.
9. PRO, TS 27/149, 'Committee on Crown and Government Lands: Memorandum by Sir Alexander Lawrence (Assistant Treasury Solicitor)', March 1922.

While divestment was the norm, even if in some instances this might entail government purchase prior to resale, a few government departments were actively engaged in post-war permanent acquisition of property formerly in private hands. For example, the scheme to extend public ownership of the licensed trade in the Carlisle district necessitated further purchases of licensed premises. The decision in *Cannon Breweries* had confirmed the applicability of the market price principles enshrined in the Lands Clauses Act 1845 and the post-Armistice Acquisition of Land (Assessment of Compensation) Act 1919, section four, embodied this approach. What the Central Control Board (Liquor Traffic) were concerned to stress was that their acquisitions were of a permanent character and should not be treated in the same way as those going before the Defence of the Realm Losses Commission (DRLC) for compensation settlements in respect to temporary government occupation. No doubt the spectre of the spectacular defeat in the House of Lords in May 1919 in the *Cannon Breweries* case haunted the department. Sir F. C. J. Sykes in a memorandum to the interdepartmental committee on the Indemnity Bill in November 1919 had warned the committee that licensed premises owners had in the past objected 'against being driven to the Losses Commission [that is, the DRLC] as their only remedy'. He warned the committee against reinstating the DRLC as the compensation forum.[10] His advice was evidently heeded and the Licensing Act 1921, Part II incorporated the compensation scheme set out in the Acquisition of Land Act 1919.[11]

Perhaps a more interesting example of post-war public utilisation of land previously requisitioned from private owners during the war concerned the activities of the peacetime Air Ministry. The Royal Air Force suffered drastic cutbacks immediately following the Armistice, shrinking from two hundred to thirty-three front-line squadrons.[12] Expansion in the early 1920s was built upon a new legitimacy of imperial policing and strategic bombing which isolated the newly independent force from the other arms of national defence.[13] Nonetheless, one of the paradoxes of the expansion of aviation after the war was that the Air Ministry contained a separate department devoted to civil aviation, placed under the direction of the Air Council as a result of section two of the Air Navigation Act 1919.[14] That statute was passed following the

10.   PRO, LCO 2/440, 'Interdepartmental Committee on Indemnity Bill and Statute of Limitations: Note by Sir F. C. J. Sykes (Central Control Board, Liquor Traffic) on effect of Bill on cases in which the Board are interested', 3 November 1919.

11.   PRO, TS 27/147, O. F. Dowson, Central Control Board (Liquor Traffic), to Sir Alexander Lawrence, Treasury Solicitor's Department, 12 January 1922.

12.   Cooper, *The Birth of Independent Air Power*, 1986, p. 155.

13.   Ibid., p. 157. See also Barry D. Powers, *Strategy Without Slide-Rule: British Air Strategy, 1914–1939* (Beckenham 1976), passim.

14.   For an analysis of the pre-1919 legal structure in respect to aerial navigation, see Hazeltine, 'The Recent and Future Growth of Aerial Law', pp. 295–96.

publication of the *Report of the Civil Aerial Transport Committee*,[15] which rejected state ownership of commercial aviation and recommended instead the expansion of the industry by private enterprise, supplemented by the assistance of the existing military organization and, where required, by the compulsory purchase of land for aerodromes.[16] The report stated that: 'The provision of aerodromes and landing stages is urgently needed, and without compulsory powers of purchase, of course, is more difficult.'[17] The report also recommended that, 'all established commercial air routes with their aerodromes and landing places should be suitable for strategical and tactical use in the event of war'.[18] In this light, the post-war concern of the Air Ministry with the scope of its legal powers of permanent land acquisition becomes understandable.

The Director-General of Lands, Sir Howard Frank, had written on 9 January 1919 to Major John Baird M.P., Parliamentary Under-Secretary of State at the Air Ministry, congratulating his department on its vision for the future. 'It is refreshing to find a Government Department so imbued with new ideas', he wrote.[19] He then raised the question of what legal powers existed for the acquisition of land for aerodromes. He pointed out the then existing defence regulation powers to take over land during the continuation of the 'war', and cited also the 1916 Act enabling the purchase of land for non-military use where the RCC so consented, especially where permanent buildings had been erected on the land. Without such consent, Frank doubted that the RAF could compulsorily purchase land for civil aviation purposes. His remark set off a flurry of brief minutes as to whether or not the military possessed powers of compulsory purchase for the expansion of civil aviation, the number of aerodromes for the post-bellum RAF apparently being adequate.[20]

The proposed retention of Doncaster aerodrome on land owned by Lord Fitzwilliam prompted a review of the existing powers in this regard and resulted in the following findings reached after consultations with A. C. B. Webb of the Treasury Solicitor's Department. First, so long as the war lasted (legally speaking), the department would not be justified in retaining the aerodrome, originally acquired under Defence Regulation 2, unless the department continued to use it for the defence of the realm. Second, on the official termination of the war, the ministry could continue to possess the property for a further two years under section one of the 1916 Act. Third, it could be used for civil aviation purposes under the auspices of the Air Council (the result of section 2 of the Air Navigation Act 1919). Fourth, the department

15. *Interim and Final Reports of the Civil Aerial Transport Committee*, P.P. 1918, v (Cd.9218), 17. For a legal analysis of the report, see H. D. Hazeltine, 'The Law of Civil Aerial Transport', *Journal of Comparative Legislation*, 3rd series, 2 (1919), pp. 76–89.
16. See also Fearon, 'The Growth of Aviation in Britain', pp. 21–40.
17. Quoted in *Flight*, 28 November 1918, p. 1351.
18. *Final Report*, chapter II, para. 15, reprinted in ibid., 12 December 1918, p. 1415.
19. PRO, AIR 2/71/A.6639, Frank to Baird, 9 January 1919.
20. Ibid., Director of Air Organization (Brig.-Gen. B. C. H. Drew) to Assistant Secretary, Air Ministry (H. W. W. McAnally?), c. 1 February 1919.

could remain in possession for a further three years under the 1916 Act subject to the consent of the RCC. Fifth, the ministry had the right during the war and for three years thereafter, to acquire permanently under section three of the 1916 Act, any properties in its possession and to be used for any Air Ministry purpose. If the purpose of acquisition were non-military, then the consent of the RCC would be required. Finally, lands so acquired permanently could be sold or leased, for example, to aviation firms, subject only to a right of pre-emption for the original owners if no government buildings of a permanent nature had been erected on the land.

With the legal position thus clarified, there appeared in the press advertisements whose wording, confided a senior civil servant at the Air Ministry, C. R. Brigstocke, 'practically amounts to an offer to sell the sites of aerodromes which do not yet belong to us'.[21] Lord Rosebery could not have put it better.

The subsequent growth of the RAF under Sir Hugh Trenchard in the early 1920s, under the programme known as the Home Defence Expansion Scheme, prompted further consideration of the permanent acquisition of aerodromes held temporarily during the war. During this planning exercise, concern was expressed within the ministry over the perceived shortcoming of the Defence Act 1842 in not apparently permitting the compulsory acquisition of land for barrack purposes, as distinct from other military uses. Lord Thomson, the Labour government's Secretary of State for Air, acknowledged in September 1924 (by which time the wartime defence regulations authorising land acquisition had expired) the strategic importance of the question but minuted that, 'owing to the agitation in connection with a *training* establishment, I am inclined to think that any legislation purporting to extend or alter our present powers of compulsory acquisition of land might meet with considerable opposition in Parliament'.[22] In 1926 the Director of Organisation and Staff Duties at the Air Ministry, J. L. B. Vesey, noted that, although hostility had been met over the acquisition of a number of sites for aerodromes, the Lands Branch had been able successfully to secure agreement, while the absence of compulsory powers for barrack service had not prevented the acquisition of a number of aerodromes, for example, at Upper Heyford, Bicester, North Weald, Sutton's Farm and Hucknall. However, 'Should insuperable difficulties be experienced in any particular case', the ministry could acquire land for an aerodrome, exclusive of barracks. Such land would then be designated a potential 'fortification' in terms of the 1842 Act, and the use of compulsory powers for barrack use would thus be justified. 'Possibly this course might be regarded as a moral evasion of the Act but legally it would appear to be valid', noted Vesey. In this way, parliamentary approval could be

---

21. Ibid., Brigstocke to Frank, 23 June 1919.
22. PRO, TS 28/122, 'Compulsory Acquisitions under Defence Acts 1842 and 1859: Prohibitions in User for Barrack Service, 1924', Lord Thomson to Sir W. Nicholson, Permanent Secretary, Air Ministry, 13 September 1924.

228   *Private Property, Government Requisition and the Constitution*

dispensed with.[23] It was another example of executive fudge and obfuscation, even if not an instance of outright lawlessness.

In January 1919 the Liberty and Property Defence League, the right-wing pressure group, proposed holding a national conference to demand:

> the removal of all restrictions during the war upon property and trade and the restoration of free conditions for commerce and industry; that land should be relieved of all unfair and oppressive burdens ... the demobilisation of the bureaucracy that has swollen to such vast proportions under the Defence of the Realm Act; that all laws should be made directly by Parliament and that powers shall not be given to Bureaucratic Departments and Boards to make laws and issue orders on their own initiative and responsibility.[24]

These were sentiments widely though not universally shared within British society after the Armistice and well-represented among the new intake of members of Parliament elected to the House of Commons in the 'coupon' election of December 1918.[25] They were the members of Parliament of whom a Conservative politician, reputed to be Stanley Baldwin (and cited by Keynes in 1919), had declared: 'They are a lot of hard-faced men ... who look as if they had done very well out of the war.'

A number of predictable targets of liberalism were singled out, which, if not neutralised, warned Lord Somerset, the president of the league, would herald 'further costly experiments in State and Municipal Socialism'.[26] All-embracing defence regulations which cramped trade, industry and commerce should go. A bloated civil service should be deflated and Parliament should reassert its sovereignty and not meekly abdicate its law-making functions to ministers or to faceless bureaucrats armed with enabling powers and immune to charges of acting beyond their legal powers. For the Coalition Liberal politician and barrister, Sir Alfred Hopkinson, the descent towards executive illiberalism had now to be halted:

> It is hardly too much to say that English Constitutional Law has been scrapped since the War ... The Reign of Law must be re-established to control the executive Government as well as the private citizen. Nothing is more infectious

23. Ibid., J. L. B. Vesey to ? Webster, 29 April 1926. For the earlier stages of the Home Defence Expansion Scheme, see PRO, TS 28/128, 'Home Defence Expansion Scheme: Progress of Works', n.d., mid 1924; ibid., 'Memorandum by Treasury Solicitor on Procedure in Purchasing Land, e.g. for an Aerodrome', A. W. L. [Lawrence], 13 August 1924.
24. *Land Agents' Record*, 4 January 1919.
25. Of necessity, this paragraph has been considerably simplified. Some in the left in British politics and society were looking for a more permanent role for the state in British society and saw in wartime state control of the economy a possible framework upon which to build. Others hoped for a more modernised version of the past. For a glimpse of the available literature, see J. M. Winter, *Socialism and the Challenge of War* (London, 1974); Gerry R. Rubin, 'Law as a Bargaining Weapon: British Labour and the Restoration of Pre-War Practices Act 1919', *Historical Journal*, 32 (1989), pp. 925–45; John N. Horne, *Labour at War: France and Britain 1914–1918* (Oxford, 1991).
26. *Land Agents' Record*, 1 March 1919.

than a habit of substituting arbitrary will for law. Tyranny breeds anarchy, and anarchy tyranny in regular succession and 'the authority of one man over another not regulated by fixed law or justified by absolute necessity is tyranny' With the advent of Peace '*Dora* must disappear'.[27]

Against this background, it is scarcely surprising that a great deal of opposition was being shown in the House of Commons to the War Emergency Laws (Continuation) Bill of 1919. This was the measure which the Committee on Emergency Legislation, chaired by Lord Cave, the previous Home Secretary, had proposed in order to assist reconstruction and to ensure that as little disruption as possible be caused to the economy in the transition from war to peace.[28] Cave himself had reported to the Cabinet's Home Affairs Committee (HAC) that his committee had first considered asking Parliament for power to continue emergency legislation by the simple means of an order in council.[29] But they had felt that such an approach would arouse parliamentary opposition and that scheduling in a statute those emergency measures desired to be continued should be the proper approach. By the time a bill had been drafted, the Attorney-General, Sir Gordon Hewart, had advised the HAC that in the light of the hostility directed towards the Bill when it was introduced in the House of Commons, it would be preferable for the government to proceed with its second reading rather than withdraw it and then to announce that, 'in view of the changed circumstances, they were prepared to cut it down very considerably'.[30]

Meanwhile, government departments would be asked to revise drastically their assessment of which defence regulations required to be retained for the following twelve months and to identify only the 'irreducible minimum of their requirements'.[31] The matter was one of urgency, Hewart indicated, as the French government were on the point of declaring that the war was at an end, in which circumstances the British government would be hard put to adopt a different line. Once an order in council was signed proclaiming the formal end of the war, the defence regulations would lapse unless, in the meantime, the Emergency Laws (Continuance) Bill had been enacted. Hewart's plea met with a positive response. The War Office, the Home Office and the Minister of Health, Christopher Addison, all indicated their support for a reconsideration and scaling down of their earlier legislative requirements. A sub-committee of the HAC was set up to examine the Bill with a view to rendering it acceptable to Parliament; the Bill as revised became law in 1920. The effect was to retain

27. Sir Alfred Hopkinson, K.C., *Rebuilding Britain: A Survey of Problems of Reconstruction after the World War* (London, 1918), p. 132.
28. PRO, CAB 24/5, G.233, 'War Cabinet. Committee of Home Affairs. Continuance of Emergency Legislation After the Termination of the War', 5 February 1919; CAB 24/5, G.242, '*ibid.*, *Second Report*', May 1919.
29. Copy in PRO, LCO 2/438. The HAC meeting was on 24 March 1919.
30. Copy in ibid. This meeting was on 15 October 1919.
31. See also P. B. Johnson, *Land Fit for Heroes: The Planning of British Reconstruction, 1916–1919* (Chicago, 1968), p. 452.

in force for a further twelve months after the official termination of the war, which occurred at midnight on 31 August 1921, a number of regulations concerned with demobilisation, reconstruction and, especially, food control. They included the important regulations 2B, 2E and 2F, and, for shipping control, Reg. 39BBB.[32]

It is no simple matter to describe in detail the widespread animosity directed against DORA and all her works, but there was a clamour immediately after the Armistice for their removal, to which the government, having established the Ministry of Reconstruction in July 1917, could not, without time to reflect, unreservedly commit itself: 'The pressure of business interests,' wrote R. H. Tawney, 'the clamour of its supporters, the noise made by the press, the advice of the Treasury, the economic situation and – still more – the prevalent illusions about the economic situation, all pushed in one direction'.[33]

It was also a nostalgic look backwards to an era which no longer existed: 'It was the last spasm of nineteenth century individualism striving to recapture on its death-bed the crude energies of its vanished youth.'[34] Even before the end of the war, the spirit of collectivism and of sacrifice was found wanting. Thus property owners, represented in a small pressure group, the Property Owners' Protection Association Ltd, had written to the Food Controller, J. R. Clynes, in September 1918, objecting to the use of DORA powers to requisition restaurants and catering establishments in order to set up national kitchens. They complained that the, 'application of what may be termed Military Law for the purpose of acquiring premises for civilian purposes, more especially when the objective is competitive trading with existing businesses, is most unfair'.[35]

On 31 July 1918 the National Union of Manufacturers implored the Prime Minister, Lloyd George, and the Chancellor of the Exchequer, Bonar Law, to lift war-time restrictions from their businesses. While Bonar Law assured the deputation that this was precisely what the government desired, Lloyd George admonished them not to ignore the beneficial lessons of state intervention in the economy.[36] Such representations from interest groups could be repeated a hundredfold, prompting government ministers to make the correct noises. Christopher Addison, for example, told representatives of the chemical industry in 1917:

> The policy of the Ministry of Reconstruction when it becomes a Ministry is not
> to interfere with your business (hear, hear). Our desire is to help so far as we

32. For the detailed statutes, regulations and orders originally scheduled for retention for twelve months after the formal termination of the war, see appendix to the Cave Committee report in PRO, CAB 24/5, G.233, above. The original intention to retain Reg. 7 for twelve months was subsequently dropped. See CAB 24/5, G.242, *'Second Report'*. See also Johnson, *Land Fit for Heroes*, pp. 306–10.

33. R. H. Tawney, 'The Abolition of Economic Controls, 1918–1921', *Economic History Review*, 1st series, xiii (1943), pp. 1–30, at p. 13.

34. Ibid., p. 17.

35. *Property Owners' Journal*, no. 186, October 1918.

36. Tawney, 'Abolition of Economic Controls', p. 11.

are able to help, and I can assure you, you need have no fear that I am at the Ministry of Reconstruction to promote nostrums of any sort or kind.[37]

The same assurances were spelt out by Winston Churchill, speaking to employers just four days before the Armistice. Though some transitional controls had to remain, he insisted, nonetheless;

> our only object is to liberate the forces of individual enterprise, to release the controls which have been found galling, to divest ourselves of responsibilities which the State has only accepted in this perilous emergency, and from which, in the overwhelming majority of cases, it had been far better to keep itself clear.[38]

The removal of threats to the property and livelihoods of small businessmen could not arrive a moment too soon after the Armistice. No doubt Tawney was partially correct when he observed that during the war, 'the public became increasingly aware of restrictions on the liberty of producers and consumers; but it thought of them in terms of particular commodities and individual trades, not of a new type of economy affecting all sides of life'.[39]

For some, indeed, the wartime experiment could have no further justification with the arrival of peace, and the dismantling of the wartime apparatus would restore not only economic freedom but mental freedom, eliminating the oppression of the individual by the state. As Johnson remarked:

> For Lloyd George, the value of decontrol was psychological: 'Even if there is no substance in it, the mere apprehension' about controls made decontrol a prime means for relieving business uncertainty. Thus every mention of uncertainty, and there were many, became an argument for decontrol as a placebo.[40]

Not all controls were quickly removed after the Armistice. In 1920 the state, as Cline pointed out, still controlled the production or manufacture of eighteen different commodities, including food, coal and wood. It oversaw a number of important industries, including mining, shipping, railways and banking, and otherwise 'directly touched on free enterprise'. When controls were finally removed, the objective was to stimulate a recovery of the economy after the dreadful slump of 1919–20.[41]

My primary concern, however, is not with the ideological, social or economic justifications for or against the retention of wartime controls, but with the extent to which their implementation by government departments

---

37. *Glasgow Herald*, 3 August 1917.
38. War Cabinet, *Report for 1918*, P.P. 1919, xxx (Cmd. 325), 453.
39. Tawney, 'Abolition of Economic Controls', p. 6.
40. Johnson, *Land Fit for Heroes*, p. 400.
41. Peter K. Cline, 'Reopening the Case of the Lloyd George Coalition and the Post-War Economic Transition, 1918–1919', *Journal of British Studies*, 10 (1970–71), pp. 162–75, at p. 173.

during the war was perceived as the exercise of state lawlessness which could brook no further toleration with the arrival of peace. We have seen how individual controversies over requisitioning under emergency legislation could flare up long into the post-war period (for obvious reasons, admittedly) when government controls still remained in place. The tenor of the opposition to the full-blooded Emergency Legislation (Continuance) Bill was one such symptom of extreme disquiet in Parliament at the retention of emergency powers of requisition. As Hopkinson wrote:

> Powers to take a person's property at the will of some executive department without any definite principle or procedure even for assessing compensation ought at once to cease when there is no longer immediate urgency for using such powers to secure the safety of the country.[42]

Lawyers often expressed their objections in classical terms of the necessity to uphold the common law against the excesses of the executive and of the very survival of the rule of law following the advent of peace:

> Doctrines have been put forward sometimes in the Courts during the War by counsel representing the Crown – i.e. in effect some Ministry – which would have seemed questionable even in the days of the Stuarts.[43]

Or the views of another legal writer:

> Such fundamental principles of the Constitution as those expressed by the phrases Government by Parliament, the Responsibility of the Executive to the Legislature, the Liberty of the Subject, Trial by Jury, Open Law Courts, Freedom of Speech, the Freedom of the Press and An Englishman's House is his Castle, were attacked, whittled down and in some cases reduced to mere shreds of their former consequence. What Dicey calls the essential characteristic of the British Constitution, namely, 'the absence of arbitrary power on the part of the Crown, of the Executive, and of every other authority in England', went into retirement and the old, long-used Prerogative was exalted as it had not been since the days of Charles I and Strafford.[44]

The objections frequently voiced, however, were not to state lawlessness per se but to perceived attacks on the shared ideals of British constitutionalism, those principles listed in the above passage. Thus it was claimed: 'When Parliament did raise any strenuous objection to the proposals of the Executive, the particular Bill or clause was dropped and the desired result obtained by departmental Regulations.'[45] Though no specific examples were cited to

42. Hopkinson, *Rebuilding Britain*, p. 132.
43. Ibid., p. 133. See also Sir John Simon's 'Introduction' to Scott and Hildesley, *The Case of Requisition*.
44. Sidney W. Clarke, 'The Rule of DORA', *Journal of Comparative Legislation*, 3rd series, 2 (1919), pp. 36–41, at p. 36.
45. Ibid., p. 37.

support the above claim, the fact that the procedure appeared to be lawful, and the end result a legally enforceable provision, perhaps added to the outrage felt by critics of the government. It was the abuse of power which was condemned, not the absence of legal authority for government actions taken, for the latter deficiency remained invisible, hidden under wraps. The complaint was about burgeoning government by regulation instead of by Act of Parliament, the failure adequately to publicise the regulations, the increasing use of provisional orders of a permanent character which did not require to be published, the dramatic increase in the number of ouster clauses aimed at outflanking the courts' power to declare regulations *ultra vires*, and the repeal or amendment of Acts of Parliament by ministerial regulations. All seemed to testify to the arrogance of ministers and to the supineness of Parliament. In Lord Hewart's explosive accusation, penned in 1929, there was in existence a 'New Despotism' (in contrast to the old despotism of the Tudors and Stuarts) composed of a faceless bureaucracy 'beyond the reach of the ordinary law'.[46] It was, moreover, a recent phenomenon, expanding 'under the greater latitude encouraged and bequeathed by the Great War'.[47] Hewart was not alone in claiming to detect unwelcome bureaucratic developments originating in the early years of the twentieth century and accelerating during the war years. Hilaire Belloc's diatribe against the 'Servile State' was a theme adopted by socialist critics of the wartime state who congregated in the rank-and-file shop stewards' movement. For the latter, the senior officials of the Ministry of Munitions, such as Sir Hubert Llewellyn Smith, William Beveridge, the architect of the modern welfare state and Humbert Wolfe – the author, incidentally, of thirty-nine novels and of one of the Carnegie Foundation official histories of the Great War, *Labour Supply and Regulation* (1923) – were the embodiment of a sinister development in capitalist exploitation which saw government ruthlessly stamp on basic liberties and more comprehensively enslave the working class.[48]

The criticisms levelled against the 'Servile State' thesis could be matched by those directed against Hewart's onslaught.[49] 'Dark and insidious conspiracies'

46. Lord Hewart, *The New Despotism* (London, 1929), p. 11.
47. Ibid., p. 21. Cf. 'Nobody is likely to deny that the necessities and emergencies of the Great War afforded a signal opportunity for departmental legislation and produced an enormous expansion in the annual output of rules, orders and regulations. But the encroachment of bureaucracy had begun well before the war, and assuredly they have survived it'. See ibid., p. 96. Pre-war fears among lawyers were exemplified by the speech of the Master of the Rolls, Lord Cozens-Hardy in the City of London in May 1911. See *The Times*, 4 May 1911, cited in Hewart, ibid., p. 144 and in Lynden Macassey, 'Law-Making by Government Departments', *Journal of Comparative Legislation*, 3rd series, 5 (1923), pp. 73–89, at p. 74. More measured criticisms of governmental legislation were expressed by Cecil T. Carr, *Delegated Legislation: Three Lectures* (Cambridge, 1921).
48. See James Hinton, *The First Shop Stewards' Movement* (London, 1973).
49. See, for example, Roger Davidson, 'The Myth of the "Servile State"', *Bulletin of the Society for the Study of Labour History*, 29 (Autumn 1974), pp. 65–67; Alastair Reid, 'Dilution, Trade Unionism and the State in Britain during the First World War', in Steven Tolliday and Jonathan Zeitlin (eds), *Shop Floor Bargaining and the State* (Cambridge, 1985), pp. 46–74; Rubin, *War, Law, and Labour*.

by civil-servants were 'sheer melodrama', wrote one (much later) critic.[50] A more exhaustive enquiry into the exercise of executive powers was set up in the wake of the publication of Hewart's book. The Committee on Ministers' Powers which reported in 1932 did, however, reject accusations of ministerial and civil service abuse of power, though it advised that the parliamentary grant of exceptional powers to ministers should be carefully supervised in future.[51] Perhaps more painful to Hewart was the reaction of the insiders in government. As Hewart's biographer noted:

> The book caused intense anger in Whitehall. Hewart's critics, remembering his days as Attorney-General, alleged that when they had asked Hewart's advice as between a more bureaucratic and a less bureaucratic course he had habitually advised the former. They pointed out with some acerbity that the type of Bill to which Hewart took exception, giving blank-cheque powers to the executive, could be illustrated by Bills which Hewart had backed personally as Attorney-General.[52]

The accusations always had a touch of conceptual confusion about them. For Hewart, the target was the despotic powers of a sinister executive. In one post-war example, Parliament had conferred powers in the Rating and Valuation Act 1925 to remove, by ministerial order, any 'difficulty' in the implementation of the Act. For Sir John Marriott M.P., writing in 1928, the target was 'quasi-Socialistic' legislative proposals exemplified by the (subsequently doomed) proposal of the Conservative government in the Rating and Valuation Bill 1928. This required the judges, not the Law Officers of the Crown, to give an opinion on a point of legal difficulty to the Minister of Health *prior* to any litigation taking place.[53] An executive engaged on legislating and the judges being recruited as an arm of the executive and thereby losing their 'independence' were part of a process, whether 'quasi-socialistic' or despotic, which had commenced prior to the war, accelerated during it and proceeded apace after it. Not so much a legacy of the wartime legal regime as a confirmation of it.

The same might be said of one other post-war development in the area dealt with in this book. That was the proposal to revamp the rules regarding the acquisition and valuation of land for public purposes. The wartime expedient was just that: a temporary, rough-and-ready measure to see the state through the acute difficulties of managing warfare on the home front, with no regard to the property owner's desire, if expressed, to secure a profit from the employment of his property by the state.

50. John E. Kersell, *Parliamentary Supervision of Delegated Legislation* (London, 1960), p. 2.
51. *Committee on Ministers' Powers* (chairman, Earl of Donoughmore), P.P. 1931–32, xii (Cmd. 4060), 345. From October 1930, the chairman was Leslie Scott.
52. Jackson, *The Chief*, p. 214.
53. Sir John Marriott, 'Law and Liberty', *Fortnightly Review*, July 1928, pp. 1–13, cited in Hewart, *The New Despotism*, p. 77.

The Ministry of Reconstruction, seeking to plan post-war Britain, recognised that grand projects, whether of housing development or of public utilities expansion, required land on which to build and to expand. Large-scale developments in forestry and in agriculture were also proposed, in some instances necessitating reclamation and drainage of land in private hands. Some members of the government, the Minister of Agriculture, R. E. Prothero (later Lord Ernle), for example, considered that land settlement for ex-servicemen and for tenant farmers should also become political imperatives.[54] The provision of effectual and well co-ordinated means of transport and access to natural and mineral resources were required, while the expanded use of electricity and of water power and developments in commercial aviation would 'give rise to many novel problems of importance in the Nation's productive capacity'.[55]

The post-war challenge was two-fold:

> Whenever the public interest really requires the expropriation of private land, that land must be made available without any unnecessary delay or expense. On the other hand, both the private owner of the particular land and others affected by the expropriation must be given a substantial protection against injustice, and the compensation to be provided must be fairly assessed.[56]

The loss basis of compensation for compulsory land acquisition deemed by the authorities adequate to the communal sacrifices of wartime would scarcely be politically acceptable in a peacetime economy. The sanctity of private property might be expected to be accorded greater respect in peacetime while the cost of acquisition might be expected to relate more closely than during the war to market value. But given that, for public projects, local or central authorities would be the major purchasers, their interest would necessarily be in acquiring land for public purposes as inexpensively as possible in peacetime circumstances. Towards this post-war objective, the 1845 Act could not oblige. As Sir Alfred Hopkinson argued in 1918, the housing situation was a scandal:

> Strong and immediate action by the State is needed. Adequate powers should be given to local authorities, and pressure put upon them, if needed, to ensure that such powers are exercised. Such action is already being taken and compulsory powers to acquire land will be given. In assessing compensation, the great urban

---

54. These latter two needs were fulfilled by the enactment of a separate Land Settlement (Facilities) Act in late 1919. See Roy Douglas, *Land, People and Politics: A History of the Land Question in the United Kingdom, 1878–1952* (London, 1976) pp. 176–77. See also Leah Leneman, *Fit for Heroes? Land Settlement in Scotland after World War One* (Aberdeen, 1989).
55. *Committee on the Acquisition and Valuation of Land for Public Purposes, First Report*, P.P. 1918, xi (Cd. 8998), 1, at p. 10.
56. Ibid.

landowner who has done nothing to contribute to the growth of the town or to promote its industries, ought not to receive the full value of the land, as enhanced by the necessary expansion of the town and thereby converted into building land, with an added amount for compulsory purchase. The manner in which the Lands Clauses Consolidation Act has been worked has added enormously to the burden of most great public undertakings. The compensation awarded has often been outrageous, and the expense incurred in assessing it one of the grossest scandals.[57]

To explore these questions and to put forward legislative proposals, the Committee on the Acquisition and Valuation of Land for Public Purposes,[58] under the auspices of the Ministry of Reconstruction, was established in July 1917 under the chairmanship of Leslie Scott. Its *First Report* was issued the following year, focusing upon simplifying the process of, and minimising the expense of, land acquisition for public purposes. The pre-war procedures of promoting a Private Act of Parliament, or the scarcely more efficient method of securing a 'provisional order' which, after a favourable local enquiry recommendation, might still require the approval of parliamentary select committees and then of Parliament itself, were condemned as dilatory and expensive. When the delays and costs were borne heavily by public departments, such as the Board of Education or the Admiralty, such obstacles required to be removed. A new sanctioning authority was therefore proposed to which every application for compulsory purchase for public purposes would be referred. As questions of policy would be involved in determining whether or not to grant permission, effective control should remain with Parliament by means of a right of appeal to that body on any question of policy, which was not the position with the Railway and Canal Commission under the Defence of the Realm (Acquisition of Land) Act 1916.[59]

Whether the proposal constituted a radical break with the previous cumbersome procedure was doubted by observers. In any case, it was argued, questions of compulsory acquisition for public purposes necessarily involved questions of policy. Under the 1845 Lands Clauses procedure, promoters were required:

> to lay before Parliament a public case before the Legislature would endow these private persons with power to purchase land, construct works, charge tolls, make bye-laws etc. It was a question whether policy, e.g., the general convenience of a travelling or trading community, made it expedient to give to the promoting company powers to take land by compulsion, or whether a man who held his land under a state guarantee of quiet possession should be made to give it up.[60]

57. Hopkinson, *Rebuilding Britain*, p. 142.
58. *Committee on the Acquisition and Valuation of Land.*
59. Ibid., sections II and III.
60. J. H. Balfour Browne, 'Compulsory Purchase of Lands', *Journal of Comparative Legislation*, 3rd series, 2 (1919), pp. 67–75, at p. 69.

No difference of principle was now involved, it was asserted. The sanctioning authority would itself be making policy decisions.

The *Second Report* of Leslie Scott's committee, which examined the question of compensation payable on compulsory purchase, was informed by a profound feeling of dissatisfaction with the Lands Clauses Act formula.[61] As the Attorney-General, Sir F. E. Smith (later Lord Birkenhead), told the Commons on 28 July 1918, in dealing with clause thirty of the Education Bill 1918, which made provision for the compulsory acquisition of land by local education authorities:

> The objections to procedure in these and cognate matters under the Lands Clauses Acts are so numerous and so universally admitted that if I were to spend time in dwelling upon them, I should rapidly exhaust the patience of the Committee. We are all familiar with the 10 per cent, with the tribunal, with the two arbitrators which are apt to develop qualities which in other tribunals would be regarded with great suspicion.[62]

The existing pre-war basis for compensation was laid down in judicial interpretations of the Lands Clauses Act, which did not in terms define the basis of valuation. That basis was what the property was worth to the owner (as distinct from its value to the community), that is, not only his loss (which was the basis for wartime compensation) but also the 'injury' he had suffered. This might be a substantial component reflecting his loss in relation to the abstract concept of property right. The committee, concerned to ensure economy in acquisition, recommended that the basis should be the market value as between a willing buyer and a willing seller. This could not be, and presumably was not intended to be, as generous and as accommodating to the owner as under the Lands Clauses Act. In one review of the committee's report this formula was attacked as being unrealistic as not possessing any existence in fact. In cases of compulsory purchase, it was pointed out, there was no willing seller, merely a coerced one. Therefore the committee's suggestion would introduce injustice which, it was suggested, could be abated by adopting an allowance of 10 per cent onto the market value. There was, in this critic's view, one consolation: 'Of course, the cheapest method of acquiring land,' he stated, 'would be to expropriate without compensation; but although many persons in these days who look upon "property as theft" would approve of such a method of acquiring land for public purposes, the Committee do not advocate confiscation.'[63]

---

61. P.P. 1918, xi (Cd. 9229), 59.
62. Cited ibid., p. 65.
63. Balfour Browne, 'Compulsory Purchase', pp. 70–71. The report dealt at length with critical aspects such as special adaptability of the land, betterment, injurious affection and recoupment, which principles, in their different ways, attempt to fix financial adjustments in the wake of the enhancement or diminution in the value of neighbouring properties following compulsory purchase. It is implicit in these adjustments that social or community values are weighed in the balance against claims of private property rights.

Perhaps the most significant feature of the report's treatment of compensation principles is what it did *not* say, rather than what it did say. As to the experience of the war years, of the Defence of the Realm Losses Commission, it was virtually silent, noting only the compulsory powers contained in the 1916 Acquisition of Land Act. Even this was treated almost as a footnote among the plethora of pre-war statutes which authorised compulsory purchase. No explicit debt to the experience of paying compensation during a period of war collectivism was noted in the report, even though the rebuilding of the post-war world in the image of the Ministry of Reconstruction was the *fons et origo* of the report, and though war collectivism was a powerful inspiration in the process of reconstruction. But the immediate post-war years, as already noted, brought dashed hopes. Philip Abrams has written movingly of the 'Failure of Social Reform, 1918–1920', as the ambitious post-war housing programme was in tatters.[64] The land tax question was no longer a live issue,[65] and even a project falling within the brief of Leslie Scott's committee, the question whether to set up a national register of legal titles to property in order to simplify conveyancing procedures, ran into obstacles. The Chief Registrar of the Land Registry, Sir Charles Brickdale, wrote on 2 August 1917 to Sir Claud Schuster, Permanent Secretary to the Lord Chancellor's Office, pointing out the importance of ridding the legal system of the encumbrances of the indenture system of conveyancing, if the government's post-war land policy were to be facilitated. Registration of title, wrote Brickdale to the Lord Chancellor, Lord Finlay, 'accords with the strong and increasing body of opinion in favour of small ownership – urban as well as rural – with the many legislative schemes having that object which are now occupying the attention of the public, and, I believe, of the Government'.[66] As with housing, while '1919–20 was a period of hope for land registration, 1921–25 was a period of humiliation'.[67]

As to Scott's committee on the Acquisition and Valuation of Land, the Cabinet failed to act on the first two reports until mid 1919. Its report had been sent to a Cabinet sub-committee under the Lord Chancellor, Lord Birkenhead, in March of that year, in order that a Bill be prepared.[68] As Johnson points out, the Bill dealt only with the question of procedure and offered, 'not a grant of new powers, not a radical redefinition of values, not an assault on such hugely important questions as betterment and injurious affection . . .',[69] whereby, in the case of betterment, owners would be required to pay for unearned gains

---

64. P. Abrams, 'The Failure of Social Reform, 1918–1920', *Past and Present* , 24 (1963), pp. 43–64.

65. Douglas, *Land, People and Politics*, p. 174.

66. Cited in Avner Offer, 'The Origins of the Law of Property Acts, 1910–1925', *Modern Law Review*, 40 (1977), pp. 505–22, at p. 512.

67. Ibid., p. 520.

68. PRO, CAB 27/63, 'Cabinet Committee: Land Acquisition Bill and Land Settlement (Facilities) Bill', March 1919.

69. Johnson, *Land Fit for Heroes*, p. 189.

resulting from socially driven development. Birkenhead's committee endorsed, however, the proposal to rely on part-time valuers in private practice who commanded high salaries, rather than employ existing full-time civil servants to assess compensation. The justification for this recommendation was that highly paid professionals would lend prestige and skill to the enterprise. Yet when Birkenhead's draft Bill reached the Prime Minister, Lloyd George, the latter's response was vituperative and damning: 'My dear Lord Chancellor,' the Prime Minister, himself an old solicitor, wrote on 15 March 1919:

> I have received the Report of your Committee on the Land Acquisition Bill with profound disappointment. The Bill was supposed to be one to facilitate acquisition of land for most urgent public purposes, speedily and at a fair price. It has been transformed into a Bill which will be represented as making sure that the landlord gets a good price, that the lawyers get their pickings and that there should be no undue delay in the completion of the transaction.
>
> To entrust the valuation of land to a man whose future prosperity and even livelihood depends on the goodwill of owners of land is to guarantee an interest and bias in favour of the landlord against the State. And as for employing lawyers to argue out the value of the land, would you or any other member of the Committee ever dream of buying an estate assessed by means of a wrangle between rival lawyers on the merits and demerits of the particular fields? . . . .
> It is these methods in the past that have rendered all housing schemes barren. It is owing to these that land producing only a few shillings an acre fetches hundreds of pounds per acre the moment it is requisitioned to build houses for the workmen whose labour has created the adjoining wealth.'[70]

In a dig at Sir Howard Frank, the unpaid, part-time professional in private practice who doubled as the War Office's Director-General of Lands, Lloyd George asked why Frank had been invited to give evidence to the committee. The co-founder of Knight, Frank & Rutley was an 'out and out landowners' man' whose testimony should have been counterbalanced with that of an opposite standpoint. 'The country is in no mood to tolerate reactionaries, high or low', the Prime Minister concluded.[71]

The superior, supercilious Birkenhead's reply was uncharacteristically respectful and subjugated:

> I have called the Committee together again tonight . . . I have no doubt that they will arrive at conclusions satisfactory to you. I can only add that if I had been at the original Cabinet, and had the slightest means of understanding what your views were and the grounds upon which they rested, the difficulty, such as it is, would never have arisen.[72]

Many revisions to the proposals were considered by the committee and

70. Cited in Lord Beaverbrook, *Men and Power, 1917–1918* (London, 1956), pp. 394–95.
71. Ibid.
72. Douglas, *Land, People and Politics*, p. 177.

by Cabinet before it was presented to Parliament.[73] Gordon Hewart, the Attorney-General, moved the Bill's second reading on April 10, 1919. But perhaps afraid of the reactions of a property-owners' parliament who seemed to be paying lip-service, but no more, to reconstruction, he chose to emphasise the limited nature of the measure.[74] The new tribunal of official valuers was accorded pride of place. This would do away with the wasteful system of magistrates, juries and surveyors in calculating compensation. Significantly, the valuers would be debarred from private practice (for soft-soaping reasons advanced by Hewart which, in the light of Lloyd George's outburst directed at Birkenhead, seem positively disingenuous). The 'sole purpose' of the measure, urged Hewart, was 'to secure fairness both as to price and as to costs'. No new additional powers of land acquisition were granted to any public authority or government department. In calculating value, Hewart pointed out, there was to be no allowance, no 10 per cent, for compulsion (the 1916 Act and others did not have any such allowance). Nor would there be additional compensation to property owners resulting from the particular suitability of the land for public purposes. Private property rights were therefore to occupy a less elevated or sacrosanct position than hitherto.

Harsh differences, nonetheless, remained. Crucially, the measure of valuation was stated to be the amount which the land, if sold in the open market by a willing seller, might be expected to realise. The objection voiced by, among others, Leslie Scott M.P., was to the omission of any statutory reference to a 'willing buyer'. For Hewart, the latter was implied. For Scott, a willing buyer would be one assuredly 'willing' to pay a price which would secure the property. But the presence of compulsory powers to back up the buyer would enable him to purchase more competitively, to the detriment of the seller. Yet paradoxically: 'A Parliament allegedly biased for property rights nevertheless voted down [Scott's] safeguard to landlords.'[75] On the other hand, no provision for a betterment levy on landowners was included in the Bill, obviating a further intrusion on private property rights. Scott's committee had advocated such an impost. It had also rejected a right to compensation for injurious affection to an owner whose land had not been taken compulsorily but which had been affected by public works. Instead, the tribunal was to have only a discretion whether to award such compensation.[76] The committee's approach was in the direction of diluting private property rights. When the Bill, already condemned for treating the state merely as a willing buyer in an open market rather than a coercive purchaser, failed to include the committee's recommendations on these matters, Scott considered that the omissions rendered the Bill so

73. Johnson, *Land Fit for Heroes*, p. 352.
74. H. C. Deb., 5th series, 114, 10 April 1919, cols. 2275–81. His speech is also reprinted in Lord Hewart, *Essays and Observations* (London, 1930), pp. 294–303.
75. Johnson, *Land Fit for Heroes*, p. 414. Unless otherwise stated, the following account is taken from ibid., pp. 413–16.
76. P.P. 1918, xi (Cd. 9229), 59, at para. 50.

flawed that he moved its rejection, having heard, minutes earlier, Hewart
pay tribute to him for his endeavours on the Reconstruction Committee. As
Johnson points out, the debate cut sharply across party lines.[77] Leslie Scott, the
Conservative, Sir Francis Acland, chairman of the Reconstruction Committee's
Forestry Committee and an Asquithian Liberal, the Labour Party, Radicals
like Ernest Benn and Josiah Wedgwood and Sir Donald Maclean (eventually
outshone by his Communist son's political exploits), and the scourge of Home
Rule, Sir Edward Carson, might be found in the same lobby on any particular
vote. A measure to free up the land for public purposes was bound to attract the
support of the Labour Party. Reform-minded Tories like Scott might repudiate
the biases of the Lands Clauses Act, but would still baulk at abject defencelessness
of small property owners confronted by compulsory powers.

One fundamental issue, however, remained: that of the compensation basis.
The market value to the 'willing seller' was passionately attacked by Maclean
almost in terms of the state offering a bloated subsidy to well-fed private
property which seemed to have done well out of the war: 'The country
will not stand the burden which the present measure seeks to impose on
communities and on Public Utilities Societies, of buying land at a market price
which largely represents the blood value of the war.'[78] The Inland Revenue
valuation assessment, he argued, ought to be the basis for compensation so
that the price which the government should be paying would reflect the
value of the property for tax purposes. Even Leslie Scott supported this
proposal in the face of his previous stance in support of small property owners.
The government held firm, however, despite being accused of promoting a
'reactionary measure' and a 'bill for profiteering.' Maclean charged that the
government's hidden agenda was to 'scrap the great machinery of land reform'
which pre-dated the war. It was an accusation which government spokesmen
rejected by pointing in the debate to Addison's Housing Bill and the Land
Settlement Bill, and by promising more fundamental reforms. Addison, and
of course Lloyd George, as was shown by his run-in with Birkenhead, were
far more ambitious and visionary.

That the accusations were well directed can be confirmed with hindsight.
In 1941 Leslie Scott, firmly ensconced on the Court of Appeal bench as
Lord Justice Scott, addressed a conference on town and country planning, and
solemnly informed his listeners that 'the Great Lands Clauses Consolidation
Act of 1845 is still law today'. Designed to protect private property rights, the
code had seen only a slight adjustment 'in favour of the nation' in 1919, but
the heavy bias towards individualism still remained.[79]

Why the damp squib? Had the war not made such a dramatic impact on
conceptions of property rights that a redrawing of the boundaries between

77. Johnson, *Land Fit for Heroes*, p. 415.
78. Cited ibid.
79. Lord Justice Scott, in F. E. Towndrow (ed.), *Replanning Britain* (London, n.d. [1941],
p. 116, cited in Johnson, *Land Fit for Heroes*, p. 416.

the public and the private might be permitted as a matter of course? If the noted right-winger, William Joynson-Hicks M.P., could question prevailing assumptions, then a sea-change could surely be detected. Recalling his writing a letter to the staunchly Conservative *Pall Mall Gazette* in 1913, warning that the Tory Party ought to grasp the nettle of land reform, Joynson-Hicks predictably aroused a storm of indignation. But, he now wrote:

> All this was before the war, when individualism was rampant, and when the last stronghold of privilege centred in the possession of the land; when, moreover, Mr Lloyd George was regarded as something a shade blacker than Satan, and when the housing of cattle was considered of more importance than that of a cottager. During the war all this has changed ... But you may say to me: 'What right has the State to compel Lord This or That to sell anything out of his 20,000 acres.' My answer, and the war has already proved it, is that the State is more than the individual ... Gone, and gone for good, are all the old individualistic ideas of the rights of property ... and I do implore my Tory friends not to shy off reforms on the ground that they are socialistic; why, the whole of the war is socialistic . . .[80]

In commenting on Leslie Scott's report, a correspondent to the *Athenaeum*, R. L. Reiss, also seemed to speak to the striking of new attitudes to property: 'the effect of the war has been to produce much greater unanimity [in the report] than would have been thought possible four years ago'.[81] For another correspondent, the transformation of attitudes had a much longer pedigree:

> The fact is that there is a great change in the last sixty or seventy years in public opinion in relation to the institution called Private Property. In the old time property in land was regarded as a sacred right, and that right could only be abrogated by the supreme power of the legislature, and that only after proof that the owner was to be ousted on the ground of public necessity or public interest, and even then only after full compensation had been paid to him for the property taken and the injury caused by the acts of the promoters ... It is obvious that, although we may not have arrived at the opinion that 'private property is theft', we no longer entertain the same views with reference to the ownership of land that our ancestors did and have, rightly or wrongly, a much more extended view of what constitutes a 'public purpose'.[82]

These remarks went further than observations such as that: 'During the war, the British Government treated the shipping industry as a national resource rather than as a private industry . . .';[83] or that: 'The war also taught the country to look at its national equipment in a new light, not as private

80. W. Joynson-Hicks, 'The Land Question', in Earl of Cromer et al., *After-War Problems* (London, 1917), pp. 187–89.
81. R.L.R. [Reiss], in the *Athenaeum*, 4628, April 1918, cited in Johnson, *Land Fit for Heroes*, p. 189.
82. Balfour Browne, 'Compulsory Purchase', pp. 67–68.
83. Armitage, *The Politics of Decontrol of Industry*, p. 39.

property alone, but as the capital helping to provide the national income.'[84] For Joynson-Hicks and Reiss thought they had detected a more permanent legacy of the war years (and in the case of Balfour Browne, a more prolonged shift). As F. M. L. Thompson has written in respect to landed society, the map had certainly been redrawn:

> The old [landed] order was indeed doomed, had in fact already passed away in many respects, but it was from causes of much longer standing than the 1919 budget [which raised death duties to 40 per cent on estates of £2,000,000 or more], though the desertion of the cause of the landed aristocracy by the Conservative Ministers in the Coalition Government no doubt was painful . . .
>
> By March 1919 a 'revolution in landowning' was proclaimed by the *Estates Gazette*. Then more and more estates were put on the market and by May an advertisement announced 'England changing hands'.[85]

Of course, Thompson is dealing here not with compulsory powers but with voluntary sales which reflected trends which had predated the war. For the political and social influence of the landed families had declined before 1914 and the war merely accelerated the process by increasing the costs of maintaining property and shifting power during the war to Lloyd George's businessmen[86] and technocratic 'men of push-and-go'.[87]

With hindsight, we know that the predictions of Joynson-Hicks, Reiss, Balfour Browne and others were mistaken as the ambitious and visionary reconstruction plans crumbled to dust. As Sir Arthur Griffith-Bowcawen, a government minister in the Pensions and Agriculture departments during this period, reminisced:

> So far as the House of Commons went, we got on well enough, the Coupon Parliament would in fact pass anything which the Government proposed and was equally ready to repeal the same resources two or three years later . . . we were all committed to a great programme of social reform; in the words of the Prime Minister we were to 'create a new Heaven and a new Earth'. We were to build 'homes for heroes' . . . Hence we embarked on these great schemes which, unhappily, later on we found we could not afford . . . Parliament in the days of poverty had to repeal measures which it had passed only a year or two before in the days of factitious prosperity.[88]

84. Sidney Pollard, *The Development of the British Economy, 1914–1967*, 2nd edn (London, 1969), p. 62.

85. F. M. L. Thompson, *English Landed Society in the Nineteenth Century* (London, 1963), p. 330.

86. Ibid., p. 335.

87. Archetypally represented by G. M. Booth who, to the distaste of the permanent civil servants, sought to organise labour regulation for a time at the Ministry of Munitions. See Duncan Crow, *A Man of Push and Go: The Life of George Macauley Booth* (London, 1965).

88. Arthur Griffith-Boscawen, *Memories* (London, 1925), pp. 216–17, cited in Johnson, *Land Fit for Heroes*, p. 431.

The late nineteenth-century 'Visions of a world transformed by some form of land exploitation in the name of the community' had to await,[89] in the first instance, the tentative schemes of slum clearance authorised under Neville Chamberlain's Housing Act 1925 before the more grandiose flowering of the 'planned environment' via compulsory development plans promulgated under the Ministry of Town and Country Planning Act 1947.[90]

89.   Cornish and Clark, *Law and Society in England, 1750–1950*, p. 191.

90.   For overviews of the historical development of land acquisition and compensation principles, see Peter Hall, 'The Land Values Problem and its Solution', in Peter Hall (ed.), *Land Values: Report of the Proceedings of a Colloquium Held in London on March 13 and 14, 1965* (London, 1965), pp. ix–xix; H. Ronald Parker, 'The History of Compensation and Betterment since 1900', ibid., pp. 53–72; Sir Frederick Corfield and R. J. A. Carnwath, *Compulsory Acquisition and Compensation* (London, 1978), pp. 1–10; and A. W. Cox, *Adversary Politics and Land: The Conflict over Land and Property in Post-War Britain* (Cambridge, 1984).

15

Conclusion

This book is not a work of jurisprudence exploring property rights theories. Nonetheless, it may be noted that the compensation bodies, the Defence of the Realm Losses Commission (DRLC) and the War Compensation Court (WCC), were not prepared to recognise a broader conception of property than one embracing merely land, buildings or physical goods. As compensation was offered, in terms of the remit, for direct and particular interference with property or business which led to direct loss, the WCC felt obliged to reject a claim for damage caused by smoke, smells, noise and unsightliness thrown up by munitions factory construction in the neighbourhood.[1] A common law claim for nuisance against a private contractor, though not against the Crown which was immune from such proceedings, would nonetheless have been competent.

Particular interference with property also failed to extend to restrictions on personal liberty. For example, a naturalised British subject ordered by the Navy to vacate a restricted area was denied compensation both for the interference with his liberty and for interference with his business as a hotelier.[2] Claims were rejected also for compensation based upon restrictions imposed on ex-enemy aliens under the Aliens Restriction Act 1914, that is, restrictions upon their persons,[3] as distinct from the occupation of their properties by government departments for which *ex gratia* payments might be made.[4]

By contrast, the trustees of a girls' school in Gravesend requisitioned by

1. War Compensation Court, *Second Report*, pp. 54–57 (cases of Mr and Mrs Bowller and Mrs E. I. M. Benjamin).
2. Ibid., pp. 34–35 (claim of W. Hatje).
3. See the list of applicants compiled in PRO, HO 45/13350/419253/5, 'Claims for Compensation based upon restrictions imposed under the Aliens Restriction Act 1914', 14 July 1921. Cf. the denial of compensation to British subjects interned under Defence Regulation 14B in chapter 12, above.
4. Although ex-enemy aliens were barred under the Indemnity Act 1920 from seeking compensation for occupation of their properties, an administrative concession was made on their behalf by the Treasury and the War Office. See also for the DRLC, Davidson, 'The Defence of the Realm Losses Commission', pp. 234–52, at pp. 257–58. For an example, see the case of Miss Luhn, an elderly German lady whose property, Pouce's House, was requisitioned for use by the commandant of the School of Observers at Manston Aerodrome in Kent. See Rocky Stockman, *The History of RAF Manston*, 3rd edn (Ramsgate, 1986), p. 12.

the Admiralty as a hospital for the treatment of venereal diseases, successfully argued that the moral stigma attaching to the premises after derequisitioning constituted a 'direct loss'.[5] Such a decision seemed to acknowledge affinities with goodwill as a form of property. Yet, no such form of property right received recognition in the jurisprudence of the compensation bodies.[6]

The coverage of the awarding bodies may therefore have been patchy. That was not out of character with the government's approach to the general question of requisitioning and to compensation. The fact is that, like much of the domestic effort during the First World War, there was a distinct lack of overall strategy and the prevalence of a muddling-through approach. This is not to argue that in some spheres of government regulation, no consistent theoretical approach can be identified.[7] As Douglas Davidson, the secretary to the DRLC and then to the WCC, opined: 'The history of compensation during the war resembles that of most other war activities in being a series of improvisations.'[8] Only the question of compensation for billeting, he thought, had been accorded consideration prior to the war. We have seen how the War Office in particular was regularly shifting its position in the early months of the war. In respect to one take-over of property it might negotiate a contractual lease at market value; on another occasion, it might requisition under Defence Regulation 2, leaving the amount of compensation legally owed to be settled in future negotiations. Or, as with Shoreham Aerodrome, and having been primed by the Treasury, it might insist that any payments made for the use of the airfield were *ex gratia*, the amounts of which would fall within the absolute discretion of the department.

The introduction of a uniform practice of compensation payments by the DRLC and by the Liquor Trade Claims Commission did not guarantee for long the routine administration of this question. The challenge to the very basis of the system – that payments were *ex gratia* whether properties were requisitioned under the prerogative or under Defence of the Realm Act (DORA) powers – forced government departments onto the defensive, ducking here, weaving there, leaving property owners frustrated and angry. For the former, nurtured in a culture of economy and of the avoidance of establishing an unfavourable precedent, the problems were administrative and organisational: how to secure that departmental and national objectives were achieved while protecting the Exchequer from 'excess claims' submitted by

5. War Compensation Court, *Second Report*, pp. 35–39 (claim of Trustees of Milton Mount College, Gravesend).
6. Property rights in inventions whose particulars were liable to compulsory communication to government departments under defence regulations were acknowledged by the establishment of another prerogative body making payments, the Royal Commission on Awards to Inventors, which issued seven reports between 1921 and 1938.
7. The present writer has argued elsewhere that government controls on labour during the First World War were informed broadly by a 'wartime-corporatist' perspective. See Rubin, *War, Law, and Labour*. Other writers on wartime labour regulation have adopted different approaches.
8. Davidson, 'The Defence of the Realm Losses Commission', p. 234.

(whisper it quietly) less than patriotic property owners with a less than perfect sense of communal sacrifice and with predatory fingers. For the latter, the predators were the government. Lord Rosebery's outrage at the light-fingeredness of the War Office and of the Ministry of Munitions could be matched by the tone of the debate on the Indemnity Bill 1920 during which one speaker felt moved to declare that: 'many of the deeds done under the Defence of the Realm Act were deeds which made the profession of a highway robber, by comparison, that of a gentleman'.[9] One suspects, nonetheless, that what may have hurt civil servants more was not the accusation of piracy or of gangsterdom but of the inefficiency of that 'gang of swankers' of which *Flight* magazine spoke so eloquently.[10] Perhaps not every participant recognised a link between constitutional politics and the payment of compensation. Whether George Wingfield or Arthur Whinney or the Cannon Brewery Co. Ltd or Newcastle Breweries Ltd or J. Hindhaugh & Co. saw themselves as 'Village Hampdens' is to be doubted though perhaps Lord Rosebery and the Southport doctor, Aeneas Henderson, may have done.[11] Legal commentators as well as parliamentarians, or, in the cases of Sir John Simon and Leslie Scott, a convergence of the two, certainly conceived of the question in terms of lofty, constitutional principle.[12] Whether Marxists are correct in arguing that the 'superstructure' of law (as well as of religion, morality and so on) is erected upon and reflects a substructural base of economic relations predicated by the forces of production, cannot be debated here. That constitutional law was conceived by property owners as a matter of pounds, shillings and pence is a more likely proposition and related to actual experience.

The 'abridging' of the royal prerogative by statute as declared in *De Keyser's Royal Hotel* was undoubtedly a constitutional landmark in reining in the Crown's discretionary powers. In searching for further legacies of the experience of requisitioning and compensation in the First World War, we may cast our eyes on the experience of the Second World War in this regard:[13] 'Constitutional lawyers' wrote D. W. (later Sir Denis) Brogan in 1944, 'would be well advised not to pass over the Compensation (Defence) Act [1939] as yet another emergency statute of no permanent importance. It is interesting, if for no other reason, because of its ancestry which can be traced back to *Att-Gen.* v. *De Keyser's Royal Hotel*.'[14]

The First World War lessons of economic conflict and of the resentment expressed in some quarters against a system of compensation whose existence

9. H. C. Deb., 5th series, 128, 3 May 1920, col. 1787 (H. N. Rae).
10. See above, p. 167.
11. See above, chapter 13.
12. See Sir John Simon's 'Introduction' to Scott and Hildesley, *The Case of Requisition*, pp. xv–xxiv.
13. For brief details, see the outline in C. M. Kohan, *Works and Buildings* (London, 1952), pp. 420–21 (in History of the Second World War, United Kingdom Civil Series, ed. W. K. Hancock). See above, chapter 14.
14. D. W. Logan, review of Eric C. Strathon, F.S.I., *Compensation (Defence)* [1943], *Modern Law Review*, 60 (1944), pp. 392–95.

was dependent on the indulgence of ministers and civil servants dressed up as the royal favour dictated a different approach during the Second World War. A statutory scheme was therefore established in the 1939 Act and the General Claims Tribunal was charged with assessing compensation on bases laid down in the Act. There the similarity with the First World War scheme begins. No compensation for loss of profits or for injury to goodwill would be made. Moreover, 'for a statute which should have been thought out in the leisurely days of peace', it was 'surprisingly inexact and indifferent to hardship'. Perhaps deliberately vague in that the Act would be applied in 'unprecedented circumstances'.[15] Rent for occupation was calculated as the sum which a tenant paying the outgoings might reasonably be expected to pay immediately prior to the imposition of emergency powers. No appreciation of values due to the emergency was to be taken into account. In respect to other provisions, it was claimed, 'it is clear that the Crown is engaged in its favourite pastime, *vis-à-vis* the subject of 'Heads I win, tails you lose', for the Crown's liability to make good damage excludes 'fair wear and tear','[16] despite the assumption that the hypothetical tenant was under a full repairing covenant.

Yet as striking in its comparison with the earlier experience is that, 'many of the most important interpretations of the Act have not been handed down by the Tribunal or by the High Court on appeal therefrom, but are to be found in statements made by the Executive'.[17] Perhaps the new despotism of the Great War and of the 1920s was still exercising its authority. Brogan remarks that the exclusion of Crown liability was modified in practice by Treasury directive. Instead of passing amending legislation, Parliament appeared to permit the executive to solve the problem by means of sleight of hand, amounting, in his view, to a constitutional innovation. Perhaps a constitutional impropriety but hardly, as the previous wartime experience demonstrated, a constitutional innovation. For compensation and the constitution, it was, indeed, *plus ça change*.

15.   Ibid., p. 393.
16.   Ibid.
17.   Ibid., p. 394.

Bibliography

1. MANUSCRIPT SOURCES

(a) Public Record Office, London

Air Ministry	AIR 2
Board of Trade	BT 31, 102, 103
Cabinet	CAB 16, 23, 24, 26, 27
High Court of Justiciary	J 13
Home Office	HO 45, 190
Lord Chancellor's Office	LCO 2
Ministry of Food	MAF 60
Ministry of Munitions	MUN 4, 5
Ministry of War Transport	MT 23, 25
Treasury	T 24, 80, 161
Treasury Solicitor	TS 27, 28
War Office	WO 32

(b) Scottish Record Office, Edinburgh

Lord Advocate's Department	AD 52, 54
Scottish Office	HH 31
Steel-Maitland Papers	GD 193, 283

(c) House of Lords Record Office, London

Brighton–Shoreham Aerodrome Ltd Main Papers.
Attorney–General v *De Keyser's Royal Hotel Ltd* Main Papers.

2. GOVERNMENT PUBLICATIONS

Board of Trade, *Report and Statistics of Bad Timekeeping in Shipbuilding, Munitions and Transport Areas*, P.P. 1914–16 (220), lv, 1915.
Central Control Board (Liquor Traffic), *Fourth Report*, P.P. 1918 (Cd. 9055), xi, 1918.

Committee on the Acquisition and Valuation of Land for Public Purposes,
   First Report, P.P. 1918 (Cd. 8998), xi, 1918.
Committee on Crown and Government Lands, *Interim and Final Reports*,
   P.P. 1922 (Cmd. 1689), vii, 1922.
Committee on Ministers' Powers, *Report*, P.P. 1931–32 (Cmd. 4060), xii,
   1932.
Defence of the Realm (Losses) Commission, *First Report*, P.P. 1916
   (Cd. 8359), vii, 1916.
–, *Schedule to First Report*, P.P. 1918 (Cd. 9048), viii, 1918.
–, *Second Report*, P.P. 1917–18 (Cd. 8751), x, 1917.
Indemnity Bill, *Proposed Amendments to the Indemnity Bill*, P.P. 1920
   (Cmd. 567), xi, 1920.
Interim and Final Report of the Civil Aerial Transport Committee, P.P. 1918
   (Cd. 9218), v, 1918.
*Report and Special Report from the Select Committee on the Indemnity Bill,
   1920*, P.P. 1920 (136), vii, 1920.
State Purchase of the Liquor Trade, *Report of the English, Scotch and Irish
   Committees*, P.P. 1918 (Cd. 9042), xi, 1918.
War Cabinet, *Report for 1918*, P.P. 1919 (Cmd. 325), xxx, 1919.
War Compensation Court, *First Report* (London, 1921).
–, *Second Report* (London, 1923).
–, *Third Report* (London, 1923).
–, *Fourth Report* (London, 1924).
–, *Seventh Report* (London, 1928).
–, *Eighth Report* (London, 1929).

3. CONTEMPORARY JOURNALS, NEWSPAPERS ETC

Athenaeum.
Citizen.
City News.
Daily Mail Year Book, 1920.
Flight.
Fortnightly Review.
Glasgow Herald.
Hansard.
Journal of Comparative Legislation, 3rd series.
Land Agents' Record.
Law Quarterly Review.
Morning Post.
Pictorial News.
Property Owners' Journal.
Scotsman.
Solicitors' Journal.

Surplus.
Vanity Fair.
Westminster Gazette.

4. BOOK AND PAMPHLETS

Allen, C.K., *Law and Orders* (London, 1947).
Armitage, S.M.H., *The Politics of Decontrol of Industry: Britain and the United States* (London, 1969).
Ashworth, Chris, *Action Stations*, 9, *Military Airfields of the Central South and South East* (Wellingborough, 1985).
Baring, Maurice, *Flying Corps Headquarters, 1914–1918* (London, 1930).
Barnett, L. Margaret, *British Food Policy During the First World War* (London, 1985).
Barton, Tilney, *The Life of a Country Lawyer in Peace and War-Time* (Oxford, n.d., *c.* 1931).
Baty, T. and Morgan, J.H., *War: Its Conduct and Legal Results* (London, 1915).
Baugh, Daniel, *British Naval Administration in the Age of Walpole* (Princeton, NJ, 1965).
Beaverbrook, Lord, *Men and Power, 1917–1918* (London, 1956).
Beveridge, Sir William H., *British Food Control* (Oxford, 1928).
Bonnett, Stanley, *The Price of Admiralty: An Indictment of the Royal Navy, 1805–1966* (London, 1968).
Carr, Cecil T., *Delegated Legislation: Three Lectures* (Cambridge, 1921).
Carter, Henry, *The Control of the Drink Trade* (London, 1918).
Clynes, J.R., *Memoirs, 1869–1924* (London, 1937).
Cole, Christopher and Cheesman, E.F., *The Air Defence of Britain, 1914–1918* (London, 1984).
Cole, G.D.H. and Postgate, Raymond, *The Common People, 1746–1946* (London, 1966 edn).
Coller, F.H., *A State Trading Adventure* (Oxford, 1925).
Cooper, Malcolm, *The Birth of Independent Air Power: British Air Policy in the First World War* (London, 1986).
Corfield, Sir Frederick and Carnwath, R.J.A., *Compulsory Acquisition and Compensation* (London, 1978).
Cornish, W.R. and Clark, G. de N., *Law and Society in England, 1750–1950* (London, 1989).
Cox, A.W., *Adversary Politics and Land: The Conflict over Land and Property in Post-War Britain* (Cambridge, 1984).
Crow, Duncan, *A Man of Push and Go: The Life of George Macauley Booth* (London, 1965).
De la Ferté, Sir Philip Joubert, *The Third Service: The Story Behind the Royal Air Force* (London, 1955).

Dewey, P.E., *British Agriculture in the First World War* (London, 1989).

Dicey, A.V., *Law of the Constitution* (6th edn, London, 1902; 8th edn, London, 1915).

Doughty, Martin, *Merchant Shipping and War* (London, 1982).

Douglas, Roy, *Land, People and Politics: A History of the Land Question in the United Kingdom, 1878–1952* (London, 1976).

Fairlie, J.A., *British War Administration* (New York, 1919).

Fayle, C. Ernest, *War and the Shipping Industry* (Oxford, 1927).

French, David, *British Economic and Strategic Planning, 1905–1915* (London, 1982).

Gough, J.W., *Fundamental Law in English Constitutional History* (Oxford, 1955).

Griffith–Boscawen, Arthur, *Memories* (London, 1925).

Hankey, Lord, *The Supreme Command, 1914–1918,* (London, 1961).

Harris, José, *William Beveridge: A Biography* (Oxford, 1977).

Henderson, Aeneas, *The Indemnity Bill: A Case of Compensation for War Loss* (Southport, 1920).

Hewart, Lord, *Essays and Observations* (London, 1930).

–, *The New Despotism* (London, 1929).

Hinton, James, *The First Shop Stewards' Movement* (London, 1973).

Hirst, F.W., *The Consequences of the War to Great Britain* (New York, 1968).

Hopkinson, Sir Alfred, *Rebuilding Britain: A Survey of Problems of Reconstruction after the World War* (London, 1918).

Horne, John N., *Labour at War: France and Britain, 1914–1918* (Oxford, 1991).

Hurwitz, S.J., *State Intervention in Great Britain: A Study of Economic Control and Social Response, 1914–1919* (New York, 1949).

Jackson, R.M., *The Chief: The Biography of Gordon Hewart, Lord Chief Justice of England, 1922–40* (London, 1959).

James, Robert Rhodes, *Rosebery* (London, 1963).

Johnson, P.B., *Land Fit for Heroes: The Planning of British Reconstruction, 1916–1919* (Chicago, 1968).

Jones, Edgar, *Accountancy and the British Economy, 1840–1980: The Evolution of Ernst & Whinney* (London, 1980).

Kersell, John E., *Parliamentary Supervision of Delegated Legislation* (London, 1960).

Kohan, C.M., *Works and Buildings* (London, 1952).

Leneman, Leah, *Fit for Heroes? Land Settlement in Scotland after World War One* (Aberdeen, 1989).

Lewis, Michael, *A Social History of the Navy, 1793–1815* (London, 1960).

Lloyd, E.M.H., *Experiments in State Control: At the War Office and the Ministry of Food* (Oxford, 1924).

Morgan, J.H., *Assize of Arms* (London, 1945).

Offer, Avner, *The First World War: An Agrarian Interpretation* (Oxford, 1989).

–, *Property and Politics, 1870–1914: Landownership, Law, Ideology and Urban Development in England* (Cambridge, 1981).

Olson, Jr., Mancur, *The Economics of the Wartime Shortage* (Durham, NC, 1963).

Pollard, Sidney, *The Development of the British Economy, 1914–1967* (2nd edn, London, 1969).

Powers, Barry D., *Strategy without Slide-Rule: British Air Strategy, 1914–1939* (Beckenham, 1976).

Rodger, N.A.M., *The Wooden World: An Anatomy of the Georgian Navy* (London, 1986).

Rosebery, Lord, *Turnhouse: An Object Lesson* (n.p., n.d., c. 1920).

Rubin, G.R., *War, Law, and Labour: The Munitions Acts, State Regulation, and the Unions, 1915–1921* (Oxford, 1987).

Salter, J.A., *Allied Shipping Control* (Oxford, 1921).

Scott, Leslie and Hildesley, Alfred, *The Case of Requisition: De Keyser's Royal Hotel Limited v. The King* (Oxford, 1920).

Simon, Viscount, *Retrospect* (London, 1952).

Simpson, A.W.B., ed., *A Biographical Dictionary of the Common Law* (London, 1984).

–, *In the Highest Degree Odious: Detention without Trial in Wartime Britain* (Oxford, 1992).

Smith, David J., *Action Stations, 7, Military Airfields of Scotland, the North–East and Northern Ireland* (Cambridge, 1983).

Stockman, Rocky, *The History of RAF Manston* (3rd edn, Ramsgate, 1986).

Sykes, Sir F.H., *Aviation in Peace and War* (London, 1922).

Thompson, F.M.L., *English Landed Society in the Nineteenth Century* (London, 1963).

Whitehouse, Arch, *The Zeppelin Fighters* (London, 1972).

Wilson, Charles, *The History of Unilever: A Study in Economic Growth and Social Change* (London, 1954).

Winter, J.M., *Socialism and the Challenge of War* (London, 1974).

5. CONTRIBUTIONS TO BOOKS

Hall, Peter, 'The Land Values Problem and its Solution', in *Land Values: Report of the Proceedings of a Colloquium Held in London on March 13 and 14, 1965*, ed. Peter Hall (London, 1965), pp. ix–xix.

Harris, José, 'Bureaucrats and Businessmen in British Food Control, 1916–19', in *War and the State: The Transformation of British Government, 1914–1919*, ed. Kathleen Burk (London, 1982), ch. 6.

Joynson–Hicks, W., 'The Land Question', in *After-War Problems*, ed. Earl of Cromer et al. (London, 1917), pp. 187–89.

Parker, H. Ronald, 'The History of Compensation and Betterment since 1900', in *Land Values*, ed. Hall, pp. 53–72.

Reid, Alastair, 'Dilution, Trade Unionism and the State in Britain during the First World War', in *Shop Floor Bargaining and the State*, ed. Steven Tolliday and Jonathan Zeitlin (Cambridge, 1985), pp. 46–74.

Roberts, P.R., 'The "Henry VIII Clause": Delegated Legislation and the Tudor Principality of Wales', in *Legal Record and Historical Reality*, ed. Thomas G. Watkin (London, 1989), ch. 3.

Rose, M.E., 'The Success of Social Reform? The Central Control Board (Liquor Traffic), 1915–1921', in *War and Society: Historical Essays in Honour and Memory of J.R. Western, 1928–1971*, ed. M.R.D. Foot (London, 1973), ch. 5.

6. ARTICLES

Abrams, P., 'The Failure of Social Reform, 1918–1920', *Past and Present*, 24 (1963), pp. 43–64.

Anon., 'RAF Turnhouse', *Aeromilitaria: The AIR BRITAIN Military Aviation Historical Quarterly*, 1 (1986), p. 15.

–, 'Requisitions – Clarendon's Opinion – "Carefully to be Repaired by the Public Stock"', *Law Times*, 180 (1935), pp. 35–36.

Browne, J.H. Balfour, 'Compulsory Purchase of Lands', *Journal of Comparative Legislation*, 3rd series, 2 (1919), pp. 67–75.

Clark, Sidney W., 'The Rule of DORA', *Journal of Comparative Legislation*, 3rd series, 2 (1919), pp. 36–41.

Cline, Peter K., 'Reopening the Case of the Lloyd George Coalition and the Post-War Economic Transition, 1918–1919', *Journal of British Studies*, 10 (1970–71), pp. 162–75.

Davidson, Douglas DuBois, 'The Defence of the Realm Losses Commission and the War Compensation Court', *Journal of Comparative Legislation*, 3rd series, 5 (1923), pp. 234–52.

Davidson, Roger, 'The Myth of the "Servile State"', *Bulletin of the Society for the Study of Labour History*, 29 (Autumn, 1974), pp. 65–67.

Donnachie, Ian, 'World War I and the Drink Question: State Control of the Drink Trade', *Scottish Labour History Society Journal*, 17 (1982), pp. 19–26.

Fearon, Peter, 'The Growth of Aviation in Britain', *Journal of Contemporary History*, 20 (1985), pp. 21–40.

George, A.D., 'Aviation and the State: The Grahame–White Aviation Company, 1912–23', *Journal of Transport History*, 9 (1988), pp. 209–14.

Hazeltine, H.D., 'The Law of Civil Aviation Transport', *Journal of Comparative Legislation*, 3rd series, 2 (1919), pp. 76–89.

–, 'The Recent and Future Growth of Aerial Law', *Flight*, 14 March 1918, pp. 295–96.

Holdsworth, W.S., 'The Power of the Crown to Requisition British Ships in a National Emergency', *Law Quarterly Review*, 35 (1919), pp. 12–42.

Logan, D.W., book review, *Modern Law Review*, 60 (1944), pp. 392–95.

Macassey, Lynden, 'Law-Making by Government Departments', *Journal of Comparative Legislation*, 3rd series, 5 (1923), pp. 73–89.

Mackenzie, V. St. Clair, 'The Royal Prerogative in War-Time', *Law Quarterly Review*, 34 (1918), pp. 152–59.

Mann, F.A., 'Outlines of a History of Expropriation', *Law Quarterly Review*, 75 (1959), pp. 188–219.

Myerscough, John, 'Airport Provision in the Inter-War Years', *Journal of Contemporary History*, 20 (1985), pp. 41–70.

Offer, Avner, 'The Origins of the Law of Property Acts, 1910–1925', *Modern Law Review*, 40 (1977), pp. 505–22.

Pollock, Sir Frederick, editorial, *Law Quarterly Review*, 32 (1916), p. 339.

Randolph, Carman F., 'The Eminent Domain', *Law Quarterly Review*, 3 (1887), pp. 314–25.

Rubin, Gerry R., 'Law as a Bargaining Weapon: British Labour and the Restoration of Pre-War Practices Act 1919', *Historical Journal*, 32 (1989), pp. 925–45.

Tawney, R.H., 'The Abolition of Economic Controls, 1918–1921', *Economic History Review*, 1st series, 13 (1943), pp. 1–30.

Townshend, Charles, 'Martial Law: Legal and Administrative Problems of Civil Emergency in Britain and the Empire, 1800–1940', *Historical Journal*, 25 (1982), pp. 167–95.

–, 'Military Force and Civil Authority in the United Kingdom, 1914–1921', *Journal of British Studies*, 28 (1989), pp. 262–92.

Tudsbery, F.C.T., 'Prerogative in Time of War', *Law Quarterly Review*, 32 (1916), pp. 384–91.

Turner, John, 'State Purchase of the Liquor Trade in the First World War', *Historical Journal*, 23 (1980), pp. 589–615.

Van Wesemael, M., 'Sir Polydoor De Keyser: Lord Mayor van Londen', *Ghendtsche Tydinghen*, 15 January 1981, pp. 28–43.

7. CASES

A. & B. Taxis Limited v. *Secretary of State for Air* [1922] 2 K.B. 328.

Ard Coasters v. *The Crown* (unreported; c. 1919?).

Attorney–General v. *Brown* [1920] 1 K.B. 773.

–, v. *De Keyser's Royal Hotel Ltd.* [1919] 2 Ch. 197 (C.A.); [1920] A.C. 508 (H.L.).

–, v. *Wilts United Diaries Ltd.*, (1921) 37 T.L.R. 884 (C.A.); (1922) 38 T.L.R. 781 (H.L.).

B. Aerodrome Ltd. v. *Dell* [1917] 2 K.B. 381.

Best & Sons Ltd (John) v. *Lord Advocate* 1918 2 S.L.T. 220.

Broadmayne [1916] P. 64.

Burmah Oil Co. Ltd v. Lord Advocate [1965] A.C. 75.

Cannon Brewery Co. Ltd v. Central Control Board (Liquor Traffic) [1918] 2 Ch. 101; *sub. nom. Central Control Board (Liquor Traffic) v. Cannon Brewery Co. Ltd.* [1919] A.C. 744 (H.L.).

Chester v. Bateson [1920] 1 K.B. 829.

China Mutual Steam Navigation Co. Ltd v. Maclay [1918] 1 K.B. 33.

Commercial Estates Company of Egypt v. Ball (J.E.B.) (1920) 36 T.L.R. 526.

Consett Iron Co. Ltd v. Clavering Trustees [1935] 2 K.B. 42.

Danish Bacon Co. Ltd v. Ministry of Food (1922) 38 T.L.R. 507.

Elliott Steam Tug Co. Ltd v. Shipping Controller [1922] 1 K.B. 127.

Entick v. Carrington (1765) 19 St. Tr. 1030.

Fowle v. Monsell (1920) 36 T.L.R. 863.

Hinde v. Allmond (1918) 34 T.L.R. 403.

Hindhaugh & Co. (J.) v. Food Controller (unreported; 1917).

Hole v. Barlow (1858) 4 C.B. (n.s.) 334.

Hudson's Bay Co. v. Maclay (1920) 36 T.L.R. 469.

Johnson v. Sargant & Sons [1918] 1 K.B. 101.

King's Prerogative in Saltpetre (1606) 12 Co. Rep. 12.

Kohl v. United States (1876) 91 U.S. 449.

Lipton Ltd v. Ford [1917] 2 K.B. 647.

Lithgow et al. v. United Kingdom (1986) 8 E.H.R.R. 329.

London & North–Western Railway Co. v. Evans [1893] 1 Ch. 16.

Longbenton (unreported; c. 1919?).

Minister of Munitions v. Mackrill [1920] 3 K.B. 513.

Monypenny v. Lords Commissioners of the Admiralty 1922 S.C. 706.

Moss Steamship Co. v. Shipping Controller [1923] 1 K.B. 447.

Newcastle Breweries Ltd v. The King [1920] 1 K.B. 854.

Petition of Right, In Re a [1915] 3 K.B. 649 (C.A.); [1916] W.N. 311; *The Times*, 28 July 1916 (H.L.).

R. v. Abbott [1887] 2 I.R. 362.

–, v. *Broadfoot* (1743) Fosters' Cr. Cas. 154.

–, v. *Halliday, ex parte Zadig* [1917] A.C. 260.

–, v. *Hampden* (1637) 3 How. St. Tr. 825.

Robinson & Co. Ltd (John) v. The King (1920) 36 T.L.R. 773.

Russian Bank of Foreign Trade v. Excess Insurance Co. [1919] 1 K.B. 39.

Sainsbury v. Saunders (1918) 35 T.L.R. 140.

Sarpen [1916] P. 306.

Secretary of State for War v. Middlesex County Council (1923) 39 T.L.R. 357.

Sheffield Conservative and Unionist Club Ltd v. Brighton (or *Brighten*) (1916) 32 T.L.R. 598.

Swift & Co. v. Board of Trade [1925] A.C. 520 (H.L.); –, v. – [1926] 2 K.B. 131 (C.A.).

Weld–Blundell v. Stephens [1920] A.C. 983.

Zamora [1916] 2 A.C. 77.

Index